Nandita Haksar and **Sebastian M. Hongray** began their political journey as human rights activists while studying in the Jawaharlal Nehru University. In the early 1980s, they began working full time in the human rights movement. They filed the first cases against the Indian Armed Forces, for committing human rights violations, in the Supreme Court and before the Guwahati High Court. They took up cases of illegal arrests, torture and also unfair compensation for development projects such as the Hundung cement factory. They have also been involved in the Indo-Naga peace process, and Haksar has represented NSCN leaders internationally, before the UNHCR, Geneva and before the courts in Thailand.

Their publications include *The Judgement That Never Came: Army Rule in North East India*; *ABC of Naga Culture and Civilization: A Resource Book* (Nandita Haksar); *Across the Chicken Neck: Travels in Northeast India* (Nandita Haksar) and *The Exodus Is Not Over: Migrations from the Ruptured Homelands of Northeast India* (Nandita Haksar).

Haksar and Hongray are married and live in Goa and Delhi and sometimes in Ukhrul.

KUKNALIM

NAGA ARMED RESISTANCE

*Testimonies of Leaders, Pastors,
Healers and Soldiers*

Nandita Haksar

and

Sebastian M. Hongray

SPEAKING
TIGER

SPEAKING TIGER PUBLISHING PVT. LTD
4381/4, Ansari Road, Daryaganj
New Delhi 110002

First published in India by Speaking Tiger in paperback 2019
Copyright © Nandita Haksar and Sebastian M. Hongray 2019

ISBN: 978-93-88874-93-9
eISBN: 978-93-88874-92-2

10 9 8 7 6 5 4 3 2 1

Typeset in Garamond Premier Pro by Jojy Philip, New Delhi

Contents

Preface: The Story of This Book   1

CHAPTER ONE: THE NAGA PEOPLE, THEIR LAND AND
THE MOVEMENT   5

CHAPTER TWO: THE POLITICAL LEADERS   37

   Isak Chishi Swu: The Statesman   42

   Thuingaleng Muivah: The Ideologue   90

   Khodao Yanthan: The Warrior   155

   Nuri (Saw Sa): The Democrat   168

CHAPTER THREE: THE NAGA ARMY   203

   Thinoselie Keyho: The General   209

   VS Wungmatem: Commander-in-Chief   229

   Khulu Eustar: The Soldier-Wife   270

   Avuli: The Barefoot Doctor   283

   Ramyola: The Soldier-Widow   299

CHAPTER FOUR: CULTURE, THE CHURCH, AND CHINA   317

   Puni: The Reverend   324

   Unice: The Oracle   346

CHAPTER FIVE: THE TRIBE, TRIBALISM AND THE NATION 363
    Medem Jamir: The Ao 368
    G Gaingam: The Rongmei 378
    Shanglow: The Konyak 388
    Zarshie Nyuthe: The Pochury 397

BY WAY OF A CONCLUSION 409

APPENDICES
i)   Angami Zapu Phizo's speech on May 16, 1951 415
ii)   NSCN Manifesto: Relevant Extracts from January 1980 435
iii)   Prime Minister Narendra Modi's speech on
    August 3, 2015 440

Notes 443
Select Bibliography 449
Acknowledgements 453

Preface
The Story of This Book

If you have come
To help me
You are wasting
Your time,
But
If you have come
Because
Your liberation
Is bound up
With mine
Then let us work together.

– Lila Watson, Australian Aboriginal

The idea of writing a book on the Naga national movement based on extensive interviews with the leaders came to us some time after the National Socialist Council of Nagaland (NSCN) signed a ceasefire agreement with the Government of India in August 1997 and began the peace process.

Before the ceasefire it would not have been possible for human rights activists like us to meet senior leaders of an underground organization.

At the beginning of the peace process there were great expectations that the Indo-Naga conflict would finally be resolved, and that resolution would lead to peace and prosperity for the Nagas and the rest of the country. We thought it was the appropriate time to write a book on the Naga national movement, to help in creating better understanding between the Nagas and the rest of the country.

We approached Thuingaleng Muivah and Isak Swu with the idea and they were open to it. Our interviews took place in 1998 and 1999, but we could not publish this book till now.

It seemed that our interviews were outdated and irrelevant, as was the original purpose for which we began our project. The interviews do not deal with the period beyond the establishment of the NSCN in 1980 and its split in 1988.

But on reading the interviews again, we realized that the stories that had been told are compelling and need to be told, otherwise a significant part of the history of the Naga national movement would be lost. We have given the political context of the movement and an update of subsequent events in the first chapter; there are also introductions to each section respectively.

In this book, leaders and members from ten Naga tribes in India and Myanmar, men and women belonging to two generations, speak directly to the reader about their childhood experiences, reasons for joining the armed resistance and their personal triumphs and tragedies.

These stories are about how men and women living in remote mountains decided to shape their own destiny, against all political odds, by sheer power of their collective will, courage, determination and audacity.

It does not matter whether we agree with or strongly disagree with the men and women who took up arms against the might of the Indian State; the significant fact is that successive Prime Ministers of India, from Jawaharlal Nehru to Narendra Modi, felt the need to personally meet the Naga leaders and sit across the table for peace talks. In part, this was dictated by the geo-political significance of the North East region and the international interest taken by various states, including Britain, America, China and Pakistan.

Even as the peace talks continue, the Naga insurgents continue to run a parallel government with legislative, judicial and executive wings;

they continue to collect taxes and settle cases. And they continue to recruit for their Naga Army while they sit across the table and negotiate a settlement which they hope will be honourable and just.

Can there be an honourable solution? This is a question not only for the Naga leaders, but a challenge also for Indian democracy.

CHAPTER ONE

The Naga People, Their Land and The Movement

They call us primitive,
civilized us in the name of Christianity.
They measured our skulls and stole our bones
Leaving spirits shrieking from cold collector' shelves
and lonely museums.
They trespassed and violated our Sacred Sites.
Their learning killed our song, our story, our dance, our voice,
our dignity, our humanity—all.
Our Mother's teaching.

– Jeanine Leane (Aboriginal poet)

They languish, these uprooted
Treasures of my heritage
Caged within imposing structures
in designated spaces

– Tensula Ao ('Heritage' 1-4)

There are 370 million indigenous peoples in the world and they constitute 5 per cent of the population. They are called tribal people or first-nation, and in India many identify with the name Adivasi. One defining feature of all tribal communities is their special relationship with their ancestral lands: their culture and society is inextricably linked with their territory.

The special relationship between indigenous people and their ancestral lands has been recognized by international human rights law as well as the domestic laws of many countries. In 2007, the United Nations passed the Declaration on the Rights of Indigenous Peoples, Article 26 of which states that:

1. Indigenous peoples have the right to the lands, territories and resources which they have traditionally owned, occupied or otherwise used or acquired.
2. Indigenous peoples have the right to own, use, develop and control the lands, territories and resources that they possess by reason of traditional ownership or other traditional occupation or use, as well as those which they have otherwise acquired.
3. States shall give legal recognition and protection to these lands, territories and resources. Such recognition shall be conducted with due respect to the customs, traditions and land tenure systems of the indigenous peoples concerned.

The focus of the Naga national movement has been the integration of all Naga-inhabited lands, and the slogan of the movement has been 'Kuknalim'—'KUK' is derived from the Tenyidie word 'KUO' meaning 'victory'; 'NA' means 'people' and 'LIMA' means 'land.' Some writers have said that the word was coined by Takatemsu and is purely an Ao derivative, and others claim that it is a word made from two Naga languages: 'Kukna' in Chang means 'victory' and 'lim' in Ao means 'land.' There is, however, no controversy over the meaning of the word: 'KUKNALIM', it is agreed, means 'Victory to our People and Land.'

The Land

When the Naga nationalists refer to Nagaland, they do not refer to the present State of Nagaland within India but to the entire Naga-inhabited parts of Indian and Myanmar.

The Naga-inhabited areas stretch from India to across the international border in Myanmar. Naga territory is a part of the North East Region of India which is situated between the Himalayas (China, Bhutan and Nepal), the Indian Ocean (Bangladesh) and wide fluvial corridors (Brahmaputra, Chindwin and the Irrawaddy rivers).

In 1963 the Indian government announced the creation of Nagaland State within the Indian union. The Naga nationalists looked at this as a measure of counter-insurgency to divide their people because a large number of Nagas lived outside the state.

Before the formation of the Nagaland State, 'Nagaland' meant all Naga-inhabited areas; but with the establishment of Nagaland State the Indian government began calling the demand for the integration of Naga-inhabited areas as a call for 'Greater Nagaland.'

The Nagas set up a commission to go into the question of nomenclature and in 1995 at the 16th General Conference of the Naga Students' Federation at Phek, it was decided that the Nagas would call their land Nagalim. In 1999 the National Socialist Council of Nagaland changed its name to National Socialist Council of Nagalim.

The actual boundaries of the territory claimed by the Nagas have changed over the years. The National Socialist Council of Nagalim (NSCN I-M) have released a map of Nagalim which includes the Karbi Anglong and North Cachar Hills, District of Assam; districts of Golaghat, Shibsagar, Dibrugarh, Tinsukia, and Jorhat. It also includes Dibang valley, Lohit, Tirap and Changlang districts of Arunachal Pradesh and five of the sixteen districts of Manipur—Tamenglong, Senapati, Kangpoki (Sadar Hills), Ukhrul and Chandel.

In Myanmar, a Naga Self-Administered Zone has been created in Sagaing Division under the 2008 Constitution. But the Nagas have challenged the boundaries defining their territory as per the Myanmar Government because only Layshi, Lahe and Namyun were included in the Naga Self-Administered Zone, whereas the Naga nationalists claim the following townships:

1. Homalin
2. Lahe with Tanbakwe sub-township
3. Layshi with Mowailut sub-township and Somrah sub-township
4. Khamti
5. Khanpat
6. Namyun with Pangsau sub-township
7. Tamu of Sagaing Division
8. Tanai of Kachin State

Map of Nagalim as claimed by Naga nationalists

Naga nationalists refer to Naga-inhabited territory in Myanmar as Eastern Nagaland; the Naga-inhabited territory in Arunachal Pradesh, Assam and Nagaland as Western Nagaland and the Naga-inhabited areas within Manipur as Southern Nagaland.

The Naga Tribes

There is debate on the exact number of tribes included within the Naga nation. In the nineteenth century this was a socio-anthropological question—now it is a political one.

The number of tribes included in the Naga nation has also changed over time. In a publication called 'Naga National Rights and Movement' brought out by the Publicity and Information Department of the Naga National Council in 1993, eighty-four tribes are listed as belonging to the Naga nation of which twenty-seven are from Myanmar.

The Naga Hoho, the apex body of the Nagas set up in 1994, brought out a 'White Paper on Naga Integration' (May 2002) in which they listed a total of sixty-six tribes, some which were spread across the international border and some which were only in either in India or Myanmar. However, they added a caveat: out of the sixty-six tribes, 50 per cent are subject to confirmation.

The tribes included within the Naga nation keep changing because some smaller tribes unite together to form one larger unit, or sometimes sub-tribes. There are tribes in in Manipur where half the members identify themselves as Naga while the other half identify with the non-Naga tribes, mainly the Zomi group of tribes. A tribe may seek recognition within a state or as a Scheduled Tribe under the Indian Constitution, and they may seek recognition from the parallel government run by the Naga insurgents.

Despite the fact that each Naga tribe has different customs, languages and histories, anthropologists have observed that 'ethno-linguistically and culturally the Naga tribes are somewhat homogenous...all Nagas are of mixed origins marked by commonness in their institutions, social structures, polity, descent systems and oral traditions.'[i]

Map of Naga Tribe Distribution

Source: Naga Students Federation.

One of the biggest challenges before the Naga national movement is to weld the different tribes into a Naga nation.

A brief history of the Nagas and their resistance to incursions into their territory is given below to give the reader a background to the reasons for Naga national movement and its ability to sustain itself over so many decades.

Origins of the Nagas

According to the oral traditions of many Naga tribes, their ancestors migrated from Yunnan in China. Some claim they were forced to leave during the construction of the Great Wall of China.

Having travelled from China through the jungles of Myanmar, the Nagas arrived at Makhel. The Naga tribes pronounce the name in different ways—Makhriffi, Meikhel, Mekroma, Mekharomei, Mekrimi, Makhel, or Makhriohfu—but there is no dispute over the exact location of the village or its significance.

Makhel is a small village near Sajouba, Tadubi village of Senapati district in Manipur on the border of Nagaland State. But Makhel existed long, long before the existence of Senapati, Manipur, or even India.

It is said this village became so prosperous that the people had to leave and migrate to different parts of the region. The community must have grown and flourished because there came a time when the land could no longer provide for all of them. It was time to move once again. It was a time of parting, a time to separate from one's loved ones, search for new lands and establish new villages.

Before they dispersed, the people of Makhel planted a pear tree and under the tree they took a solemn oath that they would one day come together again. Even today the tree stands and is called Chütebu.[ii] No one was allowed to cut even a small branch of this sacred tree. Legend has it that anyone who tries to cut a branch will instantly fall to his death and a terrible storm will follow.

However, if a branch of the tree broke on its own, the chief of

Makhel would immediately send a message to all the people of Makhel and they would observe 'genna', during which period no one could go to the fields and all had to maintain a state of ritual purity. The fallen branch would.be left to decay and return to the soil. This custom was practiced in living memory of Nagas before their conversion to Christianity.[iii] In 1880 a British army officer passing the village of Makhel noted that there was a pear tree which had stood for three or four hundred years, and was greatly venerated by the villagers. However, he did not discover the reason for this veneration.[iv]

Often Naga scholars have described the tree as an apple tree in an attempt to link it to the Garden of Eden; they have not speculated on the symbolism of the pear tree. Pears are native to China. In ancient Chinese civilization, the pear tree symbolizes longevity and immortality.

There is a Chinese superstition that pears should never be shared. In Chinese, the phrase for 'sharing a pear' is 分梨 (fēn lí). It is a homophone of 分离 (fēn lí) which means 'to separate'. Therefore, sharing a pear would mean you separate from the person with whom you share the fruit.

On January 1, 1992, a monolith was erected at the site of the pear tree (Chütebu) and the inscription on the monolith reads: 'This tree is known as the oldest tree in the history of the Nagas...This tree still stands as a symbol of unity and oneness of the whole Naga tribes...'

Beginning of Naga Resistance

Naga nationalists trace the beginning of Naga resistance against incursions into their territory to the time of the Tai-Ahom invasion in the thirteenth century. The Tai people came from what is today the border between Myanmar and China's Yunnan province. The Tai (or Shan) people are called Ahom in India.

The Ahom dynasty (1228–1826) was established by Sukaphaa, a Shan prince of Mong Mao who came to Assam after crossing the Patkai mountains. The Ahom dynasty ruled for 598 years; their rule ended with the Burmese invasion of Assam and the subsequent annexation by the British East India Company following the Treaty of Yandabo in 1826.[v]

According to a statement issued by the Naga National Council in 1955[vi] the genesis of the Naga political resistance started in 1228 A.D. when the Tai invaded Assam. This position was reiterated by Thuingaleng Muivah in an interview in 2009, when asked by journalist Subir Ghosh: 'The birth of Naga nationalism is seen by many as the submission of a memorandum to the Simon Commission in 1929. Do you agree that the formation of the Naga Club (in 1918) was the first concrete step towards Naga nationalism?'

Thuingaleng Muivah replied: 'It would be a serious mistake if one thinks that the submission of a memorandum to the Simon Commission in 1929 was the birth of Naga nationalism. The Nagas' history did not start with this incident. Alien forces in the past had met with stiff resistance from the Nagas—the Shans from the east and the Ahoms from the west, prior to the British intrusion into Nagaland. The British suffered many setbacks from the resistance put up by the Nagas. All these acts actuated from the love of their country. Indeed, Nagas were zealous of their homeland. The formation of the Naga Club and the submission of the memorandum to the Simon Commission are, of course, historic in that the Naga Club officially represented the Nagas and the memorandum expressed the national aspiration of the Nagas as a whole.'[vii]

Apart from these statements by Naga nationalist leaders, the oral tradition of the Nagas, including their songs and folk stories, testify to their resistance against Ahom incursions. For instance, Ao Nagas have a song about a warrior called Kumnatoba who led an army of Naga warriors right into Rongpur, the Ahom capital, and killed many enemies young and old, carrying back countless heads as trophies of war along with cattle, utensils and clothing.

It was in December 1228 A.D. that Sukaphaa, the first Ahom King, crossed the Patkai through the Pangchao Pass (through which the Stilwell Road was made during the World War). He faced stiff resistance from Naga warriors but they were ultimately defeated. This is how the Ahom Burranji records Sukaphaa's savagery:

> A great number of Nagas was killed and many were made captives. Some Nagas were cut to pieces and their fleshes (sic) cooked. Then the king made a younger brother eat the cooked flesh of his elder brother and a father of his son's. Thus Sukaphaa destroyed the Naga villages. The inhabitants of other villages being very much afraid acknowledged his subjugation.[viii]

However, the Nagas continued their resistance to the Ahoms. There were altogether forty Ahom Kings who ruled for six hundred years from 1228 to 1838 when the British deposed the last King and annexed Assam.

The Burranjis record confrontation between Ahoms and Nagas in the reign of sixteen Ahom kings, with the conflicts intensifying after the thirteenth king ascended the throne in 1493 and expanded his kingdom into Naga territory. The conflict was often over control of salt wells located in Naga lands.

Naga Resistance to British Colonial Rule

The Naga resistance to British incursions is well-documented by various authors including Tajenyuba Ao in his book *British Occupation of Naga Country* (1993).

The British sent ten military expeditions against the Angamis from 1839 and 1865. The tenth expedition was sent to Khonoma in 1850 when a force of 500 soldiers of Assam Light Infantry and 200 soldiers of Cachar and Jorhat Militia were sent along with two mountain guns and two mortars. The force entered the hills in December, where they were attacked by the Nagas with showers of spears and rocks, killing thirty-six sepoys.

In November 1879 the British again attacked Khonoma, and this time also the Naga warriors defended their village by throwing huge rocks and spears from their strongly built fort on top of the hill. In that battle two British officers and one native Subedar Major were killed, two British officers and two native officers were wounded, and forty-four soldiers were killed.

The British imposed a heavy penalty on the villagers as punishment for resistance. Here is a vivid description of the destruction of Khonoma village by the British:

> In 1880 the village of Khonoma had its wonderful terraced cultivation confiscated and its clans were dispersed among other villages. The result was that the dispossessed villagers found themselves not only deprived of their homes, but, by confiscation of their settled cultivation, they were during the whole year reduced to the condition of homeless wanderers, dependent to a great extent on the charity of neighbours and living in temporary huts in the jungles. The result was widespread sickness and mortality.[ix]

This was the experience of hundreds of Naga villages throughout the colonial era. There are songs about the suffering of the Nagas during colonial rule like this one composed by the people of Khonoma:

> *You from far unknown valley*
> *Looking more ghost-like than man*
> *With peculiar wooden toys*
> *Crushing neighbours without much effort*
> *Have settled in our land*
> *May we with good fortune*
> *Conquer and defeat*
> *And have our serenity once again.*

The Nagas deeply resented the rules and regulations made by the British which were both humiliating and oppressive. T Aliba Imti,[1] the first President of the Naga National Council, describes these rules in his book *Reminiscence: Impur to Naga National Council.* He states that

---

[1] T Aliba Imti (born 1919) was Joint Secretary and President of the Naga National Council from 1946-1948. He was a member of the Rajya Sabha from April 1980 to April 1986.

the regulations did not come in writing but were passed on the whims of the Deputy Commissioner. For instance, he recalls that in the Naga hills, Naga students were forbidden from dressing in Western clothes or having Western haircuts. He writes:

> They were to dress in loin cloth, as that was the dress of the tribals, and to have their hair cut in the tribal way, round the head, and anyone not found in this tribal attire and haircut was to be fined a sum of 2 rupees—a big sum in those days. In this regard, I told the Mokokchung High School boys that this was nonsense and a stupid order which should be challenged. 'I am the owner of my head' I said. This was in September 1946, and this practice was still in force. I told the boys in the hostel that if they so desired they could keep their hair cut any way they wanted. This statement was very much appreciated and applauded. I jokingly said this should not create any students unrest! Anyway, from the next day the boys went all out and cut their hair in the Western or as the British called it the Bengali style.[x]

Jadonang and Rani Gaidinliu

Many accounts of the Naga national movement are silent about the role of Jadonang, the man who gave a call for Naga Raj. In our interviews with the Naga leaders we did not have any discussion on their views of this history.

Jadonang started a movement against the British and he was released after his first arrest on December 8, 1928 a month before the Naga Club submitted its Memorandum to the Simon Commission in January 1929.

We do not know the exact date of Jadonang's birth. According to his cousin and disciple, Rani Gaidinliu, he was born in 1901; his son has calculated that Jadonang was born in 1885 while the British official records state that the year of birth was 1905.

Jadonang was born into a poor Rongmei family living in Puiluan village (called Kambiron by Meiteis) overlooking the Barak river in Zeliangrong country. His mother's name was Chunlungliu and father's name, Thiudai. The baby boy was named Mazahduanang but he became famous as Jadonang.

Jadonang was an unusual child, and there are oral traditions about his mystical experiences and long trances. On one occasion when Jadonang was barely two years old he walked into thick mist and did not return till late. He came back smiling.

There are stories of how the little toddler would wander into the forest alone and how he would sleep for so long that it worried the parents. However, little Jadonang assured them that he was visiting the house of Tingkao Raagong (the Supreme God).

Jadonang became known as a social and religious reformer with powers to heal and to predict the future. He was a deeply spiritual man who introduced many reforms in the traditional religion because many irrational and obscurantist practices had entered into peoples' religious practices. He also wrote new hymns and songs.

After he had laid the foundation for social and religious reform, Jadonang started his political campaign against the injustice and oppression of British colonial rule. Jadonang preached to his people that they should unite and fight against the British. He prophesized that British rule would end, and in its place there would be Naga Raj. People were attracted to Jadonang's idea of Naga Raj in which there would be no diseases, famines, or taxes; people would not be forced to give their labour without payment as they were compelled to do by the British rulers.

Jadonang began to train young men and women as 'Riphen' or soldiers who would carry forward the message of social reform, spiritual rejuvenation and political resistance. The soldiers learnt the use of dao, spear-hurling, gun shooting, and making of gun powder. The villagers supported the Riphen by contributing food grain, and other basic necessities.

Jadonang used to travel on a pony gifted to him by a friend, and he wore trousers and a hat. On one occasion when he met a British officer he told the officer to go away from his land. On another occasion in 1927 Jadonang refused to dismount or doff his hat when

he encountered the British SDO. He was arrested and put into jail. He
was released after a few days.

The same year he heard that Gandhiji was to visit Silchar.
Jadonang thought of joining forces with the Indian freedom fighter
and mobilized 200 boys and girls to present a dance to him. Jadonang
even composed a song in honour of Gandhiji. But he was deeply
disappointed when Gandhiji had to cancel his programme and the
two leaders never met.

Jadonang's activities were being carefully monitored by the British
rulers who began to feel threatened by his growing popularity. In
1929 Jadonang launched his first overtly anti-British agitation by
calling for a boycott of the three rupee house tax being imposed by
the colonial authorities in Naga-inhabited areas. He also protested
against the British using villagers as porters and making them carry
heavy loads. Even though Jadonang was inspired by Gandhiji, he did
not believe in non-violent struggle. Jadonang, very secretly, collected
both firearms and traditional spears to launch an armed resistance to
colonial rule.

Jadonang was framed in a false case, arrested and incarcerated in the
Imphal jail. He was denied the right to a lawyer; without a fair trial, he
was convicted and sentenced to death.

On Saturday, August 29, 1931, at 6 a.m., Jadonang was hanged at
Imphal jail. He was twenty-six years old.

Jadonang's movement did not end with his hanging. His cousin
and disciple, sixteen-year-old Gaidinliu, continued to resist British
rule. She was an extraordinary girl with little formal education but
knowledge of several languages—Rongmei, Meitei-lon, Assamese,
Hindi, Nepali, and Bengali.

It took more than a year for the British to arrest the young girl and
imprison her in October 1932. Gaidinliu was kept in jail for fourteen
long years and it was only after India won independence that she was
released.

Rani Gaidinliu was released under the care of the father-in-law of
T Aliba Imti; Imti writes that when she was first released, she could

not walk properly due to long years of imprisonment. He describes his first meeting with Rani: 'I met Rani Gaidinliu and we shared our views about the situation that was prevailing and what the youth of our generation were thinking. It was a bit difficult to converse with her as she would use all kinds of languages; a word or two in Bengali, another in Khasi and a bit later in Chang and so on. Anyway after two sittings of more than six hours I could understand in brief that she was all for the independence of India from the British.'[xi]

The Naga nationalists find it difficult to accommodate Rani Gaidinlu within the pantheon of Naga freedom fighters because in later years, she was more concerned with fighting for a Zeliangrong homeland within the Indian Union than with integration of all Naga territories. Besides, the stress on 'Nagaland for Christ' makes it virtually impossible to accommodate non-Christians as Naga nationalists.

The leaders of the National Socialist Council of Nagaland have, however, in recent years acknowledged the contribution made by Jadonang to the Naga cause. For instance, in 2010 Thuingaleng Muivah visited the Zeliangrong village Peren and acknowledged Jadonang's contribution in these words: 'Jadonang knew that British people are not the masters of the Nagas, but masters of themselves.' He added that in this Jadonang was correct, even if he 'did not know God.'

This acknowledgement of Jadonang was perhaps more in response to the need to appease the Zeliangrong sentiment than to evolve a more inclusive Naga nationalism.

The Naga Club

Many scholars and Naga nationalists trace the origins of the first political consciousness among Nagas to the establishment of the Naga Club in 1918. The Naga Club was formed mostly by those Nagas who had gone to France during the First World War (1914–1918) as a part of the Labour Corps. The British Government recruited a number of labourers and porters from the Naga tribes.

It is estimated that around 2000 Nagas were sent to France, where, alienated from the other British Indian troops, they developed a sense of unity. They agreed that after returning to their homeland they would work towards unity and friendship among the various Naga tribes. These Nagas, together with the British officials, formed the Naga Club in 1918. Later, the Club ran a co-operative store in Mokokchung which was the first of its kind. This club provided the socio-political foundation for the Naga nationalist movement.

The Naga Club members thought of themselves as the only representatives of the Naga people and therefore having a mandate to speak on their behalf. On January 10, 1929 the members of the Naga Club submitted a memorandum to the Indian Statutory Commission.

The Commission was a group of seven British Members of Parliament that had been dispatched to India in 1927 to study constitutional reform in Britain's most important colony, India. It was commonly referred to as the Simon Commission after its chairman, Sir John Simon. Indians were outraged and insulted that the Simon Commission, which was to determine the future of India, did not include a single Indian member. The Indian National Congress resolved to boycott the Commission.

The Naga memorandum read:

Sir,
We the Undersigned Nagas of the Naga Club at Kohima, who are the only persons at present who can voice for our people have heard with great regret that our Naga Hills is included in the Reformed Scheme of India without our knowledge, but as administrator of our Hills is continued to be in the hands of the British Officers and we did not consider it necessary to raise any protest in the past. Now we learnt that you have come to India as representative of the British Government to enquire into the working of the system of Government and the growth of education and we beg to submit below our view with prayer that our Hills may be withdrawn from the Reformed Scheme and placed outside the Reforms but directly under British Government. We never asked for any reforms and we do not wish for any reforms.

Before the British Government conquered our country in 1879-80, we were living in a state of intermitted warfare with the Assamese of the Assam valley to the North and West of our country and Manipuris to the South. They never conquered us nor were we subjected to their rules. On the other hand, we were always a terror to these people. Our country within the administered area consists of more than eight regions quite different from one another, with quite different languages which cannot be understood by each other, and there are more regions outside the administered area which are not known at present. We have no unity among us and it is only the British Government that is holding us together now.

Our education is poor. The occupation of our country by the British Government being so recent as 1880, we have had no chance or opportunity to improve in education and though we can boast of two three graduates of an Indian University in our country, we have not got one yet who is able to represent all our different regions or master our languages much less one to represent us in any council of a province. Moreover, our population numbering 1,02,000 is very small in comparison with the population of the plain district in the province; and any representation that may be allotted to us in the council will be negligible and will have no weight whatever. Our language is quite different from those of the plains and we have no social affinities with the Hindus or Mussalmans. We are looked down upon by the one for 'beef' and the other for our 'pork' and by both for our want in education, is not due to any fault of ours.

Our country is poor and it does not pay for any administration. Therefore if it is continued to be placed under Reformed Scheme, we are afraid new and heavy taxes will have to be imposed on us, and when we cannot pay, then all lands have to be sold and in long run we shall have no share in the land of our birth and life will not be worth living then. Though our land at present is within the British territory, Government have always recognized our private rights in it, but if we are forced to enter the council the majority of whose number is sure to belong to other districts, we also have much fear the introduction of foreign laws and customs to supersede our own customary laws which we now enjoy.

For the above reasons, we pray that the British Government will continue to safeguard our rights against all encroachment from other people who are more advanced than us by withdrawing our country that we should not be thrust to the mercy of other people who could never be subjected; but to leave us alone to determine ourselves as in ancient times. We claim not only the members of 'Naga Club' to represent all those regions to which we belong viz, Angamis, Kacha Nagas, Kukis, Semas, Lothas and Rengmas, but also other regions of Nagaland.

Some Nagas have argued that it was in response to this memorandum that parts of the Naga-inhabited areas were declared excluded and semi-excluded areas under the Government of India Act, 1935. Subsequently, Nagas have argued that the declaration of these areas as 'Excluded' meant that large tracts of Naga territory were independent of colonial rule and thus were independent.

In 2017 some Naga nationalists declared that January 10 would be observed as Naga Day to commemorate the day the memorandum was submitted to the British.

Excluded Areas and the Idea of the Crown Colony

The creation of Excluded and Partially Excluded Areas in both India and Burma by the British was a part of their ambitions in keeping the people divided and using them in their quest to control the strategically important region.

The British justified the provision for Excluded and Partially Excluded Areas on the grounds that the people living in these areas were so backward and primitive that they needed a special system of administration which would be simple and direct.

Sir Robert Reid, then Governor of Assam (composite province), wrote in *Geographical Journal* in February 1944, explaining the idea of Excluded Areas:

The title 'Excluded Areas' which has been given to this paper is, I need hardly say, indicative of nothing forbidden or mysterious, but is a purely official phrase taken from the Indian Constitution Act of 1935. It is the lineal descendant of the older phrase 'Backward Tracts', and means that the areas enumerated as such in the Government of India (Excluded and Partially Excluded Areas) Order 1936 are excluded from the operation of the said Act. They are directly administered by the Governor, and elected Ministry have no jurisdiction over them. Finance however and staff have to be found by the province as a whole.[xii]

The Indian National Congress brought out a pamphlet written by ZA Ahmad (Allahabad, 1937) which criticized the idea of Excluded Areas as an imperialist ruse: 'Special forest and game laws, land laws, excise laws and a number of other enactments are hitting at the very root of the economic life of these people, virtually reducing them to the position of chattel slaves or serfs of big landowners, tea planters and other European adventurers.'

The British had usurped large tracts of Naga territory for their tea plantations and by enactment of the Inner Line Regulation in 1873 ensured that the Nagas were confined to the hill areas.

David R. Syiemlieh in his book, *On the Edge of Empire: Four British Plans for North East India, 1941–1947*, has documented how the idea of keeping the North East region excluded was part of a secret British plan during the closing years of their rule, discussed at the highest levels of the colonial administration for setting up a Crown Colony comprising the hill areas of the North East India and the tribal areas of Burma.

The strategic and geographical location of the North East, boxed in by four countries viz., China (Tibet), Burma, East Pakistan, and Bhutan, with only a 22 km wide chicken-neck corridor of Siliguri linking it with mainland India, the region fitted well into the scheme of the colonial rulers to turn into their 'Crown Colony' under the 'Coupland Plan'.

However, the Nagas did not support the idea of a Crown Colony and in the letter to Rajagopalachari written by Phizo from Presidency jail in November 1948, he reminded the Indian leader that both Nagas and Indians endured British colonialism; the Nagas never supported the secret British plans to create a Crown Colony. However, now with the British about to leave, India should respect the right of the Nagas to independence.[xiii]

Indo-Naga Relations

The British had ensured that the Indian freedom fighters did not reach the people of the North East region by banning their entry in the Excluded areas. However, the Naga nationalists had heard of many Indian leaders and there was no hostility towards the Indians in the pre-independence period.

Among the Indian leaders who inspired many young Nagas was Subhash Chandra Bose, or Netaji as Indians called him. In 1938 Netaji visited Shillong for the first time. Bose was the President of the Indian National Congress at that time. Some Naga students went to meet Netaji, including Aliba Imti who recalls the meeting in these words:

> More out of curiosity, eight or nine of us Naga boys went to his (Subhash Chandra Bose's) lodging to meet him and he welcomed us warmly and spent about 15 minutes talking to us. In sparkling white dhoti and shirt and with a fitting Gandhi cap he struck me as one of the handsomest men I had ever met. A Naga sword was presented to him which he accepted joyfully. I was amongst the juniors in the group so I cannot recall the exact gist of the talk. But one sentence of him still remains clearly in my mind, he laughingly said, 'You Naga are very brave and so you must join us in the struggle for independence of India."

The news of this meeting reached the ears of the SDO Mokokchung H Blah who summoned Aliba Imti's father and warned him that if he did not control his son, he could lose his job.[xiv]

In 1945 when Jawaharlal Nehru became the President of the Indian National Congress, he too visited Shillong. His first meeting was organized by Naga students, including Imti. Nehru stayed in the home of Reverend Nichols Roy (the man behind the idea of the Sixth Schedule).

Aliba Imti describes his meeting with Nehru further:

Panditji's first meeting in Shillong was the one arranged by us and I was the one to escort him to the public meeting scheduled to be held at Nongthommai football ground at 9 a.m. March 1945. The rush to take Panditji to the venue was great as different groups had each arranged vehicles. I had arranged a tiny car (perhaps a Morris) said to have belonged to a prince, through some friends.... On coming out, Panditji saw the number of cars there and specially the one of the stubborn party whose car was profusely decorated and remarked that the vehicle should not follow him as it reminded him of a funeral party. I immediately opened the door of the car for him, he entered followed by Mr Gopinath Bordoloi, then ex-premier of Assam. I sat in front with the driver and we proceeded forthwith... Approaching the venue, four Naga boys dressed splendidly in native costume saluted Panditji. He got down from the car and shook hands with all of four of them and proceeded to the platform which was a short distance away. The dais itself was encircled by tribal boys in full costume. It was a very impressive meeting. The ground was packed with people. There were also many Indian and foreign correspondents covering the event. I was surprised when Panditji opened his speech by mentioning the Naga boys and Naga people...[xv]

The Nagas were still debating on their relationship with India after the British left. As Aliba Imti wrote in his memoirs, the Nagas were neither sure of their identity nor their future. There were intense debates among the Nagas on whether Nagas were Indian or not, and what the relationship should be between India and the Nagas.

There were Indians like Jaipal Singh Munda (1903-1970) who championed the rights of Nagas in the Constituent Assembly. He had said: 'I say that we, all of us, stand by them in their demand for that feeling of oneness, to have one consolidated Nagasthan within the territory of India.'[xvi] Jaipal Singh emerged as a campaigner for the causes of Adivasis and the creation of a separate homeland for them in central India.

Earlier, a Naga delegation led by Phizo had met Gandhi at the Bhangi colony in Delhi on July 19, 1947, and he had assured them, 'I will come to Kohima and ask them to shoot me before they shoot one Naga... Personally, I believe you all belong to me, to India. But if you say you don't, no one can force you.'

The Naga nationals furiously debated on whether they wanted to have a measure of autonomy within India or be an independent country. Those debates took place within the first political organization of the Nagas, the Naga National Council.

Naga National Council

Nagas see many parallels in the formation of the Naga National Council and the Indian National Congress. Just as a British administrator AO Hume founded the Indian National Congress in 1885, the British Deputy Commissioner of the Naga Hills, CR Pawsey, played a pivotal role in the formation of the Naga National Council.

Mr Pawsey's concern for the disunited Nagas led him to form the first political body called Naga Hills District Tribal Council (NHDTC) in April 1945. His ostensible objective of forming this body was to unite the Nagas and also to repair some of the damage done to the Naga villages and Naga economy by the devastations of World War II.

The following year, on 2 February 1946, the NHDTC met at Wokha and changed its name to the Naga National Council (NNC) with the aim of uniting all the Naga tribes under one political umbrella. Aliba Imti was chosen as the first President and T Sakhrie as the Secretary.

The Naga national leaders are often divided into moderates such as T Aliba Imti, Sakhrie and Suisa; in contrast to the extremists such as Phizo, Muivah and Isak Swu. This division was made by the Indian State to distinguish between those willing to accept the Constitution of India and those who did not; those who use armed resistance and those who thought use of arms would not succeed.

However, both the 'moderates' and those who took to armed resistance had a common goal: to unite all Naga-inhabited territory under one administration. The differences were of strategy and tactics.

The Naga National Council began with a commitment to non-violence and non-co-operation; but within ten years of its formation the organization moved to supporting armed resistance against what they saw as Indian occupation of their land.

The NNC was closely knitted together through the Central Council, Tribal Councils, Regional Councils and Village Councils. It was first formed with twenty-nine members representing the various tribes on proportional representation of one member for every 10,000 people. As to its membership, every Naga born of Naga blood was by virtue of birthright a member of the NNC.

The Naga National Council was supported and financed by the villages with a membership fee of two rupees; the villagers also contributed in kind such as with vegetables, paddy, cows and mithuns.

It was the fourth President of the Naga National Council, Angami Zapu Phizo, who would begin an armed movement for establishment of a sovereign independent Nagaland. When he died, he would be called the Father of Naga Nationalism.

Angami Zapu Phizo

Phizo was born on May 16, 1904 in Khonoma. He attended school in his village. When he was eleven years old, he went to Kohima where he watched the British recruit volunteers for the Labour Corps. The men were recruited to serve as porters in France during the First World War; they had no idea how terrifying their experience would be.

Later, Phizo studied at the Mission School at Kohima and was baptized by Sidney Rivenberg in December 1922 when he was eighteen years of age. He supplemented his pocket money by looking after the mission's cows and working as part-time janitor. Phizo then went to Assam Government High School at Shillong but he did not pass his matriculation.

Phizo went to Burma in 1935 where he lived for eleven years. In Burma he was in touch with the Indian National Army and met its charismatic leader Subhash Chandra Bose. Phizo never gave a full account of his activities in Burma and the extent to which he collaborated with the Japanese.[xvii]

The Japanese attack on India was launched March 1944. The two most bitter battles were fought in Imphal and Kohima, where the British with the help of the Nagas defeated the Japanese by September of the same year. Only 70,000 of the original 270,000 Japanese force survived.

Phizo was taken into custody and imprisoned in Insein jail, a few miles from Rangoon. Of his interrogation, Phizo said 'Gradually a damning picture of my dealings with the Japanese was built up. My interrogators accepted no extenuating circumstances. I was condemned as a traitor regardless of what I said. But I was certainly not a traitor to my own conscience.'[xviii]

It was while he was in prison that Phizo suffered from Bell's Palsy, a paralysis of the facial muscles causing inability to close one eye.

Phizo was released from jail in the beginning of 1946. By June, Phizo and his family sailed across the Bay of Bengal by steamer on their way home to Nagaland.

On his return Phizo involved himself in rebuilding Kohima which had been devastated by the war. He was elected Chairman of the Kohima Central Council and consequently was in the leadership of the Naga National Council. However, Phizo was impatient with the moderate attitude of the NNC and he withdrew in 1948 to found the People's Independence League, the Naga Youth Movement and the Naga Women's Society, mobilizing Naga people around the demand for full independence.

On December 11, 1950, Phizo was elected the fourth President of the Naga National Council. In May 1951 the Naga National Council organized a plebiscite on the question of independence. The plebiscite was inaugurated on May 16, 1951 and Phizo went from village to village to collect signatures and thumb impressions. Solemn oaths were taken and the results showed that 99.9 per cent of the Nagas voted for a sovereign, independent Nagaland. Some members put their thumb impression in blood.

The NNC boycotted the general elections in 1952 and by the next year Phizo organized the Naga Guards under Thungti Chang. Naga armed resistance to what the NNC called 'Indian occupation' had begun.

On March 30, 1953, Prime Minister Jawaharlal Nehru, accompanied by the Burmese Prime Minister, U Nu (1907-1995) arrived in Kohima. The NNC leaders wanted to submit a memorandum to Nehru but the Deputy Commissioner, Satyen Bakatoki, on the advice of the intelligence agents refused them permission. The NNC called for a boycott of the meeting. The Nagas turned their backs to him, slapped their buttocks and left the meeting—leaving Nehru facing an empty football field.

In September of 1954, Phizo announced the formation of the People's Sovereign Republic of Free Nagaland, popularly known as the Hongkin Government. It was short-lived. There are no accounts of who Hongkin was, except for a description by an Indian intelligence officer who met with and then wrote about his encounter with the old man.

Hongkin was a Gaon Burra (Headman) of the Khiamniungan village of Noku. He was born in 1889 and was sixty-two years old when he met the Indian officer and told him that Phizo had visited his village in 1954. Hongkin said his name meant 'Foreigner out!' He described how Phizo had made him the President of Naga State: 'He gave me a tie and a suit to wear and took photographs of me. He then told me that he was appointing me as President of a Naga State but I was not to tell this to the Indians.'

Thereafter Hongkin added indignantly, 'He then took back the suit and didn't even leave behind the tie!'

The NNC started collecting taxes and laying ambushes in his name while Hongkin went about his life undisturbed.[xix]

On March 22, 1956, Phizo created an underground government called the Naga Federal Government (NFG). There are accounts of how Phizo went from village to village mobilizing the Naga people and talking to them of freedom. On one occasion, when he was in Ningzam village in Zeliangrong country, he disguised himself as an old woman carrying bamboo pipes in a basket going to the village to collect water.

The Naga Home Guards were re-organized under General Kaito, a Sema leader. It was only in January 1964 that the armed guards were named Naga Army.

In April 1956 the Central government sent the Indian Army to crush Naga resistance in the Naga Hills District of the state of Assam. The armed forces were given extraordinary powers under a new law enacted in 1958 called the Armed Forces (Special Powers) Act, 1958.

Phizo went underground. In 1956 he escaped to East Pakistan where he was warmly welcomed and kept in a safe house in Dacca.[2] The Pakistanis gave him an El Salvador passport with which he travelled to Zurich and stayed for some time. There his passport was taken away and he flew to London in June 1960 without travel documents. When Phizo was detained at Heathrow Airport he famously said to the British: 'When you came to my Nagaland, you did not carry any passport. Why can't I visit your land without a passport?'

Phizo was allowed to stay in London and eventually given British citizenship: he lived there till his death in 1990. His body was brought back and buried in Kohima. The memorial stone erected in his honour reads: 'Here lies the father of the nation.'

Creation of Nagaland State

A month after Phizo arrived in London, nineteen Naga leaders of the Naga People's Convention headed by Imkongliba Ao were flown to Delhi to meet the Prime Minister, Jawaharlal Nehru, and there they signed the 16-Point Agreement. This was the agreement on the basis of which Nagaland State came into existence.

-----

[2] All old spellings have been retained in the text: Dacca instead of 'Dhaka', Mao Tse-tung instead of 'Mao Zedong' etc.

On August 1, 1960, Nehru announced in the Lok Sabha that a new state to be called Nagaland would be established within the Indian Union. The next year, on August 20, 1961, before the state was officially inaugurated, Dr Imkongliba Ao was assassinated. This was the way the Naga National Council warned against the creation of a state which would further divide the Nagas living in Nagaland, from those living in Manipur, Assam and North East Frontier Agency (NEFA would later become Arunachal Pradesh in 1972).

In Janaury 1956, one of the most prominent NNC leaders T Sakhrie was murdered. Sakhrie had been at the helm of decision-making of the NNC and its spokesman at important meetings, even the one with Gandhi, and he was the author of most documents. But he was condemned as a traitor to his people and murdered. Many Nagas believe he was assassinated at the insistence of Phizo, but there is no proof of that. He was undoubtedly a man of vision and keen intellect.[xx]

Perhaps what earned him the anger of a section of the NNC was that he believed in non-violent struggle or it may be that he was opposed to the NNC's Chinese connection. Murkot Ramunny quotes a letter written by T Sakhrie to Jasolkie from Shillong on March 15, 1955. In that letter, Sakhrie wrote: '...the American Press is now publicizing the news that the Naga leader is receiving his orders from Moscow... We have never suspected or at least refused to believe such things. But there may be truth... So the revolutionary wing is Communist until proved otherwise.'[xxi]

Sakhrie was assassinated in January 1956, so it would seem that the leaders of the Naga National Council were already discussing the possibility of having contacts with the Chinese. After his murder, the post of General Secretary lay vacant till 1964 when Thuingaleng Muivah was made the General Secretary of the Naga National Council.

The election of Thuingaleng Muivah has been described by an Indian journalist, Harish Chandola, who was married to Phizo's niece and was present at the election:

In Viswema village of the Southern Angamis, on the main road to Imphal, representatives of most Naga tribes gathered to fill the post through election. Participating in it were about 2000 representatives of Konyak, Chang, Mao, Imchunggar, Meluri, Zeliangrong, Tangkhul, Angami, Ao, Chakasang, Sema, Lotha and other Naga tribes, from near and far. I was at this election. This was the first instance of filling a post in the organization through an open election. The vote was unanimous and the 32-year old Thuingaleng Muivah, a graduate of St Anthony college of Shillong, was elected to it. This was the time of the ceasefire. After eight to ten years of oppression and distress the Naga society was breathing in peace. The election made people happy. Muivah belonged to the Tangkhul tribe and was a successor to Uncle Suisa. The Nagas of Manipur had greatly expanded the area of struggle.[xxii]

Nagas of Manipur

Even before India had finished drafting its Constitution, Manipur, which was a Princely State, had already drafted Manipur State Constitution Act, 1947. The Maharaja of Manipur, Bodh Chandra Singh, invited representatives from the Hills[3] including Athiko Daiho and Tiankham to participate in the drafting. Daiho demanded that a clause be incorporated in the Manipur Constitution to protect the rights of the hill people. The clause read: 'The right of any section of the hill people to secede at the end of the five-year period, should the conditions within the Constitution not be satisfactory.'

The clause was not included and the Constitution was applicable to the whole of Manipur, inclusive of the hills. The only exception was that specific provisions were made for the Administration of the Hill areas under the Manipur State Hill (Administration) Regulation, 1947 (Chapter I: 2).

---

[3] Manipur can broadly be divided into the Valley (largely inhabited by the Meitei people) and the Hills (inhabited by the tribal people), both Nagas and non-Naga tribes of the Zomi group.

The Naga National League (NNL) headed by Athiko Daiho in September 1946 was organized to consolidate Nagas of Manipur in order to bring together Naga people separated by colonial boundaries. In the colonial period, the political department of the British Crown administered Naga areas of Manipur. The Manipur Maharaja and his durbar administered the valley areas. The Naga League categorically asserted that they will not remain in Manipur since the Manipuri Maharaja had never conquered Nagas, and declared that it would be impossible for the Nagas to preserve the best of their culture, tradition, customary laws and political practices. The movement expressed their strong desire to merge with the Nagas Hill district of Assam (the present Nagaland State). In pursuance of this demand the Naga National League boycotted the preparation of the electoral rolls in the Naga areas and the first election to the Legislative Assembly of Manipur in 1948. Later Daiho declined to boycott the elections.

However, Rungsung Suisa (1907–1971), a Tangkhul Naga from the present Ukhrul District, decided to stand for elections as an independent candidate in order to take up the cause of Naga integration within the Legislative Assembly.

In the first general election in Manipur in 1948, Mr PC Deb, the Returning Officer of Manipur declared R Suisa elected uncontested to the Manipur State Assembly. He then served in that capacity till the Assembly was dissolved just after the Manipur Merger Agreement with the Union of India.

Later Suisa became an MP in the second Lok Sabha on a Congress ticket from Manipur Outer Constituency (1957–1962) and was a member of various Committees of the Parliament. He was directly involved in Naga politics in serving as Assistant to the Vice President of the Naga National Council from 1964–1966.

Suisa set out some proposals for a possible resolution of the Indo-Naga conflict in a small book he published.[xxiii] The four proposals were:

1. That Nagaland and India form a federation.
2. Nagaland and India will have a pact on defence, foreign affairs and communication.

3.   Some subjects of common concern to be selected if required.
4.   Except for the above-mentioned subjects, 'in all matters of her own affairs and self-concern, Nagaland will be sovereign.'

Rungsung Suisa's proposals were not acceptable to the Naga National Council who wanted 'nothing short of complete independence; nothing to do with India'.

The Peace Mission

The Indo-Naga conflict was at its fieriest during the years 1954 to 1964. The Director of Indian Intelligence, BN Mullik, wrote in his book *My Years with Nehru*: 'Following the plans adapted in Malaya to cut off the rebels from the civilian population, it was planned to group the villages. Grouping of villages meant that the residence of several villages were brought to one central village, which was fenced round and kept under protection of strong security forces... The plan was to break the supply and intelligence system of the rebels, who, being a guerilla force depended on their supplies and information on the villagers. This grouping of villages had also a telling effect on the Naga civilian population.'[xxiv]

The Nagas were put in these concentration camps and were not allowed to go to cultivate their fields. Isak Chishi Swu, who had joined the Naga National Council by 1959 and was the Foreign Secretary to the Federal Government of Nagaland, estimated that until December 1960 the Indian Army had burnt down 2,203 houses in thirty-six Naga villages and put 11,207 people behind barbed wire. It was estimated that 34,244 people had died in the concentration camps in the Sema areas alone.

The stories of the atrocities committed by the Indian security forces in those years have been documented and could fill volumes.

It was in this background that the church leaders took initiative to set up a peace mission. The Government of India declared a ceasefire and the Peace Mission, consisting of three people: Chaliha, Reverend

Michael Scott and Jayaprakash Narayan, who began the task of trying to resolve the conflict. However, the peace talks failed and the conflict started once again in 1966.[xxv]

Nagas in Burma

There are many stories about how Phizo travelled all over Naga-inhabited areas, in Burma and India, organizing his people. Nuri gives an account of how Phizo stayed in his village and how he met Phizo when he was a child.

The Naga national movement had a base in the jungles of Burma where the Burmese Army could not reach in those early days since there were neither roads nor any communication system. In 1962, Burma came under military rule after General Ne Win staged a coup.

The condition of the Burmese Nagas was far worse than the conditions of the Nagas in India, and for Nuri the most urgent need was to persuade the government in Rangoon to bring basic amenities to his people. He even joined General Ne Win's party but left after he saw that it would not bring any development to the Naga areas. It was after that experience that he joined the Eastern Naga Revolutionary Council (ENRC) and rose to becoming the President of that organization.

After the national uprising of 1988, Nuri wanted to make common cause with the other minority nationalities who had decided to join the movement for the restoration of democracy led by the National League for Democracy. However, SS Khaplang, another Burmese Naga leader, took a stand that the Nagas should continue to fight for their own rights and not join the Burmans (the majority community) in their fight for democracy.

This, is in, brief, the political background in which Isak Chishi Swu, Khodao Yanthan, Thuingaleng Muivah, and Nuri grew up. It was in this background that they worked in the Naga national movement and committed themselves to life-long struggle for the cause of Naga nationalism.

By the time these leaders joined the movement, the Naga National Council was well organized with a Constitution (the Yehzabo), a President (Kedage), a Parliament (the Tatar Hoho)[4] and a Government with representatives from each tribe (Federal Government of Nagaland or the FGN), a Council of Ministers (the Kilonsers) and an Administration with Deputy Commissioners (Pantong Riyam) and their assistants.

The Naga Army was well-trained both in Pakistan and on the streets of Kohima. It would be Isak Chishi Swu and Thuingaleng Muivah who would lead the Nagas to China.

---

[4] Tatar Hoho is the Parliament of the underground, while the Naga Hoho is a federation of all Naga tribes established in 1994 as an apex body of the Nagas.

CHAPTER TWO

The Political Leaders

In this small world
A few flies knock against wall.
The noise they make
Is sometimes spine-chilling
And sometimes like sobbing.
Ants climbing up an ash tree brag about a great country,
But it is easy to say that beetles can shake the roots of a stout tree.
— Mao Tse-tung

We have, in this chapter, the testimonies of four leaders of the Naga national movement: Isak Chishi Swu, Thuingaleng Muivah, Khodao Yanthan, and Nuri (Saw Sa). All four men have occupied the highest positions in political leadership.

Isak Chishi Swu was a Sema from a village which falls in present-day Nagaland State; Khodao was a Lotha from a village near the Arunachal Pradesh border; Thuingaleng Muivah, a Tangkhul Naga, grew up in Ukhrul district which was a part of the Princely State of Manipur, and Nuri (Saw Sa) from the Para tribe was born in the Somrah tracts which were and are part of Myanmar.

All the leaders became politically active during the time the Naga National Council was under the leadership of Phizo. Khodao went with Phizo to the UK and stayed there with him till the latter's death in 1990.

Isak Swu and Thuingaleng Muivah split from the Naga National
Council in 1980 when they formed the National Socialist Council of
Nagaland (NSCN) on January 31, 1980.

The primary reason for the split was the differences over the
signing of the Shillong Accord with the Government of India in 1975.
Isak Chishi Swu, Thuingaleng Muivah and SS Khaplang (1940–2017)
opposed the Shillong Accord signed by the then Naga National
Council with the Indian government and the refusal of Phizo to
condemn the Accord publicly.

We interviewed the NSCN (Isak-Muivah) leaders through 1998
and 1999 and the account in this book stops with the split in the
NSCN, which bifurcated into the NSCN (I-M) and the NSCN
(Khaplang group). According to the Khaplang group, this split was
because Khaplang was opposed to the idea of having any peace talks
with the Indian government. He suspected Isak Swu and Thuingaleng
Muivah of wanting to have a dialogue with the Indians.

Isak Swu and Muivah maintain that the split with Khaplang was
due to the latter's lack of discipline and nothing to do with differences
over the possibility of a peace process.

There is also a view that the split was a deeper ideological one rooted
in the NSCN (I-M) wanting to introduce socialist principles while
the others opposed the socialist or communist ideology. W Shapwon
even published a pamphlet calling Thuingaleng Muivah a 'terrorist'
and accusing him of bringing communism to Nagas.[i] The pamphlet
does not mention the existence of the All Nagaland Communist Party
which announced itself in 1979, a year before the formation of the
NSCN. The Maoist party was alleged to have links with the Eastern
Naga Revolutionary Council, and also the Arakan Independence
Army and the Burmese Communist Party.[ii]

However, the debates on the differences between the various Naga
armed factions are for the most part bereft of ideological depth or
political analysis.

We interviewed the leaders after they had signed a ceasefire agreement
with the Government of India and had begun the peace process which

continues till today. Nothing has been achieved by the peace process, but the NSCN has split further and today there are at least five NSCNs: the Isak-Muivah group formed in 1980; the Khaplang group formed in 1988; the NSCN (Unification) in 2007; the NSCN (KK) in 2011 (which has become NSCN NK: Neokpao-Kitovi after the death of Khaplang) and the NSCN Reformation formed in 2015.The Naga National Council too has split into several groups, with some supporting the Shillong Accord and others calling themselves the non-Accordists.

The Forum for Naga Reconciliation, formed in 2004 by church leaders, has been trying to bringing together the warring armed groups who are killing each other in deadly battles on a daily basis.

The NSCN (I-M) has blamed the Indian intelligence agencies for engineering the splits within their organization. However, it is not only the Indian intelligence agencies that have played a role but the intelligence agencies of Britain, USA, China, and Pakistan.

Many British anthropologists acted as informers or even spies for the British Empire. For instance, Ursula Violet Graham Bower (later known as UVG Betts) (1914–1988), was one of the pioneer anthropologists in the Naga Hills between 1937 to 1946 but she also was a part of British military intelligence during the World War, in which she involved the Nagas. In recognition of her courage and assistance to the British India military, she was awarded an MBE and the Lawrence of Arabia medal.

The Pakistan Intelligence Bureau, under the direction of President Ayub Khan, was the first intelligence organization to contact the rebel Naga leaders. They had arranged safe accommodation for AZ Phizo in Dacca and had arranged for his escape to the UK. It is believed by informed sources that Pakistan IB was assisted by the MI6 in arranging the escapade of AZ Phizo when earlier, CR Pawsey (Political Officer, Tuensang, in 1952), had advised that Phizo should be removed from the scene. What were the calculations they made to decide to support Phizo and allow him to stay in the UK?

British intelligence records would perhaps reveal why the British framed and hanged the Naga leader Jadonang (1905–1931) and

jailed his sixteen-year old cousin Rani Gaidinliu (1915–1993) for
nearly fourteen years while they helped Phizo (1904–1990) escape to
East Pakistan and from there to Britain where he was given a British
passport.

The declassified files of the CIA reveal how closely the Americans
were following the events in the North East. In 1960 the Director of the
Central Intelligence Agency (CIA) met Phizo in London. According
to a former CIA agent John Smith the Agency gave the Nagas several
million dollars to organize armed resistance.[iii]

In April 1967 Phizo went to America where a British nuclear
scientist, Stanton Candlin, introduced him to the American political
circles and Phizo was invited to speak at the Hudson Institute, a right-
wing think tank founded by Herman Kahn.

The declassified files of the CIA also show that the United States
of America supported the balkanization of the North East Region of
India. According to Indian intelligence reports the Americans had their
Operational Headquarters at Bangkok from where they could supply
arms to the North East insurgents. A journalist Dhruva Mazumdar,
the author of *Confessions of a Journalist*, states that he was paid by the
CIA to file reports from North East India on movements of the Indian
Army and 'barrack room gossip'.[iv]

The Americans and some other Western powers hatched a
conspiracy in 1963 to create an 'Independent Bengal' comprising East
Pakistan, West Bengal, Assam, Nagaland, Manipur, Tripura, Sikkim
and Bhutan. The British had always wanted isolation of North East
India to make it easier for them to infiltrate Tibet, as part of London's
greater geopolitical plan to upset China.

It was Moscow Radio who first broadcast that the Chinese personnel
were training the Nagas. The Chinese even offered to allow the Nagas
to form a government in exile in China with a radio station and help in
handling foreign affairs. On October 22, 1969, the Foreign Minister of
Taiwan informed the UN General Assembly that China was training
Nagas. A year earlier, the Indian External Affairs Minister summoned

the Chinese Charges d'Affairs on June 6, 1968, and officially charged them of helping the Nagas.[v]

Intelligence agencies of all these countries continue to play a role in controlling and manipulating the Naga movement, often in the guise in supporting the peace process.

How far these intelligence agencies have impacted the Naga movement is yet to be studied. But what is clear from the interviews of the leaders is that the Naga national movement always had and continues to have international dimensions which have yet to be researched.

ISAK CHISHI SWU: THE STATESMAN

Isak Chishi Swu (November 11, 1929 to June 28, 2016) was born in
Chishilimi village of Zunheboto District of present Nagaland State.
He belonged to the Sema (Sumi) Naga tribe. His father was the first
Christian and evangelist in the Sumi Community.

Isak joined the Naga National Council in December 1958. Within
a year he was appointed the foreign secretary to the Naga Government,[5]
a post in which he served for seven years i.e. 1 March 1959 to 1966. He
was then appointed and served as Chaplee Kilonser (Finance Minister)
NNC in 1966 and he was elevated to the post of Vice President NNC,
a post he held from 1977 to 1980.

In 1980 Isak Chishi Swu along with Thuingaleng Muivah and SS
Khaplang founded the National Socialist Council of Nagaland (NSCN)
on January 31, 1980. He was the Chairman of the NSCN from the
inception of the organization to the time he died. The office of the
Chairman is equivalent to the office of the President of Naga Nagalim.

After Isak's death the post of President of the NSCN (I-M) lay vacant
till February 2019 when Qhehezu Tuccu was appointed the President.

Isak was married to Eustar and they had five sons and one daughter.

The interviews with Isak Chishi Swu were conducted in April
1998 in Bangkok.

Testimony of Isak Chishi Swu

I was born in 1929, the same year that Simon Commission came.
My father was not a member of the Naga Club because he was not a
political person. The Speaker of the Naga Club was a Sema. He was a
Dubashi and he danced in front of the Commission to demonstrate
that this was the way of our life. He said before the British came, we
lived like this and after the British go we want to live in the same way.
His name was Nizevi.

---

[5] On March 22, 1956 Phizo formed the Naga Central Government which was
later renamed to Federal Government of Nagaland (FGN) in 1959.

That night the Deputy Commissioner called him and asked which Babu had told him to say all that, and the DC threatened to put him in jail. The Dubashi said he was willing to go to jail but he said the right thing. The DC said he had done well and gave him a bottle of whisky and a packet of Akbar cigarettes and five rupees and told him to have a feast.

We did not want to be a part of India, Burma, Pakistan or Assam. And then the Naga Club drafted a Memorandum to the Simon Commission. So you see the Naga movement did not have only Angamis.

Early Childhood

The name of the village in which I was born is called Chishilimi and it was in Kohima district at the time. Now it is in Zunheboto district. My village had around a hundred households and it was about 50 miles from Kohima which seemed very far away because there were no roads or public transport in those days. My village was a small one but like other Naga villages it was self-sufficient. We did not need to import anything. But just before I was born there was a great change in our society with the coming of Christianity.

Naga social life is centred around the village and the working and singing together in the fields. We have a traditional training institute called the morung. There is a morung for every Khel. In the morung old men come and tell stories, and the boys are taught songs, skills and our ancestry. By the time I grew up there was a morung only for the women so I did not go to the morung but my father did.

The chief owned everything but no longer. Now land is mostly privately owned. My great grandfather founded the village of Chishi and we have kept some land for the public. There is some community owned land and some is owned by the clans. And lakes or rivers belong to the entire village. The Village Authority will allot the common land to people to cultivate. People cannot cut trees at random; they must have a purpose. The same is true for killing animals; you can kill only if you want to eat the animal.

It is said there was fierce fighting between Nagas and the Ahoms. In the Western side we had salt. The Semas got it from the Tangkhuls who had salt at Kharasom. But when the British came, the Angami, Zeliangrong people had to go down to Chittagong to fetch salt. It used to take one and half months to reach and then the same to return. There are stories of the men getting sick and dying and when the children asked their mothers where their father was, she would say he has gone to fetch salt—which meant he had died.

The Meiteis brought rice and there was trade between them and the Nagas. We ate on wooden plates. I remember when my father first bought aluminum plates home from Kohima—we were so happy!

My Father

I learnt all these things from my father, Kushe Chishi Swu. I wrote a small book on him.[vi] He had memorized all the names of my forefathers from the time of Khezakeno[6] until now. We are the twenty-fifth generation. I also memorized the names. My father knew three hundred songs. He had a tremendous memory.

After he became a Christian, he used to put Christian words into two or three traditional songs. The songs are sung in the village even today. After he became a Christian, he started teaching how to love one another. Even before Christianity, we used to take care of the poor because Nagas don't hate the poor. There was equality. Of course there are some cruel people, some bad chiefs who harassed the

---

[6] Khezakeno, a village in Phek district of Nagaland State also known as Kezakenoma or Khezakenoma was initially home to many Naga tribes when they left Makhel, presently part of Manipur. According to the history of Naga migration, a particular wave of Naga tribes crossed Burma and wandered through the valley of Imphal, Manipur, lived in Makhel and after some time moved northward to finally settle at the present site of Khezakeno. This group stayed in and around Khezakeno for a considerable period of time and finally dispersed to different regions for further settlement. Some of the Naga tribes that are known to have dispersed from Khezakeno are Angami, Chakhesang, Lotha, and Sumi.

people, but that happens in every society. But in general Naga society is very sound.

I have a story about how my father became Christian. In fact my grandfather was told by angels to observe Yihovah religion. My grandfather was a traditional priest in the old religion (animism). After the dream he tried to observe the new religion but he did not know how. So he sacrificed pigs and mithuns and made wine and they gave a feast to the whole village. But the entire male population of the village died. They were shocked. They thought it was a terrible religion and they thought they do not know how to observe it.

Then an angel came to my father in his dream and told him to follow the Yivohah's religion. This was in 1921. But my father said his father had already tried and now he was frightened. For a long time he said he cannot do it; he refused. Then one day when he was returning from the field he was shown a vision. The whole mountain range became flat and there was light. And my father heard a voice saying, 'I am this kind of God. I can do this, that is why I am telling you to believe me. But you still continue to refuse.'

So, after a few days the angel threw an earthen pot at my father's chest and he became rich. He was lying on his bed but his soul was taken up to Heaven and he came to a place where Angelic police were watching and he asked what they were doing and he was told they were watching over the people on the planet.

Then my father was taken to another place and it was very quiet and people were walking around but there was absolute silence. The angel told him this is the place of God. But nobody can see God because if you see him you will die. These are the ministering angels who serve God unceasingly.

Then my father was taken to another place where there was a lot of noise like thunder. When my father asked, the angel told him that the people were practicing a song to celebrate when Jesus Christ will come back to earth. He was shown the Scriptures.

Then my father was shown the River of Life, the living water flowing from the Throne of God and of the Lamb. Then the Tree of

Life was shown to him, the tree that bears fruits twelve times a year and whose leaves are for healing of the nations.

Then my father said he would practice the new religion and he asked how. The angel told him to work on his field for six days and rest on the seventh. The angel said he would send someone to teach the new religion. Till then we did not have concept of week but we calculated the seasons accurately by the lunar cycle and the villagers knew when it was time for hunting or when birds would flock, and also when to catch fish.

Later he was formally baptized by a missionary. He was the first convert to the new religion and my grandfather was angry and disinherited him.

After my father converted, people in the village boycotted my parents. Even my grandfather was angry with them. This was the time before the children were born so my mother and father were almost outcasts; nobody helped us in our fields. Some evangelists would come from Kohima to help us but the field was not a good one and did not yield much. But then a miracle happened and our field yielded the richest harvest. People were really surprised.

After seeing the miracle, the people in our village realized that the new religion was a good religion and it spread like wildfire and they all converted to Christianity. My grandfather also subsided and he too converted. My father said he had a wireless connection with God and that God spoke to him. My father was a determined person so Christianity superseded animism.

The missionaries came and then my father read the Bible and he could memorize the Bible. Then my father went to different villages, and to the neighboring tribes such as the Rengma, Chakhesang, Angami and Yimchunger. Sometimes I went with him and I learnt a lot. I met missionaries such as BI Anderson and Robert Delano but the foreign missionaries left by 1956. I was supported by Reverend Delano and that is why he came to see me at Barapani (Meghalaya) before he left for America and after that I lost touch with him.

My Family

My mother Shokhali Swu and her family converted much later. We were altogether four brothers and two sisters. My older sister Henili supported the whole family of eight and my younger sister Hekhuli Jakha became the first woman evangelist in the Sema area. My younger brother was also in the Naga Army and he was so badly beaten by the Indian Army during their combing operations that he cannot walk even now. He just sits and prays.

My mother was the first to mix the fur of the sheep and cotton to make shawls. Before that we just had wild cotton and we used to help gather the cotton and separate the seeds from the cotton. My mother also used different roots for dying the cotton. Yes, we reared sheep.

We have nine different kinds of patterns in Sema shawls and each has a different meaning. Some are for those rich people who have fed the whole village in several feasts of merit. In our tradition if someone who has not killed anyone and he wore a warrior's shawl he would face death. Because of that fear no one wore the warrior's shawl.

We use sea shells in our shawls. We have to do more research to find out where we are from. It may be that we lived near the Chindwin river and the shells are from there. Semas live near Irrawaddy and Chindwin. Angamis and Zeliangrong people used to go down to Chittagong for trade and brought salt.

My mother and my oldest sister worked in the fields while my father spent time in preaching. I was deeply influenced by my father and we learnt early in life how to sacrifice and help other people. My father taught me the message of salvation and the teachings of Jesus Christ inspired us most.

My father taught us to live by Christian principles such as not to lie, not to steal, not to fight with other people, to love ones' friends as one loves oneself, and most important of all to love other people. The verse in the Bible that influenced me most was John I 4:20.

My father used to tell village authorities to always tell the truth. There were many boundary disputes between clans and it was the village authority which settled the matter.

My father said it was the will of God that the Nagas should be united. He would discuss the future of all Nagas, Rengma, Chakhesang, Yimchunger, Pochury, every tribe. We did not have an apex body for the whole tribe like the Tangkhul Long at the time.

My father passed away in 1951. He had prayed that he wanted to go to the Yimchunger area and God answered his prayer and sent him there. He preached there and it was there he fell sick. But he did not call me.

My mother passed away in 1987. She was a wonderful woman and very hard-working. She used to love to help people. Whatever she had she sacrificed and finally she knew it was better for her to go away. So she told my sister, 'Don't pray anymore to lengthen my days but pray to God to relieve me.' My brother told me she dressed herself carefully and then lay down and passed away peacefully.

I had told my brother to take care of my mother but he too went and joined the movement. He was active for three years but he got injured in his leg and from that time he had been at home. My next brother Jacob was active in the movement from the beginning. He came up to rank of Major. He was to be promoted to Lieutenant Colonel but he was arrested and beaten very badly. His spine, his ribs were broken and his eyesight was affected. That was in 1972.

Some people reported that my brother was commanding the Naga Army which attacked Hokishe Sema[7] in August 1972. He was in hospital for a long time. Then he was taken to court and when he was asked whether it was right to fight the government, he said it was not

---

[7] Hokishe Sema was the third Chief Minister of Nagaland and in his career went on to hold that post four times, serving from 1967–69, 1969–74, 1982–87 and 1987-88. He was the first Chief Minister of Nagaland to complete two full terms in office in a state known for its political instability and defections. In 1994 he left the Indian National Congress owing to differences with Chief Minister SC Jamir and formed the Nationalist Democratic Movement. He joined the Bharatiya Janata Party in 1999 and went on to become that party's National Executive Member. There was an unsuccessful assassination attempt on Hokishe Sema on August 8, 1972. He died in 2007.

wrong on the part of the Nagas to fight. They asked him whether he had anything to confess and he said, 'I have done nothing wrong so I have nothing to confess.' Then at last he was released unconditionally. But he was so badly tortured that he could not work in the fields and he is now just staying at home.

My sister is an evangelist and even during operations she used to go into the jungles and from village to village without being afraid. She went to places where there was no evangelist or missionary. Her husband is also an evangelist. She has sacrificed a lot. During the time when I was studying, she was earning sixty rupees and she sent me thirty rupees and the rest she used for my two brothers. I used to get fifty rupees from a reverend so altogether I had eighty rupees.

Early Education

I attended the Baptist Elementary School in our village but I wanted to go to school in Kohima. I started crying and after that my father decided to take me. That was in 1937. It was a long journey for him, about 50 miles going and another 50 coming back. When we had to climb up my father carried me on his back.

I stayed with the family of the headmaster of the Kohima Mission School. He happened to be the drafter of the Memorandum to the Simon Commission. My father's young brother was also in the same school.

I learnt Angami language. We also had music lessons and we used to play together and sometimes quarrel with the other boys but we learnt to love one another.

It was a new world for me with some pucca houses, and for the first time I saw vehicles and bullock carts which used to come from Manipur carrying rice. But the roads were not tarred. That happened only after the Second World War. When they were building roads, I worked three months in construction to earn some money.

It was totally different world from the village. There was no electricity but the mission compound had paraffin lamps.

Then the Second World War[8] came and I had to go back to the village. I attended Atukuzu School.

I worked in the fields for two years before going to college. Those were my happiest days because I was with the Naga society—we worked together in the fields, sang together and ate together; we ate five times. We would go to the fields after a meal and then while working we had three breaks and then when we returned home from work, we had another meal. It was that experience of living with my people that inspired me.

Then I went back again to Kohima and I passed High School in 1956 from the Mission School in Kohima which later became the Government High School.

During the British time we were not allowed to wear Western clothes; neither half-pant nor the full pants. And we had to have our hair cut in the traditional manner. The Semas were particularly discriminated against by the British and not allowed to study beyond Class Six and after that they were sent to teach in the LP (Lower Primary) schools. I do not know the reason why the Semas were singled out because the Aos and Angamis were allowed to study up to graduation. I was in the Mission School so nobody stopped me from wearing pants. But the students in the Government High School were not allowed to wear Western clothes. I do not know why. Maybe they wanted to encourage the old culture. Perhaps that was the reason.

In 1947 I was eighteen years old. Till then I had not seen any Indians or even Assamese. The British used to come on annual visits to instruct the Dubashis and they went from village to village. They would settle those cases which the Dubashis could not settle. They would hold court in the Inspection Bungalows. These IBs were only in some villages.

Before the British left they started forming ranges so the following were formed: Pughboto, Atukuzu, Atoizu, Akuluto, Suruhuto,

---

[8] One of the bloodiest battles of Second World War was fought in Kohima in 1944. Many Nagas helped the British win the battle, but they remember the Japanese army with admiration for their courage and the way they treated the local people with respect.

Aghunato and Satoi. And there was a school in each range and also a court at the range level. This was also around 1943.

I saw Japanese troops and they behaved very well in Naga areas. Our President (Phizo) and his brother met Subhash Chandra Bose in Burma. But no one else had met him. Our President had told the Indian National Army that the Naga people will fight against the British but no proper message was sent to the people so they did not support the Japanese.

There was no case of rape by the Japanese army. The Japanese behaved badly in the Philippines and in Korea but in the Naga areas they behaved very well. There were rare cases in which the Japanese took rations forcibly but most times they paid for the rations.

There was major fighting over the Jessami post and the miserable Nagas fought on the side of the Allies so the Japanese were helpless.

I saw the Americans when the American army came to our village. I was very young at the time. My Uncle could speak a few words of English so he could talk to them. We children went to their camp because they distributed biscuits and chocolates. We used to stare at them with admiration because they were so big and tall.

Naga National Council

It is not known on which exact date the Naga National Council was formed but it was in the year 1946. I was too young to remember but I think there was a public rally in Kohima to mark the occasion. Representations from all the ranges were sent to the newly formed Council.

I began attending meetings by the Naga National Council from the time I was in Class Seven. There were several public rallies and we were encouraged to attend by Visar Angami (1913–1976), who was the third President of the NNC, and our teacher. He would instill in us the need to maintain our culture, our way of life and not imitate other people; and to be brave. He started Boy Scouts and told us to be prepared to fight with courage.

Uncle Phizo's daughter (Adino) who is in London with him was in school with me so I met Phizo in his house. He did not talk much. He used to tell people that we must maintain our identity. Phizo did not talk to us because he was busy talking to elderly people so he did not have time to talk to us personally; he would generally tell us what the youth should do.

I was in Class Nine when Phizo was elected as President in 1951. He called the youth and students to organize together for a movement to preserve Naga identity. Phizo started campaigning in Wokha, Zunheboto, Mokokchung and other parts of Naga territory. He said whenever there is any dangerous work the youth had to be ready to sacrifice their lives. We knew there would be a reaction from the Government and so we worked hard to raise the consciousness of the people. For the first few years the youth ran a paper called Naga Nation.

From this time, I was in the picture all the time. I remember a minor boy by the name of Zasibuto was accused of theft and he was beaten to death in police custody. We took out a procession to protest against this brutality. Jasokie[9] was also there. At that time Borkotoki was the Deputy Commissioner and we told him whatever the facts the case should be settled properly. Our people did not trust the Indians as they were not honest, whether it was the police or the administration.

Nagas Reject Sixth Schedule

It was during this time that JJM Nichols Roy[10] visited Kohima. He met the youth and told him about the proposals being discussed by the Bordoloi Committee.[11] The Nagas said they were fighting for

---

[9] John Bosco Jasokie was a guide for the Allied forces during the Second World War and a member of the NNC till he was expelled by Phizo and later elected as the Chief Minister of Nagaland. He died in 2005.

[10] Reverend James Joy Mohan Nichols Roy (1884–1959) was the grandnephew of the Khasi freedom fighter U Tirot Singh and a member of the Constituent Assembly.

[11] The primary objective behind the provisions of the Sixth Schedule was to see that the aspirations of the people of the area are met and simultaneously these areas

independence. After hearing the Naga youth, he asked what would happen if a knife was given to a monkey—what would a monkey do except to cut himself? We asked him whether he thought Nagas were monkeys, and he said we did not know the meaning of independence. He was really backward and we started quarrelling with him. And next morning we held rallies, saying 'GO BACK NICHOLS ROY'. He was helpless and he said he was trying to raise the Nagas' standards. He had hoped to persuade the Nagas in the Naga Hills District of Assam to accept the Sixth Schedule but the elders refused. People regarded Nichols Roy as very advanced or educated but politically he was backward. The Naga National Council decided to declare Independence after the Indians betrayed the promise made in the 9-Point Agreement[12] which had the signature of Gopinath Bordoloi[13] and Rustamji.[14]

---

are assimilated in the mainstream of the country. A Sub-Committee was created on 27 February 1947 to report on the North East Frontier (Assam) Tribal and Excluded Areas. Its chairman was Mr Gopinath Bordoloi who was then the Premier of Assam.

The Sub-Committee extensively toured the Assam Province (as the region was known then). It submitted its report on July 28, 1949 to the Chairman, Advisory Committee on Fundamental Rights, Vallabhbhai Patel. The draft was debated in the Constituent Assembly in the first week of September 1949 and passed.

[12] Aliba Imti continued to strive for a settlement between the Government and the NNC members. As a result of his efforts, on June 26, 1947, Sir Muhammad Saleh Akbar Hydari, the Governor of Assam, reached a 9-Point Agreement with the Naga leaders. It was agreed that the Nagas would be granted judicial, executive and legislative powers, as well as autonomy in land-related matters. There was a ten-year guarantee of these provisions at the end of which the Nagas could choose between extending the agreement or a new agreement. The Naga leaders were also promised unification of Naga territories from nearby districts into the Naga Hills District. However, the Constituent Assembly refused to ratify the Hydari accord. The Naga leaders envisaged a sovereign state with India as a 'Guardian Power' for ten years, while the Indian Constituent Assembly concluded that the Nine Points Agreement guaranteed only a 'district autonomy within the Indian Constitution'.

[13] Gopinath Bordoloi (1890-1950) was a freedom fighter and was imprisoned several times; he was a follower of Gandhi's principles of non-violence. Bordoloi was the first Chief Minister of Assam. He was awarded the Bharat Ratna.

[14] Nari K Rustomji studied classical Latin and Greek, played the piano and violin and was a member of the Indian Civil Service. He administered the North East

A delegation of nine members of the NNC met Mahatma Gandhi on July 19, 1947 at the Bhangi colony. They asked him whether India would use force to make the Nagas give up their right to complete independence. And he said to them: 'Nagas have every right to be independent. We did not want to live under the domination of the British and they are leaving us. I want you to feel that India is yours, I feel the hills are mine, but the matter must stop there. I believe in the brotherhood of man, but I do not believe in force or forced union. If you do not wish to join the Union of India, nobody will force you to do that.'

We told Mahatma Gandhi that the Governor of Assam was threatening us Nagas with force and he said, 'I will come to Nagaland and let them shoot me first before any Naga is shot'. So we trusted Gandhiji and we believed in non-violent policy. In those days non-violent policy was successful and the whole world was admiring it. But unfortunately, Gandhiji was assassinated.

It was for the Indians to exercise their wisdom to solve the Naga problem through a proper perspective. Even today if they think they can use force or devious means, they cannot solve the problem. It is not wise to use force against a small people.

When we declared independence the Assam police started harassing our people. On August 14, 1947 the mood of the people was happy. We thought Indians would also listen. Our intention was made known to the United Nations organization and we received an acknowledgement. There was a flag hoisting ceremony in Kohima mission compound. Since our flag was not decided we had the Angami cloth but afterwards we designed a proper flag. We sang 'God Bless our Nagaland'. But I was not present at the ceremony although I was in Kohima. Kughato Sukhai and Kevichusa[15] were present.

Frontier Agency in 1950s, was the first Chief Secretary of Meghalaya State and wrote several books on the North East.

[15] Kughato Sukhai was the Prime Minister of the Federal Government and elder brother of legendary General of Naga Army, Kaito Sukhai. A Kevichusa from Khonoma Village, the first Naga graduate, the first Naga officer and Magistrate of

I was in Kohima during the visit of Nehru. I was there as a cameraman. It was in 1953. The Naga National Council wanted to submit a Memorandum to the Indian Prime Minister but the Deputy Commissioner refused to let us present it. So we left and asked everyone to leave. That is how the first time Nehru came to Naga territory, his meeting was boycotted by the Nagas.

When I was in high school in Kohima I was the busiest person and I participated in nine parts: I was Secretary of the Kohima High School Union, I was Chairman of local Sema Church, President of the Sema Students' Union, Football Captain and Class Captain , and I was in Boy Scouts but we had to go camping and that took too much time so I gave that up. But the discipline and marching helped later on. All this meant I had no time to study at all.

Shillong

I was in college in 1956. I studied at the Union Christian college at Barapani and then at St Anthony's in Shillong.

We are four brothers and I told my younger brother to take care of my mother. My second brother Jacob joined the Naga Home Guards and the youngest was still in school while I was in college. My parents could not support me and the conditions were becoming harsh so I started working in the Assam Secretariat.[16]

I never attended the Indian flag hoisting ceremony either in school or in college. I felt if I attended it would mean we are under the Indian flag so I avoided it. But I did not organize a boycott of the ceremony; it was an individual act.

British India; Honorary Captain of the British Army; a recipient Member of the Most Excellent Order of the British Empire (MBE); the first Naga Indian Administrative Service (IAS) officer; Founding Member and first Chairman of the first regional party of Nagaland, the Democratic Party of Nagaland; a Member of Parliament (Lok Sabha); and one of the first translators of the initial Angami Bible.

[16] Shillong was the capital of undivided Assam until the creation of the new state of Meghalaya in 1972 when it became capital of Meghalaya and Assam's capital became Dispur.

After 1958 I thought of going to the United States for theological studies and I arranged for my airfare and passport. But then Scato Swu, the President of the Federal Government, told me that I should stay at home. And he appointed me the Foreign Secretary to his government.

When the persecution started and Assam police battalion attacked us our people started collecting Second World War guns and weapons lying around. Semas made bows and arrows while others made dao and spears. The Nagas formed the Home Guards with two battalions with strength of around 500 people. My brother was the adjunct Captain in the second battalion. For ten years he held that post and started with muzzle loading guns. Some Nagas ran away from the Assam police and joined the Home Guards.

We fought and captured arms and then fought again. The fighting forces used guerilla tactics learnt from practical fighting. The heavy weapons were kept in front. We would lay an ambush and then deploy people to capture the arms. The enemy was very nervous so some of our people would take their weapons from their hands. Some of our people were shot down.

At first the Indians deployed the Assam police, then the Indian Army was also deployed. In March 1956 Sema fighters captured seventy-eight men of the Assam Police at Satakha village. After taking away their weapons the men were released. Nagas did not beat or torture their captives. It was not Naga tradition. After disarming the police, they were sent marching back. The Indian papers like *The Assam Tribune* and *The Statesman* reported the incident. I was not a witness but I read of this in the papers and my brother told me about the incident. I was at the time still in college.

I studied in Barapani and then in Shillong between 1953 and 1958.

In Shillong we used to have discussions with other students. There were about a hundred Naga students there. The Khasis and Mizos thought that the Naga struggle was useless. In the beginning we informed all the people but, in those days, their political consciousness was very low. They did not have political wisdom or foresight.

We said even Assam was not a part of India; it was a part of the

Ahom kingdom. Ahoms fought with the Bodos and defeated them. We sent a Goodwill Mission to Assam in 1953 to make the various sections of the Assamese people understand our position. Chaliha understood us and he said you are the people who can fight for all of us. He said the fate of Assam is linked to Nagaland in the future.

However other Assamese leaders were too proud and they despised the Nagas as 'kukur-khazat' or dog-eaters and naked headhunters. By the grace of God we Nagas could speak out for our rights from the very beginning and we continued to resist. It was much later that the Mizos and the Assamese spoke out as well.

I met some of the Mizo nationalist leaders in Shillong in 1968, and the ULFA and Bodo leaders much later in Peking and Dacca.

In the beginning Mr Phizo did try to contact all these other people, especially Mizos. They laughed at us. They asked, 'How can Nagas separate when even Assam cannot?' People regarded Nichols Roy with respect because he was educated but politically, he was backward. Only because of the Naga movement the Khasis got Meghalaya otherwise they would not have got that. Lyngdoh and Swell came to meet us after the ceasefire. Uncle Suisa, the first time he stood for elections he stood as a Naga nationalist.

In 1959 I attended the Naga People's Convention[17] at Mokokchung. It was the final session of the Convention and my intention was to stop the Semas from joining the meeting. I detained them for three days.

Martial Law

In 1958 after I graduated from college I went home to my village. During my stay at home the Indian Army conducted an

---

[17] The first meeting of the Naga People's Convention was held in August 1956 at Kohima; the second meeting was held in May 1958 in Ungma and the third was held in October 1959. It was the NPC which passed the 16-Point Agreement in July 1960 which was the basis for the creation of the Nagaland State. The meeting was chaired by Imkongliba Ao who was a doctor by profession. In August 1961 he was assassinated by suspected followers of Phizo who opposed the creation of Nagaland State.

operation.[18] They came after an encounter between the Indian Army
and the Naga Home Guards in which 200 Indian Army men died,
including one of their best doctors. They started making enquiries
about who was in the Home Guards and they found it was the Sema
group from southern Sema area. So they declared martial law in the
area and that is how they entered my village.

That day, somehow, I was holding a copy of the Indian Constitution
and the Major in charge was a little bit sensible but he still said he was
carrying out orders. He herded everyone to the football ground and
then he announced that he was going to set fire to all the houses. I
objected and said at least allow the people to take out their belongings
so he allowed one person from each house to take out their belongings
such as utensils, clothing etc. The people ran towards their homes
which were around 1 km away from the football field but by the time
they reached, their homes were ablaze. Some people did manage to
save a few things but most could not.

Then all the people from my village were herded to the next village
where they had to stay in a concentration camp. A shoot-at-sight order
was given and the soldiers started to shoot at random. Many people
were killed but luckily because I was there no one from my village was
killed. The soldiers wanted to burn down the church but I objected
and said that according to your constitution you cannot burn a church.

The following day we were all taken to the next village called Kiloni.
Even before we reached, they had set fire to the thatched roofs and

---

[18] The NNC was to begin with committed to non-violence and non-co-operation,
and in pursuance of those principles had given a call for a boycott of the first elections
in independent India, boycott of school and government institutions but by 1956–57
had decided to take to arms. The Government of India passed the Armed Forces (Assam
and Manipur) Special Powers Act in 1958 to deal with 'misguided Nagas' and restore
normalcy. Under the Act the Indian Armed Forces were given unfettered powers to
arrest, search, seize and even shoot. The Indian Armed Forces committed wide scale
human rights violations in the Naga-inhabited areas which included burning down of
villages, torture and killing of civilians, rape and sexual assault on women, desecration
of churches and forced labour. Under the Act, large parts of Naga-inhabited areas were
under virtual military rule.

wooden floor of the village houses. The soldiers had kerosene which they poured over the thatch and set it on fire.

People lived in those concentration camps for two years. The village chief was killed and one chief was starved to death. My village had eighty houses but it was reduced to only thirty houses; the rest were burnt down. The villagers were not allowed to cultivate and they were not given any rations. Instead they were forced to work for the Indian Army doing jobs like cleaning the compound, raising the stockade; if they were sent out of the concentration camp they were shamelessly stamped on their bodies, and women were stamped on their breasts just to humiliate them.

Many villagers died. Our village chief also died. Some villagers had managed to escape into the jungles. They lived in the jungles but many starved to death there. About 300 to 400 people died in the jungles. The Indians even dropped locusts from helicopters to destroy our crops.

The press was not allowed to enter so the world did not know what was happening to the Nagas. And our paper *The Naga Nation* also had stopped.

The Nagas started hating the Indians after seeing the brutality of the Indian Army. Generally, we were not dominated by any outsiders—either the Chinese, the Burmese or anyone else. So our attitude to foreigners was always to welcome them. We don't have any kind of hate towards the foreigners.

I wrote out a report of what I had seen and sent it to Uncle Phizo to submit to the United Nations. That was the only such incident I witnessed because I went underground after the Indian Army operation in my village.

The Naga Army

In 1954 an ex-havaldar of the Assam Rifles called Thungti Chang organized the Naga Home Guards who were loyal to Phizo. There was some misunderstanding so General Kaito[19] organized the Safe Guards.[20] Later Thungti was arrested by the Indians.

In terms of military strategy and force, General Kaito did much better. I went with him to East Pakistan. It was there that we first got our formal training. General Ayub Khan[21] had Nagas under him when he was the Commander of 1st Assam Regiment so because of their discipline he liked them. When our boys went to Pakistan for training when he became President, they were treated very well. I am not sure whether he ever came to Nagaland but during the World War he might have gone through.

But our people had already got a lot of practical training so we knew guerilla tactics. There were former instructors from the Assam Rifles and from the Assam Regiment who trained our people. They taught our people discipline. First thing is to learn discipline, then fighting.

There was a Nepali who joined the Naga Army and took a Sema name. He became a Lieutenant Colonel in the Naga Army and was caught and spent twenty-three years in the Indian jail. His name was Hoto (Hoitoi) and when he came out of jail, he became a Gram Burra in a Western Sema village.

There were many Nagas in the 3rd Assam Rifles and they were very helpful to us. There were some Meiteis and some of them even went to China with us. Some of them were Irabot Singh's men who joined us.

Guerilla fighting, in fact all fighting, depends on the courage of the

---

[19] General Kaito Sukhai (1933–1968) was a Sema celebrated by Naga nationalists as the youngest General in the world. He was assassinated in 1968 in Kohima, aged thirty-five.

[20] This is a reflection of inter-tribal rivalries between the Angamis (followers of Phizo) and Semas (followers of Kaito).

[21] Mohammed Ayub Khan (14 May 1907–19 April 1974) was the first native four-star General and the only Field Marshal of the Pakistan Army. He was the first military dictator and also the second President of Pakistan who assumed power in the 1958 coup d'etat, serving in office until his forced resignation amid a popular uprising in 1969. Ayub Khan fought in World War II as an officer in the British Indian Army. He joined the armed forces of the newly formed state of Pakistan upon independence in 1947, and became its chief military commander in East Bengal.

person. If he is not courageous then even if he knows the tactics, he will forget them. That is the main secret of victory. When our people fought and won against the Indian Army, they felt encouraged. But sometimes they fought amongst themselves also.

In the beginning each person was given just three to five bullets and when ammunition was in short supply, they were given just one bullet per person. We used bows and arrows also. The Indian Army was very much afraid of the arrow because when it enters you have to pull it out of the other side. If you pull it back it is dangerous. We did not use poison; the iron is itself dangerous. In the old days we used to get iron from Burma and Assam. We had our own blacksmiths.

Pakistan

I was in Eastern Nagaland during the 1962 war. I was staying in the Somrah area. I went to East Pakistan in 1963. That time we went through Zeliangrong and Mizoram. We crossed the Kaladin river by boat. We were 300 of us.

We did not burden the villages and we always paid for the rations. We even paid extra. We did not employ them much while going but coming back we had heavy load with arms and ammunition so we employed porters.

The first week is difficult but after that walking becomes very easy and you don't feel the load. The first week you suffer. But when people become hungry it is very difficult to control people; they become very angry and unruly. We all reached Pakistan.

In the beginning the Burmese did not attack us. They were friendly and we could talk to them. They said if no villagers reported or complained against us, they would remain neutral. We would give them a present. But after 1962 Ne Win came and in 1964 the Eastern Naga Revolutionary Council[22] (ENRC) attacked the Layshi post, then the Burmese Army became very cruel.

---

[22] The Eastern Naga Revolutionary Naga Council was formed by Nagas in Burma in April 1964.

The ENRC used to consult us and used to talk to us and we used to tell them we cannot fight on two fronts at one time. We told them it was not time to fight with the Burmese. But they did not take our advice and without our knowledge they attacked the Layshi camp.

So when we were coming back from East Pakistan via Burma the Burmese Army attacked us. One of our boys got injured when they threw a two-inch mortar. But we had mounted machine guns and we could chase them and capture some of their arms. But the Indian Army was just below us and perhaps some of them got injured. The Indian Army also attacked us. But we were able to come back, except a few who were injured or were sick.

In Pakistan we had three months training and they taught us how to use arms, assemble and dissemble them blindfolded. There were three Assam Rifles men who joined us and many of us had already been fighting in the Home Guards and some had been fighting without training. General Mowu and General Dosai were also there. I did not take military training in Pakistan but I took when I went to China.

The 3rd Assam Rifles was very helpful to us. Their headquarters was in Kohima and many of the Nepalis joined us and came with us to Pakistan.

Peace Process

When Scato Swu[23] became President of the Federal Government of Nagaland he had a meeting to discuss the issue of China. It was at that meeting we decided to send Mr Muivah to China.[24] Whatever it may be, we cannot ignore this superpower and we must make our

---

[23] Scato Swu (1927–2014) was the second president of the Federal Government of Nagaland and later became a member of the Rajya Sabha in 1974.

[24] Nirmal Nibedon quotes Scato confirming that Phizo and the Tatar Hoho agreed to send a delegation to China and he then approved of sending Muivah to China because 'I found him to be a very, very honest man. Ramyo was nothing compared to this man.' *Nagaland: The Night of the Guerillas* (New Delhi: Lancer Publishers, 1978), 382.

position clear to them or it will be dangerous for India also. If we agree to completely stay in India, China will one day claim us. But if Nagaland is a buffer zone between India and China it will profit everybody.

It was very difficult to communicate to Mr Phizo. I had to write to his nephew in the United States and then the letter would be sent to him in London.

In 1964 I was a part of the Naga delegation involved in the peace talks. The Indian delegation was led by YD Gundevia,[25] the Foreign Secretary and Naga delegation was led by Zashie Huire,[26] the President of the Naga Federal Government. We had twelve rounds of talks in Chedema (Kohima district) and Khensa (in Mokokchung district).

In the beginning Mr Gundevia was very arrogant. He treated the problem as a law and order problem. We said we are not Indian so you cannot impose your Constitution on us.

We objected to Shilu Ao[27] being included in the delegation to represent Nagas. We said he could not represent the Naga people. We did not go for the talks for two days and after that Shilu Ao was included in the Government of India team, not as a Naga representative.

The peace talk was initiated by the Nagaland Baptist Church Council which set up a Peace Commission with Jayaprakash Narayan, Chaliha and Reverend Michael Scott[28] as members. We had a Tatar Hoho session in Wokha and invited the Peace Mission and asked them

[25] YD Gundevia (1908–1986) was an ICS officer and Nehru's last Foreign Secretary. He said the talks led to truce without a political settlement.

[26] Zashie Huire was from the Chakhesang tribe and was in the Indian Air Force before he joined the Naga national movement.

[27] Shilu Ao (1916–1988) was involved in the creation of Nagaland State and became the first Chief Minister of the state from 1963 to 1966.

[28] Jayaprakash Narayan (1902–1979) was a member of the CIA-funded Congress of Cultural Freedom, Bimal Prasad Chaliha (1912–1971) was the Chief Minister of Assam who imposed one language, Assamese, on the state and Reverend Michael Scott (1907–1983) was finally expelled from India partly because it was suspected he worked for British intelligence. These three men were chosen by the Baptist Church to negotiate peace between the Indian government and the Nagas.

whether they think it is a law and order problem or a political problem, and they said it was a political problem.

We spent the first round explaining our history. We asked Indira Gandhi: when did India conquer Nagaland? And when did Nagas consent to join the Indian Union? She could not answer.

I was there till the fifth round of talks but when the sixth round of talks were starting, I went to China. The sixth round of talks with Prime Minister Indira Gandhi started in October 1967.

While I was in China the Revolutionary Government [29] was set up. Mr Phizo wanted to remove the leadership of the Semas even though I myself said we accept Mr Phizo as our leader. But Mr Phizo wanted to completely remove the Sema leadership.

Before I left for China I was at the so-called international border between India and Burma, but then because I was involved in the talks I went back to Kohima and made a public appearance to show I have not gone underground. But the Indian authorities were looking for me.

March Through Kachin Lands

I started in a jeep and the jeep broke down near Jessami. The Indian Army helped repair it! I just got down from the jeep and walked to the next village right past the Indian Army patrol. Since I was not armed, they thought I was just another villager. I waited for General Mowu. That was in December 1967.

I had some Eastern Nagaland people with me. One of the Generals from the Eastern Nagaland Revolutionary Council was also with me. We crossed the Tizu river on foot. I was leading 150 people and General Mowu led another 150.

We had an encounter with the Burmese Army. The Burmese Army attacked us because the Eastern Nagaland people were with us. But at

---

[29] The Revolutionary Government of Nagaland with its political wing, the Council of Naga People, was set up under Sema leadership in November 1968. Kughato Sukhai became President, and Scato Swu the Prime Minister. In August 1973 the Government surrendered to the Indian authorities and Scato Swu was made a Rajya Sabha member.

that point General Mowu arrived and he could deal with them. One or two of our people got injured but it was not difficult for them to go back home since they were Yimchunger and lived nearby.

Before entering Kachin[30] area we had to purchase rice for six days because during those days we would go through jungle and not pass any village. Then we met the Kachin leaders and surprised one American missionary. He had been driven out by the Burmese Army for being Christian. I met him again in Thailand.

We all marched together to the 2nd Brigade Headquarters of the Kachin Independent Army. We had told the ENRC people not to identify themselves as Nagas from Eastern Nagaland and instead say they were from the West, but unfortunately Brigadier Simon revealed everything to the Kachins and they objected to Eastern Nagas going to China. And because of that Simon went back and surrendered to the Indian (sic) side. He was involved in the agar business. That is how Nuri came to be President of ENRC but his wife was sick for so many years. His wife was in Dibrugarh for more than twenty years. Then Khaplang became Chairman.[31]

Then Khaplang stayed with the Kachins on the condition he stays for five years and helps them. The Eastern Nagas fought for the Kachins and helped them bring arms from Chiangmai, Thailand. Many of the Nagas lost their lives.

We reached the China border and stayed for three days. They were expecting us because Mr Muivah had gone ahead and there were interpreters there. We had plenty of rice and we camped there and then the Chinese took us by vehicles straight to our training centre and gave us clothing and everything. It was cold and we were given cotton padded trousers. They gave us soap, hair oil, toothbrush, toothpaste, and after we changed into our new clothes, we could not recognize each other!

---

[30] The Kachin State is the northernmost state in Myanmar, bordering Tibet and Yunnan provinces in China. Kachins began their armed struggle for independence from 1960, under the leadership of the Kachin Independence Organization. Kachins are Christian, and mostly Baptist.

[31] The full story is in the testimony of Nuri.

We could not sleep on the soft bed because we had got used to
sleeping on the hard ground. So we were laughing about that.

In China

Then the training started and they taught us a revolutionary song.
General Mowu, myself and my personal secretary, and two others were
taken to meet the Chinese leaders. Mr Muivah came to meet us. We
were given a very warm welcome by the Chinese Foreign Minister.
He was there with us almost every day. We were taken to Bangkok
also. Our boys were brought to us batch by batch. We learnt to use
chopsticks and we visited many places in China.

The Chinese told us about how much they had suffered in the past
and how they had fought the enemy. We were shown their bases and
where General (sic) Mao sat to rest and which bunker he used, and
how he used to carry his own rice. They have preserved all these places.
They are intact. They showed us the places where the Communists
fought with Chiang Kai-shek and where they arrested him. They also
gave us General (sic) Mao's books. The army tactics they taught were
not very difficult to learn.

They also taught us how to make propaganda and write pamphlets.
They took us to a place on top of a mountain where there was no soil
for miles around. They carried soil up to the mountain, dug ditches
and filled them with the soil. And they brought water by pipeline
and planted fruit trees and now it is a beautiful garden. They planted
millet and rice also. In this way through hard work they have created a
beautiful garden. This they taught us. And in the field of fighting also
they taught us we have to help each other as friends. If they were sick,
we must look after them.

The Chinese also gave us medical training and many of our ladies
were trained. My wife also got training—no, we were not married
then. She went to China with Mr Muivah, not the first batch; then
there were no ladies.

When I went to China, I saw how Mao Tse-tung encouraged his

army to work in the fields and farmers would be brought to teach the army. By getting university education you cannot know many things. They think once they get education, they will wear suits and not go to the field. I used to encourage our boys and girls to go to the village during holidays and learn to catch fish and birds, learn from the villagers. There are many good things we can learn from the communists. There are many good points and bad points.

Phizo and China

In 1968 I went from China to Pakistan and from there I was taken to Paris to meet Phizo. I stayed with him for six days and we discussed what our next programme should be. Phizo wanted to come to China. But in 1962 he had issued a statement from London that he would mobilize 40,000 Nagas to fight the Chinese and that statement had become a stumbling block. He had issued the statement on the insistence of the British but he had also thought he would be able to convince the West in that way to help the Nagas. The Chinese were very hurt so we discussed and we—my friend and me—kept insisting that he should come to China.

Phizo sent word to the Chinese that he wants to come to their country. He told them he wants to take treatment for the paralysis on his face. But in reality, it was for political reasons that he wanted to go to China.

When I went to China I had a long talk with Marshal Chen Yi[32], who was Foreign Minister at the time. He said they would consider and let him come in the winter. I went back. But afterwards the Chinese changed their mind. I do not know the reason why they changed their mind about allowing him to come to China. There must have been some reason. The Chinese seemed to have no good opinion of Phizo because in a way he could not influence the West also.

---

[32] Marshal Chen Yi (1901-1972) was Foreign Minister of China from 1958 to 1972.

Another March to China

In 1974 I went to China again. That was the time I was the Finance Minister and I had gone to the camp to give them money. They were camping somewhere in the southern Sema area and we were praying and the Spirit said that I had to go. I said I was not ready. I told them I have been to China and also Burma. I went up to Rangoon so I should give other friends a chance to go to China so that they may also experience it.

But the Spirit said I must go, and if I go back my life would be in danger. The Vice President of NNC Imkongmeren also sent his consent. And Vice President of the Federal Government Merhupfu was with us.

So we started and it was really a miserable trip. Some of the boys went to the village to get rations and the enemy detected their movement and followed them and they were attacked. So that night we ran away. One Captain was killed but the rest escaped.

We arrived at the next village. We sent our men to contact the Pastor and the elders for rations. The village was opposed to our movement so instead of bringing rations they brought the Assam Rifles to attack us the next morning. It was a village which supported Zashie Huire, the proprietor of statehood.[33]

In that attack we scattered. We did not know the number of casualties. The Indian Army deployed a whole brigade to do combing operations, so the next night when we were in the camp the Spirit told us to go to the fields and collect the roots of sweet potatoes. The Spirit said it would open the way for us. So we stayed there and one Angami boy who was stationed below the mountain surrendered.

It started raining so we could not sleep and the next morning they attacked us. I was saved by the grace of God because bullets were coming from all sides. That evening I had loose motions after eating roots. I was so weak I could not move my legs and we were attacked and my two bodyguards pushed me up the hill.

---

[33] Zashie Huire supported the establishment of Nagaland State.

We kept climbing up and our boys took position and fired. The firing stopped for a while and we told our boys to rush down to the river and we followed its course towards a village. The Spirit told us to pass the woodland and then cross the road.

Then we came to the highway. I told the commander to go in a certain direction but instead he went below and the Indian Army post was there. The Indian Army started to follow us. The Angami boy who had surrendered started shouting in the loudspeaker that no harm would come to us if we came out.

I told the group to pray. I told them don't look in the direction of the firing but just pray, and I continued to pray. The rest of the group scattered or were captured and only thirteen of us were left. The people were very much frightened and I told them just to keep praying.

Then we moved ahead. We had just one submachine gun and an automatic rifle. One Sema boy was holding the submachine gun. He came to me and said, 'Sir, I do not know what has happened to me but I am feeling so weak.' I encouraged him and at one point he was sent to guard but we made some sound that the Indian Army heard and they captured the boy holding the submachine gun. So now we were just twelve of us.

The Spirit told us to keep going without sleeping and we then came to the area which is between the Ao and Phom. We collected leaves and slept but the next morning, we saw that the enemy had covered the whole area. We moved only in the dark and it was after a month I think we reached Burma. We did not get any rice and we used to eat leaves.

We reached the Konyak area. We came to the village of Brigadier Ngamlo. He had already gone with the General Secretary. Eastern Nagaland had not been mobilized so there were some people who were not friendly with us.

Then we came to a Lao village.[34] We were in the jungle and I sent

---

[34] Lao village is in Sagaing Division, Khamti District, Lahe Township on the border of India. The Lao Naga, also spelt Law or Loh, are many times included under

word to them that we were coming. They said, 'No! Don't come.' I sent word that I want to come and explain things to you. So we went to the village and there I purchased one buffalo and shared with the entire village and we ate together.

Then we discussed together and I told them why we had come and what was our mission. Brigadier Kholi was there; at the time he was Lieutenant Colonel. He had been suspended by Ngamlo. I asked Kholi why he was suspended and he said there was no reason only because Ngamlo wanted his younger brother to be put in charge.

So I told Kholi to come with us and let the younger brother take charge of the brigade. So he came with thirty-eight of his men who were a part of the Naga Army. So then we were fifty of us altogether.

Lao is a very strong village and they are the strongest supporters of the nation. We are going to award them because they fought the Burmese and they never betrayed. The village volunteers would go with our army.

The Lao Naga are closer to Konyak and there are differences between Khaplang and the Konyak people. The Khaplang people try to dominate the Konyak. Khaplang is from Rangpan tribe. Later, in the 1980s, Khaplang told the Rangpan and Heimi tribes to merge and call themselves Pangmei.

So we started marching, the fifty of us, but three more were killed on the banks of the Chindwin river. That included one Sema woman and one Captain and one Sergeant Major. It was a surprise attack so we could not do anything and we could not recover the bodies. After a year we came back to dig their graves but the area was flooded so we could do nothing.

When we reached the Kachin area, they did not want us to continue and they had also detained Mr Muivah. We had a spiritual programme because the Spirit encouraged us and said we will be allowed to go. So we fasted and prayed and we fasted and prayed.

Konyak Naga or Leinong Naga but they have a distinct language. Lao village has some 200 households.

We were in the Kachin area for three months, I think. Then Mr Muivah and I went to the Kachin General Headquarters and talked to Brangsen, their Finance Minister. He was a bit friendly with us so at last they allowed us to go.

We arrived in China in August 1975. The Chinese authorities were very good to us. The commander and interpreter were very good to us. We discussed about our needs and what was necessary. We discussed the idea of training pilots, engineers to repair the arms, and mechanical training.

During the discussions we were told Mao Tse-tung had ordered them to build a church for us. We used to dig for them and we had helped build the training centre. They knew whenever we dig, we make a lot of noise but the work gets done quickly. They liked the way we worked together.

Shillong Accord[35]

Just as we were in the midst of all these discussions, we heard that the Shillong Accord was signed on 11 November 1975. That date I remember well.

So all our plans were blown up and the Chinese said your home government has failed and now you have to go back and build everything by yourselves. They said even if you stay here it will not profit you. They wanted to help us. They said it was their international duty to help all revolutions over the world. If Nagas fail, it affects many other people as well. We must go back and convince more people.

---

[35] Shillong Accord was an Accord signed by the members of the Naga underground and the Government of India whereby the members of the Naga underground accepted the Constitution of India and also agreed to deposit their arms. The Agreement was signed on November 10, 1975 at Shillong. Phizo's brother Kevi Yalley was one of the signatories on behalf of the underground. The Accord was condemned by Isak and Muivah and ultimately led them to leave NNC and form the NSCN in 1980. The NSCN blamed Phizo for not condemning the Accord. The NNC said the organization was not a signatory to the Accord, only some members of the underground. The Accord continues to be one of the most contentious issues among the Naga nationalists.

We wrote three letters to Uncle Phizo telling him the situation and requesting him to condemn the Shillong Accord. Two were written in Angami. I wrote them myself. The third letter was signed by all seven of us and we said, 'If you don't condemn the Shillong Accord then we shall take it that you are also party to it. History will never forgive you and we will never surrender.'

We asked Phizo to give us directions and instructions on what we should do. But he never replied. It was very difficult to understand what was happening. If Angami and Chakhesang unite what would happen to whole of Nagaland? So, with a heavy heart we began our journey back.

We were ambushed on the way but it did not affect us seriously. On the way we gave 30 per cent of our arms to the Kachins. I think altogether 700 arms; before when General Mowu and I had passed we had already given them 123 pieces of arms on our way to China. We gave them the arms because it was no use taking them to China and also we helped the Kachins to strengthen their organization. The Kachins had promised to return our arms but they did not; we did not ask them. The Kachins are not reliable. The Chinese had also told the Kachins not to give us trouble.

The last trip to China was in 1978. The Kachins stopped us on the way. We warned them not to get too close to the Indians. The Kachins were taking arms from China which had its own tactics and gave them arms through the Burmese Communist party, but they were not allowed to purchase arms. They could purchase as much as they liked from China but they thought they would get more from India. So we told them that now you are trying to undermine our position but one day it will be suicide for you. They wanted to take Khaplang with them.

When the Kachins opened their office in New Delhi then the Chinese started helping the Shan. The Kachin don't understand the importance of NGOs.

We reached the Khiamniungan area and settled at Lakhiang village. We had a meeting for thirteen days on what we should do next.

Reflections on China

The Chinese civilization is the oldest in the world. And according to history they consider themselves as the only civilized people in the world. In the matter of religion, they think that God is so high that only the Emperor can worship Him. Common people were not given a chance to worship God. That was left to high ranking priests to pray on behalf of the public once or twice a year.

So there was longing in the people to worship God and soul of human being cannot be happy unless it has communication with its creator so it is said by historian that when Buddhism came it was like melting of butter in a hot pan—people accepted it and everybody could worship.

If it was not for Mao, China would not be as it is today. Before he came, there was the emperor and landowners who lived like God and people were treated as sub-human. Some people were given land to cultivate and the owner will take their share so the peasant never had enough for his family and he had to borrow from the owner again. They had nothing to eat so they had to sell their children. Some had to commit suicide instead of selling his boy or girl. There are so many cases like that. It is said the emperor and landowners would take the women's milk and the child would starve. These are the stories we heard. They rose up in revolt but they were crushed. Mao studied communism and then he organized.

Mao taught people how to love each other, how to help each other, and he said in the beginning the people coming from the provinces quarrelled over petty matters such as too much salt in the curry or too much chilli in the curry. He used to calmly call them and ask them, 'What is the trouble, what is the problem? Tell me.' Then when they told him, he would explain to them that they must learn to appreciate each other.

He taught the people how to rise up against the rulers. And they started to form a people's army and Mao himself and other two leaders were very good leaders. They participated in the revolution and carried loads like a soldier. They suffered the same way. The army was taught how to raise chicken, how to raise pigs, how to take care of the horses, how to milk cows, how to make butter, how to cultivate, and practical lessons from the university when they formed the people's army. They were happy because they were united.

They have a love for fellow human beings. And they have concern for the poor people; the Chinese Army used to work in the fields and according to Mao's teachings they went to villages and helped people. So people consider them a People's Army. That is something we can learn from them.

If Mao had not been there and given proper education to his people then China would not be like it is now. Then the landowners were arrested and some of them were executed. And the lands were divided among the people. So everywhere people became happy since they had their own land to cultivate. And where possible twenty to thirty families made a commune and worked together; sometimes even 100 families. In the commune they were given common land and they cultivated that. They kept enough for the village and the rest they sold to the government. Then the people purchased one bicycle and one radio and one television set for each family. But now people complain that they do not have private property and private ownership.

Under Mao Tse-tung the morality in China was the highest in the world. We saw it. There were no love affairs among boys and girls, there was age limit so they just get married but there was no moral degradation among the people. During Mao's time they did not expose the body. The people dressed properly. But now the Chinese are becoming the worst —following the West, they expose the whole body. So many becoming prostitutes and gambling and old people started drinking heavily and gambling and it is going to be dangerous because if China becomes a bad country with bad people it can influence us, or it can destroy us easily. So human beings will have to think about it and how to correct society.

Man cannot live by bread alone. Why did Marilyn Monroe commit suicide? She had everything. She had all the money but she did not have a relationship with her Creator and did not know the value of the soul. Like that Russia also thought just because everyone had food everybody will be happy. No! Man cannot live by bread alone, so happiness is not having plenty but happiness comes from the heart and in the mind.

What happened in Russia is happening now in China. But the Chinese are not like the Russians, and China will not totally collapse.

The Soviet Union has collapsed. There are many causes. But one is that they tried to subsume nationalism under communism. Our nationalism will never die because it is the creation of God. God has created every nation, even small groups like Tarao which has only three villages. When you think of it, it is a wonderful thing. If the Soviet Union has collapsed then there is a possibility that India too will collapse.

When we met Deve Gowda[36] I read out John 8: 32 which says the truth will set you free. India's national symbol is 'Satyamave Jayate'. Like Gandhi fought for independence and his achievement and his non-violence is followed by the whole world, so if Nagas stick to the truth and win victory and have an understanding with Government of India and we practice the truth we will be set free. God has a purpose for Nagaland. And it will help not only Nagas but also India, China and Burma—also the world.

Some people used to say we should have no connection with India. But we used to say no, because no nation can be entirely independent of each other. We have to establish a relationship with India.

So we have to see a different platform to correct human society. Whether it is social, religious or political then we can contribute at least something to humanity. But if we consider only for profit how to become rich and dominate people, then the world will become the worst hell for everybody and it will be difficult to live.

---

[36] Haradanahalli Doddegowda Deve Gowda (born 18 May 1933) was the eleventh Prime Minister of India from 1 June 1996 to 21 April 1997. He was previously the Chief Minister of Karnataka from 1994 to 1996. He became the National President of the Janata Dal (Secular) Party.

Even in case of religion and culture we cannot blindly follow others. Whatever is possible by us we must do, and what our people cannot do we have to slowly change. We have to slowly change, otherwise people will commit suicide. Let everybody learn that change is coming. In this way we improve our society.

When Mao died we had half-mast flag and we stood together and had a word of prayer and observed silence for two weeks just to pay respects to him because he was the person who fully helped our people.

Now the greatest fear of India is that if we are to free Nagas, then they will come closer to China because racially we are one and so one day China will claim the Nagas and that will be the most dangerous thing for India. But we used to tell the Indians: 'No! That is not the case. We know that we are Christian.'

My Marriage

I got married in Eastern Nagaland in our base camp in 1976. The Spirit told us to get married by the month of March but there was no means to get married then so we had an engagement on 25 March. The Spirit told us we must get married within that month but we had no means. We had only a few hundred rupees. But it was the will of God, so what to do?

We went in search of a mithun and we caught it. We asked the villagers to contribute one pig. Then we asked for another and we finally got two more. There was fighting with the Burmese Army so we captured the rations of the Burmese Army and we got rice, sugar and milk. And the group who had gone to capture the rations also came back and joined the ceremony. God's work is so wonderful.

The Spirit gave my wife the name 'Eustar' which means light-bearer. Her formal name is Khulu. She is from Lazami, the biggest Sema village. They have six or seven thousand houses in the village.

The marriage ceremony was conducted by Reverend Puni. We do not have any photograph of the ceremony. We had taken one photograph and we sent it to Kachin State to develop it but we lost it. It would have been a remarkable memory for us.

Aftermath of the Shillong Accord

In February 1976 we decided to send a fact-finding mission to find out who was supporting the Accord. We heard that many Nagas were not satisfied with the Accord, especially with the surrender of arms. So we thought we would take our Army and bring them to the Eastern side.

Two people were given the task of contacting leaders at various levels to ascertain their stand on the Shillong Accord. We could not take any step unless we had a proper assessment of the situation, and knew which of the leaders and which tribes were supporting the Accord. This was not a small problem but a problem which affected the entire nation. Many people were under the spell of Ramyo,[37] Kevi Yalley (Phizo's brother), and the church leaders who were threatening people. Ramyo and Kevi Yalley would tell anyone who wanted to oppose the Accord that it would be of no use fighting individually because everyone had surrendered. So, in this way they would discourage the individuals who wanted to continue fighting for independence. Yalley contacted Indian intelligence people and told them where he would be going. So wherever he went the Indian Army would not carry out their operation while he was there and that is how he escaped being arrested.

The Peace Mission was formed by the church leaders like Longri Ao and Kenneth Kerhuo and later it was renamed Nagaland Peace Council. Indira Gandhi had invited them for talks to Shillong with the Governor LP Singh. It was then that the Governor told them to lay down their arms. They were in the hands of the enemy so what could they do? They were made to say they accept the Indian Constitution unconditionally. They were helpless and our President (Phizo) did

---

[37] Ramyo Zimik (1929–1994) was a Tangkhul Naga from Talui village in present-day Ukhrul district of Manipur. He was a Kilonser in the Federal Government and a signatory to the Shillong Accord. He went to America where he lived in exile and later died in a car accident. He is buried in his village.

not condemn it so it made it worse. If he had condemned it the whole world would know that the Shillong Accord was not legitimate.

After Phizo died many of his followers called a meeting and condemned the Shillong Accord, including Yanthan Lotha, General Thinoselie and Biseto.[vii] It was in 1994 or 95. Twenty years later! Till then they were not bold enough to join us but they did not mind joining the Accordists who wanted to eliminate us.

A New Government

The leaders who did not support the Shillong Accord met and we set up a caretaker government. I was made the Chairman of the Caretaker Government, and Brigadier Vedai was the Commander-in-Chief. The General Secretary remained Muivah. And then he called the National Assembly in August 1976. He was the only one authorized to do so in the absence of the President and Vice President. The National Assembly is the highest body, it can even recall the Tatar Hoho or Parliament. The National Assembly was held in Suphao Village.

In the National Assembly we passed some resolutions:

1.   to uphold the national movement
2.   Shillong Accord was condemned
3.   condemn the Ministry which had signed the Shillong Accord and sold out the nation
4.   I was elected the Vice President of the NNC and the government.

It was a historic meeting and about 500 people came, including people from nearby villages. Khaplang was not in the picture because he had not yet come back from Kachin area. He was serving them for five years[38] but some of his people came for the meeting. We also raised a battalion.

---

[38] Kachins had insisted that, as a Burmese, he had to stay with them and work with them.

Around seventy to eighty Tangkhuls, both civil and army, came and joined us. The Khiamniungan people, including one battalion was there; but some had surrendered.

The Aos wanted to have a separate northern command and we had a lot of discussion. Not many Aos had gone to China to fetch arms so we said it is important to have a centralized command. We re-organized the army. From the federal times it was based on tribes but we centralized it.

While we were in the process of re-organization some of the men who supported the Accord came pretending to support us. They said Uncle Phizo should be made the President of the Federal Government in addition to being the President of the Naga National Council. While we were busy trying to save the organization, they started propagating that we wanted to topple Phizo and capture power of both the Party and the Government. This was what they— Ramyo, Kevi Yalley and the Peace Council—propagated. The Peace Council also started saying we are bringing communism. In the midst of this confusion we were arrested by these men who had pretended to be anti-Accord.

We were detained and kept at a separate place and there was a plot to eliminate us. Our graves were dug but by the grace of God we were saved. Instead they were eliminated.

There was a difference of opinion between those who arrested us, Muivah and me; the Leinong said they would not allow their national leaders to be eliminated in their area. The Konyaks supported us and also the Aos. So it was the Khiamniungan, the Angami and Chakhesang who wanted to eliminate us.

Khaplang returned. He was not given any arms by the Kachins. The Americans and Taiwan were helping the Kachins. The Kachins were angry with U Nu, the Burmese Prime Minister, for giving a big chunk of their land to China.[39]

---

[39] U Nu gave three Kachin villages to China as a part of settlement of the border dispute with China and signed a mutual no-aggression pact on October 1, 1960.

They, the Accordists had a second plan. They would pretend to attack the Indian Army post but in fact they would hand both of us to the Indian Army. But the news of the attack was leaked. Then they had a third plan to get the Indians to send a helicopter to Lao village where they would hand us over but the helicopter got lost and so that plan also failed.

Finally they decided to elect Mr Khaplang to be President of the Federal Government. He accepted it and after that he came to meet us. He said he would release us. But we said since he had not arrested us how could he release us?

Finally, we were released in March 1979 and we had a long meeting. It was a three-month long meeting and at the end of which we decided to form an organization in which East and West Nagaland could merge and four of us were the leaders: I was the Chairman, Khaplang became the Vice Chairman, Muivah was the General Secretary and General Thungbo would be the Commander-in-Chief of our Army. He is a very reasonable man and from Eastern side.

While we were under arrest, we wrote the manifesto of our new organization called National Socialist Council of Nagaland.

Role of the Church Leaders

The church leaders started preaching against us saying we are communists and communists had everything in common, even common wives, and children were also common property. They said even families were not privatized—it was quite a frightening future.

The church leaders started preaching against us and said whoever went to China must be killed. The Government of India had agents who educated the church leaders. One of those agents was Dr Aram.[40] He misled the church leaders. He knew Jayaprakash Narayan and he opened peace centres in two or three places. Some of the

---

[40] Dr M Aram (1927–1997) was part of the Nagaland Peace Mission from 1964 to 1980 and he helped to design the Shillong Peace Accord. His full name was Muthukumaraswamy Aramvalarthanathan.

Christian Nagas were paid by the Indians. They said we were bringing communism to Nagaland. They had organized Christ's soldiers and General Assa was their leader.

These people did not know what we were doing when we were in China or what we did while we were staying in Eastern Nagaland.

When we were in China, we had regular church service and even the Chinese Army used to ask us about Christianity and our beliefs. They asked why we do not smoke or drink. Both from the religious point of view and the revolutionary point of view it is a matter of discipline not to smoke or drink because then the enemy cannot distract us or take advantage of us. Then the Chinese said, 'Oh! This is a good thing!' and some of them also gave up smoking because it was bad for health. They don't drink and particularly their drivers were not allowed to drink.

These Peace Mission people started saying that NSCN people are killing all pastors and deacons and burning down churches in Eastern Nagaland. They sent a fact-finding mission to Eastern Nagaland consisting of Reverend Rangkam and Reverend Chinang. When they came, they saw how many people we were converting and how many churches we had built in the villages. We had opened three Mission Centres and fifteen Mission Schools. We had converted more than 40,000 people. They went back and told the church leaders that NSCN is doing more than them. So, how can the NSCN be communist?

Even today when one pastor was killed by the Burmese Army, they accused us of killing him. They wrote in the papers that he was killed by us. In fact, the pastor was sponsored by the Ao Baptist Church to evangelize the Khiamniungan people. The Burmese Army came while he was preaching and they rounded up the village and he made a mistake of trying to run away and they shot him. His name was Rameses.

Those who are spiritual people and were praying were told by the Spirit that we were not Communist. The Spirit told them that we were working for the spread of Christianity and then they subsided. They believed in the Spirit of God.

I met Reverend Longri and Kenneth[41] myself when I first returned from China. That time the Indian Army was searching for me everywhere but I went to the Chedema Peace Camp[42] and met them and told them about our stay in China and how we worshipped and how the Chinese were very much impressed with us. I told them how the Chinese public was also impressed because there were many Christians who secretly worshipped there.

Longri was a very emotional person and he said 'Oh! We did not know it and we have been criticizing, but do you have any picture of yourself there?'

NSCN in Burma

After we formed the NSCN and before the split with Khaplang, we re-organized the army. We centralized the whole army and the command and divided it region-wise.

Our other concern was with the unreached people (sic)—those who were enemies and those who do not know the meaning of religion and the message of salvation. That was the toughest area and the darkest area. One of our objectives was to evangelize where no gospel had been preached. Nobody had come there to teach them. Even as late as 1978 few villages were practicing headhunting. We had to control it and then convert the whole area to Christianity so that was one of the biggest challenges.

No Forced Conversions[43]

NH: It is said you forcibly converted the people.

---

[41] Reverend Longri Ao (1906–1981) and Reverend Kenneth Kerhuo were both involved in the peace process which led to the signing of the Shillong Accord.

[42] Chedema Peace Camp was set up in September 1964 after the first ceasefire and was the venue for the peace talks; after the Shillong Accord, 150 arms were deposited in the custody of Nagaland Peace Council at Chedema.

[43] We reproduce the exact exchange on this charge against the NSCN leaders made by various writers.

IS: No that is not true. We went to the villages and for days together we preached and when we got the consent of the people and when they said yes, we converted them.

NH: But you went with an army.

IS: If we do not go with the Naga Army, the Indian Army and the Burmese Army were here and there and they could attack us at any time. But the Naga Army was not there to threaten the villagers but to guard us, and it was not a big army—mostly they were my guards and some Kilonsers.

NH: Was the preaching done by you?

IS: The preaching is done according to the programme given by the Spirit; the Spirit would tell us that this fellow will pray and this fellow will speak first. Of course I used to speak every time, I was the main speaker. But I would speak last after giving the others a chance to preach. The others who preached included an ordained Chakhesang pastor called Vedai. He was in the Naga Army of Brigadier rank. His wife was also one of the prophecies[44] and my wife was also there. They were guided by visions.

God told us to evangelize as soon as possible because the people were perishing so whenever we came to a village we got together with the sick people.

We started praying for them and healed them. That was quite a surprise for them because the blind could see and the paralyzed could be healed. And we could drive away the demon possessing the people. Leprosy could be healed instantly. Even their old animist religion had rituals to drive away demons possessing people. So we could help many people to get released from the bondage of the devil. And many people were happy with us.

We started three Mission Centres and then we started fifteen Mission Schools in different villages. The children were put in the schools and we started teaching them to read and write.

---

[44] The NSCN call the oracles who are a part of their organization 'prophecies'. This is explained further in our interview with Unice.

My children[45] were sent to the Western side but my adopted children went to these schools. My children were very young so we just taught them A-B-C at home but they were not able to learn much so we sent them to the Western side.

That is how God performed miracles and we came to one of the biggest villages in the Burma side called Ranchi (sic). A paralyzed man sent for us. He had gone to his field and the devil had attacked him and he had been lying paralyzed for years.

We went to his house and prayed for him and suddenly all his veins started moving—the paralyzed side of his body started moving. And he stood up and started walking. So we called a meeting of the people who started coming to see him and we started preaching to them and said how the world is cursed and salvation can come. We told the story of Noah which they knew because they knew of floods. We told them how the entire humanity was punished because of the sins of the people. And then Jesus Christ had to come and he has given a new life to us. So those who believe in Jesus Christ would be saved. And they said they would change their master but they needed a pastor and they said no one will be left who has not been baptized—even a new-born baby would be baptized.

The only sad thing was that we could not provide a pastor to teach them. Of course we have a few who go from time to time to teach them. But even today they are suffering because of that. We could not provide a pastor to all the villages and a pastor cannot be an ordinary person and he must know how to teach the people. Anyway they learnt how to pray and that was the main step for them. They learnt to pray to God: 'God we want this and this; we want to lead a righteous life, have a happy and good family.' They could pray better than our people in Western Nagaland.

In Eastern Nagaland the main source of income for many villages was poppy cultivation. They made khaini or opium and then took

---

[45] Isak Swu's oldest son Ikato said he met his father for the first time in 1993 when he was fifteen years old and this was trying for the other children.

it to Khamti and also to Arunachal side and they sold it there. So we discussed this problem. We could not allow all the people to smoke because it would create a problem. But we could not stop the old people from having opium so we gave them a license and told them not to take in excess. In this way we had to control them and the poppy plantation.

We introduced terrace cultivation and taught them to grow potatoes and cabbage, chicken and pig-rearing, and the women's organization were sent from village to village to teach sanitation. We taught them how to plant chillies and soya beans and the people were very happy and our students were brilliant. Many of our boys from the Eastern side who went to the Western side to study occupy good positions. Many have passed matric and also some have graduated. Before we went, they had not been given any education.

Armed Resistance

There is a prophecy that Burmese and Nagas were brothers and many in the Indian and Burmese Armies were Nagas so we never took the offensive. But the Burmese Army did attack and burn down Naga villages and finish the domestic animals. These attacks were two or three times a year. After the attack the Burmese Army did not occupy the village but went back.

We needed money to buy arms. We wanted to continue our armed resistance so that Indian government would know that the Naga movement is not over after the Accord.

So we captured money from a bank at Phutsero. We do not call it bank robbery. This is warfare so whatever we capture from the enemy it is not a sin. So it is not wrong. So instead of burdening the villagers we decided to capture the bank so the load on the public would be lighter. We can capture everything and they cannot accuse us because when they attack, they loot everything from us and we cannot blame them. This is warfare. It is not robbery or murder but warfare. The Indian government is trying to occupy our land and we are trying to push them out. So whatever action we take is justified.

Self-Reliance

NH: So would you give an official statement that NSCN does not raise money from anywhere except from its own people?[46]

IS: Yes, we do not have any foreign help.

NH: But people are criticizing the younger members of NSCN who seem to have a lot of money and a lifestyle very different from the life your generation lived. People are asking from where is the money coming. So how do you explain this change in lifestyle?

IS: Yes, it is one of our problems and we are trying to correct this by intense political training and intense military training. And reduce the number of vehicles and reduce the expenditure. Otherwise it will be suicidal. This started two or three years back. It has not happened for long. And our enemy is taking advantage of our weakness.

Khaplang[47]

He was the Vice Chairman but he cannot be disciplined. We have strict rules and regulations for the leaders such as no drinking, no smoking, no womanizing but he cannot avoid any of these. He continued to smoke and drink all the time. It will spread to the Tatars (Members of the Tatar Hoho or Members of Parliament).

Khaplang would go to the village and preach that the Western and Eastern should be separated. Sometimes he would go to church and

---

[46] We had a long discussion on the impact of money on the Naga national movement. According to our understanding, this money had come through western based NGOs with their own hidden agenda. We wrote about it in our book: *The Judgement That Never Came: Army Rule in North East India* (New Delhi: Bibliophile South Asia, 2011).

[47] SS Khaplang (1940-2017) founded the Naga Defence Force in 1964 and the Eastern Naga Revolutionary Council in 1965. He was the Vice Chairman of the NSCN from the time of its foundation in 1980 to 1988 when he split and formed the NSCN (K).

say that drinking is not bad and if we all become Christian we will lose our culture. And the villagers came and told us that they were confused by what Khaplang told them and what we had taught them. And the villagers said that there must be some misunderstanding between them and us.

Then we had a council meeting at the headquarters and he was sent a letter to come, but he had gone back to his village saying that his wife was sick. But he wrote back that he would accept whatever decision we made. He told us not to worry about his absence. This was in 1987. But actually he was preparing to separate his men. And Khaplang called all the Konyak boys under Kholi.[48]

Our organization took the decision to send me to China and if possible to other countries to explain the position of NSCN. I went along with my wife who was pregnant. Our baby was born in Kachin side. We reached the Kachin headquarters but there was propaganda that I had gone to New Delhi to surrender with twenty-nine people. A Konyak MLA told Kholi that Muivah and I had gone to Delhi to surrender.

Rumours were also spread that Muivah has lots of houses in Arunachal, Dimapur, Guwahati, Jorhat while Nagas were dying for nothing and the leaders were enjoying themselves in Delhi. In fact, Muivah was at the headquarters.

I was on my way to China and I was detained by the Kachins on the request of Khaplang. Khaplang had told them to send me back to Burma. I negotiated with the Kachin authorities to allow me to go Arunachal and they allowed us. We were all together, twenty-nine of us, but I sent back eighteen of them to our headquarters along with the arms that we were carrying. We kept one submachine gun and one pistol. We carried three tins of rice for the eleven of us.

---

[48] General Kholi Chetkoh Konyak joined the Naga movement in 1956. Later he joined Khaplang but worked tirelessly for unification of the NSCN (I-M) and NSCN (K); in 2016 he re-joined Isak Swu and Thuingaleng Muivah shortly before his death in December 2018.

We had to walk for twenty-two days through the jungles to reach the last Kachin village. They escorted us to that point. After that there are Naga villages. By that time the rice had finished. We had to go without food for nine days. I told my men to go hunting and by God's grace within fifteen minutes they shot a stag. So we dried the meat and then we cut down a big palm tree and from the stem inside we made flour. People used to survive on this when there was no rice.

At the last Kachin village, we were detained for five days because it started to rain. The rain stopped and then we followed the river course. We arrived at a Naga village and contacted the Christian houses. In that village there was a teacher who was an intelligence agent but on the day we arrived, he had gone on holiday so we were saved. That is why God had detained us with rain.

My daughter became very sick because of the mosquitoes and leeches. She became bloodless. So there was no way out but to kill a monkey and give her monkey blood. We gave the fresh blood of two monkeys and she survived.

We arrived in Tinsukia and from there to Dimapur. It was a struggle all the way but with the grace of God we got help everywhere. Then there was a village with the Brigadier HQ of the Indian Army. There I asked the pastor to provide a vehicle but he said there were only two and one had gone to Digboi and the other was under repair. The pastor and his wife helped us and we reached a doctor's house. I had a letter from Paresh[49] which I gave to the doctor's wife and the doctor told us to wait at the bus stand and we had to wait for the whole day; seven of us hiding our submachine gun and then in the evening he bought train tickets for us. We tried to get first-class tickets but they were sold out so we got second-class. I did not disclose my identity to the doctor.

Even the second-class was full and we had to push our way into the compartment, but my biggest worry was about reaching Dimapur. If we reached in the morning then we would be exposed. We met a Kuki

---

[49] Paresh Barua (born 1957) is a leader of the ULFA said to be living in China. In 2017, he warned the Dalai Lama to stop speaking against China.

from Manipur and he was a Christian and he told us that the train would reach at three in the morning so we decided it was safe to go by the train.

When we reached Dimapur I went to the house of my cousin brother and then I tried to find out what was happening. I sent Captain Akhui and within an hour Hanshi came and said Muivah was in Calcutta, so we went to Calcutta and three of us were admitted to hospital. My wife and I had malaria and my baby was not well. We were in hospital for two weeks.

After that we printed a pamphlet and distributed it. It was a joint statement of Mr Muivah and myself on the differences between us and Khaplang.

Peace Talks

Jamir said he wanted to be a bridge between us and the Government of India and people came to us from two directions—from Jamir and from Rishang Keishing. Mrs Gandhi agreed to have unconditional talks but then she was assassinated and Rajiv Gandhi too agreed but he too was assassinated.

Then we had a meeting with the Indian Prime Minister PV Narasimha Rao in Paris in 1995. And now we have started the peace process.

THUINGALENG MUIVAH: THE IDEOLOGUE

Thuingaleng Muivah was born on March 23, 1935[50] in Somdal village of present-day Ukhrul District, Manipur. He is a Tangkhul Naga.

Muivah joined the Naga National Council in 1964. The next year he was elected as General Secretary. He was the first plenipotentiary to China in 1966.

Thuingaleng Muivah stayed in China close to ten years, and visited Vietnam and North Korea.[viii] He remained in the NNC till he broke with them in 1975 regarding disagreements over signing of the Shillong Accord.

Thuingaleng Muivah along with Isak Chishi Swu and SS Khaplang established the National Socialist Council of Nagaland (NSCN) on January 31, 1980. He was the General Secretary of the NSCN from its inception to the present time. The General Secretary is also the Ato Kilonser or Prime Minister in the Government of People's Republic of Nagalim (GPRN).

Thuingaleng Muivah has been involved in negotiations for a honourable settlement with the Government of India ever since the ceasefire agreement was signed in 1997.

This interview was conducted in April of 1998 in Bangkok.

Testimony of Thuingaleng Muivah

Shongran is the village where I was born.

It has been so long since I visited Shongran,[51] the village where I was born, but the exact date, month and year are forgotten. My father noted down the date on the Holy Bible; it was on the first page. But later the page got torn because the Bible was used by so many people.

---

[50] Thuingaleng Muivah was not sure of the exact date, but his birthday is celebrated on March 23, 1935. Perhaps that is the date on his passport, but he told us he thinks it was March 1934, a year after the death of Ruichamhao in 1933.

[51] Somdal is the exonym given by the dominant Meitei community but the Tangkhuls are increasingly renaming the villages by their autonyms, in this case 'Shongran.'

I am blessed that I was born in a village where prominent leaders such as Uncle Suisa[52] and Rungsung Ruichamhao[53] were born. Among them all it was from Ruichamhao that I drew the most inspiration. He was a great educationalist and also a pioneering missionary. Unfortunately, he died one year before I was born but I learnt about him because of my father, Shangkathan Muivah, who was a disciple of Ruichamhao. My father was deeply spiritual while my mother was more practical.

My Family

Our family was very poor. Sometimes we had nothing to eat. My sister Longrungla was the oldest of us. She has a deep love hidden for me in her heart. Even now she always prays for me and for all national workers. She would always give something for my education. When I was in the eighth standard my sister wanted to get married but my parents could only arrange for seventy rupees. She went with that money to Imphal to buy things for her wedding. Fortunately, my brother was there and he was able to borrow money so she could get married. But when she came back, she had saved forty rupees for the education of my brother and me. And that money lasted for one whole year! I was studying in the village school and luckily I passed.

My older brother, Shangreihan, he is economically better off. He supported Yangmaso Shaiza[54] at one time but Rishang Keishing[55] put

---

[52] Rungsung Suisa (1907-1971) Member of the Naga National Council; he stood for elections and was elected to the Indian parliament in 1957. He strongly advocated a peaceful negotiated settlement to the Indo-Naga conflict.

[53] Ruichamhao (1896–1933) was born on May 7 in Shongran, the same year that Reverend Pettigrew arrived in the district.

[54] Yangmaso Shaiza (1923–1984) was the fourth Chief Minister of Manipur and the first tribal politician to hold that post. His party was called the Manipur Hills Union and gave full autonomy to District Councils. He was shot by militants.

[55] Rishang Keishing (1920–2017) was Chief Minister of Manipur in the 1980s and 90s, a member of the Indian National Congress since 1964. He was the longest-serving parliamentarian in the world.

him in jail three times because he was my brother. He sacrificed so much for me. My other brothers also always supported me.

I have the deepest respect for my mother, Ramangla. She was not like other mothers. I know some mothers take great care about cleanliness of their children and about their health. Not my mother. I used to be the dirtiest among my friends and they made fun of me and joked at my cost.

My mother was illiterate and did not ever go to school. But she was a deep thinker, a philosopher, you could say. She was orphaned when she was little and she had a miserable life. But she was tough even though she was short in size. My elder brother was critical of my mother but I learnt a lot from her.

To my mother, life was all about struggle. Before she set out to do anything, she would think out the best way to do the task. She did not like to beg from others but she said we must share whatever we have.

She always said everything that happens in the world happens for a reason. My mother could be difficult but her thinking was always scientific. She always thought deeply and pondered over everything. She said, 'My son, everything has a reason. Life is not emotion. You must approach any problem seriously, precisely and realistically. Some trees are green, others are red. River waters flow down, not up. Everything is governed by laws of nature. Until and unless you grasp these laws, you will not be wise. Our Maker has created the universe with some thought so you cannot just have your own interpretations and presumptions.'

My mother always said there was a season for everything and every season also has an end. She would take me to the field and we would cultivate it together. There she would again lecture to me about the importance of doing things correctly. How the earth must be ready for the sowing; and the seeds could be sowed only at the right time. She said you can never be independent from these conditions. For instance, you have to ensure that the water supply should be regular and the water must reach every nook and corner of the field.

So, it was from my mother I learnt to interpret the world around me. My mother said it is through our efforts we can achieve anything.

She said: 'You will know, my son—the greatest enemy will always from within, not from outside. Sometimes the people inside your own home are more dangerous than any enemy. Do you know the Maharaja of Manipur was poisoned by his own cook?' My mother said, 'Don't depend on others, otherwise you will never win. Remember, you yourself are the most important thing in everything you do.' And my mother also said that the world may forgive you, but it will not forget your wrongs.

I remember how all of us sat around the fire in the kitchen and listened to my mother. She told us how poor we were. Our grandfather was perhaps the poorest in the village but he was very popular because he was generous with whatever little he had. One day he caught a little chicken and a hen. Then the chicken and the hen gave lots of eggs and that became the mainstay of the family.

When my mother began working in the field, she would plan everything meticulously; and when she had a programme my father also followed. People would sometimes criticize her plan and say she is taking on too much but she would not pay heed. She would keep working slowly and in the end my parents had the best paddy fields.

So with her hard work she raised the status of our family from the lowest point to the highest and that is why my parents named me Thuingaleng which means raising up, equal to the highest.

I heard many stories from my mother but the one I remember to this day is about hunting. A group of young people from a village went hunting. They had hoped to catch a tiger but after spending days in the jungle they came back empty-handed. A young man who had not accompanied them thought to himself, 'Ah good I did not go with them'.

The next time a hunting party went the young man did not go. But this time the hunting party returned with a big deer. The whole village celebrated and then the young man who had not gone regretted not accompanying the hunting party. He felt if he had only gone with them, he too would have had a share in the meat.

The story teaches us that the person who does not struggle and does not experience bitterness or shame will never know the glory of achievement. That is exactly what history teaches us. Of course I did not understand the real meaning of the story when I first heard it from my mother.

Uncle Suisa used to say to me: 'Your mother is a politician. She is illiterate but she is wise and far-sighted.' I told my mother what Uncle Suisa said and asked her whether he was a wise man. She said Uncle Suisa was wise but he would never be successful. I asked why she said this. She said he preaches down to the people and he knows a lot but he does not explain things to them. So there will be no one to take his message to the people.

That was what Mao Tse-tung also taught. We have to make the people understand what you want and then they will back you; unless the people back you nothing can be achieved. My mother said Ruichamhao inspired the people and she thought of him almost equal to Christ.

My mother said I would always remember her words and understand their meaning later in life, and that is true. But there were things my mother never understood. For instance, she called airplanes balloons and wondered how they could fly people across the world. For her it was an example of how people could achieve unimaginable heights.

When I was in China she had no idea where that was. She was told there a man called Mao Tse-tung who was a wise and great man and he was changing the whole world; it was that wise man who was taking care of her son. She could not pronounce Mao Tse-tung so she called him Paosaitung which sounded like a Tangkhul name!

I met my parents once after I returned from China after five years. I was with two boys and we had spent the night in the jungles and the next evening after dark I went to my house. My parents were so surprised to see me standing there at their house. All of us could not say anything and we just looked at each other. I sat down. My mother was sitting there; it was too much for her to see me and the emotion ran high and tears started running down her cheeks. I said, 'Yes mummy, I am your son.' She said, 'Yes, my son I know. I recognize your voice; I cannot believe you are alive.' She killed two chicken and made me chutney and my father prayed for me. My mother also prayed although it was not something she did often.

I learnt my father had been beaten by the Assam Rifles. Then I had to leave. It was not safe for me to spend a night in their house. I could not stay and so I left.

On another occasion we had made a camp near our village but I could not go to meet my parents. I heard my father shouting. He was on his way to his field which was near the camp where I was. Later, I asked him why he had shouted and he said he wanted me to know that I was not alone and my father was with me, even if we could not meet.

I am not sure which year my mother died, it was either 1980 or 1981. But I could not meet her or visit her grave. I was deep in the jungles. When my mother was dying, she told the family that she would wait for me in Paradise. She told the family to tell me not to return halfway. That would be a disgrace to the family: 'I want to be a proud mother.'[56]

Shongran Ruichamhao

As I said, I was inspired by the life of Ruichamhao. He was born in May 1896 in our village. But Ruichumhao's father treated our family very badly. My father told me how the father oppressed our people and I was not at all happy when I heard these stories. But my father said Ruichamhao was totally against his father and openly condemned his own father.

He was a brilliant student and went to study in Assam. But when he was eighteen years old and studying in Class Ten the British called him back from Shillong to lead our people who were sent to fight in the First World War. Ruichamhao could speak very good English so he was sent as an interpreter.

Ruichamhao even defied the British SDO LL Peter who was known as Peter Saheb. This Peter made the Tangkhuls work on road

---

[56] In 2010 Thuingaleng Muivah was to visit his ancestral village after forty years but the Manipur Government objected on the ground that the visit would be used by the NSCN to strengthen their demand for integration of Naga-inhabited areas.

construction during the time they needed to work in the paddy fields and made them work as porters carrying army rations from Ukhrul to Imphal. He also demanded that he be provided Tangkhul girls so he could have sex with them.

Ruichamhao was angry and he thought this was an insult to the Tangkhuls and it showed a lack of respect to the community. He said he would defy Peter Saheb and even if it meant imprisonment he would go to jail; if it meant he had to face death, he would rather die than allow such an insult to his people. And he fought and fought and fought even though he was alone.

Ruichamhao went to Imphal and reported the SDO to the Political Agent—I have forgotten his name, it was perhaps Higgins. That was something no one ever imagined could be done. Even reporting against the local Lambu[57] was unimaginable. Lambus were treated like small tigers. The Political Agent was impressed with Ruichumhao's courage and after a while Peter Saheb was transferred. At that time Tangkhuls composed two songs on Ruichumhao's brave act.

I do not remember the exact words but it said 'Oh! Ruichamhao, he sent leaves to the people and the leaves used to speak to the parents.' At that time people probably did not know what letters were and they had never seen paper. I cannot remember the exact words but it went something like this:

> *Thangmeiya chi akha Shongran Ruichamhao*
> *Maning akha khipa lei!*
> *Pingnha Shongran Ruichamhao*
> *Maningla khipa lei?*
> *Saheb li kasham kho?*
> *Saheb khayeklak eina thinhao kho!*

---

[57] Under the colonial system, the Lambu was an interpreter, a process-server and a peon combined in one. The counterpart in the Naga hills was the Dubashi, or the interpreter. The Lambu was employed in all aspects of the colonial administration, keeping law and order, administration of justice, supervision of public works. He was the ear and eye of the government. During the period of British direct management of Manipur (1891-1906), the Lambus oppressed the people.

The translation is something like this:

Witty and wise man means Shongran Ruichamhao
If not who else!
Brave man Shongran Ruichamhao
If not he who else?
He who chased away the white man
White man went away in shame!

The song speaks of the greatness and wisdom of Ruichamhao of Shongran village and how he defeated Peter Saheb's power.

Early School

I studied in the Middle English Christian School in our village which was established by Ruichamhao. Many Tangkhuls and Maos also came to study in the school. While I was in school in the village, many students from the Somrah region also attended classes.

Our Headmaster, Chiri Khamrang, was interested in international politics and he used to tell us about the French Revolution, the Bolshevik Revolution led by Lenin, and the American Revolution led by George Washington and the Chinese Revolution led by Mao Tse-tung. But he never said Indian 'revolution' but Indian 'struggle'. He told us about Mahatma Gandhi and Subhash Chandra Bose. I remember he told us that Bose said: 'Give me your blood and I will give you your freedom.'

The Headmaster was political-minded and he told us a little about Phizo and the Naga national movement. But the Headmaster was a bit of a coward. He passed away in 1998.

When Ruichamhao returned from France he became a teacher and later was the Headmaster of the Ukhrul Mission School but he died in 1933 at the age of thirty-seven so I never had an opportunity to meet him.

However, I felt I knew Ruichamhao well because, as I said, my father was his disciple. My father was his orderly and carried his things from village to village so he had an opportunity to listen to the great man who understood Christianity and could prove himself with principles. My father was so impressed that he could not stop talking about him.

I Am Taught a Lesson

My father was the church treasurer and our church used to help the children who came from Somrah, Mao and Zeliangrong areas. Our village took it as a kind of responsibility to make sure they got free education. My father collected the money and he buried the coins in the earth. Some hostellers from the village were maimed or handicapped. I loved them very much and I did not like to see them suffer so much. So I stole some money for those boys. Some took the money but others were too scared to take it.

I was discovered and arrested by my villagers. I was beaten up and taken to the church pulpit and made to confess. I could not sleep that night in my house because I was afraid of my father. I suspected that he would kill me. So I slept in the granary for two or three days and had nothing to eat.

My father would explain the purpose of God sending his son to save sinners; how God saved Daniel from the lions and how He led Moses to the Promised Land and Joshua took over from Moses who led the people across the river Jordan and how Jericho fell. My father was deeply concerned with the problem of salvation and he taught me about the wholeness of Christ.

My parents would teach us never to steal, or tell lies and never to hurt orphans because their tears were precious to God. Because of the stories I heard about Ruichamhao, and how intelligent and wise he was, I was inspired to follow Jesus. I did not always understand all this and it would trouble me so I would go into the jungles with my dao and sit quietly and think seriously. When I start to think of something deeply, I prefer to be alone and I stay aloof from my friends. I would ask why there is a heaven and why there is crime. It was a kind of torture—this struggle within oneself.

These moral lessons were not always easy to learn but I found the stories about our history very interesting. I was deeply touched by the history of our people.

Life in a Tangkhul village

The British called the northern Tangkhul as Lahupa and the southern as Tangkhuls. But we had our own names. We called the northern Tangkhuls Raphei; south-east Tangkhuls as Kamo and we called Mao, Chakhesang and Angami as Kharao. But these terms were sometimes used in a derogatory sense by the Ukhrul people.[58] The Ukhrul people made fun of others; they composed stories and counter stories about the other Tangkhuls! We would enjoy this. The Ukhrul people are very intelligent and have a presence of mind but they do not go down deep into matters. We have such a saying about them, 'Ningleikak chiena thangmi lak kachmida.' But the younger generation go deeper into things and analyze much better.

When I was in my village the Longshim[59] was still functioning. But for us boys there was no separate building since we were all studying in school. But we had our yarnao and we worked according to our age group in the fields.

Because we worked in the fields in the sun my complexion was dark, almost black. At present it is okay but then it was exceptionally dark.

One day I remember our yarnao was working in a field. My friends whispered that the ladies would be joining us during the

[58] Muivah is referring to the people from Ukhrul village which became the headquarters of the Tangkhul-inhabited Ukhrul district. This is a glimpse into the making of the Tangkhul tribe.

[59] Longshim or a morung was an educational institution where the boys and girls entered at the time of adolescence till the time of marriage. The boys' dormitory was called Mayarlong; the girls' dormitory was called Ngalalong. It was in the Longshim the youth learnt various skills such as weaving for women and warfare for the boys. They learnt the laws of the tribe, etiquette and values. After the coming of Christianity, the institution slowly disappeared. Yarnao is the age group in which a Tangkhul Naga belongs; that age group works together and also helps each other throughout life.

lunch break. I had already fallen in love with one of them but not had the courage to declare my love for her. I did not know how to talk to ladies and was embarrassed by my dark complexion. So as to hide my complexion I covered myself with the soil of the field. I plastered myself with the soil!

On our way back, climbing up a hill I told my friends why I had done that and they all laughed. They told me that I did not know how to behave with ladies.

So, you know we had a good life. Our society was excellent. For fifty to sixty years before my time there was no incident of misbehavior among boys and girls. There was no prostitution. That is why we do not want our society to be polluted from anywhere. That is why my attachment to society is such that I do not want to part with our society. That is why I love our society and that is the other reason for my determination to resist any external interference in our society.

I wanted to know more about my society. In Ukhrul there were some historians but no one was there to tell me about our history. My mother told me about our Kashong Riyan, which is like the Constitution of the Tangkhuls. It has a section on rules of war and also on how to make peace and reconciliation with the enemy. These were rules we made for ourselves during the days of headhunting.

Headhunting does not profit us in any way but if we examine it properly it has its merits because it encouraged the values of bravery and courage. It was a necessity for the protection of the village. It was a way to make the youth prove themselves. Of course there is no justification to chop off someone's head to prove one's bravery, but it had a context.

You know, Tangkhuls had a big hunting dog which was available only in our part. It was known as a Tangkhul hui or Tangkhul dog.

The western Tangkhuls were good in weaving. We used to make cloth from cotton and I remember we used to call the thread 'Bombay lang.' Some Nagas made cloth from wood. I remember when the woollen thread came, we laughed at it. Wool came very late. It was a modern thing and ours was the first generation that saw it, but the patterns on the cloth were much older.

Learning the History of My People

My mother would say, you know my son, our Tangkhul people were humiliated by the Meitei people and she would cite examples. She said Kuki raided our villages and killed us and we had to go into hiding. The British also treated us badly. I remember my mother telling me, 'My son, don't dance like a fool in front of the white people.'

This history hurt me deeply even when I was very young. I would ask why we had no right to exist even on our own land, and why the whites dominate us.

But the Japanese were different.[60]I was really fascinated by the Japanese. I went to their camp even though we were strictly forbidden from going to the Japanese. Only the members of the Village Authority were allowed to meet them.

I cooked for the Japanese. I met an officer and he smiled at me. I asked him through gestures to give me one of his three stars but he just smiled. I even learnt some Japanese songs from the soldiers and they were amazed that I could sing them.

I also cooked for the elite force of the Allies. They gave me sugar and that was how I tasted sugar for the first time. One American officer called me, 'Hey boy! Bakshish! Bakshish!' I did not forget that Indian term.

I did not understand why we had such a history of humiliation and why so many forces could come to our land—Meitei, Kuki, British, American missionaries, Japanese and later Indian—and our people had to live in humiliation. I thought to myself even at a young age that I will not accept this history of humiliation; my people have a right to live with dignity and self-respect.

---

[60] This must have been around March 1944 during World War II when the Japanese and the Allies fought several battles.

Imphal By Foot

The first time I went to Imphal was with my father. We went by foot
from the village.[61] I remember looking at the valley from Mahadev.
It was not called by that name. We called it Ngashanphung which
means 'a place where you get a view.' It was called Mahadev after the
Assam Rifles made a temple at that point. It was like looking down at a
different world. Of course I had heard a lot about Imphal even before
we went there. We did not call it Imphal but Keithei[62].

My father and I went to work in the fields in Imphal and our job
was to make channels in the paddy fields for better drainage of water.
And we made tracks for the bullock carts. We used to work for a month
every year. It was during the cold season, either January or February.
And I remember earning five rupees. I held five rupees in my hand and
I forgot the whole world; I was so happy!

I bought one shirt and one underwear and one half-pant. I had
taken some seven or eight rupees from my mother so I bought all
this plus textbook for twelve rupees. And also a lead pencil. I was the
happiest boy.

The Meiteis in those days knew how to struggle. The Meitei
women were good in small businesses. They were not proud and many
Tangkhuls loved them. Tangkhuls did not hate them at all. Now it may
be a little bit different.

We went to the same Meitei families from the time of my
grandfather. We went in a big group. Sometimes we dug a tank or
pond. But when those Brahmans see us, they shout from far: 'Mange
mange lak kanu hao, hao!' (We will get polluted, don't come, tribals.)

Even though they respected my father they would wash themselves
even if we left a footprint. And if they had to give us anything, they
would drop it into our hands from far without touching us. If we used
their utensil, they would clean them again and again.

---

[61] A journey of two days.

[62] Keithei means market. The distance from Somdal to Imphal by road is about 86
kms by road.

It is not only the Brahmans—the general Meitei also practiced this untouchability. The Meiteis would not allow Tangkhuls to enter their homes, especially their kitchens. We were allowed to sit or sleep on mats on the verandah.

I am told some such incident happened even with Rishang Keishing.

It was with the Sanamahi[63] movement and the revolutionary groups like PLA and PREPAK that the situation improved.[64]

As for the Indians, we saw them in the shops. The Marwaris were not bad—they would take out many things so we could choose. And they would explain things. I used to buy school bags from them.

You see if you do not have a political consciousness then you can tolerate these things. My parents tolerated many things because they did not have the political consciousness. But I knew we cannot be treated in this way. The Communist Party did a lot to change things. The transformation was started by the Communist Party but not really effective because it did not take strong roots in society. The UNLF, PLA and PREPAK[65] have come up but they also treat hill people with disdain.

Yes, I learnt Manipuri language but I told the teacher I did not want to learn Manipuri or Hindi. I got just two marks in Manipuri language but they allowed me to absent myself. I also did not learn Hindi. I had hatred against Hindi. But it is also true I am not good at languages otherwise I would have learnt Manipuri and Hindi. But I was just not interested.

---

[63] Sanamahi religion was a pre-Hindu religion. Meiteis were converted to Vaishnavism during the reign of Meidingu Pamhieba (1690–1751) who was converted to Vaishnavism by Hindu missionaries and made it the official religion in 1717. The Hindu missionaries were Shantidas Adhikari and Guru Gopal Das. They introduced the caste-based concept of purity and impurity.

[64] The Meitei nationalist movement asserts its pre-Hindu identity and observes the day the Meitei sacred texts were burnt by Hindu missionaries.

[65] People's Revolutionary Party of Kangleipak (PREPAK) started in 1977 to oust outsiders from the state and restore the old Meitei script; People's Liberation Army (PLA) started in 1978 and the United National Liberation Front (UNLF) started in 1964 with the aim to establish a sovereign, socialist Manipur.

Government High School, Ukhrul

After Class Eight I went to study in Ukhrul at the Government High School. It was called Mission School before Indian Independence. I learnt much more when I went to study in Ukhrul Government High School. By the time I went there I was already nationalist-minded.

We had to walk to Ukhrul as there was no proper road. I had to walk up and down the road cutting through the jungle. Sometimes the climb was steep and I had to carry a tin of rice, which is roughly 20 kgs, for my consumption. I went with friends but they were senior to me and I could not keep up with them. I found it so hard that I cried; but I was ashamed to admit that tears had come to my eyes so I said I was sweating. It was a long way—perhaps 25 kms or so. Now I am told there is public transport but, in those days, there was no other way than going by foot.

The Ao Naga were more advanced than us. They came to study in Ukhrul but more Aos passed matric than Tangkhuls. I was little bit quick to pick up English so I spoke to the Ao students in English and several of them spoke Tangkhul fluently. I did not know Nagamese. I could speak Tangkhul of Ukhrul because our village dialect is very close to the Ukhrul Tangkhul. Because of Pettigrew[66] a common language had evolved so all Tangkhuls knew Ukhrul language. In my village in the church when reading the Bible, we read and spoke in the Ukhrul dialect. The Ao students came to Ukhrul rather than go to Shillong or Guwahati because Ukhrul was cheaper. With twenty rupees we could manage for half a year. Do you know we could buy one tin of rice for one rupee?

My mother would also come and she would carry two tins of potatoes which she would sell for one rupee and she would give me four annas for my education. I was in a hostel and sometimes I did not have a shirt or even footwear. But since it was my native town I could manage somehow.

---

[66] Reverend William Pettigrew (1869–1943) was a missionary who started his work as an educationist in Ukhrul in 1897. Pettigrew brought out the first Tangkhul dictionary and standardized the Tangkhul language.

By the time I joined the Government High School, Rishang was no longer the Headmaster and Mission School was taken over by the Government of India. I do not remember the exact year but I was no longer a child so it must have been 1950 or 1951 when I joined the Ukhrul school.

In those days the Ukhrul people were very proud, rather arrogant. They looked down on the villagers. They would say: 'Lawai macha na hili khiphazat li?' (Country bumpkin, what have you come in search for?)

This arrogance became a habit of the people of Ukhrul. But still I have a great attachment to Ukhrul. At that time they were not politically conscious, but that was true for the whole of the Tangkhul people.

Despite all this I had a very good time in Ukhrul. For the first time I came in contact with and interacted with Indians, Bengalis, and Meiteis. Our teacher Roy loved me very much. He taught mathematics but I was not interested in the subject and I did not want to be forced into learning the subject. He called me Aleng.[67]

By that time, I was already Naga nationalist and had decided I would join the movement one day. In Ukhrul High School I started singing 'God Bless my Nagaland.'[68] Actually, it is not really our anthem, we borrowed it from an American song.

But when we sang 'God Bless my Nagaland' some of our Bengali teachers objected. They wanted us to sing 'Jana Gana Mana', the Indian national anthem, before the classes began. I would argue with the teachers and ask why should I not sing 'I li phara sang kahai ngalei' which means in Tangkhul, 'The land where I was born.'

I took the decision then that I would only sing that song and not 'Jana Gana Mana.' I began singing the song and all the Tangkhul students joined in and so you see I was a bit of a rebel. I became a hero in school. My headmaster was not happy with me.

---

[67] The diminutive of Thuingaleng in Tangkhul would be Aleng.

[68] Naga national anthem based on American song written by Irving Berlin in 1918 and revised in 1938.

When the teacher asked the students in my class what they wanted to be when they grew up, someone said he wanted to be an engineer, someone said missionary, and some students said they wanted to be doctors. I said, 'Politician,' and everyone laughed at me. Then the teacher asked why I wanted to be a politician and I replied because I love my people and if we do not establish ourselves as a people, we will be a lost people. I do not want our people to be a lost people.

In the beginning the Headmaster was a Bengali but after that it was Acheiyo[69] Luikham. I think his name was Ramyo Luikham. There were several Bengali teachers like Ghosh, Roy and one called Pulin Das. They were excellent teachers and they loved me very much. I would fetch water and chop firewood for them but I would never allow them to insult our villagers.

Sometimes the villagers would bring rice to sell. Pulin Das started bargaining with the Nungbi villagers. I shouted that if he did not want to buy the rice, he need not buy but he should not treat the villagers like that. Then he took me aside and asked whether I was hurt and I said no, but I did not want my people to be insulted. And he said, 'Understood, understood.' He was quite a sensible man. He told me once I passed matric, I would shine like a star. Bengali teachers were very good and I learnt a lot from them but not on political matters.

At the time Rishang was a popular leader. He had joined the socialist movement. He was leading an agitation at the time in which the slogan was, 'The plains and hills are one'. That meant that the Indians and the Nagas are one. There is no difference between them. This was around 1953 or 1954. I was doing construction work in Ukhrul and people came and asked why I had not joined Rishang's movement when I wanted to be a politician. I said I do not want to join this kind of movement. My politics is different.

When I was in Class Ten I remember Rishang's politics of unity between the people of the hills and the people of the plains: 'ching-taam amatmay.' There was a gathering of 10,000 Manipuri women at the polo

---

[69] Elder Luikham.

ground when Rishang spoke and the women shed tears. I was there and I saw how he spoke in a sweet manner. He would also shed tears. The Meiteis worshipped him like a god. Sometimes he would speak deadly against the Nagas. He was not standing properly for the Indian nation but for himself. The Nagas were with Uncle Suisa and then for a time Yangmaso came up. Irabot Singh[70] had no influence in the hills and the Nagas were not attracted to the Communist Party of India.

I said I support the Naga national movement, not this kind of movement led by Rishang. I want to know more about my own people and have our own history and identity. I wanted to establish the identity of my people. Those people like Rishang did not like what I said. They wanted to eat me up but I stood my ground. I told them: 'You go your way and I will go my way. You decide your history and I will decide mine.'

Luckily, I got through my examinations. I was the youngest among the Tangkhuls to finish my matriculation. I had not met anyone from the Naga National Council but I had met Uncle Suisa and my father was close to him. Even if my father did not understand everything that was discussed, it was from him I heard the name of Phizo and the NNC. I decided I would join them. I did not yet understand history but I did know that the Naga national movement represented the future.

St Anthony's College, Shillong

I joined the Union Christian College at Barapani in 1957.[71] There we had very good teachers. In the college equality was practiced. From Barapani I went to Shillong where I joined St Anthony's College and was there from 1958 to 1961. At that time my father was in prison. Isak Swu was my senior in both these colleges.

---

[70] Hijam Irabot Singh (1896–1951) was a freedom fighter from Manipur who was jailed several times. In jail he was influenced by communists and became one himself; later he was one of the founders of the Communist Party in Manipur.

[71] Union Christian College was established in 1952. The Barapani lake was not made till 1960s.

My brother was doing a little bit okay so he could support me. I became very much independent and even did not attend all the classes but I read on my own.

I went from Imphal to Silchar by Kalinga Airlines.[72] The ticket was less than one hundred rupees. I had a friend with me; he was an engineer. His name was Siraphui. I could not go by bus because our movement was ambushing buses. It was the first time I went by plane and I could not believe it. I entered the plane and kept looking around and the seats were so good.

We reached Silchar and then we did not know where to go. We found a rickshaw and luckily he dropped us to town where we were told we could pick up our luggage. There was no facility for picking up luggage at the airport. We found the luggage just outside the building.

From Silchar we went to Guwahati by train. We had never been by train either and we did know Hindi, Bengali or Assamese, only broken English. We asked for the train without realizing that the train was already standing there and it was full. We were suspected of being Naga underground but we said we were students so they allowed us into the train but we could not find any place to sit. We stood all the way to Guwahati. From Guwahati I took a bus to Barapani. At the time the lake was not there. I walked all the way from Barapani to Shillong carrying my luggage.

In St Anthony's I shared a room with a Garo student. He was a very quiet person and better in studies than me. In St Anthony's I saw Isak Swu for the first time. He was a very keen sportsman and his record in high jump was the best in Assam. His record was not beaten for a long time. He played football also; he played gracefully, not at all roughly. He used to dress up properly and he always carried the Holy Bible.

---

[72] Kalinga Airlines was a private airline based in Calcutta, India. It was founded in 1947 by aviator and politician Biju Patnaik, who was also the airline's chief pilot. The airline was nationalized and merged into Indian Airlines in 1953. It restarted operations as a non-scheduled charter operator in 1957 and flew passengers and cargo until 1972.

I did not have political discussion with him. Most of the other students were supporting the idea of a Nagaland State; Isak was not. In fact he and some other students wrote a letter saying that if the demand for a Nagaland State is accepted it would be a blunder. They wrote the letter to the Naga People's Convention. Then he was called by the Federal Government and he went into the jungles and did not come back.

There were other Naga students such as Ramyo. He was a good football player. But he was too much into the Indian Constitution. He interpreted political issues in terms of law. Ramyo was jealous of Uncle Suisa and betrayed him by worshipping and accepting the Indian Constitution.

It was in St Anthony's that I first read about Communist philosophy and I was very excited and it was as if a new world had opened for me. I read the writings of Karl Marx, Hegel and Rousseau. I still remember Rousseau's famous words: 'Man is born free but he is in chains everywhere'. It made me think a lot and I was happy because I could grasp the meaning. I understood the truth. I also read Rousseau's *Emile*.[73] I think he said that one is not born right or wrong, it is education that makes a man. I felt that now I could hear the voice of the people in the voice of God.

I read Marxism and I began to think Communist philosophy would shape the whole universe. I liked the dialectical analysis and could understand what Marx meant by the synthesis between thesis and anti-thesis. I understood that everything is in a process of change; nothing remains still. Society keeps changing. I felt if you approach any problem you cannot lose sight of the class aspect. I used to say that don't kick Marx away because Marx still has a lot to do with us.

---

[73] *Emile, or On Education* or *Émile* is a discourse on the nature of man and education written by Jean-Jacques Rousseau. Due to a section of the book entitled 'Profession of Faith of the Savoyard Vicar', *Emile* was banned in Paris and Geneva and was publicly burned in 1762, the year of its first publication.

I used to tell my friends that Moses was a nationalist and God endorsed the existence of different nations. But we have to make analysis of what kind of nationalism we want—without that kind of analysis we will be making a mistake. Being a Naga nationalist does not mean we must kill Indians. Killing Indians is not the principle of our politics. We should not kill or touch innocent people.

It is true that there are no classes in our society. But there were already some people who were much better off than others. My mother used to say Daiho was the richest man in the world. Of course by our standards my mother was not wrong. Daiho was much older than me. He had already constructed a big building in Mao during the Second World War. He was educated and came from a family little bit richer. They say the British people used him and Indian government also used him for construction work. He was a contractor and he got the tender to make the Kohima-Imphal road. He was looked up to and he was a little bit conscious so he started the Naga National League in 1946 but later he became against the movement.

Then I noticed how the Naga people admired the students even though they had not organized themselves but just because they were educated. I myself was admired just because I was a graduate. So people really looked up to people like Rishang, he was one generation older than me. I also realized that just because someone has done an MA and is coming from America does not mean he is right.

The village chief and people of higher status have a superiority complex. And I come from a poor family. I identified with the poor and with the orphans. I had noticed that the children belonging to people with higher status treated the poor children differently.

During Christmas time the children of rich people put on good clothes but my parents could not afford to buy new clothes for me. We did not have the big woollen shawls, only cheap cotton ones and loin cloths in childhood. Children of the rich kids were given respect and we the poor children were not treated well.

So, although there was no class in our society but there were differences between the rich and the poor. The Jews say, 'The fear of the Lord is the beginning of wisdom,' but the Greeks will depend on investigation. And I would depend on investigation into causes of social problems so I could get to the truth.

I could not always discuss all these new ideas because I was perhaps the wisest among the fools and other students were not interested in these political questions.

Uncle Suisa

Reading the writings of philosophers like Hegel and Engels helped me understand many things. The world condemns Karl Marx—I have great admiration for him. But when I read Solomon in the Ecclesiastes in the Old Testament, I was disturbed by the philosophical discourse. Solomon seemed to lament that everything is vanity under the sun and life seems to be futile.

I was so disturbed after reading Solomon that I sought out Uncle Suisa who was at the time admitted to the Guwahati Christian Hospital recovering from an operation. I went to him and said: 'I have a problem, Uncle.' He asked what it was and I said I had been reading philosophy and trying to develop my own understanding of the world but when I read Solomon I felt very troubled.

Uncle Suisa thought for a while and said: 'Solomon wrote about vanities under the sun after his bitter experience when he betrayed God. For that reason God had to punish him and he was reduced to nothingness. It was then that he thought everything was due to vanity. But what is not vanity is the word of God.'

After Uncle Suisa's explanation I felt liberated. I realized I had to re-examine my faith in God. I wanted to understand the preciousness of existence. God had created the Universe and I can live with that thought. God has created the Universe, what is behind this creation? There must be a reason, a purpose. If God has a purpose for the whole universe then God must have a purpose behind the creation of Nagaland because Nagaland is a part of that universe. So I tried to interpret what was the purpose of the creation of Nagaland in the light of Marx's writings.

I used to go back to my village during the holidays. When I went back I would help my parents in the fields and also with other work like chopping firewood. When I came home after graduating Uncle Suisa was elected to the Indian Parliament. He was Member of Parliament from 1957 to 1962. During that time I had heated discussions with him. I asked him to explain his politics to me and why he had contested in the Indian elections. I asked him to teach me the things I needed to know. And I told him he did not know everything.

In those days he just laughed at me. He said to me, 'The bad man has come to teach me eh?' He knew how to provoke me. He had a very bad habit of laughing outright.

Tangkhul people would also ask many things from him but he felt they would not understand so a discussion with them would be in vain. He would instead ask them how many tins of rice they had produced that year and then tell the person to produce more. He was a peculiar man and people were not happy with him.

Uncle Suisa kept provoking me and I kept accusing him but finally one night he talked to me in earnest. Then I listened to him carefully. He said we Nagas are confronting a force which is far stronger than us. It is superior in strength and the more we fight the more we will be aggrieved, and more people will be killed and no one in the world will know why we fought. If we fight like two confronting bulls, we will not be able to explain to the Indian leadership our point of view. He said he had spoken to the Indian Home Minister Pandit Pant who reacted angrily to Uncle Suisa but that did not deter him. Uncle Suisa talked to Jawaharlal Nehru who banged on his desk in anger when Uncle Suisa said the issue had to be settled between his Government and the Nagas, and instead the Indian Armed Forces were killing Nagas.

Uncle Suisa did not give up and he continued to tell Nehru that he should talk to the Nagas. At last Nehru agreed. Uncle Suisa said he did not represent the Naga people, Phizo and the Naga National Council did. He suggested that the Government of India talk to the NNC. Uncle Suisa said, 'I am nobody. The sole representative of the Naga people is Phizo and the Naga National Council.' He asked the

Indians why they were talking to the Naga People's Convention when the leader of the Nagas is Phizo? Uncle Suisa was dead against the Naga People's Convention.[74]

The difference between Uncle Suisa and Uncle Phizo was that Uncle Suisa did not want to go straightaway for independence. He thought the one thing the British should have done was put all Naga areas under one administration. He wanted an agreement with Burma that after fifty years the Nagas could be free.[75] Outside of the official talks with Government of India, there was a proposal of giving Nagas the same status as Bhutan.

Uncle Suisa said it was important to understand the Indian leaders. His biggest achievement was that he made the Government of India accept that Phizo was the leader of the Naga people, even though the Government of India said they could not negotiate with Phizo because he was a British citizen. Before Uncle Suisa died, he said Nagas had achieved so much but we did not value our achievements and so we would destroy ourselves. Uncle Suisa published a small pamphlet setting out his proposals for a resolution to the conflict. He said if the Nagas accepted anything less than his proposals he would rise up from his grave.

Phizo threatened Uncle Suisa with the same fate as Sakhrie. I was told this by others because I did not meet Uncle Suisa before he died in 1971.

T Sakhrie lost confidence in himself and opted for co-operation with India. He thought the idea of sovereignty could be delayed. Nehru

---

[74] Naga People's Convention was set up in 1957 with Dr Imkongliba Ao as first President. The NPC was formed on the initiative of the church leaders and led to the 16-Point Agreement between the NPC and the Government of India which resulted in the establishment of the Nagaland State and the assassination of Imkongliba in September 1961, allegedly by the NNC who were opposed to the formation of a Nagaland State which did not include all Naga-inhabited areas.

[75] The Burmese Constitution under General Aung provided an option for the Shans to leave the Union of Burma after thirty years—perhaps Suisa wanted a similar arrangement for the Nagas.

sent Purwar[76] to convince Sakhrie that the Nagas could get some kind of autonomy and then they would not have to suffer. So Sakhrie believed that without undergoing hardship and suffering, the Naga goal could be achieved. Much depends on the lifestyle of a person.

Influence of Political Parties

Nagas were not much interested in ideological matters. Some like Longri Ao joined the Congress Party but that was in British times. Uncle Suisa also joined the Congress Party. Lohia influenced some Nagas and there was some contact with the Socialist Party. Rishang was also influenced by Lohia. But the Congress Party could only come after Nagaland State was created. There was some friendly contact with the Communist Party. Even Uncle Phizo was accused of having connection with communists. He was very much questioned by his villagers and he had to take an oath that he had no connection with the communists.

At last the Government of India agreed to a ceasefire in September 1964. Of course the ceasefire was the result of the intervention of the church leaders. Before the ceasefire came into place, I met Reverend Michael Scott[77] when he came to Shillong. I think Uncle Phizo must have sent him to do a survey of the situation. There was a lot of CID but I managed to meet Reverend Scott. Soon after my meeting, the Principal of St Anthony's Fr. Joseph called me and told me that the intelligence department had been asking after me. Fr. Joseph provoked me and told me that he could expel me but I said if he wanted he could do so but nothing would stop me from asserting my Naga identity. But Fr. Joseph said, 'Well done my boy, you have done well.' Fr. Joseph was from Madras.

---

[76] Triloknath Purwar was a Gandhian and independent political worker who befriended Sakhrie. Purwar's role is discussed in Chapter Seven of Nibedon's *Nagaland* (1978).

[77] Reverend Michael Scott (1907–1983) was an Anglican priest and anti-apartheid activist; first white man to go to jail for defying racist laws in South Africa.

By this time Isak Swu was already in Pakistan although I did not know it at the time. He had joined the NNC in December 1959. He was a very religious kind of person and moral while I was more revolutionary and rougher.

But there was no time to discuss the peace proposals set forth by Uncle Suisa because the Naga leaders did not understand their relevance and also because soon after Nehru died in 1964, the year I joined the Naga National Council. I would have joined earlier but the leadership wanted me to finish my MA. I thought my study of international politics would help us in our movement. I finished my post-graduation from Guwahati University in 1962 or 1963 and then went back to the village to teach in the school. Then in 1964 I joined the Naga national movement.

The China Factor

When the leaders first asked me to go to China I refused to go. I said I was a nobody. I felt it was not the right time to send anyone to China since the peace talks were going on full swing. And I felt we had still not understood India and India had not understood us. But if India is reasonable and sincere, then it would be unwise to provoke India by going to China. I felt it would not be right to antagonize India unnecessarily when India was trying to understand us. So at that stage I opposed the idea of going to China.

Mr Isak may have his version, but this is what my position was in the beginning. But when we came to know the reality of the Indian position, yes, I said it is time for us to go to China. You know that politics is not only about arms. We needed support from as many countries as we could get and that included China.

The NNC did not have any policy on China. In 1962 Mr Ramyo drafted a statement on behalf of the Federal Government supporting India in the war with China. Fortunately or unfortunately I was also a part of the nine-member delegation which sent the statement to the

Government of India. They thought India would be happy and would leave us alone.

I opposed giving such a statement. So, Ramyo was not happy with my position.

In political matters we should be very cautious, we must analyze carefully and anticipate the consequences of our actions. The Indians and the Western people were glad to read our statement supporting India but the Chinese were hurt by our support for India. Phizo gained nothing. In fact he was the loser and the Nagas were the losers because after all it was Pakistan and China and others through them who were behind us. We should have taken that into account before issuing our statement. I felt there would be no point for the Nagas to remain antagonistic to China. I say this because I saw that despite the statement made by Uncle Phizo during the Indo-China war, the Chinese were not against him, Chinese were not against us. That is, in the real sense, the beginning of my disagreement with Phizo.

The then President of the Federal Government of Nagaland, Scato Swu, told me to go to China. He said I must go. But I was reluctant; I said I was just a twenty-nine-year-old child. How can such a young person be sent to China, a country whose people were shaping the whole world? The world is afraid of them, who am I to talk with these people?

I told him it would be wrong on his part to place such confidence in me. It was like placing the fate of the Nagas in the hands of a small boy like me. This is going to be a historical meeting between Chinese and the Nagas.

Scatu Swu just laughed. He said, 'I understand, I understand.' He told me that in a year from now we will be discussing ideological matters, communist philosophy, international policies and politics. I didn't know whether he had been studying these matters. He was very happy with me.

I suggested to him to send Mr Isak or Ramyo, my seniors, to China. Scato was not willing. He said it was very important that the person who went knew communist philosophy, ideological matters and international complexities.

Scato Swu asked me many questions about international relations. He wanted to know the position of the West in Asia and Africa. I told him, if there was a global war China could occupy the whole North East region from Siliguri to Naga territory. Chinese are the strongest especially in comparison to India. USA could not do that unless they come by sea.

The rise of the Chinese Communist Party is the most formidable force in Asia; not Japan, USA or Soviet Union. So there is an absolute political necessity that we have some form of friendship with the Chinese.

You ask me about Tibet. The BBC asked me the same question in their interview. I said I am sorry I don't know very much about Tibetan history; there will be people from Tibet who can talk about it. But for me I know the Naga history.

From the human rights point of view, you may have a right to talk about the violation of human rights in Tibet but human rights violations alone don't constitute the right to self-determination. If you say that the Chinese do not have the right to suppress the Tibetans, well and good. But the Chinese also say, well we won't suppress them but they have to admit the fact that Tibet is a part of China as a historical fact.

So President Scato and Uncle Suisa were very serious about our establishing relations with China. I explained that we should not wait for the circumstance to come before we establish relations with China. China has helped Vietnam, Laos, Cambodia and Thailand and the Americans could do nothing. We cannot rely on Burma because the political situation there is very uncertain. Uncle Suisa was present during my discussions with President Scato. Being a Christian, he was no doubt against China yet he understood the necessity of having relations with China.

I felt if we had the blessing of China in some form or the other the Indo-Naga conflict would be automatically internationalized. The Western powers would put pressure on India to settle the issue through peaceful way and to stop killing the Nagas. That pressure we can expect from the Western powers. Scato and Uncle Suisa were very happy with my analysis. They said: 'God bless you, you have to go.' I said once I go I will stay there. So finally it was decided that Thinoselie and myself would go; Ramyo didn't go, but Isak came afterwards. The authorities decided that there would be altogether 133 of us who would go to China in the first batch. We were mostly Angami, Konyaks and some Aos. There were no Nepalis but there were some Mao Nagas and five Tangkhuls, including me. In that first batch there were no women.

The Long March to China

Once the decision was taken, I was determined to reach China even though I was physically weak. I did not have formal military training. But I had practice walking all over the Naga areas and I had already participated several times in pitched battles. So walking would not be a problem for me but since I was not strong physically it would be difficult for me to carry heavy loads...but then I was determined.

We carried our own rice and slept on grass in a clearing in the jungles. The government gave us one plastic sheet each and each of us carried our own cotton cloth to cover ourselves and we had to manage with that. I had the privilege of having two long pants, two shirts, one cloth and one plastic sheet. The most important thing for all of us were of course was our boots. Boots are the number one priority for an army.

All the way to China I complained about pain in various parts of my body! I could not stand the hunger because there were days when we did not have food and sometimes we were thirsty because there was no water to drink. We had a thermos flask for water but mine broke. Two boys looked after me and helped me.

We had the same uniform as the Indian Army. I wore jeans and a cowboy hat. The Kachin used to joke that the Nagas' General Secretary is a cowboy.

We started from Konyak area. We sent some scouts to survey that area. We had to find out how many Burmese Army outposts there were before we crossed the international border into Burma. The Nagas in the Eastern part are wild and rough so we had to be careful. But our biggest worry was crossing the Chindwin river. You know the Nagas are not very brave when it comes to crossing rivers because most of the Nagas cannot swim. They do not like to even wade across the river.

We began our march after the two scouts returned. I do not remember the exact date but it was in the last week of October of 1966, of that I am sure. We began marching at night.

It took us a long time to cross the border because we had to be very careful to avoid both the Indian military posts and the Burmese posts. We did not want the news of our crossing to leak out so we pretended to be going on survey duties along the border. Finally when we felt safe we crossed the border into Burma. The two people who had gone ahead for reconnaissance took us very close to a village. We passed through without stopping and arrived at another village located on top of a mountain. We were trying to get as far away from the India-Burma border as possible. So we crossed the border and then we proceeded for quite a distance till we reached a village whose name I forget. There we cooked during daytime[78] and then we proceeded and reached another village where we suddenly came across a section of Burmese troops. But they were not very bad to us, rather they were very friendly. We talked and talked and they gave us meat and sugar.

Even if the Burmese had wanted to attack us, they could not have because we were very well-armed and they were just a small group. So the officer invited us for a meal and we ate together. We talked in English. We told him that the Indian government had been accusing us of violating the ceasefire rules so we were inspecting the border to see if there had been any violations. We got two guides and they took us along the villages but then they were afraid and we allowed them to

---

[78] The Naga Army could not cook at night because the fire and the smoke would have given away their position.

go back. So in this way we reached the Hukawng valley.[79] There in the Hukawng valley we found a Burmese military post.

We wrote a letter to the Burmese commander saying that we are Nagas and are friends of the Burmese and we have lost our way and that is how we arrived there. Then the commander came and he took us to his camp and gave us good food. In the meanwhile, he contacted his headquarters. Then he gave us an ultimatum, ordering us to immediately go back, otherwise face the consequences of defying the Burmese Government. We said we did not come with any bad intention, otherwise we would not have gone to their camp. We said you can kill us, you can shoot us, we do not mind. We said we had told him the true purpose of our coming was to check the border.

We told him if we went the way he was suggesting we would have to face the Indian military post and we talked and talked; finally, we persuaded the commander to let us go.

Quickly we cut across and arrived at the Chindwin river which is quite a big river. It is the main tributary of the Irrawaddy river.

By the time we were crossing the river on bamboo rafts the Burmese commander came and tried to call us back. I think he had been told to get us back and finish us. After all Burma was under military rule at that time. The boys saw him and asked what we should do and I said just wave back to the Commander.

Across the river we kept walking through the jungle and cutting the undergrowth and marching ahead without realizing that we were lost. We had been walking like that for two days when we came to a stream. There we saw the large footprints of an elephant and we started following the footprints and then we saw a Kachin riding an elephant. He must have come in search of gold. There was a lot of gold in streams in the Hukawng Valley and also mines with precious stones like jades.

I think he must have known that we were lost because it was all thick jungle. It was a huge tract of land where no human being was to

---

[79] Hukawng valley covers 17,890 square kms and falls in Sagaing division of Kachin State. It has several gold mines and the floodplains of the Chindwin river.

be seen for miles. The Kachin came on his elephant and told us said he would help us find our way.

Throughout the journey I wore just pants and shirt. We had to carry rations for a week in case of any eventuality. It was very heavy and I am weak. I was looked after by two boys nicely and the commander took special care, that's why I never suffered. Sometimes they carried my rations and sometimes I carried them myself. We carried four or five pawa of rice; one pawa is equal to 250 grams. We used to use empty Milkmaid tins to measure out one pawa of rice. So we carried around two kilograms of rice each. It was very cold and the temperature reached below zero. The two boys who looked after me collected firewood and made a fire to keep me warm at night so I could manage to sleep.

On Reaching China

As we were nearing the China border there were a lot of Burmese armed forces moving around. We had to climb up the mountain again and follow a route leading to China. We suddenly reached a point where we found the border stone; on one side something was written in Burmese and on the other side in Chinese. We stopped and took photos there; we were overjoyed. It was thrilling, and suddenly the boys learnt that we are going to China and that we had finally reached our destination! Till that point of time we had not disclosed our final destination as we had been told not to tell the boys. Of course on the way they started guessing and speculating. They may have suspected that we were going to China.

Ah! Everyone was excited and three senior officers of the Kachin Independence Army escorted us to the border. Of course I disclosed everything to them. So we established a good understanding with them. We also shared some of our arms with them and they were very happy. On our way back they told us that with the help of the arms we gave them, three light machine guns, they captured a Burmese outpost and with that they captured thirty more pieces of arms. So, with the arms we gave them they were able to penetrate into the jade mines area.

They had wanted to capture the mines but they did not have arms till we gave them some. The Kachins also got some arms from the Chinese afterwards. At that time they had only an army but no government.

So there we were standing at the border of Burma and China. Most of our boys had never seen Chinese writing. That was the first time they set their eyes on the Chinese characters at the border stone. You know it was a wonderful place. We had climbed right down the mountain and come to an excellent area, beautiful spot, with pine trees and beautiful green shrubs.

The Chinese came to us and we handed our letter of introduction. But they could not read it since it was in English and they could not read English. But they took us across the border into China and allowed us to stay in the jungle. They kept the letter on a table with a submachine gun. The Chinese Army kept guards at the spot and we had to stay there for several days. Then two Chinese came with a dictionary. They were schoolteachers from a nearby village. They asked us our names and where we came from. Those two questions were asked very clearly but then we realized that was the extent of their knowledge of the English language!

Then they told us to write down what we wanted to convey so it would be easier to translate with the help of their dictionary. So, I wrote down two to three sentences:

1.   we are Nagas
2.   coming to China for help, and
3.   we are fighting against Indian government.

I wrote only that much and the whole night they tried to understand those three sentences with the help of torchlight. They looked up their dictionary but they could not understand. I sat up the whole night without any sleep struggling to communicate.

The People's Liberation Army personnel were also there, anxiously waiting for them to make sense of what we were trying to communicate. Everyone was feeling very confused and helpless but the two teachers were sent away.

I think they must have sent word to Kunming and in the morning two other men arrived; one was a student from an engineering college and the other was a high school teacher. This time they understood us and the People's Liberation Army men were also happy now. Now they could communicate to Peking and they received information that Chairman Mao is considering the matter.

The PLA men were so impressed! And we felt the whole Chinese people were behind us. We were treated with the same respect given to the People's Liberation Army because we were to be considered friends.

The PLA issued us warm clothes and took us down to a big Buddhist temple where we stayed for a month till they made arrangements for our stay. We were given good food and they started teaching us songs in praise of Chairman Mao, but they did not force us to do anything we did not want. Our boys picked up very easily and we started singing very well so the Chinese were really happy. This was before our formal training began.

Then one morning we were taken to Tengchong (new spelling Tanzhong) in southwest Yunnan. We were disarmed and escorted by the Chinese Army to the place where our training began. We were given proper instructions.

The first lectures were about how to distinguish between our friends and our enemies;[ix] also the difference between tactics and strategy. We also learnt how education must have a revolutionary philosophy.

Mao emphasized that people are like water and the people's army must be like fish which swim in the water.[80]

In Peking

General Thinoselie and I were flown to Peking to have long political talks. At first we talked to junior party officers and then senior officers came to talk to us. They asked us about Naga history, about our

---

[80] The popular masses are like water, and the army is like a fish: 'The guerrilla must move amongst the people as a fish swims in the sea.' —Mao Tse-tung.

conditions, our customs and traditions and everything possible. They wrote it all down. They asked why we had decided to come to China. In this matter the Chinese are very thorough. I think this is to do with Chairman Mao's thinking that they really tried to understand us. That is what I liked the best about the Chinese.

General Thinoselie was an army man; of course he tried to answer their questions but otherwise he did not talk. He just sat quietly. Whereas I asked for full liberty to talk, to speak, and they said yes, you are free to speak your mind, in that there is no restriction.

I told them about my reading of socialism and communism and how I had read Marx and Lenin in college. I said I had read about the Chinese liberation movement and I praised their movement and they were very happy. All of them started shaking hands with me. But sometimes we could not understand what they said.

The word Naga is not found in the Chinese dictionary or any other dictionary. They called us 'nazah.' I think there must have been some Nagas in China but now they are totally absorbed in the Chinese nationality. So they just called us 'nazah.' We also found cloth with designs similar to ours.[81]

In Peking we stayed in a big hotel meant for the PLA and by our standards it was very good. After that we were taken to Nanking (Nanjing). We stayed there for three months. There we had discussions on strategy and tactics. They told us how Chairman Mao dealt with Chiang Kai-shek and also with the Japanese imperialists. They told us about Korea and the role of the USA in South Korea. And we discussed the war with India. I asked for permission to go to Tibet but they said it is forbidden to foreigners. The Tibetans must have their own history but the Chinese are dead against the interference of the external powers in Tibet whether it is the Americans, other Western powers, Indians or the Russians. I was warned not to talk too much about Tibet.

---

[81] Muivah was in Yunnan which is home to more than twenty ethnic minorities, of which some have similar textile designs to the Nagas.

They called us friends, not comrades. They knew we would not be easily converted to communism.

They said everyone in China was willing to sacrifice his life if Chairman Mao asked. No Chinese would defy Chairman Mao. I could see the massive support for Chairman Mao during the processions on the streets and at important public functions where we were taken.

General Thinoselie saw things differently. His was a narrow military point of view. I was interested in knowing how so many people could be mobilized. I found it inspiring to see so many people out on the streets and I wanted to know more about the movement. I could not understand how they got such big crowds. I had never seen such a scene.[82]

During the meetings held in the evenings or at night when Chairman Mao was to personally appear, there would be a flash of light and then everybody would know that Chairman Mao was coming. Everyone would rise up and many people would shed tears, when they saw him. 'Ah! Chairman Mao, our saviour, you are our saviour,' everyone shouted, because everybody had a sad and bitter experience before the Revolution, so Chairman Mao led the Revolution and saved them all. So when Chairman Mao appeared they could not help shedding tears. I cannot put into words the experience of seeing all those people and their deep feelings for their leader.

The first time I saw Chairman Mao was in the main square of Peking, on October 1 which the Chinese celebrate as their National Day. My friend who was doing the interpretation for me also stopped as he looked at the Chairman and was lost in awe. Of course, I know Chairman Mao does not inspire such awe any more. But at that time he would be able to speak to Chinese people about their most bitter experiences and that is why he was able to mobilize so many people.

I think Chairman Mao really applied Marxism-Leninism to analyze China correctly so nobody could question him. At the same time, he

---

[82] The Cultural Revolution was launched by Mao Zedong in 1966, a year before the Nagas arrived in China.

was cautious because he was aware he was leading a movement which had far-reaching consequences for the future of mankind.

Joseph Stalin made a lot of mistakes, but Mao didn't make many mistakes except, in my view, the Great Leap Forward.[83] But you know he also thought that the communism could be achieved during his lifetime; that was a mistake. His thinking became too emotional and presumptuous and so he made that kind of mistake. They called it left adventurism or left opportunism. Otherwise, well, nobody can deny that he really had wisdom.

Chairman Mao had a deep love for the poor people, nobody can question that. Christians and others may criticise him but that is only from their point of view because of some incidents. But he was able to save millions of people who were oppressed. I saw how people were oppressed in people's museum in which they reproduced scenes of oppression in the village before the revolution.

They chartered a plane for us so we could visit many places. I visited villages as well and heard from people about their lives before the revolution. Stories of how people died of starvation and people committed suicide, the parents committed suicide. They spoke of how the People's Liberation Army rescued them. The people would cry and I could not help the tears in my eyes also. It is no exaggeration about the sufferings of the Chinese people under the Emperor and his fanatic rule.

I stayed in China for five years continuously without going back. I was given a chance to study the revolution and I was taken to different places. It was up to me to ask questions and if I wanted a discussion, they would bring experts and we had discussions for a week and sometimes for a month.

They can teach well and also they have traditional ways of teaching

---

[83] The Great Leap Forward was the economic and social campaign undertaken by the Chinese Communist Party from 1958–1964 to rapidly transform China's agrarian economy into an industrial one. This hasty industrialization and collectivization caused the Great Chinese Famine.

and people were encouraged to memorize Mao's Red Book. I did not have the capacity to learn 3000 characters of the Chinese language so I did not learn Chinese language.

They allowed me to go everywhere except to Tibet. Yes we had discussions on nationalism, especially minority nationalism.

They gave much attention to the requirement of the minorities, so the minorities were satisfied. Yes, the Han Chinese are the majority but the minorities were given fine opportunities, and if I am not mistaken many Tibetans were there in Peking and they firmly identified with the Chinese. I don't mean to say that they are Chinese.

The Dalai Lama managed to get out and shout to the foreign places against the Chinese military atrocities, so the world is shouting for Tibet; but the Chinese were also very good to the Tibetans. This is one of the reasons why the Dalai Lama had to give up his claim of independence, not that the Chinese were pushing him, but because Chinese had already won over the great part of Tibet. They say the Dalai Lama is a fugitive and he cannot speak on behalf of all the Tibetan people.

But you know from our point of view any form of government that goes against religion is a problem.

You know the Chinese would say, don't interfere in our internal affairs; India and America also say the same thing. So Americans wants to speak many things against China but what about their treatment of the Native Americans? So the Chinese have a saying that, 'Clean your compound first, then the whole world will be clean.'

In Geneva, during discussions and debates on human rights Americans speak in a proud and arrogant way as if they have the authority to teach the world. The Chinese point out that the USA has a history of human rights violations against negroes and the indigenous people. Even today many people in USA are suffering.

General Thinoselie was also very much impressed by the discipline of the PLA. It was good to see their discipline and their courage. The PLA was always prepared to face any situation. So General Thinoselie told his boys: 'Don't complain, ask yourselves whether you can act like the men of the People's Liberation Army. The PLA will sacrifice without complaining.'

General Thinoselie is a fine man, he has a sense of integrity in many ways but you know when it comes to the question of philosophy and politics he does not understand much. I think he would realise his own limitations. So politically of course we cannot expect much from him. But he won't betray the nation.

General Thinoselie[84] and the NNC

The last time I met him and we talked, he wanted me to go back to NNC. He said you are the only elected General Secretary, we are waiting for you. I said I saved the NNC from the tragedy of the Shillong Accord. But General Thinoselie did not join us when the Accord was signed; how can he expect me to join NNC now? Now I have no connection with NNC. He said I was right to condemn the Shillong Accord but the NNC is a national cause.

I told him that the NNC is for the nation, the nation is not for NNC; please don't try to place the NNC above the nation. Yes the Naga people passed a resolution at Lakhuti village in 1953 to look upon the NNC as a national institution but if that institution sells the nation, then how can the Naga people support the NNC?

Nationalism isn't enough. There must be a love of the people but NNC is rough with the people. In those days national workers had a kind of Brahmin attitude towards the people. General Thinoselie made a mistake in China by making certain remarks and I had to apologize to the Chinese. Some religious minded people said undesirable things to which the Chinese took offence.

General Thinoselie and myself urged the Chinese authorities to allow Uncle Phizo to stay in China. We felt at that stage all he needed to do was to talk to the Chinese authority and if need be offer sincere

---

[84] General Thinoselie M Keyho was elected President of the Naga National Council in May 2016. See his interview below.

apology for his statement during the Indo-China war; that must be the beginning of relationship between us.

The moment Phizo came to China the whole politics of Asia would change. There would be international alarm; the Western world may not support us openly but they will ask Government of India to solve Indo-Naga problem. This is the upper hand we can have if the issue gets internationalized.

But Phizo did not realise the full political significance of what we were asking him to do.

Return from China

I returned from China in winter of 1971. I came back with thirteen of our boys. Then I found some of our boys who had been wounded or fallen sick with the Kachins, they too joined us and we started back. We were attacked by the Burmese troops and five boys got hit. It hurt me very much to see them screaming and I could do nothing for them.

After two days we were ambushed again and the villagers cautioned so we did not follow the paths but went through the jungles. It was at that time Nuri came and he took us to his camp. His wife was not well. He is a peculiar man. He speaks English, Burmese, Angami, Manipuri and Tangkhul. He looks ordinary but he is the best among the Burmese Nagas for writing and to work out strategies. I am told he was brought up by U Nu.

Nuri happened to be there at that time and he was carrying two kilograms of rice so he gave us that. He looked after his wife for twenty years. I love him very much. He is a Para from the southern side whereas Khaplang is from the northern side. He was Buddhist before, then one day he told me he has become Christian and we laughed together.

I continued my journey and had to climb the Saramati which is the highest peak in the Patkai range. Then we saw an Indian Army post so we could not cross for two days. We passed a Pochury village and they gave us small, small pigs and we made soup and then arrived at a small Sema village. The Semas have very small villages because everyone wants to be a chief. So whenever anyone falls out with the chief he starts his own village. We told them we were Naga Army and the chief cooked some rice and brought a curry with leaves and a chicken, not very well-cooked.

When I reached back I heard Ramyo had made contact with the Indian Army. NNC had given orders to eliminate him but I stopped it.

I along with three boys managed to reach the deep jungles where there was a meeting, a sort of Christian revival meeting. In that meeting I was told I had to go back to China. I protested but it was decided, so in September 1974 I started for China again. It was at that meeting I met Atem, he was still a student. He used to make moorahs (stools) and give them to people like teachers and accept whatever they gave in return for the movement.

Back to China (1974)

When we started from the camp, we were 200 of us, and that included twenty ladies. The Indians got wind of our going so we were ambushed but no one got killed. We did not carry sufficient rations so we planned to buy from the villages we passed. At the first village they cooked some rice, and gave us salt and green chillies; and gave us one small pig. We laughed and said don't worry, everyone will get their share.

We would send one man to climb up to the highest point and look out and if he saw a village we would go there. Often it was the ladies in the villages who came out and showed us the way. But we did not get any food. And it was raining throughout the night. I have never seen rain like that. We could not sleep so some fell down from exhaustion and the new recruits lost their way.

We came to a river and stayed near the river for a week. We made a porridge with leaves and some rice which we took from the fields where we left money for the owner. The boys made a raft and two tried to cross but one boy floated down; he reached the plains of Assam. Yes, he was alive. The other held on to the bamboo and saved himself. We made another attempt to cross but one boy got washed away.

Then we saw a bridge and found no one was guarding it and we crossed it. We reached Longkhum Imkongmeren's village.[85] I met him in his camp in the jungle. That was the last time I met him.

We did not have anything to eat and on one occasion I took out my glucose packet and distributed it among everyone to sustain ourselves. The Chaplain Puni was there and he made many sermons out of this incident.

At one point we found beans in a jhum field and we all ate the beans. People started vomiting and got stomach ache. I think they use the beans to ferment and make wine. We got sick because we ate on empty stomachs and beans cause gas.

Finally we reached the border. It was the second highest peak in Nagaland and the sun was bright and I told them to see the beautiful land that God had given to us.

By this time, we were only eighty-two or eighty-three of us. Some had lost their way when we were ambushed, some went back without surrendering. They were the new recruits.

We continued our march but there was little food. The Burmese Nagas live on millet and maize, there is almost no rice. Eating that maize we got gas in our stomach. We had a terrible time. I came to know if we do not have sufficient salt in our body, we get lice. The boys took off their pants and shirts and killed the lice with a stone. But despite all this suffering no one wanted to go back.

We reached the Chindwin river. We met a Naga officer from the civil side. He was carrying rice and was probably on a tour and we bought rice from him. He supported our movement. He helped us cross the river.

In our group there was a young girl, a high school student. She was the fiancé of one of our men. When we were approaching the river,

---

[85] Imkongmeren (1900–1979) was at the time the Vice President of the NNC; his village Longkhum is some 17 kms from Mokokchung in Nagaland. The river they crossed was Doyang. He was arrested in 1974 and released in 1976.

I sang a song. It is a sentimental song: 'I will go away, and if you love me marry me now.' She also joined in the song. And her fiancé was anxious about crossing the river because our people do not know how to swim and he crossed at the wrong place, taking her with him. The commander was shouting, saying do not cross there. And in that process, she drowned. We pulled her out and buried her.

Kachins

Finally we reached the Kachin area. In those days the Kachins were very helpful and the people were very kind. Without their help it would have been impossible to reach China. We would have been finished without their help in crossing roads and rivers. But when we reached this time something undesirable happened. The Kachins insisted we sign a contract by which we would give them 30 per cent of the arms we get from China. Most of our people wanted me to sign it because they wanted to reach China. I told the Kachins we could sign but that is not the way revolutionaries should treat each other. They said if we did not sign they had orders to kill us. But they also wanted me to agree to give them a substantial part of our territory.

We signed under duress. But despite signing the agreement the Kachins detained me. The others were allowed to proceed to China.

When they reached China and told the Chinese about the Kachins they were not happy. Indirectly they gave us extra arms. Later the Kachin leaders apologized. The reason for that incident was the power struggle going on within the Kachin Independence Organization. Most of the Kachins wanted good relations with China but some leaders did not. At the time this fight was going on and Kachins detained me at their headquarters at Pajau for a year while the in-fighting was going on. I was not told that Brang Sen had already taken over the leadership of the Kachin Independence Organization. He was a close friend of mine.[86]

---

[86] Maran Brang Seng (1930–1994) was elected the Chairman of the Kachin

Shillong Accord[87]

I was in China when we heard over the radio that the Shillong Accord had been signed. The others had already reached by May of 1975. Our people were having their military training and political classes and we in the meanwhile wrote to Phizo. Unfortunately, Phizo wrote a letter, (probably his daughter wrote it) that Angamis and Chakhesang must be united because the others are not reliable. It was written to Thepuse Venuh[88] but not shown to me although I was the leader of the delegation.

All seven of us wrote a letter to Phizo from China and waited for his reply and condemnation of the Accord. We said we would never surrender.

I knew that this was serious. There was no point my having trust in them (the NNC leadership) because they were politically bankrupt, no morality, no policy, no confidence in the people or even in the cause. So I knew we needed to get back home. We reached safe and sound but the Shillong Accord people had already come overground.

We held a meeting at Supao village in the Khiamniungan village in Eastern Nagaland. The meeting started on August 14 to celebrate Naga Independence Day and then I called a National Assembly on August 15, 16 and 17. At the meeting we condemned the Shillong Accord and Zashie Huire and his government. Zashie was the Kedage (President) of the Federal Government of Nagaland and party to the Shillong Accord although he did not sign the Accord.

Independence Organization (KIO) in 1976 and he reached an agreement with the Communist Party of Burma on co-operation.

[87] According to the NNC, the Shillong Accord was signed under dire circumstances: the Indian Government abrogated the Ceasefire Agreement in August 1971 and five divisions of the Indian Army moved into Nagaland. President's Rule was declared in March 1975 and a National Emergency in June 1975. The sweeping powers given to the Indian security forces under the Armed Forces (Special Powers) Act, 1958 led to widescale repression and ultimately the signing of the Accord.

[88] Thepuse Venuh, a Chakhesang and Vice President of the NNC, was eliminated later in November 1979 allegedly by supporters of the Isak-Muivah group.

In that meeting we formed a new government. We still accepted Phizo as our President, we made Isak the Vice President and I continued as General Secretary. Even before our condemnation, the Tangkhuls had condemned the Accord.

We had to make our base in Burma. You know starting must be in an impressive way. So the army was given instructions that the first fighting must be an impressive one. It must be a victory. So in one go fifty-four Burmese troops were just wiped out. And that included one Major, one Captain and one Lieutenant. So our men did very well and two of our men sacrificed themselves because of the chase firing. They did very well.

After that we were left alone by the Burmese. We captured sixty arms and started to mobilize the people. We were successful and in a short time we mobilized people from the Khiamniungan area to the Konyak area. Khaplang had just ten to fifteen villages but we extended our base to include his area as well.

On one occasion in 1976 when we were attacking a Burmese post I got injured when a hand grenade exploded right near me. I was carried away from there and I heard the boys saying after one or two days he will die. They thought I could not hear. I replied, 'I will not die, don't talk like that.' Then they gave me a drop of water. I could bear the pain because my mother used to say you should not cry and you should not weep. Just bear it. Don't let the devil take advantage. She was a little bit superstitious. I still have shrapnel inside my leg and when I went to China I showed it to the doctors; they said it would not be good to operate because it would mean amputation so it remains there.

Martial Law (August 1978 – March 1979)

As I said, the Shillong Accord people had come to our camp. They shook hands with us, talked nicely and gradually started winning over our boys in the name of Phizo. They said Phizo was the President of the Nation and Muivah wanted to topple him. They even tried to win over Isak.

Then at a meeting at the Sector II Headquarters in August 1978, these people came with submachine guns and demanded all the powers of the Federal Government be handed over to them. Mayanger, who was Imkongmeren's brother's son was one of the leaders. They also won over one of our Tangkhuls, Ngathingkui.

At first they kept us at the camp then they moved us from village to village and then we made our camp in the jungles. Three times they made plans to eliminate us or to hand us over to the Indian Army. But the Konyaks refused to co-operate.

They had plans to do away with us. Khaplang was made the President of the NNC and he accepted. The Shillong Accordists wanted to entrap him. But we spoke to him. We explained to him that if we were eliminated, he would be blamed since he was now President.

We had many meetings with him and we also needed time to prepare ourselves. We discussed the terms for unification of Khaplang's organization with ours. I drafted a statement to save his face. Khaplang wanted to be Chairman and we had to discuss that also. He gave us an ultimatum and I had to talk to him with guns pointing at me. I said I won't accept Khaplang as President.

I said Isak was the most senior amongst us, in terms of service to the nation and sacrifice, he was also the most educated, so he should be the Chairman. Khaplang tried to say the Semas had brought disgrace to the movement (referring to the Revolutionary Government of Sukhai which had surrendered). I said Isak had proven himself not because he was a Sema but because he was a Naga.

Then I explained that Isak would not be able to make decisions on his own because we would have a Collective Leadership, so we would not be in the same position as the NNC, with Phizo who was above everything.

Khaplang had been giving the Shillong Accord people shelter in his area. So we told him to deal with them. He had to face practical confrontation. It was a challenge to him not to betray us again. He issued orders in December 1979 to his people to eliminate the Shillong Accordists; without eliminating them there would have been danger to us.

We had tried to save the Naga National Council from the Shillong Accord. We had condemned the Accord in the name of the NNC and the Federal Government; we did not take the post of President and continued to accept Phizo as our President. But the Federal Government wanted to brand us anti-Phizo and so justify killing us. The leaders on the Western side were supporting the Accord in one way or the other. What alternative was left to us? We had to form our own organization.

National Socialist Council of Nagalim (NSCN)

I called a meeting of the national workers in January 1980 and I addressed the meeting and told them why the Shillong Accord had to be condemned, why the Federal Government had to be condemned and also the Naga National Council.

I explained why we have to establish our own organization and our own institutions to prove that we are no longer a part of the NNC which has already surrendered to the Government of India.

I then spoke about the reason for having a manifesto. I told them the NNC did not have a manifesto because it was guided by one man. We need a manifesto which will guide the organization. NNC never had a manifesto because they went by whatever Phizo said. That is very dangerous.

It took a long time for our people to understand. They understood a little bit at a time. We explained we could not allow any leadership to be above the people or above the organization or above the nation and the cause. That is the reason we have introduced the concept of Collective Leadership.[x]

So at that meeting the Eastern Nagaland Revolutionary Council and the former NNC agreed to merge; we passed the manifesto and thus the National Socialist Council of Nagaland was born on January 31, 1980. And the Government of People's Republic of Nagalim (GRPN) was created a few days later.

My Marriage

A bitter thing occurred during the days of my detention under martial law. I asked my fiancé, now my wife, to join me. Even though we had not met for nine years, she was there waiting for me. So I had to call her and she came to join me. Unfortunately, she fell sick. In our areas we eat rice but in the Konyak areas the mainstay is maize or millet. In the jungles you won't get rice. And we ate with chopsticks, corn and millet. In the West we eat corn as a snack, not as mainstay. Anyway she fell sick.

My close friend, I trusted him and he had knowledge of medicine so among us he was the most reliable. I had to move up and down so I asked him to look after her. You know they went wrong and she became pregnant. I was given the news while I was in custody. I worried not so much for me but about her life, because in our society these things are taken very seriously. It will become a life and death issue for her. And so also for my friend. Why, you know because he had earned so much credibility and now it would be pulled down on account of a woman. So I was the only person on earth who could save the two of them.

In the name of God, I could forgive her but he would have to make a public confession. He would have to respect our society and ask their forgiveness. He had been a leader. I told him I had forgiven him without any condition in the name of our Saviour, Jesus Christ. I will forgive him and I will forgive Pakahao (that is her name). But I told her don't try to justify yourself. God does not like it. It broke my heart.

Pakahao was pregnant. Nobody liked her because she had disgraced the leader. Everybody condemned her. We could be attacked by the Burmese Army and also the Indians and they would have left her. So I had to take care of her even though she carried the child of someone else.

For seven years I took care of her but I told her we could not have any relationship. She became a teacher and she was a very good teacher. She became very active and many villages became Christian.

Then I got a vision repeatedly telling me to marry her. I told God, you know best for me. I said I was not after beauty or physical appearance. I will gladly marry someone blind or invalid. I rejected the vision but when it was repeated, I said alright I will marry. Everyone pitied me.

We got married in 1985.[89]

The NSCN Manifesto

In the midst of this painful incident I had to carry on writing the manifesto. I wrote most of it in candle light at night. The Accordists would keep shifting us from one place to another and the guards would check us. I would draft one paragraph on one page and leave it in the village with my friends who hid it. So I went on writing and writing. I think it took me 105 days of writing. Luckily Angelus[90] was there with me. Angelus was very helpful because his language was very good. He was very gifted.

The conditions of detention were relaxed and he could come and meet me and I would show him the draft. He was not very serious about the manifesto but he was very serious about my safety. So we would read together and discuss the issues. Every sentence had some meaning. He would type it out. Once when the Burmese came we had to rush but I did not forget to hide the manifesto and we had to come back after many days to retrieve it.

Angelus never kept idle. He would go with his catapult and kill a bird or catch fish in the stream and once he shot a deer with a pistol. So we had a good time.

Writing the manifesto was taking time but we completed it. I showed it to Chairman Isak and he encouraged me and said it was very good. Once it was completed, he read every sentence and said it was good. This was our one achievement during the time we were under the custody of the Shillong Accordists.

---

[89] Pakahao Muivah made her first public appearance in March 2003 and since then she has been seen at various meetings. She is now known as Ikhreo Muivah.

[90] Angelus Paiza Shimray was a member of the NSCN who died in April 2009.

Isak was unfortunate because he did not have people around him who understood him. I had the blessing of that kind of people with me at every stage in history.

NSCN Programmes and Policies

When we started constructing our base in Burma, we had to face a number of problems. The first was the question of how to deal with the people and make them understand the mission for which we were there. We had to have a policy about how to deal with the people correctly. Our cadres had to be taught not to be rough with the people but understand them—without this understanding our movement would not be popular.

Our cadres understood, but you know it is difficult to bring up people from most primitive level to the twentieth century. We set up our administration at the village level. We went to the Village Authority and gave them the powers to deal with problems themselves.

And along with organizational set up in every village we also spread Christianity and that helped to make our progress effective. They did not resist very much and their churches are better than the churches in the west.

We also set up schools. It took a year to be accepted but people realized the benefit of schools. The teachers were from amongst our own cadres. Our own children did not go to these schools.

We also introduced terrace cultivation but the people were used to poppy cultivation and it was a source of their livelihood. A lot of them were opium addicts. And this addiction was from a long time so it was difficult to wipe out because we did not have an alternative source of income to offer them.

But on the whole the people were quite satisfied with us. They realized that the Nagas are one big family. The people from the west had of course a sense of superiority so there was undeniable contradiction which Khaplang took advantage of.

But we also provided medicines. We had one woman who we called Doctor. Her name was Unice[91] and she is from my village. Her prayers helped us a lot. She would pray and have visions and that is how the Spirit told her of herbs. I have seen how she cured a man who had been in bed lying paralyzed for twenty-two years; another with advanced TB.

Many of the people died of malaria and we used to get quinine injections from Western Nagaland.

We believe in self-reliance so we began capturing banks. We know that we cannot be dependent on foreign help to sustain us. That is what the NNC did because they would tell people that Phizo would get help from foreigners. We saw in the seventeen years Phizo was abroad, there was no help except a little bit from Pakistan. But that help was not out of solidarity for our cause but because the Pakistanis had their own agenda.

I am not saying we should not take any foreign help, but we must have our own programme to raise funds.

We also had a programme of a united front with other people who wanted to fight the monster. It became a matter of strategy. The NNC fought alone with India and they did not want to have alliances as a matter of principle but this united front is not a question of principle but of strategy.

Anthony,[92] I am very grateful to him. He organized the ULFA. He recruited Paresh and the others. Then others also came up, like the Garos and Bodos and even the People's War Group. Khalistanis also came but we could not speak to them because they only spoke Punjabi.

The Burmese armed groups formed a united front with Aung

---

[91] See her interview below.

[92] Anthony Ningkhan Shimray was arrested in 2011. According to the Indian media he confessed that NSCN continued to have links with China. https://www.outlookindia.com/magazine/story/the-great-claw-of-china/270223.

In 2017 Anthony was made the Chief of the Naga Army while he was on bail.

San Suu Kyi. We did not think that was right.[93] During the time the enemy was so afraid of them. They did not make the right political calculation.

The Manipuri groups sometimes came and stayed with us or we allowed them to pass through. The PLA, PREPAK and UNLF all came but we did not allow them to fight against each other in our camp.

The Burmese Army sometimes carried out operations against us. In one village at least three hundred people died. The Burmese Army burnt down their granaries. We would help with medicine but what could we do? We did not have doctors or the amounts of medicines needed at the time.

The outside world did not know about the Burmese operations against Naga people. No one knew, no human rights groups from either Burma or India side visited those areas. Only one journalist[94] came and he was in our camp when the Burmese attacked, but we were able to resist. Our boys fought very well.

But he was actually on the side of the Shillong Accord. We had a tense confrontation with him and actually we did not welcome him very much. He carried a letter from a Kachin General like a certificate for him. The journalist has written negatively about the Nagas. He wrote that had already got Nagaland State so what are we fighting for?

---

[93] See Nuri's interview in which he joins the united front of ethnic armed groups to fight for restoration of democracy in Burma. Muivah probably felt the ethnic minorities should have carried on their armed struggles for sovereignty instead forming an alliance with Aung Saan Suu Kyi's National League for Democracy which was dominated by the majority Burman community and at that time weak. Many of these groups entered into ceasefire agreements with the NLD.

[94] Muivah is referring to Bertil Lintner, a Swedish journalist and author of *Land of Jade: A Journey through Insurgent Burma* (1990) in which he writes in which he writes: 'At the age of 83, Phizo was still adamantly advocating Naga independence. I could not help feeling sorry for him and the plight of his people, although I found their intransigence hard to understand. After all, the Nagas in India have managed to get from the Indian government exactly what Rangoon denies its national minorities: a separate state with high degree of self-government, aid from the centre and the right to preserve their own customs and culture.' (Gartmore: Kiscadale Publications, 1990), 314.

He said he supports Nagaland State. He was deadly against Christianity
and he said we did forceful conversions. That is not true. He wrote so
much ill about us but thought highly of Kachins.

China Again

The last group to go to China was in 1977. The Accord group also tried
to go to China and they reached Tibet but the Chinese did not give
them arms.

In 1986 I was sent to China again[95] but the Kachins did not allow
us to pass and I was detained at the Kachin headquarters for seven or
eight months. I sent a letter to the Chinese but there was no reply.
They said it was the Chinese policy to help revolutionaries to rise up
but after that we must sustain ourselves. Of course we got a few pieces
of arms but not directly from China.

Phizo made a mistake by giving that press conference and saying
he would fight against China. He may have said it to get the support
of the west but we lost an opportunity. Americans are retreating from
everywhere—Cambodia, Laos and even Thailand. China has the
potential to occupy almost all of South Asia from Siliguri to Vietnam
if there is a global war. We should have good relations with China.

It is no use shouting that Nagaland belongs to the Nagas when we
do not take the opportunity and take the initiative to create a situation
where we have the control. We lost the opportunity and we defeated
ourselves.

NSCN Makes Base in Ukhrul

If we want to prove ourselves in a meaningful way, we have to mobilize
the people, show them that we are really something to be relied upon.

---

[95] Thuingaleng Muivah went to China three times: in October 1966 when he
stayed in China for five years; then in September 1974 when he returned just after
the signing of the Shillong Accord; then for the third time in October 1976 reaching
China in 1977.

We had to show them that we will continue the fight and we had to send a message to the Indians as well. We had to show them that our fight is not over after Shillong Accord.

We had to do something which was historic and had to be a grand success. Our boys chose the spot well. It was at Namthilok and they were just six or seven of them led by Atem. They did not even take position when they attacked the Indian Army.[96] It was successful operation and it gave out a beautiful message to the Naga people and to the Indians also.

Then the Naga Army did actions in various places in so-called State of Nagaland, including in Khonoma; then at the Lumding Junction and at Haflong. One group led by Ningkhan Anthony were sent to Assam to organize the Assamese and they were successful. They could organize them into the ULFA and did action in Naogaon, Jorhat, Shibsagar and Golaghat.

The Tangkhul people started supporting and admiring us. Rishang still had support in the southern side of Ukhrul. Not as a fighting force, but as a man who could talk to the people. Our side Livingstone was selected. He was a good soldier and at the same time he was good at mobilization of people by talking to them. 80 per cent people under Rishang's influence were won over. Only about ten villages at the foothills of Imphal valley were left. They were not touched. After that Hanshi along with other boys also mobilized the people and, in that way, Ukhrul became a base for us to operate from.

We had the people's support. I taught our boys that if anyone is standing in our way just do away with them and I would take responsibility for their actions. It was really a matter of necessity for the survival of the nation to have a sound base. That is why we unfortunately had to deal with Yangmaso Shaiza and his brother Lungshim Shaiza; Rishang escaped several times as did Stanhope who escaped to a Kabui village and he spoke in the church praising us.

---

[96] The NSCN ambush at Namthilok in February 1982 is described in detail in testimony of Atem.

High-ranking officers from our organization criticized me very much and asked why only Tangkhuls were done away with and not others, whereas the biggest mistakes of high treason were committed by other people, not by Tangkhuls. It took me a long time to explain the reason to them. It is for the interest of the national strategy and it is not a question of killing this tribe or that tribe or killing this man or that man; if we are to be successful in our national resistance movement, we have to see that there is a safe base area under our control. So as long as the base area is there, the nation can survive. The future of Naga people depends on a base.

Khaplang

Things were going smoothly and our base in Burma was secure.

Indian and Burmese started joint military operations against us; this collaboration was something new. But it was not a problem because how could they operate there in the jungles? They were strangers to the terrain. So we had nothing to fear and we were secure in the jungles.

We started working together with Khaplang who was from the east but we have rules to maintain discipline which is really important to the organization. Certain things are forbidden within our organization: drinking, immorality, misappropriation, taking drugs and smoking. We have suffered much in the past because of lack of discipline in these matters. And those who commit fornication we have to punish them with capital punishment.

Khaplang smoked, chewed tobacco and even raped women. He did some things that are too dirty to talk about. And the worst part of his indiscipline was if he was not happy with someone, he would have them eliminated.

Khaplang's father was a Chief, or close to that position, so Khaplang was used to being listened to, he did not listen to others. That was his mentality.

I did not know these things before we started working closely together. I know it was foolish to trust him. We should not take our friends for granted.

So this was the beginning of our differences between us.

Split in the NSCN

People started demanding that Khaplang confess during the budget session his mistakes because everybody must bear responsibility for their own mistakes. He refused. This was in 1985.

Khaplang started saying there was a power struggle between ourselves. The first propaganda he made was that the eastern side was going to be totally dominated by the westerners. But the people did not believe him; they did not listen to him because they knew him. So you know even the leaders from his own tribe were against him. During that time, you know I was sent out to go to China in August 1986 and I was detained by the Kachins for nearly a year and returned only in December 1987. Khaplang had time to arrange many things during the time I was away.

The Indian intelligence agencies also took advantage of the situation. They spread the rumour that Isak had flown to New Delhi along with twenty-nine persons to have negotiations with the Indian union. That was in 1987. And another rumour was that Mr Muivah has already accepted huge amount of money from the Indians and he has already put up several buildings; one in Shillong, another in Dimapur, one at Golaghat and one at Jorhat and another in Arunachal.

Khaplang spread these lies in big, big public meetings which he held in our absence and he gave emotional speeches.

Our people wanted to physically eliminate him but it would have been dangerous to do away with him so we called a meeting during the budget session and we sent two reliable people, one Konyak and one Yimchunger, to invite Khaplang to the meeting but he did not come to our meeting although he was staying nearby.

I explained to our people that the day will come when the Government of India will say military solution is not possible and they will have to have political peaceful negotiations as a matter of necessity which was very different from a sellout. And many people in the Western side will accept but the Indian intelligence will try to divide one tribe against another so we must be aware of these things.

I went on lecturing about this possibility and preparing our people for the possibility of political negotiations but Khaplang did not see the context and he distorted my words to create trouble.

The Escape

I think that night after the meeting, or the next day, I do not remember—I am not sure, he sent those Konyaks and the Pangmi to surround our headquarters and started firing.

This was in April 1988. There was a Manipuri boy who came running to my camp and said: 'Avakharer (Uncle) the camp is surrounded and they are firing openly but I escaped, nothing happened to me.' The Meitei boy has been very good to us. Even now he is alright and twice he has saved us. And so you know that was the beginning.

I was sleeping inside my camp. By the grace of God nothing hit me and I was able to escape. The Deputy Commander-in-Chief Ashiho was there with a boy of five or six years and he tried to stop the firing and he said it is wrong but he was killed along with the boy he was holding.

We went out of the camp and cut through the jungle. It was night and we were trying to spend the night in the thick jungle but the Burmese Army also entered. They tried to ambush us near the riverbank which was near the camp.

Along with the Burmese Army there were villagers and we overheard then saying it is not good to shoot women and children so a very brave little boy with us shouted and the Burmese shot him there.

One of our Kilonsers, Hanong, was with his wife who was pregnant. We also had small children with us. The pregnant woman could not walk so she just rolled down through the jungles and we arrived by the river and managed to cross the river but we lost the direction. It is difficult to have orientation and the jungle is so thick we cannot see the sky. We reached a village which was deserted so we could stay. The officer took his wife and kids to another village called Kako because the situation was too much for them to bear. We gave good guards to him and he talked to the villagers nicely and responsibly to take care of the family but unfortunately as he was leaving Khaplang's people came and rounded up the villagers and arrested him. His tongue was chopped saying, 'You speak Muivah's words', and ears chopped saying, 'You listen to him,' and eyes poked out and he died a miserable death.

Hanong was from the Burma side from Khaplang's tribe. He was the Finance Minister. He sacrificed without surrendering even a little. One boy from my village Taothing was commander. He tried to save the others but they were made to dig their graves and if they refused, they were shot dead.

The next day they attacked the deserted village where we were. Thirteen of the boys were killed. We had to leave and we had only one weapon. We went round and round and round. Then accidentally we reached Hukawng valley. I noticed a bird—that bird is found only in the plains and not in the hills. So we realized there would a river nearby because the bird lives near the river. I was with Atem and thirty others. We sent two boys to see. That river I knew because I had seen it on my way to China. We were very close to Chindwin. We thought we could cross it and reach the Kachin side. But before we went, we had to give information to their people.

We spent the night near a small stream near thick bush and we had no food. But Atem and his wife went out to catch fish and they brought four or five fish. One was big; others were small, small ones. My wife had no energy anymore. She had some fish and then I had to support her as we walked. And one of our boys who had crossed the river before found a small wooden boat. We were a few men and more women. We crossed and then got rice. It was like we had reached paradise; we could not be happier.

We tried to construct a small camp but Khaplang's men came again to chase us. We contacted the Kachin authorities but they would not support us, they supported Khaplang because you know they wanted Hukawng valley. The Kachins allowed us to stay a few days and then we were asked to leave the place. There were four ladies with us and they were very sick and our boys had carried them but it was not possible to go on carrying them; so we left them with the Kachins and the ladies trusted us. The Kachins were treacherous. The ladies died after a few months.

After we left the Kachins other ladies with us also got sick. One lady became thin and she would have died no doubt, but her mind was clear. She fell and I rushed to raise her. She said, 'I know your love for me and you have done your best for me but I know I will not live, I will not survive. Just leave me somewhere. I will not mind.' She told me. She was from Khangkhui village. But it was too painful to leave a human being like that.

The boys were also exhausted. They had been carrying two ladies through high jungles and mountains up and down. The ladies knew that also. So alright we prayed, if it is the will of God we are sure to come back and find them. You know we left her just by the stream with one small pot of rice, some salt and one thin cloth to cover and she did not worry at all. She said 'I know you have done the best for me. I understand, don't worry.' Ash! We had to leave her. Sometimes it is too much to bear.

The other lady, we had to drag her. And we reached one place we took rest there but she could not recover. She could not walk again. What could we do? Khaplang's people were also close. But we somehow got her to walk with the help of two boys; she dragged her legs and it was painful and we left her at a village and prayed that we would be able to come back for her. She was from Jimmy Stanhope's village.

We learnt that Khaplang people killed her afterwards.

And then we came out cutting through the jungle and then Khaplang people again attacked us there—one boy and one lady got killed. All of us scattered again.

I thought my wife was also lost in the attack. But suddenly she was just behind me. I did not recognize her. And when I stood thinking she said go, go. It was her voice. She was herself. 'So you are alive?' She said yes. I asked who else was alive and she said she did not know. Then around fifteen of our group came together and we came to a river and it was very narrow but very deep and rough, I think it is one of the biggest of the Naga rivers. We crossed the river but Khaplang's men were there so we crossed back and started walking and walking for two or three weeks and we observed Christmas in the jungles with some villagers we met and they helped us.

We reached Chalam, our old headquarters. We used to call it Kesan Chalam. The Spirit had told us to go and worship there because that was our prayer centre. It was the will of God that we reached there but it took us three months to reach after going through the Kachin area and the Khaplang area.

After we reached there, we prayed and we fasted for three days. We thought even if the Khaplang people came it's alright we will simply die. After fasting and praying I sent some people to contact the Chalam villagers. Some Khaplang people were there and started firing at us; we escaped but one of the villagers was killed.

That very night we had to move. It was a day's journey from there to the border and we had to cross a stream and around there we found a wide-open area of jhum cultivation. It was risky to cross the area so we had to rest there. We were too tired and hungry, with Khaplang people still chasing us and they attacked us. In that attack our only gun dropped and we lost it. Five ladies died there, including Ramsan's wife. But I escaped along with my wife and we found Samson, he was still alive. We all accidentally met and we were just seven of us left.

My wife was also there and she told me to drop all the luggage and just walk. And as we walked my wife saw Khaplang's men there ready to ambush. They thought we would go to the village since we have nothing to eat. Khaplang's men had mobilized the villagers so we crossed the village silently. Now we were near Tirap in Arunachal. I warned our group that we were in Khaplang's territory and the villagers would not support us.

Quietly we passed though and climbed up and up; and from the top we could see the last outpost and we avoided it and walked on till we reached the Konyak area and from there to Jorhat in Assam. In Jorhat we got some fruits and like monkeys we ate without cleaning ourselves; myself included. Human beings are no better than monkeys at such times! In my heart I said: 'God, you have brought us safe and sound, thank you. We will not betray you.'

I think this was the last week of February 1989. We stayed twenty days in a village with our friends in the ULFA. Although ULFA helped us they were in alliance with Khaplang. Their alliance was more to do with having safe passage to the Kachins and to China than any disagreement with us; they did not do any harm to us.

Aftermath of the Split with Khaplang[97]

Isak Swu had gone to China with twenty-nine people. That was after I had gone and come back without being able to reach. We wanted to explore possibilities because there was a lot of confusion with regard to our relations with China and also the Chinese relationship with the Kachins. Isak was going to China when Khaplang spread the rumour that we were having talks with Delhi.

Isak and I sent a message to our boys and told them to organize with full authority and strengthen our position. We sent a message to Angelus, Raising and Hanshi.[98] Raising came to meet us and Yaopei.[99] That was the first time I met Yaopei.

---

[97] The NSCN split in April 1988 into two; one group led by Isak Swu and Thuingaleng Muivah (NSCN I-M) and the other was led by Khaplang and Kholi. (NSCN K).

[98] Senior leaders of the NSCN.

[99] Yaopei, a Tangkhul lawyer based in Dimapur, was assassinated by unknown assailants soon after.

Yaopei was very happy to meet me and he never believed people who said that I had died. He said he was confident that I would return after he had a dream that a mother hen was flying and calling her small, small chicken and they came running and the chicken were collected together. And they became happy and active again. After that dream Yaopei told his friends that he knew Avakharer would come back alive!

We then went through Assam, Karbi areas and finally reached Dimapur at night and went to my cousin's place. He wanted me to sleep at his place but I said, 'No, I will sleep in the jungle,' so we were taken to the jungle and we slept there. And then we were taken to Shillong.

I was in the bus and two Indian Army people came. I do not know if they had information or they got wind of my movement but they got into the bus. I was in a white coat, suit and tie. They looked at me but they did not suspect me because my wife was with me. In Guwahati, accidentally my wife met a classmate from Theological College and she shouted, 'Pakahao, Pakahao,' but my wife pretended she did not hear in case intelligence people were there; of course it pained her not to be able to respond to her friend but she could not help it.

In Shillong we stayed in Broadway Hotel for three nights and left for Calcutta and just after we left, they came to check the hotel but by then we were in the flight. That was the first time for me to be in Calcutta. We stayed in a hotel near Chowringhee Road. I did not know about the practice of giving tips so I did not give any. After two or three weeks, I heard of the practice; I went back and paid a tip to the doorman.

For three months we stayed in a hotel. We held the Jordan camp meeting and we passed a resolution and decided what to do and then we went to Bhutan side. We stayed in the Bodo camp. We had given training to their men.[100] We stayed three months and then we went to

---

[100] The NSCN trained the Bodo Security Force formed in 1986 with the objective of establishing a sovereign Bodoland; the organization's name was changed to National Democratic Front of Bodoland in 1994 and by the 1990s they had established their camps in Bhutan which border the Bodo areas. The camps were wiped out by the Bhutanese and Indian Armies in 2005.

Nepal. From there we came here to Bangkok, then to Bangladesh and back to Bangkok and started functioning from here in Bangkok finally.

Khaplang and Indian Intelligence

When the Indian Army came to know of our split with Khaplang they rushed to meet him. This was around 1988. It was no surprise that the Indians would take advantage. Khaplang had no alternative but to have an understanding either with the Government of India or with their puppets, the Government of Nagaland, if not with both. He had to do that.

The Indian government already had contact with the Kachins; and the Kukis and Meiteis supported Khaplang. It was a convergence of similar interests.

The Indians knew that the only people genuinely standing for the Naga people were Isak and myself, so if they could do away with us it would be a real victory. It was the first time for them to make use of all these people against us. But to me it was a challenge. We had confidence within ourselves—in the people, in the cause, in the future. So it was something like an oasis which cannot be dried up.

The Government of India made their calculations and for them it was the first opportunity to crush us. They had Khaplang with them. They had Kachins with them. They had Kukis with them. They have directly or indirectly the Meiteis with them and the Assamese with them. The puppet forces were with them, with Jamir who was determined to destroy us. So they declared it disturbed area again, and along with that sent an additional 50,000 strong troops to crush us. It was a funny calculation according to me because they had completely failed to understand who we were, and who we still are.

The Indian government had already sown the seeds of tribalism with the creation of the so-called State of Nagaland and now they were going to create more divisions.

Despite all these events our boys were never disheartened so they fought against the Shillong Accordists, they had to fight against

Khaplang people, they had to fight against the puppet forces, they had to fight against the Indian Armed Forces, against Kukis, against even Meiteis...so against everybody. On top of that we had no money and limited arms. It was a challenge. It was very difficult. But we have a cause we are fighting for and we have our party. So long as we have confidence in oneself there is no force that can defeat us or destroy us.

I told our boys don't worry; the Indian government will have to admit that a military solution is not possible. There must be a search for a positive political solution. Surely they will realize that they have to negotiate with us.

The fanatics opposed the talks because they could not understand the objective realities. I said if we refuse to talk to the Indians this time, we are fanatic and for me I don't believe in fanaticism, so it is time to understand them.

The Peace Process

The Indian government started sending feelers to us. They used Tangkhuls. They sent Ram Khathing. They used Rishang, he came to meet my brother. Finally it was through Deepak Dewan, an Indian journalist who was in touch with my nephew Grinder, and through Deepak to Rajesh Pilot.[101]

But life here in Bangkok is difficult. I sometimes want to go back to the jungles. There is life in the jungles. We did not have money but we could fish in the stream by throwing dynamite or setting a trap; we could hunt and catch something and share with our friends. We could eat nicely. Sometimes we shot an elephant but it did not die and ran away; there were tigers and rhinos in the forests. The most dangerous are poisonous snakes.

---

[101] The meeting between Grinder Muivah and Deepak Dewan took place in 1993 and Thuingaleng Muivah gave an interview to Deepak; it was his first interview to an Indian journalist.

There was no necessity of using money. We just bought rice from villagers. I used to have just one hundred rupees on me. And that was enough for a year.

I remember there were pythons in the jungles. Once the boys found a big python, and thinking it was wood they sat on it. Then they went around collecting firewood and made a fire and the python got warm and got up. Then they realized it was a python. Of course they killed it and ate it!

Life is much more complicated here in Bangkok. We hope the peace talks will lead to a honourable solution.

KHODAO YANTHAN: THE NOBLE WARRIOR

Khodao Yanthan (1923–2010) was a Lotha Naga. His grandfather, Moyuthung Yanthan, was the last chief of the Kyong (erstwhile Lotha) tribe.

In 1942, his studies were interrupted by the Second Word War. He joined the 10,000 Naga Labour Corps as a Quartermaster with the Allied forces to combat the advancing Japanese forces.

In 1951, he was elected President of Lotha Tribal Council and a member of the central executive body of NNC. He was imprisoned in Kohima, Golaghat, Jorhat, Dacca, and Commila. Six years later Khodao left for East Pakistan along with three other leaders to join Phizo in London.

Khodao and his three other Naga leaders reached London in 1962 from Karachi and were detained at the airport. They were finally allowed to stay in London along with Phizo. Khodao lived in London and worked for the Naga cause till Phizo's death in 1990.

After Phizo's passing away Khodao returned from England and settled in his native village. On September 18, 1990, he was elected the President of the NNC at a meeting in Wokha. His immediate task as the President was to try and unite the NNC and NSCN.

In 1994, Khodao joined the NSCN (I-M) and two years later he was elected its Vice President. Since then he continued in that post till his death.

Khodao did not get married and did not own anything. He died in his brother's home in his village at the age of eight-seven.

The interview with Khodao Yanthan was conducted at the NSCN camp at Dimapur on July 31, 1999.

Testimony of Khodao Yanthan

I was born in Lakhuti village which is today in Wokha district of Nagaland. It is situated on top of the hill and we can see the Himalayan mountains from there and the Brahmaputra river. The climatic condition is wonderful.

We were altogether five brothers, but no sister. One brother died at an early age. I am the second oldest. My mother used to say, 'Oh I wish I had one daughter.'

My parents were not political, they were just villagers. I converted them to Christianity.

I know Assamese, I studied the language in Jorhat. I can understand and speak Bengali and Urdu. But among the Naga languages, I only know my own Lotha language. But I can catch the meaning of other Naga languages.

I grew up in the village and was there for the first thirty years of my life. Village life was full of interesting things like the singing of the birds and the screeching of the monkeys. I used to enjoy playing with my friends and going hunting. I recall my life in the village whenever I go to bed.

The morung was still there at that time. I was in the dormitory till I went to school. Yes, we were told so many stories. I remember the story of Ranphan. We were taught how to defend the village.

All of us came originally from Yunnan province because we did not like the system of Chinese imperialism. And Apatanis, Mishmis, Daflas[102] all of us came from there. The people went in search of land and they occupied the land and took various names without understanding the implication; in fact, all the tribes in Arunachal Pradesh are Naga. They all arrived from same place. I won't say same tribe but same race, same family. No demarcated boundary.

The Hindu Indians never reached Nagaland. The Ahoms and we Nagas had a good relationship and there was never any dispute. There were stories of dispute between some Khamti Nagas who charged too much price for elephants but not with us. In that case sometimes Ahoms tried to take the elephants by force.

---

[102] Apatani and Daflas are tribes from present-day Arunachal Pradesh and not recognized as part of the Naga group of tribes.

Tea Gardens Established on Naga Lands

Do you know why the British called it Naga Hills?[103] The reason was because the East India Company started tea gardens in the Naga lands which extended to Shibsagar (now Sivasagar). It was to prevent the hill people from going to the plains like a buffer zone.

Within thirty to forty years more than 100 gardens were cultivated.[104] The Nagas tried to stop the British, and the British then annexed our land. They first annexed Lotha lands in 1875 and then they annexed the other Naga territories.

The tea gardens were made in Lotha lands, Ao lands, Angami lands and Konyak lands. Sometimes the tea garden was half in the Naga areas and half in Assam.

But the Naga Hills District had nothing to do with the Nagas. Nagas had nothing to do with the administration which was entirely in the hands of the Deputy Commissioner and the Assam Governor.

We went to survey the land. I was part of the team, appointed President of the Lotha Tribal Council around 1952, before Nehru visited Kohima; but we found they had removed the stone pillars which the Nagas had put to mark their territory. I went right up from Dimapur to Tinsukia.

School in Jorhat

In 1932, at the age of eight, I was admitted to a village lower primary school and in 1943, I joined Mission High School in Jorhat in Assam.

I was caught with cigarettes in school. I was called by the teacher to have a long, serious discussion but all they asked me was to write

---

[103] Naga Hills District was created by the British in 1866; the boundaries of the district were expanded by annexation of Naga territories: first the Lothas in 1875, then Ao territory in 1889, Sema in 1904 and the Konyak in 1910. In 1912 Naga Hills District was made a part of Assam province.

[104] Maniram Dewan (1806–1858) was the first Indian tea planter, and is credited with establishing the first commercial plantations of the Assamese variety of tea. He learnt of the tea plant from the Singhpos who are known as Kachins in Myanmar

one sentence: 'On my honour I will not smoke as long as I am in Jorhat.'

My friends and I used to share everything. We four shared one cigarette till the very end. We even shared chewing gum and our rations. We even drank from the same bottle.

Second World War

In 1942, my studies were interrupted by the Second World War and I joined the 10,000 Naga Labour Corps as a Quartermaster with the Allied forces to combat the advancing Japanese forces. We were posted at Tamu. During the war I saw the Indian refugees. They were mostly South Indians—Tamils. They were running away from Burma and there was no transport by sea so they walked and some of them even walked from Mandalay through to Imphal, Kohima to Dimapur. My heart was broken seeing them.[xi] We gave them cold water and any remains of food we had.

When I was studying in Class Nine the Japanese troops were going to reach Kohima in 1944. At that time one Mr Lambert[105] a British officer came to our school and asked us, 'Come on, how many of you can speak in English?'

I along with three Lotha police constables helped to show the 14th Division of the British Army the way from Mariani through the tea gardens and reserved forests. It was a fully British battalion.

We stayed at the tea garden. We reached the second range of Lotha area and the Japanese were already there.

I was a scout for the British although I did have some sympathy for the Japanese but we helped the British.

On one occasion the Japanese were cooking food in the Inspection House and the British surrounded them and finished them all. I think only two escaped. After that, the British told the Rengma Naga to

---

[105] ETD Lambert was a police officer and Chief Intelligence officer posted in Jorhat in February 1942. The Japanese occupied Burma in 1942 and the British retreated to Assam; the Japanese entered Kohima from May 16 to June 22, 1944.

chop off the heads of the Japanese and throw the heads on the road. Such wickedness. To chop off the heads from the dead bodies!

Mr Phizo and my story are different. Yes he was with the Japanese but I do not think he was with them whole-heartedly; it was a tactical support.

We arrested a lot of Subhash Chandra's army but we did not kill them. We blindfolded the Indian National Army and made them walk from Kohima to Nakachari. I enjoyed singing their song, 'Door Hato Aye Duniya Waalon, Hindustan Hamaara Hai.'[106] I respect and support Subhash Chandra because he was fighting for the liberation of India, but no I didn't support Japan.

I too have walked from Imphal to Kohima. It took nine days to walk because there were no roads. There was no civilian transport and we even had to walk from Kohima to Dimapur. That took two days. That was when I was in school.

After the war, I finished my matriculation in 1949 from Jorhat Mission School and then studied in Intermediate Arts at Serampore Christian College in West Bengal. Then I went back home and was elected as the President of the Lotha Tribal Council and told to take up a teaching post in the Wokha High School in March 1951; I also became a member of the central executive body of Naga National Council.

Yes I was there for the plebiscite in May 1951, the same year that I returned to Wokha. I went to meet Mr Phizo in Kohima. He told me, 'Khodao, take this petition and go around not only in the Lotha area, but also in Ao and Rengma areas and make sure everyone knows about this petition.'

Before we started the plebiscite, we invited everyone to come to see; we invited the press and outsiders as well.

In the plebiscite form every Naga had two options: either to be independent or to join the Indian Union. I put my thumb impression in blood for independence.

---

[106] Written by Kavi Pradeep for film *Kismet* (1943), this was Bollywood's first patriotic song which took the country by storm.

Meeting Nehru

In 1952 after the plebiscite we went to New Delhi to meet Nehru.[107] We were only three of us: Phizo, Imkongmeren and myself.

But we could not meet him. We waited and waited and waited. The Indian press wrote that we were waiting to meet him and after that at last, Nehru met us. There was no one else there in the room except his private secretary.

We explained everything. He got angry. He said it is inconceivable for Nagas not to join the Indian Union. So we invited him to come to Nagaland and see for himself.

So Nehru came to Kohima[xii] in 1953 and had to return shamefaced. It was then he decided to send the army to crush the Nagas. Even before he left Kohima, he ordered the arrest of all NNC leaders. Nehru's policy was to finish off the Nagas. Nehru told U Nu to treat the Nagas in Burma the way he treated them in Assam. So it was a conspiracy.

India tried psychological warfare to wear down the Nagas. That was their idea but no, Nagas can't be put down by such methods.

Working for the NNC

Yes T Sakhrei was very intelligent and he was an executive member of the NNC like I was. He could speak and write English like no other Naga could. He started to believe there was some other way to resolve the Naga issue other than with arms. He had friendship with Indian intelligence officers so he was shot.

Before the Indian Army was sent, I was working openly and after that I went underground and we went from village to village telling people not to be afraid and stay united.

Although the Home Guards were already formed it was in a Lotha village, Sanis, that we formed the Federal Government of Nagaland and made Thungti Chang a Colonel and Chief of the Naga Army. At

---

[107] We have not found any reference to this meeting in any other account.

that time after the Battle of Kohima it was easy to pick up Japanese rifles. I myself had two rifles. You could pick up different kinds of arms.

Of course I met Gavin Young the journalist. He is still there although he is getting old.

In 1956 Phizo and I started together through Lotha area for East Pakistan but when we reached the Zeliangrong area we found there was heavy presence of the Indian Army so we decided to travel separately. At Haflong one of the policemen was Lotha so he helped me cross to East Pakistan. In Pakistan they took me to Dacca. They asked me why I had entered Pakistan so I explained to them that Indian Armed Forces had occupied Nagaland and we needed protection, so after that Pakistanis and Nagas shook hands. The Pakistanis said they would help us and so would the Chinese.

Mr Phizo was not against the British. Yes he clashed with the Deputy Commissioner CR Pawsey when he was a young man. But later we met him in London and he became our friend. We did not have travel papers and we wanted to escape to any country from where we could tell the world about our condition. We even thought of going to South Africa.

Reverend Michael Scott arranged for Mr Phizo and he went to Switzerland and then to London. Dr Haralu explained everything to Reverend Scott. Phizo reached London in 1961.

I was still waiting in Dacca. Other Naga leaders like General Kaito, Yongkong and others came escorted by the Naga Home Guards.

In London[108]

I did not find it difficult to adjust to living in London. I had already met the British Army and I don't feel strange when I go anywhere whether it is Japan, America or China. Yes, geography books say they are more civilized but I didn't find any difference between us Nagas and other people.

---

[108] Khodao was reluctant to discuss either the specifics of their lives in London or details of Phizo's life there.

We lived like a family with no differences or arguments. I found Phizo really good. We would discuss things and sometimes if we had disagreement Phizo would say: 'Khodao, please don't feel bad.' That's all.

Of course we had to find a job otherwise who would feed us? For five to six months they gave us fast food but finally I took up a job. I had no academic qualifications so I worked as a labourer at a construction site. A labourer in India is different than in Britain. In India he is treated like a servant.

Then for some time I worked as a porter at a hotel, then at a restaurant, then at a shop and a chemist and finally I settled down in the BBC office. That was around 1971.

I used to cycle, sometimes 10 kms, but then I found a place to live near the place of work. I lived alone and sometimes I ate only once a day. I used to eat rice but then I gave it up and had bread with meat. There was no question of eating dog. British people treat dogs like humans—they brush them, teach them human language—even their cats understand human language!

At the BBC office the work was not very hard. I reached office around eight in the morning and had to work till half past four or five in the evening with the weekends off. I was an office attendant with 500 staff under me, mostly ladies. They had to do whatever I told them. They called me 'Yani!' Staff and supervisors were friends so no problem. I was bit of a joker and I made jokes and they liked it. Sometimes they called me Tony and even Charlie. I was much older than them. Of course I used to talk about our people. I retired in 1988. I still get some money. But I am not a rich man.[109]

Phizo did not work. We did not allow him to take up a job. While in Britain we celebrated the Battle of Kohima.[110]

---

[109] Khodao had no house and when he returned, he lived in his brother's home. He did not get married but he said he once 'almost got married to an Assamese girl'.

[110] He did not mention the fact that he received three gallantry awards: the Burma Star Medal, the Southeast Pacific Force Medal and the King George V Medal for active participation during the Second World War.

Phizo went out for exercise twice a day. He did heavy exercise roaming all over London. He used to read a lot—mostly philosophy, history and politics. Mr Phizo used to say India is the most greedy country in the world. He admired the French. He used to say if there was no French Revolution there would be no democracy. He also admired the Russian Revolution, because the USSR was a union of independent socialist countries.

We were well-connected with the embassies in London. Mr Phizo went to America but I did not go. We had correspondence through the Chinese embassy.

Nagas can't really support the Tibetans when we are getting help from China. But the Tibetan people and Naga people are the same. If I put Tibetan girl and Naga girl you cannot tell the difference. But you know we have difference in religion. We don't believe in their Lama and that he is chosen by God. United States is supporting Dalai Lama.

No, no, Phizo had no objection to Muivah going to China. He was willing to take help from any country willing to support the Nagas; whether they were devils or angels it did not matter. We don't find much difference between communist and non-communist.

Britain would not do anything for the Nagas. I have found out that Britain is still India's second country (sic). We rejected the British plan for North East because Britain wants to take the whole world. No, I do not agree with what the IRA is doing. The British people planted Protestants in Ireland so automatically the Irish people will not like it. So they tried to become a single nation, a single country. It is simple.

Mr Phizo called the Nagaland Peace Council[111] the Killer Council. They worked for cheating the villagers. The so-called educated Nagas did this to confuse the people. We call them Naga Indian.

During the ceasefire in 1966 we thought we would go back. All the time we were in Britain, Mr Phizo and I thought we would go home

---

[111] The Naga Peace Council was formed in 1974 and helped to bring about the Shillong Accord.

soon. We thought Mr Nehru or Mr Morarji Desai[112] would listen to the Nagas and understand.

Every people or nation have their own country and are entitled to live in their own country. The Nagas are not Indians and Indians are not Nagas. Why should Indians interfere in Naga affairs and hold the destiny of Naga people as if they have the authority?

Shillong Accord

Twice they came to meet Mr Phizo, both from the Federal Government and the church leaders, to explain that Shillong Accord was something good. Zashie Huire was misguided by the Killer Council, the Nagaland Peace Council and the yes men to Government of India. These people were just thinking of peace, peace, peace.

NH: This statement about the Killer Council was never a signed statement which Phizo gave in public?

Khodao: No, not publicly.

NH: But why?

Khodao: No official written statement, yeah. Only verbally. I also recorded it on tape recorder and he called it 'the Killer Council'. Phizo repeatedly said 'Killer Council'. He said: 'What do you think you have done?' He told Kenneth Kerhuo, the Chairman of the Nagaland Peace Council, and of course the main leader was Nagaland Baptist Church Council.

I personally told Mr Phizo, 'It's better for you to condemn it officially in writing.' But perhaps he thought if he condemned the Accord, he would close the possibility of further discussion with the Government of India. Phizo thought that after the Accord the Indian Prime Minister

---

[112] PM Morarji Desai met Phizo in London in June 1977 when Phizo felt snubbed and humiliated and the Indians said Phizo distorted the tape of the conversations. See also Lok Sabha debates on July 20, 1977.

would have talks with him.[113] In the third clause of the Shillong Accord it was written that the peace process would continue.[114] Phizo thought this because the Indian Prime Minister had been sending emissaries to him, but India was cheating us. There were to be no more talks.

Everyone was confused in Nagaland because every time an agreement was signed there were different interpretations by Indians and Nagas. When the 9-Point Agreement was signed there was different interpretation of clause nine. Nagas thought it meant that after a period of ten years Nagas would have the right to decide their own political status,[115] but Indians had a different interpretation.

Even now Swaraj Kaushal was negotiating and he was given full authority by the Government of India; but recently he was suddenly asked to resign.[116] Something secretly goes on behind the scenes.

On China

Britain had nothing to do with Phizo's stand on China.[117]

The reason why Phizo did not go to China...there were many reasons. If he had gone to China, he would not have been able to go back to Britain.

---

[113] Khodao Yanthan made a public statement condemning the Shillong Accord after the death of Phizo.

[114] Clause (iii) It was agreed that the representatives of the underground organizations should have reasonable time to formulate other issues for discussion for final settlement.

[115] Clause (ix) of the 9-Point Agreement of 1947: The Governor of Assam as the Agent of the Government of the Indian Union will have special responsibility for the period of ten (10) years to ensure the due observance to this agreement, at the end of this period.

[116] Swaraj Kaushal is a senior advocate and had a role in engineering the Mizo Accord in 1987 and was appointed as the special emissary of the Indian Prime Minister for the Indo-Naga peace process. He was withdrawn just a few weeks before our interview. He was replaced by K Padmanabhaiah, the former Home Secretary closer to intelligence agencies.

[117] We asked whether the British prevented him from going to China.

We received many letters from Isak and Muivah from China. We didn't criticize them. We did not ask them not to go to China. Ah! One Naga leader has to do things one way and the other must do in another way from a different side. I have already mentioned that the Indian Prime Minister's emissaries were coming to meet Phizo. But India is a pure, pure bureaucratic government. But when we listen to the emissaries and their sweet, sweet words one is bound to believe them. I have already mentioned the psychological war going on against Nagas. Nagas are a very small nation and not educated; children of headhunters and not united.

I want you to tell the Indians there is only one way to solve the Naga problem. There is no alternative way. 'Leave Nagaland alone.' We can have something like European Union or Commonwealth but of course without any political string attached.

Coming Back

Whenever I said something about feeling sad about not going back home Mr Phizo used to say to me: 'Just wait! Khodao, don't worry we will go home very soon. Yes.'

Even after the Shillong Accord he would say this.

Mrs Gandhi said she could not talk to Phizo because he had a British passport. I also wanted to come back but the British said I should go back on an Indian passport. The Indian High Commissioner was informed by the British.

Phizo had never had an Indian passport so he did not want to travel to Nagaland on an Indian passport. The Indian embassy refused him a visa.

Waiting in a foreign country is the main problem. Naga people ignorantly think that Phizo and Khodao are sitting in armchairs in London and enjoying life like Barra Sahebs. Some foolish Indian agent must have told them that the leaders are neglecting you.

After the death of Mr Phizo his son could not pay the mortgage of the house they had bought. To buy a house on mortgage is a big sin so some of our British friends helped to pay back the loan.

Just two days before he died, I was sitting by his side. Adino did not allow me to go upstairs to meet him. But I said: 'Adino, please try to understand. I must see him. There are very few days left. Indians are going to finish the Naga people.'

Mr Phizo was a perfect Naga leader. I don't believe there will be any Naga leader like Mr Phizo.

NURI (SAW SA): THE DEMOCRAT

Nuri, known as Saw Sa (or Sosa), in Myanmar has been the President of the Eastern Naga Revolutionary Council (ENRC) with SS Khaplang as the Vice President.

Nuri is also the founder of a political party, the Naga National League for Democracy (NNLD) formed in 1998. NNLD supports federalism in a democratic Myanmar while the ENRC is fighting for a sovereign Nagaland.

Nuri speaks Burmese, English, Manipuri, Tangkhul, Nagamese and his own mother tongue, Para.

Nuri was interviewed in August 28, 1998 in Goa.

Testimony of Nuri

I belong to the Para Naga community of Burma. It is a part of the Tisary group along with Pochury, Sangtam and the others. My great grandfather was the founder of the land (sic). They searched for new land to make a new village in the Somrah area. He was one of the four who established the village, called Tinglingaway. Because he founded the village he was respected. I am not sure but they came from Layshi.

I must have been born around 1940's, so I am around fifty-five or fifty-six years old, but I am not sure because I don't have any proper certificate with my date of birth. My parents were illiterate. I became Christian only after I joined the underground. Till then we were Buddhist but followed our own Naga religion.

In those days there were few Christians, our village already had many but Lahe did not have. The conversions were done by our own people, not white missionaries. There was discussion about the new religion but the newly converted were not thrown out of their villages like in India side.

If we had been converted during British time we would not be so backward. Going to heaven or hell is another matter but at least people would have had education quickly. So many villages do not even have civic sense. In our side the conversions were done by our own people.

My parents did not mind my becoming a Christian but I followed our religious practices so that after I die, I could be with my father. That is our belief and I wanted to be with him after I die since I could not be with him while he was alive. My father resisted conversion because he liked his drink.

Childhood

Up to the time I was six or seven years old I was with my parents but they did not send me to school. After that I stayed with my older cousin who taught me the alphabet in Burmese and A-B-C in English. He taught me whenever he had spare time. He was an SI in the police.

Then after some time a small Lower Primary (LP) School was built with bamboo and thatch in a village which was about a mile from mine. I was sent to that school to study there. But it was not like going to school like today. There were no regular classes. The classes were just three or four months a year; sometimes the master was absent and sometimes we the students did not attend. So in this way I finished LP school.

I cannot remember now the exact year, but the Deputy Commissioner of the Naga Hills who was a British man came to our village and stayed in our house. I have forgotten his full name but his name was Mr Carrot. Mr Carrot was touring Khamti side covering the entire Naga area.[118]

Even though Mr Carrot was a European man, he ate anything we ate and lived like we lived. He lay down on our bed and he drank rice beer like we Nagas; he did not want a special cup for himself. Mr Carrot happened to meet me in my house. Mr Carrot asked my father, 'Is this your son?'

---

[118] Hkamti District or Khamti District (sometimes Naga Hills District) is a district in northern Sagaing Division of Burma (Myanmar). It was a part of the Excluded Areas in British times and brought under British administration only in 1940.

When my father said yes, I was his son then Mr Carrot asked my father whether he would give his son to him so he could study. My father replied, 'No I can't.' When Mr Carrot asked him why, my father replied: 'Ah! This is the only son I have, if he happens to die who will look after all my property?' Then the DC said: 'No, no, I have medicines with me. If he is here, he may die. But with me he won't die. You must send him for studies.'

Father was not willing but DC was the king; Mr Carrot's word was final. My father had to send me with the English man. My father and two sisters came with me up to Thamanthi. The trip usually takes two days but we were carrying a heavy load so we had to walk for three days. We had to carry everything: rations, blankets, clothes and everything else we needed on the way. My father and sisters dropped me to Thamanthi which is on the bank of the Chindwin river.

From there I went by streamer to Khamti town, the district headquarters. I was there for one and half years, studying and living in the DC's house. Then the DC was promoted as Commissioner so he had to go to Sagaing. Mr Carrot told me he was going to Sagaing and since my father had been so reluctant to send me to Khamti he would never allow him to take me to Sagaing which was much further away; he said Father would be very angry with him if he took me along.

My father was always against my wish to study. I wanted to go to Thamanthi for study but he stopped me. Then my cousin came back on leave. He was working in the Burmese BSF (they called it UMB). My cousin asked me why I had stopped studying? I said 'Areah, Papa did not allow me to go.'

Then my cousin said: 'I'll take you quietly.' I said I will surely go if he helped me.

So, that night I packed a small bag with one or two clothes and was going out of the house when my father returned from his friend's house and found me. He asked me where I was going. I said I am going to Thamanthi to study. He told me I was not allowed to go and took away my bag.

Then my cousin said he would take me to his house which was in a village about a mile from our village. We went at night carrying torch made from pine. Then we slept at my cousin's village. Next day early in the morning my sister came to call me back. She said father is calling you to return immediately. My cousin brother told her we would come just after finishing our meal; at that time we were eating. My sister went away; as she went she said: 'Okay you must come quickly'.

The moment my sister went, we—my cousin brother and I—started running towards Thamanthi. It was in the first week of July and it had rained heavily. We ran all the 23 miles. My mother and sister came after us and they saw our footprints. But they saw that the rainwater collected in our footprints was clear which meant we had gone far and they would not be able to catch up with us. My mother went weeping back and cursing my cousin brother.

I studied in Thamanthi for a year. Then the next year my cousin became a Member of Parliament. It was the time U Nu was Prime Minister. So I and some other students were invited by the Burmese government to study in Rangoon. That information was brought by my cousin brother to me. So I went back to my village to ask my father for permission to study in Rangoon. But Papa did not consent. I wondered what I should do? Areah! Papa is such a man, I cannot convince him. I was helpless so I decided to do what I like and the way I like. I decided to go along with some other friends who were going to Rangoon. Someone told my father that I was going to Rangoon.

The day we left for Rangoon my father and mother came after me. They kept calling out my name: 'Ari, Ari!' (Diminutive of Nuri) My father called out and threatened to shoot me if I did not stop. He was carrying the gun gifted to him by the Deputy Commissioner. I ran for a mile and came to the plain just below my village and from there the footpath runs straight and I looked back and saw my father pointing his gun at me and he was shouting for me to stop. I was very small and I thought if he fired at me I would die, and my friends passed me and my father shouted to them that they should not expect me to go with them. He told them they could do what they liked but he would not allow his son to go with them. They all quickly ran past me.

Then I went back with my father, the whole way weeping loudly. Father told me: 'Ari, for whom are you crying? Have you no shame? Your father and mother are alive; no one has died, why are you crying like this?'

I stayed at home and cried the whole day. My Mummy tried everything to comfort me. She offered me eggs and meat. They were my favourites. Eggs was a big treat at that time. I said I did not want anything. That year I could not study.

Next year in May or June the time for admissions came again. I decided I would go to Rangoon come what may. I would do or die. I had made up my mind. My father also became restless, and he thought the only way to stop my son from going would be to use black magic. At that time, we Nagas depended on black magic even when we went hunting. My father went to consult the man whose predictions were normally correct. He went with a bottle of wine. After a discussion with the man, they decided to let me go.

My father sent me to Homalin[119] and there we were waiting for a steamer to take us to Monywa. When I was in the town I heard that one Naga had drowned because he did not know how to swim. I came running back, then I came to know it's my first cousin who had drowned. All the Nagas serving in the UMB including my cousin brother started diving and searching and within ten minutes they found the body.

I went to Rangoon along with seventy to eighty other Naga students.

We went up to Monywa by steamer and then we went by vehicle to Mandalay and from there by train to Rangoon which is far south. At that time many parents did not want to send their children to study and so students had to be forced to study. It was 1953 when I reached Rangoon. It was quite comfortable to stay there.

---

[119] Homalin is in Khamti district in Sagaing region on the banks of the Chindwin river.

From Monywa to Mandalay the area was under the Red Flag. So we were very scared. We stayed in a Buddhist monastery. I heard people saying at the monastery that look at these small, small boys. They are Nagas and their parents produce so many children and send them so far away. What kind of parents are these? I could speak Burmese fluently so I could understand what they were saying. I had learnt the language while staying in Khamti.

But the other Naga boys did not know Burmese and they spoke different languages since they had been picked up from the village. It took them a year to pick up Burmese and after that it was easier for them.

Before I went to Rangoon, I knew we were Nagas. Even before I was born, we were known as Nagas. I had not heard of NNC but I had heard the name of Phizo. One day I saw a man in our home in the village and I found he had a different face so I asked my father why the man's face was funny and he told me to shut up and not embarrass him in front of his guests. I was very naughty. But I could not speak to Phizo because I only spoke Para language, my mother tongue. My father spoke Manipuri and Burmese.

Phizo and the NNC

When I returned from Rangoon, my father told me that Phizo had also asked him for his son. Phizo wanted to take me with him. Phizo had contacted my father because he was Area Chairman appointed by the government.

I asked my father what was the difference between Phizo and the other government officials who came to our house and he said Phizo's words are like the words of parents. Phizo told us how to maintain the forests nicely because the bamboo will become money; this stone will become money. Everything will become money so maintain everything properly and don't damage the forest. He told them to stop jhumming. My father was illiterate and not political at the time.

In my village they still do jhum and the cycle used to be twenty to twenty-five years but it is coming down. I keep telling them to do terrace cultivation. The jhum destroys the forest.

My father told me when Phizo came he would discuss these things unlike other people who came to ask for things, like give me coolie etc. It was then Phizo asked my father to give me to him but my father said, 'No, he is my only son,' and Phizo being a Naga knows when a Naga says no it means no.

Phizo came with Kughato. I did not know who he was. But I enjoyed going around with him. I saw that he was looking at everything carefully. Uncle Phizo's man came to Rangoon as Ambassador of the NNC and I met him there.

By the time I was in Class Seven or Eight, the Naga National Council people started coming to our village regularly and I would meet them when I went home. Apart from Kughato, his brother Kaito and Isak Swu also came. And they had some understanding with the Burmese authorities so they made a big camp in the thick jungle. I met the NNC leaders when they came to our village to buy rations and I helped them.

Once my friend and I were invited to go to their camp by General Kaito and at that time I was in Class Eight or Nine and Kaito gave us a lecture in English. At that time I could understand English but not speak English. I learnt to speak English only when I went to India. I had to make the sentence in my mind before I could speak!

Kaito gave us a lecture on unity and disunity. He took an Indian ten rupee note. He said if he gives us the note, we would take it because it has value; then he tore the ten rupee note to pieces and he said now nobody would take the note because it had no value. So in the same way Nagas must stand united and not disunited. He asked us to help them in every way possible. Not with arms but with food. He said they would pay for the food but we could help them access rations.

General Kaito told us that if the Indian government did not understand Naga peoples' rights then we would have to go to China. The Chinese may be Communist but they are like our brothers and they will help us. Kaito told us to study and they would fight for our rights and we would win. He was a very dynamic speaker.

They, the NNC, bought a pig from our village. The villagers carried it into the jungles but then at one point they took the pig because they would go by the security path to the camp which the villagers did not know. General Kaito carried the pig himself and my friend and I said, 'Please allow us to help you,' and he said, 'No, you two are very young; you cannot bear this kind of hardship.' General Maken was with him. At that time Kaito was not yet a General. General Maken, who was an Ao, offered to carry the pig but Kaito did not allow him and he carried it to the end of the path and then they left it at the bottom of the mountain and they sent some boys to carry it up to the camp.

I stayed in the camp for a few days and Kaito gave me money; it was one hundred rupees in Indian money.

Even before I met General Kaito I met Isak Swu. He was the first leader of the Naga freedom movement I met. He was also very young at the time. He was very youthful and always smiling and he was the one who took me to Kughato.

So whenever we came back from Rangoon I contacted the Naga leaders and started working for them doing the job of a postman. I would post their letters to Uncle Phizo in Rangoon and bring back his letters from Rangoon (written from London). Many of the leaders came to Rangoon, like Isak and General Mowu.

Even before I went to Rangoon the NNC was collecting all the arms left behind by the Japanese. Our village also collected the arms left by the Japanese and the British and some we donated to the NNC and some they bought from us.

Naga Student in Rangoon

The scholarship the Burmese government gave was sixty-two kyats,[120] today it will be very funny but those days it was sufficient. Out of sixty-

---

[120] Approximately three rupees and ten paise at today's exchange rate.

two kyats, ten we used to get in hand, the rest deducted for Mess fee, medical and sports—all things. All together they deducted fifty-two kyat. And then ten kyats, that also we could buy so many things. Those days hair oil, toothpaste, Colgate small-size we can use one month.

It was U Nu's government. He is no more and I think U Nu may not have been a very smart man, but he had a good amount of love for all his citizens; not only the Burmese[121] but also the tribals. He loved everyone equally. He used to invite us, all the tribal students for lunch also. He invited the Chin, the Kachin, the Shan and Karen—but the biggest numbers were the Nagas. We were a hundred students while the rest were twenty to thirty. There was a special scheme for the poor and good students to have an opportunity to study in Rangoon.

We had a Naga Students' Union in Rangoon but we did not talk much politics. Sometimes we talked about Naga freedom movement on the Indian side. But that was two or three students together, there was no meeting. We did not talk about high political ideology. Time to time something came out in the papers, like it came out that General Mowu and General Kaito were in London. It said, 'Top Naga leaders in London.'

Yes, we made a seal for the Naga Students' Union. We must have seen the same by Shan, Karen and Chin Students' Unions so we had a seal and a logo, but there was no demand for a Naga State like Shan State, Karen State.

There was a lot of discussion among the Karen, Kachin and Chin when U Nu declared Burma a Buddhist state. I remember the debate and how we laughed at the Chin pronunciation of Burmese words! Even though U Nu declared Burma a Buddhist state, we still had other religions.

There was no demand for autonomy by the Naga students. But we sent an application with some grievance to the Education Minister and he must have thought that we were planning to make such a demand, so he called us and told us to study and not worry about

---

[121] By 'Burmese' he means the majority Burman community.

those things. But at that time, we did not ask for a separate state and we thought it was too early.

The first time I went for a picnic was in Rangoon. The Naga Students' Union organized a picnic to Inle lake and we invited our Karen, Kachin and Chin friends. We felt closest to the Karen people. Whenever I went to their homes in Rangoon, they were very simple and not formal, like the Nagas. Even though the Karens were more educated and civilized than us, they were very humble. They had no jealousy and their help was loving, not the way the Burmese behaved. The Burmese behaviour towards people depended on whether the person was rich or poor. Karens are more democratic.

I stayed in Rangoon for ten years from 1953 to 1962. We all spoke Burmese.

But it seemed a short time because I was so happy and so comfortable. My father said, 'Don't play football because you may break your leg and do not swim in case you drown,' but those are my favourite sports! So my father keeps telling me not to do things and I keep doing them. I played football, basketball, volleyball and did running and jumping and swimming. In Thamanthi we did not have footballs so we played with a fruit. It was round fruit and hard so we beat it with a stick to make it soft before playing, but in Rangoon we had real footballs! Only older children had footballs.

We had two Naga football teams, also basketball and volleyball teams. In football we would pool in money and buy a ball. There were different sizes of balls. We usually buy size three.

There were more Naga students in Rangoon because the others, like the Kachins, had schools in their own areas and also because Nagas were more backward. We were in one of the best schools in Rangoon. It was called Central State High School. Rangoon being the capital, many foreign dignitaries used to come and we would be lined up on the road to welcome them. I remember one Marshal Tito had come and we had to shout, 'Long Live Marshal Tito!'

Many engineers, doctors, police officers were from our school so that was very useful. Every year the old students got together and these people were a lot of help. And every year we had a special dinner. Then we had dancers come and we invited jokers and for the whole night we sat and enjoyed their performances. And then we would sleep the whole day. Then there was the water festival when the Burmese would invite everyone and offer them tea, cold drinks or food. You offer from four directions—it is called 'Saduditas'. I think it is a Sanskrit word. There was no caste system but there was a feeling that Burmese people give and tribal people receive. And the power was totally in the hands of the Burmese people.

In the years I was in Rangoon we walked from one place to another so we knew the city well, and if we took a taxi we would insist on going by the shortest routes and that is why taxi drivers did not like taking us.

In Class Three, one day the Headmaster came and found us Naga students sitting with a candle stick and reading and he said, 'Go back to sleep, all of you will pass.' So we all passed. I think that was a way of encouraging us. The Headmaster was a pure Burmese and a Christian. I cannot spell his name.

One day I remember one Naga student was running after a Burmese student with a dao and the Burmese was running like anything. Then the Headmaster stopped the Naga student and told him that dao was not allowed in the school. The Headmaster told the Naga student if there was any problem he could tell him. Then he told the Burmese student that Naga people are very different people, they are very straight, what they like they like and what they don't they don't. The Headmaster told the Burmese student to leave the Nagas alone.

We used to hear debates about federalism. General Ne Win was already powerful by 1957-58 and he did not bother much about the tribal people. Ne Win[122] said that this federalism will break the

---

[122] General Ne Win (1911-2002) was a Burmese politician and military commander who served as Prime Minister of Burma from 1958 to 1960 and 1962 to 1974; he was also President of Burma from 1962 to 1981. Ne Win was Burma's dictator during the Socialist Burma period from 1962 to 1988.

country into pieces and the majority of the Burmese started thinking if that happened it would be unbearable for them.

Eastern Naga Revolutionary Council

In early 1960s some leaders formed the Eastern Naga Revolutionary Council but I was not involved. It was not formed with students but by villagers who were not educated.

The President was Jopoh from Somrah area and Khaplang was the Vice President and I do not remember who the General Secretary was. Jopoh was a very nice man, very simple. I do not know much about his early involvement except that he had joined U Nu's party. He thought he could help Nagas by joining his party. But then the Anti-Fascist People's League[123] split. At that time Ba Swe's party arrested U Nu's supporters so my friend Jopoh was also arrested.

It was during that time Khaplang met Jopoh and they decided to form a party or organization for the Nagas. At that time very few Nagas took part in any politics. We Nagas were behind by a century.

Jopoh was from Somrah area. I think he did his education from Shillong. He spoke Tangkhul and Manipuri fluently and also Hindi and English. He was a very nice man. He was working with the NNC and he was arrested in Imphal and put in jail.

In those days an underground person put in jail means he was finished. No one would come and meet him or do anything for him. The only option he had was to escape. So, Jopoh jumped down from the wall and he hurt his back. Even later he suffered from back pain.

Jopoh was a very sincere and honest man. There was no one else like him from Somrah. The people in Somrah have good qualities but they

---

[123] The Anti-Fascist People's Freedom League, or 'hpa hsa pa la' by its Burmese acronym, was founded in 1945 and was the main political alliance in Burma from 1945 until 1958. The founder was General Aung San and the Chairman of the party was U Nu. In July 1958 it formally split, with one group led by Prime Minister U Nu, which he named the Clean AFPFL, the other led by Kyaw Nyein and Ba Swe which was known as the Stable AFPFL.

are too much business-minded and even political activity they turn it into a business. This is the drawback and so it is difficult to trust them. But Jopoh was an exception.

I met the President Jopoh when I went underground, not during my student days. When I was at Rangoon Jopoh was in Shillong, I think.

Jopoh was a man much shorter than me. He may be five feet two or three inches but he was very patient. People say short people are short-tempered but that is not true. I used to say we have to speed things up but he would say to me, 'You are so tall but so impatient!' But I said if you are slow people will take advantage of you. But he used to trust me. Now his children are coming up. They are doing well in studies except for his daughter who is abnormal. They are in a Pochury village. He passed away in 1994.

Khaplang is a little older than me. He studied in a school near his village. He is from Hemi tribe. Once when he came back for holidays there was a dispute between the Nagas and Kachins over land. In those days the Kachins were also very backward and they started attacking the Nagas. So Khaplang got the idea of protecting his people. I think that is how he got involved in politics. Even now Nagas have a land dispute with the Kachins.

Khaplang studied in a village in Mizoram—it may be Darlawn but I do not know the spelling. He could speak Mizo language.

Khaplang has two sons. They have been smoking opium. The eldest son was educated by Mr Muivah's eldest brother, Shangreihan, in Imphal. I do not know whether he has finished graduation or post-graduation. He spoke Manipuri and Tangkhul fluently.

Khaplang visited the NNC camps, both the one near my village and the one near Pangsha, but I did not meet him in the camps. I met Khaplang for the first time in Khamti but it was a casual meeting and I was not underground. Just hello-hello. We talked normally, nothing special, but of course we talked about how to develop our people who are so backward and that we need to educate our people.

General Ne Win and the Burmese Road to Socialism

I passed my school in Second Division. Only those who passed in First Division were allowed to go to university. In any case I had become involved in politics. My father also was politicized by the Naga leaders and he was introduced to the leaders.

I was working for the Naga movement by then. I used to buy army officers' uniforms, stationary or do other marketing in Rangoon and I would drop it to Thamanthi and rush back to Rangoon.

After Ne Win took over power, the programmes for tribal students were all cancelled. The students studying in Rangoon were sent to Homalin. Even training programmes were cancelled. They did not explain why but I think it was to stop the tribal students from organizing politically. Politicians were organizing the students and that could be a threat to Ne Win.

I used to tell the Burmese that they are eating all the meat and throwing bones to the tribals. I told them we had no roads, nothing and they should be ashamed of this. It is a shame on them. They would say that they were also suffering under military rule and when they get democracy they would definitely develop the tribal areas.

After I finished school, I came back to my village. I thought of doing something political because I had seen the condition of my people. At least in our village we had clothes although we had only cotton, no woollens, but Lahe side people had no clothes at all. All those Nagas remained naked. I did not want to see them in that condition. I was a little bit educated and I could feed myself and my family, but if I joined politics then I could feed everyone.

General Ne Win had already imposed military rule so I did not want to join his party and we used to talk about what we could do for our people. They, the Naga leaders, used to say that if you stay outside the party and you talk you will be arrested. If you join the party you will have some democratic space.

So for a few years I stayed like that without doing anything. I did not want to get a job. During that time, I used to meet friends in the

Naga underground and I would advise them to do this or not to do that. But they were so careless they wrote down everything, even the small, small things I gave them. And when there was an ambush of their camp by the Burmese Army they scattered and left behind those notes. Burmese Army suspected me but I talked my way out from being arrested. The Burmese Army said, 'You bloody fellow, you talk so well.'

Then one day one group of officers came for a discussion in two helicopters. We all lined up to greet them. I was also there. They asked me what I was doing and I said, 'Nothing, but I like the old way of life so I stay in the village.' But they said I must do something to help my people and they appointed me in charge of the co-operative. I said I am not interested but they appointed me. After some time they said all those in service must apply for membership of Ne Win's Socialist Party.[124] Then they said I must go for training. There are three categories of training: farmer cadre training, worker cadre training and political training in Burmese Way to Socialism. I went to Rangoon for six months training. The training was not bad because we got a lot of knowledge. We were taught world history, Asian history, covering India, China and Japan. We had seven or eight hours of lectures. I almost went mad with so many lectures. It was too much to digest. The lectures were all given by Burmese.

There was no question of raising any questions about Naga nationalism!

When I went back to the village I resigned from the co-operative and joined the party, Burmese Way to Socialism, and I was posted to Homalin. The co-operative was good and it sold things at fixed prices but there was corruption so it did not work.

In Homalin I started asking for development of the Naga areas, especially education and communication, also production. I told the senior Army officers what was the point of keeping the Nagas like wild people without any facilities? How can they catch up with others? See, I always fight and quarrel so I became target of the army officers.

[124] The Burma Socialist Programme Party

I had a fight in a party meeting with a Lieutenant Colonel because I wanted to go to Rangoon to represent Nagas and I was not chosen and so no Nagas were sent for the meeting in Rangoon where Ne Win was also to come. I was chosen to be member of the workers' central committee but I did not take oath, I just was silent. And in my mind I said I won't take your oath and I won't work for your party. So I returned from Homalin to my village and joined the underground.

Life in the Underground

It was in 1968 or 1969 that I joined and I must have been twenty-seven or twenty-eight years old. I joined the Eastern Naga Revolutionary Council. In 1964 I got married to a girl in my village. Her name was Dhowla. She came with me to the underground. Since I was the sole person to leave the Burma Socialist Party it was no longer possible to live overground without being arrested.

When General Secretary returned from China I invited him to lunch in the jungle and we killed a dog. That was in 1968. We could not offer him much in comfort but we could keep him secure. In that part it was difficult to hide him and I gave him a guide but he was not happy because the man was very short. I assured the General Secretary that the man was a very good hunter and expert in finding his way in the jungles. It was my responsibility to take Mr Muivah back to Nagaland because his life was in danger; this is the time after the formation of the Revolutionary Government.

We were only about fifteen people staying in the jungle together. Khaplang's men were staying in the upper side and some people were staying in the lower side so we were in the middle. We got rice from the villages. They gave us rations. And we could hunt for animals for our curry and there were leaves to be eaten so our curry was always good. Apart from my wife, my secretary also had his wife and the rest were young men who were not married.

During that time I could not meet Khaplang or Jopoh because the situation was very tense since the China-trained Nagas were coming back. The border was sealed. I think Burma and India had some understanding so the Burmese Army had made it very difficult for us to move about.

Layshi Army Post attacked

Even before I had joined the underground, I attended a meeting of the Burmese underground Nagas in a village near Layshi where I opposed military actions for some time because I thought we were politically inexperienced. I said we should educate our people and we could collect twenty rupees from every house and give it to the full time Naga national workers to survive. I warned them if they did any armed operation it would be suicide because we would be attacked from both sides—Indian and Burmese Army.

At that meeting we passed a resolution that we will not take any military action and we will do work of political mobilization through political education. And we will get contributions from our supporters from the overground.

Despite the decision, one of my friends made plans with the Nagas working in the Burmese Army to attack the Layshi post and they captured all the arms and ammunition. The attack was done by Simon who was a Brigadier, now he lives in Imphal under the name of Somi. Hopeless fellow—he did not follow the resolution. Just after the attack I ran to General Kaito and told him about the attack on Layshi post and he said, 'Yes, I know.' He asked who was behind the attack and I said Simon and he asked me whether I was involved in the decision and I said no. He asked me about the resolution at the meeting where we had resolved not to undertake military operations. I said the ones involved in the Layshi attack knew of the resolution. I spent one night with Kaito at the camp and returned to the village. After a few days Kaito arrested Simon and Jopoh.

The Burmese Government started putting pressure on the NNC to hand over the two and General Kaito was so angry that he wanted to kill those two but Isak and others intervened. They said killing them would affect the future and they have spoiled the whole situation and now we cannot stay here peacefully.

Then the NNC took the arms and ammunition captured from the Layshi post and returned it to the Burmese Government. The arms were returned by General Mowu who put the arms in Naga baskets, including a machine gun, an LMG, a pistol and some other arms. On his way to return the arms, he spent one night in our village. The arms were put in several baskets carried by the villagers, accompanied by two or three boys of the Naga Army. They handed over the arms to the Burmese and came back. I remember General Mowu! He liked his drink! He spent one night in my house and went back to the camp.

Then the Indian Army attacked the camp. They may have been brought by some informers. So that time Simon and Jopoh were released. Then this Simon went along with Isak to China and he is an arrogant type and he had a quarrel with the Kachins. I do not know exactly what happened but Kachins stopped the Burmese Nagas from going to China.

In 1968 General Kaito was killed. That was one factor that brought disunity among the Nagas. Uncle Phizo might have given orders for his assassination.

Some Burmese Nagas did go to China but not from the Eastern Naga Revolutionary Council (ENRC). The ENRC cadres were given arms training by the Kachins. I do not know whether they were given arms. KIA used to get arms from Thailand and they made money from jade stone business. They did not get Chinese arms but they had American arms.

Some Burmese Nagas went to Pakistan for training with the group of 999 but they did not go from the ENRC. General Kaito said General Ayub was in Nagaland and that is how the Nagas had contact with Pakistan. Ayub Khan liked the Nagas so he helped them.

Arrested by Indian Army

I was working in the political wing of the ENRC and I used to go to Indian side to consult with the NNC leaders. Towards the end of 1969

I went to the India side. I left my wife in the jungles where she was looked after by the villagers.

I was going to India with the Chinese returned NNC. One of them, by the name of Kochu, was wounded. He was in General Mowu's group so we were bringing him back and we were arrested when we went through the Pochury area. We were arrested by the Revolutionary Government[125] and they took away all our arms and ammunition and then handed us over to the Indian Army.

In the Indian Army camp we were given a parachute to cover ourselves since there were no blankets. I told everyone to eat all the documents. So the whole group was lying under the parachute and chewing the documents which included our accounts. The boys started teasing each other, 'Ash! You are eating too much, share some with me.' The next day we were taken to Melory and finally to Zakhama, near Kohima. I was kept in the army camp for six months so I learnt a little bit of Hindi!

They tried to find out whether we were from Burma but we did not tell them. I had given training to my boys while we were in the lock-up. One Sardarji spoke to us in Burmese and I pretended not to know what he was speaking. He was a tricky officer and I think from intelligence. He would say 'come' in Burmese and we would stand as if we did not understand; he would say 'stand' and we would move as if we did not understand. We were afraid of being handed over to the Burmese Army. We had to remember our names and village names in India.

The Indian Army did not treat us badly because we were handed over and after six months, they released us to the civil authorities. But when we were going in the army truck, we were handcuffed two together so it was like chicken tied up by the wings. And one person stood up to vomit but he vomited in another fellow's mouth! Instead of feeling pity we laughed.

---

[125] Kughato Sukhai and others formed the Revolutionary Government of Nagaland in 1966 and it continued till 1973.

So we were in jail and we did not know anyone in the Indian overground. We could not pass messages because the jail and police authorities were backward politically and would not help us. They were just boozing and getting fat. One sweeper helped us. I wrote to Uncle Vihoto, he was the Ambassador of Federal Government. He had been in jail and bailed out and after that he was in Kohima. Uncle Vihoto and Hokishe Sema[126] were classmates. Uncle Vihoto asked Hokishe to release ten of us. Hokishe asked him whether they were in the underground but Uncle Vihoto said that was none of his business, the Burmese Nagas were not killing other Nagas.

We were released by the court in Kohima. But when we came out, we did not know where to go. I told my friends we should go two by two and not look lost.

Then I remembered there was an Angami in jail with us called Thomas and he told us his name was Peselie and if we needed help, we should go to him. He said we should ask for Papa Peselie and we found him. At the time there was a revival crusade going on in Kohima so he introduced us to the Mess Maintaining Committee and told them to give us food, so we got food for four days. He told us to attend the crusade like other people and in the meanwhile he will make arrangements for us.

Finally we took a truck from Kohima to Dimapur which cost us two or three rupees each, and then we went to meet Uncle Suisa.[127] He had stomach cancer. He said he did not have money but he would help us. He sent someone to buy basic things for us like plates and a saw and tools. Then a Mao Naga gentleman got us work of jungle cutting so we could earn our living. So after six to seven months we managed to earn enough and we managed to reach the border through Zunheboto.

When we returned, we found that our President Jopoh and Simon had surrendered to the Indian Army. I was chosen as President of

---

[126] Hokishe Sema was the Chief Minister of Nagaland State at that time.

[127] Rungsung Suisa passed away in 1971, so Nuri must have met him in his last days.

the Eastern Naga Revolutionary Council, Khaplang remained Vice President, and the General Secretary was one Muang Aye, he was my cousin sister's husband.

I told our people that they should learn to pay the organization house tax. I told them that they should not grumble because it was a way of being involved in the freedom struggle. From our side the underground must not make our people suffer unnecessarily. But sometimes we cannot help it: when you save one freedom fighter in your house then you may be beaten or you may be put in jail. Such things will happen. This is called sacrifice.

We also told the people to settle the disputes within themselves and not spend money going to court. But we in the ERNC did not have a judicial wing like in the NNC; only a political wing and an army. Ours is much smaller organization than the NNC.

My Wife Falls Sick

Soon after I became President of the ENRC, my wife fell sick. This was before the Shillong Accord. I did not realize then, but for the next twenty years I would be looking after her.

I was new to Nagaland and I had no job. And my wife had TB and she needed a good diet. I had to approach officers and well-to-do people to help me and for ten years with their help I survived. And after I got to know engineers, I started to get small contract jobs.

Life in the underground, mostly hiding in the jungles, was very tough but life in cities and towns without money is much worse. In the town I could see plenty of food but I could not afford to buy and eat it; I could see clothes in the shops but could not afford to buy them, and the most difficult thing of all was that I had to behave like a normal person who had enough food to eat. I have struggled in the underground, I have been in jail, but the struggle I did for my wife was the most difficult.

I took her to Tuensang and the doctor said she needed to be operated on. They said there is something wrong with her intestines, but actually she had TB in the womb. It was the TB which affected her intestines. But the doctor in Tuensang did not diagnose her illness correctly.

They did the operation and she was on drip and then she was allowed to have some liquid and her stomach started swelling. One day she vomited violently and the stitches came apart. And her stool came out. Her stool was leaking and she was lying like that for two months. The doctors were inexperienced although they were supposed to be specialists. They just tried to repair it but could not so they just stitched her back again.

Then the doctors told me to take her to Dibrugarh because they could not do anything. I took my wife to Dibrugarh and she was there and for a whole year from 1973 to 1974 I went all over Nagaland from Tuensang to Mokokchung to Wokha and Zunheboto doing business to earn for my wife's treatment. Sometimes I bought chillies in Imphal and sold them in Nagaland. I also bought bullets for hunting from Imphal and the packet was very heavy. I collected seventeen licenses for the guns so I could buy the bullets and sold them; sometimes I bought a two-in-one radio from Moreh and sold it in Nagaland. I went to Moreh in part to do business but also to get news of what is happening in Burma.

In Dibrugarh they operated on my wife three times unsuccessfully, so I thought of taking her to Vellore but before going there I needed money. To make money I went to Miao in Arunachal Pradesh to get agar (plant highly valued for medicinal qualities) but I was arrested and put in the lock-up for ten months. I think it was in 1979. I was caught with Burmese money so they thought I had contact with the underground but I told them I am doing Agar business to make money for the treatment of my sick wife. They must have done a thorough investigation because my wife told me some people came to see her in Dibrugarh and told her they were friends of her husband's.

So when I was released from the lock-up I had no money. This agar business is good because I could sell 2 or 3 kilos for fifty to sixty thousand rupees in Imphal or Dimapur. I struggled for three years to get almost thirty thousand rupees and some politicians helped me with five thousand rupees, one gave two thousand rupees, another three thousand rupees. Also I did small, small contract works and with that money I took my wife to Vellore in 1983. There she was better but she still had to take medicines for TB.

In Vellore I met a Naga IAS officer. He had come there for his mother's treatment. We became friends. He used to drink. I told him we should not drink like that because the mission hospital does not like it and it spoils the reputation of Nagas. He did not like me scolding him, since he felt he was an officer. He later became a DC in Phek and he got me arrested. But I was released soon after my arrest.

Even after NSCN was formed in 1980 I did not get in touch with Isak Swu and Thuingaleng Muivah, because if I got arrested who would look after my wife?

I took my wife back from Vellore to Dibrugarh and she had to remain there for two or three years. After that she became completely alright but after undergoing six operations and being on such heavy medication she could not go back to normal life. In 1992 she had a kidney failure and so I knew she could not go underground again. And if I joined the movement there would be no one to take care of her. Then I thought I can help the movement even while staying overground. I went to Moreh from time to time and did log business.

My wife had kidney failure and I had to run around for her dialysis which is very expensive. In the beginning she needed it just once and it cost three thousand to four thousand rupees, then she needed it once a week, and then twice a week—it was horrible! She suffered throughout 1993 and finally in January 1994 she passed away.

Sometimes people would greet me and say, 'How is your wife? Areah, you are so faithful to your wife.' It was not said in a good way to encourage me but in a bad way. I did not like it.

Creation of Nagaland State and SC Jamir

Nagas of the so-called State of Nagaland and the Nagas living outside the state are getting to be little bit different. The ones inside the state are getting opportunities so they want to fight to keep their privileges. I challenged my Nagaland friends and told them they got the state because of our sacrifices. There are so many things happening that I do not like. The Indian government is sending so many of its intelligence agencies like SIB and SSB but that is the job of the Indian Government and our job is to resist it.

I heard about the Shillong Accord. I knew Ramyo very well, I knew Phizo and Uncle Yalley (Phizo's brother) but I did not contact them. If they are making an agreement within the Constitution of India then we have no part in it. We condemned it, but not publicly.

Before the crisis of 1988 my friend who was a Cabinet Minister in Congress government, a Sangtam, told me Jamir[128] started talking about a split in the NSCN. The Sangtam fellow, although he was in Congress, he was patriotic and he told Jamir, 'Saheb, please don't say that, even if they become disunited we should make them united.'

Jamir answered that let them fight and we can do development. There is no harm, let them fight. The next time Jamir formed a Cabinet in 1989 my friend was out.

There is a saying: 'Seeing is better than hearing, and touching is better than seeing.' So if we look at Jamir's life he did not make a drop of sacrifice. He was the son of a Dubashi so he did not know much hardship. He could study and come to civilized modern age earlier. He became MLA, MP and Chief Minister but he did not struggle. I do not think he is doing good for the Nagas.

So Nagas started saying that Jamir is selling Naga's flesh and blood and India gave him awards. He is the most trusted Naga politician for the Central government. He is playing tribalism and he has smashed the Naga national movement.

---

[128] SC Jamir (born 1931) was Chief Minister of Nagaland from November 1982 to October 1986; Hokishe Sema was Chief Minister from October 1986 to August 1988. President's Rule was imposed from August 1988 to January 1989. Jamir opposed the NSCN (I-M) who accused him of causing divisions among the Nagas and allegedly made several attempts on his life.

The most painful thing is that he is using my friend Khaplang. If Jamir is really concerned about the Nagas of Burma he could help build a school. He does not know about the suffering of the Naga people either in the West or in the Eastern side.

Jamir has a lot of money and even if he cannot liberate the Nagas, he could start a lower primary school, or a high school. He used Khaplang to smash the movement to make himself comfortable.

Jamir used Khaplang in dark, unseen ways so the common people could not see. People say Jamir used to go around wearing army or police dress. Jamir sent his people and planted them in the movement. He sent Dally Mungro.[129] Dally was an MA, that is what we heard. Khaplang thought he is more qualified. And Jamir also offered money and arms so Khaplang thought he was really helping.

So Khaplang became a puppet in the hands of Jamir. Jamir sent Khaplang to the Atlanta meeting.[130] I quarrelled with friends in Kohima. I asked the Naga Hoho members: would Naga unity be made in the USA? I told them Naga unity can be made only by Nagas. I said the Atlanta meeting was just deceiving the Nagas. They told me I am always suspicious and I replied: 'Don't say that, I am much more broad-minded than you are. You have to think things properly through.' I said this 'America chalo, America chalo' is not going to solve any problem.

I had this argument sitting in a hotel in Kohima. I said don't do this. It is a national issue. Then they said, 'Okay, let us go and see what happens.' We argued and argued and at last Khaplang was silent. Then he said but everything is arranged. And I said you will see that no result will come out of it.

At that time, I could not speak to Khaplang. But earlier I had told him—quarrelling like that the wounds won't heal.

---

[129] Dally Mungro was the General Secretary of the NSCN (Khaplang) and was assassinated on August 18, 1999 allegedly by the NSCN (I-M).

[130] Baptist Peace Fellowship of North America convened a meeting of Naga leaders to foster unity among the Nagas in Atlanta (Georgia) between July 28 to August 3, 1997. NSCN (I-M) called the meeting a congregation of traitors and did not attend partly because Jamir was expected to attend.

In my understanding Khaplang is a (Naga) nationalist. But his nationalism has been misdirected by others. He was deceived by others for their own benefit.

Khaplang and the General Secretary Muivah were very good friends. Khaplang still has a soft corner for him even now. I do not think Khaplang did all that on his own. It is because of Jamir. These Ao are very well educated but not sincere. That is what I have observed. I have seen how they were worried that the Tangkhuls would compete with them and how the Ao officers manipulated things. But there are the anti-Jamir Aos who are real nationalists. Those Aos are always sacrificing for the nation but they do not come to power. The Ao public do not understand them.

Impact of NSCN Split on Eastern Nagaland

In between I met Khaplang and told him that although I am the head of the organization, I have not been able to do anything because my wife has been sick. I told him the moment my wife dies or is fit to be left alone I will come back to the movement.

In 1988, the year when there was the split in the NSCN, in Burma there was an uprising against military dictatorship and General Ne Win was gone.

It was all a complicated situation and it all needed to be studied. I could not take any sides in the NSCN crisis and the situation in Burma was such that tribals could do little. And then we had another military regime in Burma. Khaplang asked me to come but I said I could not go immediately.

The Eastern Naga Revolutionary Council became irrelevant once Khaplang merged with the NSCN in 1980. The ENRC and the NSCN became one party. So I decided to work in the Burmese democracy movement. If there were Burmese Nagas in the NSCN (I-M) then they were there as individuals, not representing any organization.

The time NSCN was present in Burma there was some improvement in the condition of the Burmese Nagas. Opium cultivation came down. They have become Christian—yes it was not the right way to forcefully convert but there is more cleanliness. But still drinking is there. When people come to know the advantages of not drinking then they stop.

I was watching all this from Moreh. In 1989 I went to Bangkok where the tribals have made an organization called National Democratic Front. Then they made another organization called Democratic Alliance of Burma.[131]

I went to Bangkok on my Indian passport. A Naga in Indian intelligence helped me get it after I convinced him that we Burmese Nagas were not doing anything against India.

I was two months in Thailand discussing the political situation in Burma. I came to the conclusion that democracy is much better than military rule so we should support the Burmese movement for democracy. In a democracy we have some freedom politically and even if we do not have a political status at least we can have development, communication and education.

I met the Karen people; they are gentle and patient people and very humble unlike the Burmese who are arrogant.

Khaplang and Burmese Democracy

In 1992 I went to meet Khaplang and discuss the developments in Burma.

I told Khaplang that we should work for democracy and forget the divisions among the Nagas. We need to do something for the Nagas in the east who are illiterate, naked and backward. Then Khaplang introduced me to his friends Dally Mungro, Kitovi and others. Then Khaplang started comparing me to T Sakhrie.

I told Khaplang I was not opposed to him but if two groups of Nagas fight each other, the only result will be that Nagas will be wiped

---

[131] National Democratic Front was formed in 1976 with the political wings of ethnic groups; the Democratic Alliance of Burma was formed after the 1988 uprising and is an alliance of armed groups, but in 1994 Kachins pulled out.

out. That is the situation and I can foresee it. I said he may not accept it but it would happen.

After that Khaplang invited me to a party. They were going to another camp. I went with him and had lunch and then I had to leave because my wife's condition had become very serious. Khaplang gave me a little money.

I used to tell Khaplang, 'Let us work for the Burmese Nagas. We should do something to dress up our naked brothers and sisters and let them have sufficient food, which is hygienic food, and get communication. We can do that. We should not worry about what they do in the western side; let them do anything, we should concentrate on improving the conditions of Burmese Nagas.'

I told Khaplang I had no interest in the west side. I am not doing politics to kill my brothers. I told Khaplang if he wanted my position in the movement that too is alright, and if he wants me to work under his leadership that too is okay by me. But our people must be benefited. When I said all this Khaplang was silent.

Then I tell our people on the western side that let us not kill our own people.

Khaplang and the Burmese Government

Then in 1996 I went to Bangkok again. I was following the democracy movement in Burma but Khaplang did not want to be involved in that. He kept saying all he wants is independence for the Nagas. I sent him documents relating to the Burmese democracy movement from time to time and tried to talk to him about the necessity of supporting the Burmese movement.

On one occasion the Burmese Government sent a Konyak who spoke English to talk to Khaplang. The Burmese Government asked Khaplang to work together with them for development of the Nagas. But Khaplang replied that it was the government 's job to do development work and he had never been an impediment in any of their development works; the Nagas had never broken a bridge or burnt a school. Then they said, 'Okay, if you do not want to discuss development then let us not kill each other.' They told him he would be free unless he went in a uniform and had arms. He has not been arrested but others have been. One Naga nationalist was tortured and died in jail.

The Burmese Government has not done much for the Nagas. If you love someone you should do something for them, isn't it? But they have not bothered about the Nagas. So by not bringing education and awareness, indirectly they are killing the Nagas, no?

Khaplang's source of funds is not opium. When I was with him one year, we did not have money even for bus fare, let alone rickshaw, so we went everywhere by foot even in Rangoon. He may have small fields of opium and sell it in Arunachal Pradesh or to Konyaks for personal consumption but that is not his source of funds. Khaplang's main source of funds is Jamir.

Democracy and Federalism in Burma

I believe it is very important to establish federalism in Burma and that is why we started a political party and called it the Naga National League for Democracy (NNLD). We formed it in July 1998. The NNLD has been formed to fight against military rule in Burma and for the restoration of democracy in the country and the establishment of a federal state.

Our party, the NNLD, is a part of the Democratic Alliance of Burma.[132] The DAB is an alliance of all tribal communities in Burma.

Before we formed the NNLD there was a Naga Hills Progressive

---

[132] The Democratic Alliance of Burma (DAB), was founded on November 18, 1988, in Klerday at the Thai border. The DAB included the National Democratic Front, the All Burma Students' Democratic Front (ABSDF), the Committee for Restoration of Democracy in Burma (a US-based Burmese exile organization), the All Burma Young Monks' Union (ABYMU), the Chin National Front (CNF) and many other groups. The aim of DAB included the overthrow of the State Law and Order Restoration Council (SLORC).

Party but that was abolished by the Burmese military. They had fought in the 1990 elections and won two seats.[133] The MPs are still there. I wrote to them to discuss our party but they were too scared. They are cowards. Even before the Progressive Party there was a Naga MP from U Nu's party.

Nagas have resisted the Burmese administration being imposed on them. One Leinong Naga village resisted. It was right on top of a hill. They had a few self-loading guns and they rolled down stones on the Burmese Army. The Burmese Army used two-inch mortars and destroyed the village.

I met the leader of that village, his name was Pathien and he later joined the Burmese Army. He was a Sergeant when he came to my village. He was strong like a lion. He told me the story of how his village was blown up and how they suffered. We became very close like brothers. He advised me that if we loved our people we must plan properly. He said learning to read and write was not enough, you have to learn so many things. Without planning the people suffered unnecessarily.

Naga Areas of Burma

Khaplang has alliance with revolutionary groups from Assam and Manipur.[134] I do not think the alliances have benefitted the Burmese Nagas. The villagers are being forced to carry their luggage without getting paid even one paisa. If I could convince Khaplang I would

---

[133] The Naga Hills Regional Progressive Party, following the reintroduction of multi-party democracy after the 8888 Uprising, contested six seats in the 1990 general elections. It received 0.08% of the vote, winning two seats; U Khapo Kailon in Lahe and U Dwe Pawt in Layshi. The party was abolished by the military government on 18 March 1992.

[134] The latest such alliance was the coming together in 2015 of the anti-talks faction of the United Liberation Front of Asom (ULFA), the NSCN (K), the Kamtapur Liberation Organization (KLO) and a faction of the National Democratic Front of Bodoland (NDFB), to form the United National Liberation Front of Western South East Asia (UNLFW) which is committed to liberate North East India, North Bengal and Myanmar. It is reported that the UNLFW has the backing of China.

stop this practice. I do not know if these groups are giving financial assistance to Khaplang.

Yes, we want a Naga State in Burma like Karen State, Kachin State etc. but it must include all the Naga townships: Homalin, Layshi, Khamti, Lahe, Nanyun and Shingbwiyang.[135] It is true that other tribes have settled on our lands but that cannot be stopped in today's world.

In Homalin, many Nagas joined the Shans. Human nature is such people want to identify with the advanced group so these Nagas said they were Shan but now they are thinking about their origins. I have visited Homalin and stayed there for a year. That is when I have seen Naga ornaments and necklaces with the Nagas who call themselves Shan.

The Myanmar Government has a policy that wherever a people are not a Majority then they cannot claim the area. So Homalin is very much beyond our control population-wise, but we have historical claims.

Naga National Movement

I told my Angami friends that Muivah is the only fellow who has thinking power in Naga politics. I have met all the Naga leaders and politicians. Of course Uncle Phizo and Imkongmeren thought deeply. None of the others know anything about Burma but Muivah could tell me about Burmese history. Because our people are in two countries, it is good to know the history of both India and Burma.

I tell my friends that we cannot have settlement in both Burma and India together. We have to understand international politics and we have to go part by part. If we take on both India and Burma, we will make our enemies stronger.

---

[135] Naga Self-Administered Zone has been created under the 2008 Constitution of Burma and includes only three townships: Lahe, Layshi and Nanyun. The Nagas in Myanmar continue their struggle to include Homalin and Shingbwiyang (the latter being a part of Kachin State).

I started supporting the NSCN (I-M) after they got recognition from the UNPO[136] in 1994. It is very important to get international support without which we cannot achieve our goal.

Phizo and the Naga National Council

When Uncle Phizo died, Biseto[137] and I said he should be buried in London so people from other countries can also see his grave. We would be able to say our President is lying there till his country is free from the rule of foreigners. We tried to talk to people quietly but Uncle Biseto even told Phizo's relatives and the Angamis were out to kill him. He had to go underground again. Our idea was to keep the Naga issue alive internationally so we thought he should be buried there in London.

So now they have buried Uncle Phizo in Kohima with a big monument. And they say Phizo is the Father of the Nation. That is not the title because that title should go to the person who achieves sovereignty for the nation. Of course after the Shillong Accord Uncle Phizo had to suffer a lot.

Phizo's daughter Adino knows nothing about politics. Not even A-B-C of politics. How can she lead the organization, i.e. the Naga National Council? One young Angami woman interviewed Adino in London and she told me that Adino told her not to speak in Nagamese.[138]

---

[136] The Unrepresented Nations and Peoples Organization (UNPO) is an international pro-democracy organization. It was formed on 11 February 1991 in The Hague, Netherlands. Its purpose is to facilitate the voices of unrepresented and marginalized nations and peoples worldwide. Some of its members are governments or government agencies of unrecognized states. NSCN (I-M) became a member of the UNPO in January 1993. On the UNPO website, it is stated that Nagas originally came from Mongolia in the tenth century B.C.

[137] Biseto Medom Keyho was the Home Minister in the Federal Government at the time of the signing of the Shillong Accord.

[138] Nagamese is a creole based on Assamese, Hindi, English and Naga languages. Nagamese is used as a lingua franca in schools, markets, hospitals, the legislative assembly and churches by the peoples of Nagaland, who speak more than twenty other

How can she say such a thing? We must have a common language to communicate with each other.

Ideology and Religion

China and India can never be friends. We have to understand this. Western Nagas have a political advantage over us Eastern Nagas.

I told Khaplang not to mention the word 'socialist' in the name of our organization or party. When we declare we are socialist, and Naga way of life was originally socialist, that cannot be denied but just now it is no point in causing divisions amongst ourselves. After we get independence, we can have different parties.

I do not know what we gain by the slogan of 'Nagaland for Christ' and I do not know what we will lose if we drop it. We need the help of Buddhists, Muslims and other non-Christians as well. That is what I feel. Yes, religion and politics should not be mixed.

I do not know much about Mao Tse-Tung but the way the communists did revolution was very good. They captured power and helped the people. They provided food to the people, helped people in the fields—after capturing the whole of China they did good for the people. China was in a horrible situation before the Revolution with so many beggars, prostitutes and opium eaters. That is what we read in school. Rich people reached heaven but the poor were living like animals. Beggars were dying on the roadside. In India if poor are not helped, then communism will come to India.

Americans are helping India so India does not become Communist. It is not out of love for the people.

So we have to try to understand socialism and communism. But our people are so backward. And this anti-India policy of the Nagas is not good. It is a very narrow way of thinking. We have equal rights to express ourselves, to speak. I am not supporting Indian Army or

mutually unintelligible languages. It is also the language spoken by the NSCN but they do not advocate making it an official or national language, and it is seen as inferior to English and Naga languages.

Burmese Army but if we think properly, we will see the Burmese Army is much worse than the Indian Army.

We cannot ask why are they killing us because we are also killing them. Naga freedom fighters are fighting the Indian Army. We can say we don't like Indian government because they are forcibly ruling us but we cannot be against the Indian people. That is what I think.

CHAPTER THREE

The Naga Army

'The soldiers should be like gardeners—they should tend their gardens, the nation, and not let cattle from outside get in. Instead, they are destroying the beauty in the gardens they ought to protect.'

—Woodcutter of Ukhrul

Naga men were trained to be warriors and protect the village from attack. The Naga warrior in the past was to fight in the men's dormitory called the morung; they were also trained in the rules which govern wars and peace-making.

The Naga warriors of the past have been praised in songs and legends in the villages they were born, and sometimes their deeds of courage and valour have reached across the mountains and their fame has spread far and wide.

The Konyaks even made guns and gunpowder which they used for hunting, and their fierce resistance to colonial incursions led to the British planting opium on Veda hill, the highest peak in Mon District, and making so many of that tribe into opium addicts.

Every village has stories and songs of its famous Naga warriors. In most tribes the warriors were entitled to wear special shawls, or ornaments indicating how many heads they had taken.

In many ways the modern Naga soldier is continuing the tradition except that he is now trained in modern warfare and from a traditional warrior he has become a highly trained guerilla using sophisticated weapons. And there is another difference, now there are women soldiers and officers—just as well-trained and lethal in the battlefield.

In 1954, under the guidance of Phizo, the first armed group was organized and it was called the Home Guards under the command of Thungti Chang, and around the same time Kaito Sukhai organized his Safe Guards. Two years later the two forces were united and called the Country Guards.

In April 1956 the Central Government sent the Indian Army to crush the insurgency in the Naga Hills District of the state of Assam. The Indian Armed Forces were given extraordinary powers to shoot, arrest, detain and seize under a new law enacted in 1958 called the Armed Forces (Special Powers) Act. Everywhere the Indian Army was met with tough resistance from the Nagas who were not as yet trained and had few weapons.

For instance, in Tusom village in present-day Ukhrul district of Manipur, Captain Phungtha Horam (1920–1967) engaged the Indians in armed combat in January 1958. He had collected the old rifles left by the Japanese during the Second World War and he is credited with manufacturing a home-made canon which catapulted stones on to the Indian security forces.

By 1958 batches of Nagas were going to East Pakistan for arms training and weapons. We were able to interview the man who acted as guide to Phizo and other Naga officers and take them safely to East Pakistan. The man's name was Gangmei Tadingpau or Taodaijang (1934–2016) and we interviewed him on July 16, 1999 in Dimapur.

Tadingpau was born in a Rongmei family in Fulertom village in Cachar, Assam in 1934. His mother died early and he gave up school after Class Five so that he could help his father support his five brothers and one sister.

Tadingpau joined the Burrows Memorial Christian Hospital at Alipur in 1950 and was given some medical training by Dr Kenoyer for three years, after which he began his work of selling medicines all over the Zeliangrong area of Manipur.

It was difficult travelling to distant villages when there were no roads or public transport. For three years, from 1953 to 1956, he did this work and that is how he knew the roads and could lead the batches of Naga Army to East Pakistan by different routes.

In March 1956 he joined the Naga movement after his father reassured him that if he was ever arrested, he would visit him in jail. The first task Tadingpau was given was to contact the Pakistani authorities and to act as guide to Phizo, taking him across to East Pakistan.

Tadingpau told us: 'I met Phizo the first time in Tausem village in Tamenglong district of Manipur. I told him there were many ways to go to East Pakistan, and my house was just 60 kms from the border. We could go to East Pakistan from the NC Hills or from Haflong or catch a train from Silchar to Karimgunj and then walk. Other times I had to go across the river Barak. I can speak a little Bengali but Phizo spoke English, Nagamese and Hindi.'

Tadingpau went on to testify: 'I went to East Pakistan several times. Phizo had sent a message from London via the Federal Headquarters that as soon as possible and as many as possible should go to Pakistan for training. Even Indian, Nepali, Kuki and Meiteis went for training.

'In 1960 I escorted General Mowu who came with around 250 to 300 people; General Kaito came with 400 to 500 people to Zeliangrong. It was around 700 who went for training at that time. That was the time when the Nagas had captured the Indian pilots in Burma.'[139]

Tadingpau said that, 'Bengali miyas gave us tea and snacks,' and they were taken by the Pakistani army to a camp in Sylhet. He did not get training since he was not in the Naga Army but he did help carry arms and ammunition from East Pakistan from 1958 to 1963. Later, he joined the NSCN.

General Kaito of the Naga Army went to East Pakistan for training and there in the Sylhet camp, Colonel SG Mehdi (1921–2015), a veteran of Pakistan's Special Service Group observed that: 'The

---

[139] We interviewed Tadingpao on July 16, 1999 in Hindi in Dimapur.

Nagas are far better fighters than the Kashmiri Mujahids. They were disciplined and dedicated and quickly picked up tactics and weapons skills. They clearly had a cause. The Mujahids of Azad Kashmir were unruly. It was clear they had more interest in women and loot waiting for them in the Srinagar valley. And morale—the Mujahids would flee at the first sight of an Indian counter-attack but the Nagas would fight until the bitter end.'[i]

Even Indian intelligence officers posted to the Naga-inhabited areas, such as Maloy Krishna Dhar, acknowledged the ethical behavior of the Naga Army. In his book *Open Secrets: India's Intelligence Unveiled*, Dhar wrote that: 'In those golden days the Naga rebels, so also the Meitei militants, observed strict codes of warfare. They did not attack civilians and hardly disturbed a lady. An Indian traveller, alone or with a lady companion, was more secure in the highly disturbed Naga area than he was in the streets of Calcutta.'[ii]

The most celebrated action by the Naga Army was shooting down of an Indian transport plane (Dakota) trying to drop relief materials and ammunitions to the besieged post.

The Naga Army captured all the nine airmen including Fl. Lieutenant AS Singh. The captured airmen, none of whom were harmed in any way, were later set free through the Red Cross.

RN Kulkarni, an Indian intelligence officer, describes in his book *Sin of National Conscience*[iii] the audacity of the Nagas. Kulkarni describes how General Dusoi Chakhesang of Yanomami village living in the jurisdiction of the intelligence officer 'maintained a very cordial relationship with CIVINT as well as with the bosses of SIB.' Dusoi allowed the intelligence officers to come to his home and hinted that he was suffering from TB; then Dusoi slipped under the very noses of the intelligence officers and went to China in 1968.[140]

---

[140] Dusoi was in the group that left for China in February 1968 but did not reach. On the way they stopped at a Konyak village and many became victims of headhunting; those who survived were captured by the Burmese Army in June the same year.

The training given by the Chinese was a contrast to the training given by the Pakistanis. Pakistan taught the Nagas that all Indians were their enemy whereas the Chinese said only the Indian State was the enemy, not the Indian people.

The Chinese also taught the Nagas the concept of a People's Army which helped ordinary people instead of looking down at them. The NSCN calls its armed wing the People's Army of Nagaland.

The Chinese training also included special training for handling medical problems in the battlefield. Avuli's testimony gives an account of how the Chinese developed the concept of barefoot doctors by which peasants were given basic medical and paramedical training to work in China's villages correcting the urban bias of the healthcare system.[iv]

According to Indian intelligence sources, the NSCN has received millions of dollars from Pakistan and USA to buy arms and ammunition; for instance, in 1994 the finance secretary of the NSCN, Khayao Huray, was alleged to have confessed that Pakistan had provided 1.7 million US dollars to them to procure arms.

Another source of money for the organization has been fees collected from other insurgent organizations for training their cadres, and when they go on joint operations the NSCN keeps 70 per cent of the captured money from banks.

The split in the National Socialist Council of Nagalim has meant that the Naga Army too has split. This has resulted in deadly conflict between the groups and an added burden on the Naga public who have to pay taxes to each of these groups, so tax collection becomes extortion.

In 2013 the Naga public formed the Action Committee Against Unabated Taxation (ACAUT) and have taken up the issue of multiple taxes imposed by the various armed groups and especially the distress of farmers.

Despite the splits, the NSCN (I-M) continues to recruit cadres for its army. Each year, the organization holds a passing out parade of newly trained armed cadres in its designated camp, set up under

Ceasefire Ground Rules, called 'Camp Hebron' which is about 40 kms from Dimapur. The recruitment and training of its army is undertaken by the General Field Training Department (GFTD) at the Hebron Mount Gilead Training Centre. This training has continued throughout the Indo-Naga peace process.

THINOSELIE KEYHO: THE GENERAL

Thinoselie M Keyho is an Angami General of the Naga Army who commanded the first group of Nagas led by Thuingaleng Muivah to China in October 1966. He returned to Nagaland in January 1968.

Thinoselie went to meet Phizo in Paris with the help of the Pakistanis. From Paris he flew to Dacca, East Pakistan, and landed in the midst of the Bangladesh War of 1971. He was arrested and detained by the Indians for five years and released in May 1976 after the signing of the Shillong Accord.

His older brother Biseto Medom Keyho[v] was the Home Minister in the Naga Federal Government and one of the signatories to the Shillong Accord.

Presently he is the elected President of the Naga National Council (non-Accordists) from 2016.

We interviewed General Thinoselie M Keyho between August 12 to 14, 1999 at a hotel in Kathmandu, Nepal.

Testimony of General Thinoselie:

I am from Chedema village. I was around twenty or twenty-one years old at the time of the plebiscite in 1951 so I must have been born in the 1930s.

I studied in Kohima High School and after passing I went to Shillong for matriculation. During the plebiscite we made two gates— one India gate and one Naga gate. Those who wanted to go with India had to go through the India gate and those who wanted independence went through the Naga gate. This was in Kohima but I could not take part in the plebiscite.

I feel if the British people had not come, the Naga story would have been different. It is they who betrayed our people. They kept us isolated. They totally ignored our people. But on the other hand, I appreciate the British people because they have safeguarded our way of life, traditions and customs. During the British time we had to pay a simple house tax of two or three rupees.

The British knew that one day they would have to give up their empire, so they set up Simon Commission. The Memorandum to the Commission is written without hurting the sentiment of either the Hindu people, who do not eat beef, or the Muslim people, who do not eat pork. It was written in a simple beautiful language. As a result of the Memorandum, Naga areas were put under Excluded Area.

It was the Naga people who saved British and Indian lives during the Second World War. The British burned down my village to prevent the Japanese from entering.

If the American Baptist missionaries had not come, our history would be very different. It was because of them we were converted to Christianity. The British wanted to keep the Nagas backward but the American missionaries wanted to introduce Western ways, so we lost our culture.

Phizo talked about independence. He hated the White Man. He and his brother wanted to join the British army[141] so they declared themselves as Anglo-Indian because they did not want to call themselves Indian and they were not allowed to call themselves Naga. It is said he met Subhash Chandra Bose in Burma.[142]

---

[141] Neither Thinoselie nor Phizo seem aware of the contradiction in their positions of not liking the White Man in general on one hand, but supporting the British or taking their help on the other.

[142] Gavin Young (1928–2001), a British journalist who visited the Nagas in 1960, noted: 'But Christianity is one of the factors which has led most Nagas to feel closer affinities with the Christian West than with what some of them describe as 'the dark, empty faiths' of their immediate neighbours—a feeling shared by other Christian peoples in Asia notably the Karens and the Shans in Burma. The Nagas may secretly despise Hindus unenlightened, but they have no wish to convert them, still less destroy them as infidels. The Naga War is not a jihad. But their Christianity is undoubtedly one reason why, for the moment, the Nagas are seeking sympathy from the West rather than elsewhere and why Mr Phizo is in London rather than Peking.' *The Nagas: An Unknown War* (London: Naga National Council, 1962), 87.

I used to attend NNC meetings and hear them talk about the movement. But it was my Uncle who influenced me. He was a good footballer. I remember there used to be water scarcity in 1945 and we got water only for one or two hours. The Nepalese would take it away and I fought with them. And my Uncle encouraged me saying it is our land and so I took away the water from them.

I remember seeing Reverend Longri Ao and he got to know me and was very friendly. I liked and admired him very much. But I did not know or understand politics. Then an incident happened in my village which compelled me to join the movement.

One day the Assam Rifles came to our village and killed two Gaon Burras. They tied them on a bamboo pole and carried them as if they were carrying pigs and brought them in front of all the people. And the police were standing there and making a joke. The Indians said, 'See what will happen to Naga people who ask for independence.'

I have seen our people beaten so badly that they could not open their eyes. I have seen how our villages were burnt and our women were raped. That is when the youth decided to defend themselves and started collecting arms even though the elders tried to stop them, because all the youth could think of was revenge. So the NNC wanted to channelize the youth and they declared the formation of a government on March 22, 1956. The President of the Government was one Hongkin. But I do not know much about him.[143]

Seeing the beatings and torture made me angry and I joined the Home Guards. The moment we joined the Home Guards we went to the battlefield. Guns are like toys in our hands and we were good in hunting.

To begin with, Angami, Lotha, Chakhesang and Semas joined but later Semas were recalled by General Kaito. Semas claimed that Phizo had promised to make Kaito the Commander-in-Chief but Phizo said Kaito had failed to come to the Federal Government meeting so he made Thungti the Commander of the Home Guards. Kaito felt Phizo had not been sincere.

---

[143] See Chapter One on Hongkin.

Later Thungti was suspended and Kaito was made the Chief of
the Safe Guards. It was alleged that Thungti had run away from the
battlefield but I am not sure whether that is true.

At that time the Indian Army was very scared because they thought
Nagas were headhunting cannibals and we would eat them!

All through this period the Women's Society (of the NNC) were
cooking almost twenty-four hours a day non-stop to feed all of us.
They were not allowed to take rest. They had to feed the entire village
hiding in the jungles and the men fighting.

At that time Yusuf Ali, officer of Assam Rifles, was there in
Nagaland. He had married an Angami lady. He was very persuasive
in getting many officers to surrender. If he had been allowed to stay
in Kohima, more and more Nagas would have surrendered but he was
posted out because Government of India began suspecting him of
helping the Nagas.[144]

Phizo sent a message saying that whosoever was willing to join the
Naga Army should be allowed to do so; some Meiteis, Nepalis and
some Madrasis also joined the Naga Army. I think within the Indian
Army there were a lot of differences and the officers beat the soldiers
very badly and called them coolie. In 1964 I myself had a request from
one person working in the border roads and he said he had a quarrel
with his officer but I did not recruit him.

Yes there were differences between Phizo and Sakhrie. Both
happened to be from Khonoma village. Sakhrie was General Secretary
of the NNC from earlier times so even after Phizo became President
he continued. Sakhrie said we should develop ourselves first, then ask
for independence. There was pressure on him from the government
of India.

There was serious debate between the two. Phizo asked Sakhrie

---

[144] Rashid Yusuf Ali was military advisor to the Governor of Assam and
then joined the Indian Frontier Administrative Service created by Nehru for the
administration of North East region. The IFAS was created in 1953-54 but became
effective from 1957.

one last question: 'Okay, suppose we Naga people co-operate with this government of India and we can educate and develop, then how can we begin the movement for independence?'

Sakhrie had no answer. Phizo said once a man dies, he cannot be revived. So once we join the Indian union we cannot come out. From that time Sakhrie became a minority. Somebody kidnapped him and killed him. We did not. Sakhrie's friends said it was Mr Phizo's responsibility.

In August 1960 I was in our camp in Burma. We did not have any written agreement with the Burmese government but we did not carry out ambushes on the Burmese side. The Burmese told us not to go into the villages in our uniform with our arms and ammunition. They knew the people we were staying with were our people, i.e. the Nagas of Burma.

When I was at the Burma camp, I met the Indian prisoners who were kept there by the Naga Home Guards. It was in the Pochury area. We captured two Dakota planes and I remember one of the pilots was Fl. Lieutenant Anand Singha. He was the personal pilot of the Governor of Assam and he told me he was not supposed to fly the plane that day but he did it on the request of a friend. They flew over Indian posts to drop rations and ammunition.

After their plane was shot by us with an LMG he asked the other men to eject but they were afraid and refused to jump. They were afraid that their heads would be chopped off. Singha managed to land the plane in a small clearing. Our Home Guards surrounded them and asked them to surrender.

The prisoners were Flying Officer Chandrashekhar Misra, Flying Officer RE Ratphael and Sergeant JC Chowdhury. And there was Rafi. We kept only the officers and released the other men. I think we had captured eleven of their men and kept only four officers.

I was there for three to four months and I met the pilots every day and we exchanged many stories. I used to get small, small things like sugar and tobacco and I shared it with them.

Phizo was trying to get the Red Cross to accept the prisoners so the matter would become international. But General Kaito released them to representatives of India and Burma in May 1962.[145]

We did not agree with the Naga Peace Convention. We arrested all the Angami members and warned them against signing. The NPC had all the educated people and to stop them we would have had to kill all the educated people.

Nagas of this side (Nagaland) became impatient and accepted so-called Nagaland State because they wanted power. That is why they did not include Nagas from Manipur. They could have brought all the Nagas together.

Nagas from Manipur were active in the movement. I know Phanitphang from 1962 and many from Zeliangrong area. People from Tamenglong were with us from the beginning, and also Mao Nagas.

On January 3, 1964, the Home Guards and Safe Guards were merged to form the Naga Army. We celebrate Naga Army Raising Day every year. We had centralized command in the army, it was not organized on the basis of tribes. We were organizing the army under southern command and all tribes were included from the region but then came the ceasefire in 1964 and it put a stop to our efforts.

We did not really know what this ceasefire was. Some of our people were very suspicious and did not want to talk to the peace mission. But some of the younger generation persuaded the elders to accept the peace mission. They said we could show the world that we wanted peace.

The Indian government knew we were bringing arms and then the Indian government realized that Nagas could not be defeated by

---

[145] Gavin Young described his meeting with the prisoners: 'Singha and his fellow prisoners—Flying Officer Chandrashekhar Misra, 23; Flying Officer R.E. Ratphael, 24; and Sergeant J.C. Chowdhury, 32—were bearded and thin but cheerful. They were keen. to know the results of last year's Olympic Games. For months they had received virtually no news of the outside world. For more than seven months, Indian Army units in Nagaland (believed to comprise three divisions or 20,000 men) have been searching for the men in vain.' (Ibid.).

military repression. That is why they decided to have a ceasefire and start the peace process.

At that time Suisa had a peace proposal. He was given the post of Assistant to Vice President of the NNC. Muivah was made the General Secretary right after he finished his MA in political science. I do not know exactly what Suisa's proposal was but I know Phizo did not like it. He was angry not because he had a proposal but because he published it before showing it to Phizo. Suisa circulated his proposals before going to London to show it to Phizo.

We thought government of India would consider us human beings and recognize our rights so the dialogue would be fruitful. The Indian delegate will address us, the NNC members, and say 'a section of the people' which made me angry because it meant that they did not consider that we represented all our people, as a nation. Our Naga people are also vengeful.

Mr Chaliha[146] was not the right person to deal with us because he never considered us as human beings. We realized that the government of India was not going to talk to us as equal human beings. We felt they wanted to weaken the Naga people in the name of peace. They are strengthening their position and exploiting whoever was close to us. General Mowu Gwizan told the president of the Federal Government Scato Swu (1927–2014) that it was better to go to China. And the president told General Mowu to give money to me and start preparing for China.

I was a Brigadier at the time and I was to lead with my team of soldiers. Mr Thuingaleng Muivah was to head the civil side and he had special powers.

At that time no one knew anything about China. The only thing we knew was that it is a communist country. That's all we knew. And

---

[146] Bimala Prasad Chaliha (1912-1971) was Chief Minister of Assam for three terms, from 1957 to 1970. He introduced Assamese as the sole official language which angered the Mizos. Chaliha opposed the division of Assam into smaller states such as Nagaland, Mizoram etc.

we believed we would reach that land. I asked Scato: 'Now what we are planning is not known to the Indian government. We do not know whether we will be able to reach China and we do not know whether the Chinese will welcome us. But supposing by the grace of God we reach China and the Chinese accept us, and then government of India finds out—they may do anything out of shock. Out of anger or emotion they may do anything and if that happens what will you do, will you reject us?'

He replied that they would not reject us. If they could not resist the pressure of the government of India, they would find other ways to continue the struggle.

So, with that assurance I started preparing for the China trip.

We started in the wrong season. We arrived in Mon in the month of July when it was raining. So we were in the Konyak area and I asked the authorities for rations. I said I could manage vegetables. The 24th battalion of the Naga Army was posted there. Two or three battalions make a brigade.

I had heard that if we give some beedis and cigarettes to the Konyak boys they will help us so I carried beedis, cigarette packets and also some underwear.

Several times the Konyak misunderstood our intention and tried to ambush us. When we tried to enter a Konyak village the men would stand at their doors with daos in their hand and refuse to let us in. Then my boys would offer beedis and cigarettes and the doors would open. But there was no incident. Even on our way to China we were not attacked by either Burmese or Indian armies.

One day two of my boys were buying rations from the villagers on the Burmese side when they saw Burmese troops. They told me. I told them not to move but hang down their weapons and bring the Burmese to me. One Burmese Sergeant came to me with his sten gun. I signaled to him to sit down and offered him a cigarette; he took it and lit it with a match, then he sat down and we offered tea. He did not show any emotion.

Then in the evening one Captain came to ask what we were doing.

The commandant and other officers were attending a meeting so he was in charge. I told him there were some people who want to create misunderstanding between Burmese and Naga people and I had come to check that. I bought a fat pig and I gave them half and kept the other half. I said we want to be friends.

That is how I convinced him. But he informed his seniors about what happened and asked for reinforcements. The villagers all ran away. The women and children ran away into the jungles thinking that there would be a fight between us and the Burmese. But that was a false rumour.

It was in a Konyak village. I told him (the Captain) I wanted to cross the mountain range. He suspected we wanted to contact the Kachins but I pretended that I did not know anything about the Kachins. He said he could not allow me to cross that range which was under his charge, but he allowed us to cross another range going into the Hukawng valley.

In Hukawng valley there were no people in the villages. They were in the jungles. The Burmese Army was carrying out operation against the Kachins, so the villages were empty. There was an army post in the village.

We sent a message to the Post Commander that we are coming and we have no intention other than to make peace. We said we were 300 to 400 but actually we were only 130. We spoke to them in English. I went disarmed to their camp and they were nervous because we had occupied the entire village. By midnight the reinforcement came.

A Burmese Army Lieutenant woke us up and asked why we were coming with arms. He said it was disrespectful to their government. He told us to go back immediately or he would have to either arrest us or kill us. He told us to go to Myitkyina, the headquarters of the Burmese Army in Kachin state. He was communicating with their headquarters through wireless. The Lieutenant said he was just a mediator.

That night we went back to sleep. The next morning, I bought a chicken and we cooked it to share with the Burmese Lieutenant and got cold drinks. Again he asked us to go to Myitkyina but I said if they want peace talks they should ask my government to send a representative. That way I escaped.

Then the Lieutenant asked our purpose of coming. I said we were visiting to see the Naga and Kachin border. They told us there were no villages this side; only jungles. He refused us permission to go further. I said I have to go to the villages where people are living because I have no rations. I think they were not thinking properly so they allowed us to go. They wrote a letter giving us permission but the note said we were not to go near the security posts.

We entered the Hukawng valley. The headman of the village happened to be a Naga. I think Naga is a magic word. I do not know to which tribe he belonged. We told him, 'You are Naga and we are Naga.' Only that much. They had sentimental attachment to Nagas so we could communicate on our first meeting.

I asked him whether he could give us a guide. He asked whether we had got permission from the police; without the permission the villagers were likely to be tortured for giving us a guide. So I went to the Burmese authorities and asked and they told us to ask the villagers. I asked them if we take the villagers will you torture them? And they said 'No, no.' I told this to the villagers and they gave us two guides, one Naga and another Kachin.

The headman spoke Assamese fluently. They do marketing this side of the border. There were some ex-servicemen also.

Despite the guides we got lost in the Hukawng valley. There were big, big trees so we lost the way. We had a compass but it did not work.

I asked one of my men to climb up a tree and asked whether he could see a village and he said 'No.' Then I asked him whether he could see a field and he said 'No'; then I asked whether he could hear a dog barking and he said 'No' and finally I asked whether he could hear a cock crowing and he said 'No' but he said he could see two elephants coming towards us. The man quickly climbed down the tree.

We thought it was the Burmese Army so we took positions. Our Kachin guide went up to them and talked to them. They talked and talked and talked. Actually those on the elephants were Kachins.

I offered them money but they refused. They also refused the cigarettes. We arrived at a village which seemed deserted.

In that village we found one woman who could speak Assamese. Through her we got rations. The next day we found ourselves on the banks of the Chindwin river. We were really tired and we got a message that we must not move from there. We thought the Burmese troops were coming so we moved away and after marching for two days we met the Kachins. At first they thought we were Burmese so they ran away.

The Kachins then realized that we are not Burmese but Nagas. The Kachins were confused. One Sergeant of the Kachin Independence Army said he would take over command and he took us to their battalion camp. The Burmese found out that we are linked to the Kachins and started operations but we had left by then. Our group did not suffer much.

We had sent a message to the Chinese outpost through a Kachin. But they did not know how to read the message and it came back to us. So I led my men to the small town in China. It had taken us ninety-three days in addition to the three months we had spent in Mon district.

The PLA man came out and waved. I thought he was welcoming us so I also waved to him but he was telling us to move back. We were not surprised and I told my men to move back. The Kachins told us to stay. The Chinese did not know English and they kept saying something like 'Nogao'—possibly it meant 'Who are you?' They spoke broken English. They had Mao Tse-tung badge. Mr Muivah saw the badge and pointed to it. Probably they thought we know their Mao Tse-tung. Then they asked for our flag. We did not have a Naga flag. We had Indian currency but we did not want to show them that. Then on the ground we draw a map and pointed out: This is India, this is China, this is Burma and this is Naga territory. But they could not make out what we were saying.

That night we were allowed to stay there at the border but within China. We made a big fire because it was very cold. The boys were taken to a place where there was water and they could eat. It was very cold, either December or January.

Then at night two young Chinese boys came and their first sentence was whether we knew English. We said yes and were very, very happy. But later we realized they could not really speak English. They had an English-Chinese dictionary. I had to hold the torch on the dictionary and the whole night we tried to communicate but we could not make much sense of each other.

Then at around seven or eight in the morning two little men came and they could speak English fluently. I think they had been called for us. After that we understood each other very well. We were told to stay at the border for some more time. The first thing they did was to bring us rations and the second thing was clothes to wear. We stayed around ten days while they made arrangements for us. Then they took us to an isolated temple. I think they meant to give us security. I asked to let my men have exercise and requested to make a volleyball court. I explained what that was and I said we would make it ourselves.

Then they gave us material and two gardens so we levelled the ground and as we worked the Naga way, shouting and joking, the villagers heard the noise and came to see. Some climbed the trees and others the wall to see us. The PLA took the branches and hit those who came around because it was in their security zone.

Once we levelled the ground, we had wrestling matches, high jump and long jump contests. After spending four to five hours we came back to the camp. And the Chinese people said we were a good team. While digging the ground one of our soldiers cut himself and he was taken to a Chinese hospital.

Then the officers came to interrogate us. I think it was for eight or nine days daily they interrogated us. After that Muivah and I were taken to Peking (Beijing) where we met the deputy chief of the PLA. I forgot his name but he had only one arm. He and eight others interrogated us for eight or nine days. After that we were taken sightseeing and shown important monuments. We saw where Chang Kai-shek was caught.

After that we were allowed to go to Dacca by flight to meet Pakistani officers. We came back to China and then we had to get ready to return in October.

We felt more comfortable with the Chinese. Pakistanis were also friendly but maybe because of race or religion we felt more at home in China.

The training the Chinese gave us was very different from the Pakistani training. Instead of putting us altogether and asking to fire, they gave each man a loaded gun and asked us to fire. So they separated those with experience and those who could not fire properly. In Pakistan they gave us lessons on how to aim and how to fire. I think the Chinese sent us the best person to teach us.

At one point they mixed the parts of several arms and then asked us to put them together. We had to do this wearing a blindfold. I think they mixed the parts of seven weapons and we learnt to put them together with our eyes blindfolded. They said if we are to fire in the dark or in the night, we must know how to assemble the weapons. They also taught us how to send messages by wireless through high speed.

The relationship between the Chinese officers and men was equal. At the time of the revolution there were no ranks and we could not differentiate between the soldiers and the officers. Then the one thing I found strange was the higher the officer, the humbler he was. They said they could differentiate between a soldier and an officer by the badges they wore but we could not.

As for the Naga Army, I do not know what it is like nowadays. I have not been in service for a long time. But at that time, it was very democratic. We all had the same Mess, we ate the same food and slept in the same camp.

It is very difficult to deal with men. It all depends on the attitude of the officer. Otherwise all kinds of complaints come in.

We also learnt that the relationship between the army and the people must be that they love each other. The army must take care of the civilians. We learnt this in our military training but also in the political training. We also got political training and learnt Mao Tse-tung's thoughts. Yes, it was very interesting.

We learnt that the guerilla is like a fish and the people are like water. More water there is the better the guerilla can move. That explains all. We learnt to help the villagers. Once the Chinese could persuade the villagers, they were able to isolate the government.

I read a book by a Vietnamese General but I did not go to Vietnam. As far as I know Muivah did not go there. When I was arrested by the Indian Army, they kept asking whether I had been to Vietnam. The Indian press also wrote that we had been to Vietnam. I told my interrogators that I wanted to go to Vietnam but I did not go there. But they did not believe me.

Mao Tse-tung's thoughts also taught us to distinguish our enemy from our friend. I thought that is very important. They told us to distinguish between the Indian people and the Indian government. Chinese taught us that the Indian people were not our enemies.

We never thought that their ideology was against Christianity. We went for service every Sunday. They used to look at us while we prayed but they did not stop us. When we went to Beijing we could not go for service because the churches were closed but we were free to pray in our camp. Our Chinese interpreter said he felt there must be a god, a real god. But when everybody claims their god is the real god, then it was difficult to differentiate who is the real god.

On our return there was no incident till we reached Phek. By that time the Indians came to know we had returned from China. The Phek people said they would cook for us. We were hiding in the jungles. One intelligence officer came from Kohima and he saw the women cooking and he asked casually: 'Oh, our friends have come already? I saw two of them guarding on the road.' And they answered: 'Yes! Yes! They have come. We are cooking for these people.'

He told the women to quickly make arrangements and then he went away. He reported to his headquarters. On that I had gone to the Chedema peace camp. Of course by then I had changed into my civilian clothes. It was on the same road, and I was told the Indian

Army is patrolling. I wondered how they could know about my boys. No one knew except the women who were cooking for us.

My boys had taken off their uniforms and were wearing just their underwear and an Angami shawl and mixing with the villagers. I was not with them, since I had come to Chedema.

There was fighting between the Indian Army and our boys. One of our boys was killed. According to the All India Radio both sides suffered but, on our side, only one was killed. One was injured but because of a lack of medical facilities he died.

Indian soldiers were killed. One of our officers shot a seriously wounded soldier because he did not want him to suffer. The Indians captured seventeen to eighteen guns and our wireless. But they could not pick up all the arms because they had to run for their lives!

At this time General Kaito had declared martial law. Later he was assassinated in Kohima town in 1968. I do not know all the details but he wanted to be the Commander-in-Chief and was not satisfied with being the Defence Minister. But General Mowu became the Commander-in-Chief. Kaito also wanted to go to China and asked permission from the Federal Government but they did not allow him.

The second time I was going to China I was again in Mon. The Federal Government gave me a very big dao, it's the biggest dao I had ever handled in my life and it cost sixteen thousand rupees. After spending the money, I did not have enough to buy meat for the boys. I had to give them meat at least once or twice a week. So I had to go to Chedema to get more money. I went to Kohima and there Kaito met me and asked how the preparations were going. He said he was behind me and supported me. I was surprised how he knew of our programme when even the Kilonsers did not know. I said 75 per cent preparations were done. I took ten thousand rupees and went back to Mon.

The whole trip from Kohima to China cost around thirty to forty thousand rupees. In those days money had a lot of value.

When we came back from China there had been a coup and the Semas had taken over. Kughato Sukhai, brother of Kaito, resigned after a No Confidence motion was passed against his government when the peace talks failed. And then the Semas formed the Revolutionary Government of Nagaland (RGN). There was a debate on whether we should have a Parliamentary form of government or a Presidential form of government.

General Mowu was betrayed and captured on his way back from China in 1968 and he was in jail till 1976.

Our Sema brothers are the bravest and have a best record but they did the worst things. I think it is a part of God's plan to bring down those who are proud.

After I was released from jail, I went to meet Kughato and he thought I was not happy with him. But I said what has happened has happened. It's all history. From his side there was no plan to take revenge for Kaito's assassination. One day he was in Dimapur and I bought food and we ate together and he realized we must work together.

How was I arrested? Actually, when I went the second time to China we decided that some of us should return via Burma and some via Dacca. I suggested to Muivah that he would be the best person to meet Mr Phizo but Mr Muivah felt that the Pakistani authorities were not keen to allow him to meet Phizo. He felt the Pakistani authorities had more confidence in me than in him. We debated this for very long and we talked over the plan. At last it was decided that he should go via Eastern Nagaland and I was to go to Dacca and from there fly to London to meet Phizo. Pakistani government allowed me to meet Phizo in Paris. This was in 1970.

I used to write to Phizo and my letters were carried by the Kachins. But if they did not like the contents, they burnt the letters. Luckily my letters did reach him. He had information that we were going to China and he had told the Chinese ambassador in London that his people were going to China.

In Paris I asked him many questions but he did not give me all the answers. I am forgetting all the things we talked about, but we talked politics and about the possibility of negotiating with the Indian government and also about taking our case to the United Nations.

Then I came back to Pakistan and asked the Pakistani government to let me meet Laldenga, the Mizo leader, but they were reluctant. I had met Laldenga in Dacca. He had been to China but I met him in Pakistan.

I asked the Pakistani government to allow me to go to London and stay with Uncle Phizo and they refused. In Dacca, I had a good friend, an Angami missionary, and through him I contacted the American ambassador. I did this secretly without the Pakistanis knowing. At that time the Bangladesh war had started in December 1971 so I could not return to Nagaland from that side. But if I took shelter with the Americans without Pakistani approval it would not be good.

I had no idea about Bangladesh and I was a guest of Pakistan so I was waiting for them to allow us to go. I was in Dacca and curfew was imposed. On the loudspeaker it was announced that Pakistanis must surrender and leaflets were also dropped. Then we heard that the Pakistanis had surrendered.

I was in the cantonment under the Inter Service Intelligence. Of course I was staying under a different name. The Indian troops entered and I was afraid so I went to my American friend and he said if I was alone he could smuggle me out, but I said I was not alone. There were quite a few of us Nagas and it was not our culture to leave friends behind. Then we divided ourselves and some stayed with Christian leaders working among the Bangladeshis.

There were raids on the homes of the Christians and I escaped. They took me to a Bishop's house. There I met many Indian officers and I even told them my real name but they did not realize who I was. The Bishop said he could take me to Chittagong but I said that would be no use. He said he could take me to Garo hills. But at the time we had no money, no Indian currency. I had only Pakistani currency. So it was no use going anywhere without money.

Then this missionary took me to the Chairman of the Red Cross but he was not there. And then I met a British journalist. I explained my position to him. He said, 'If a soldier will not surrender, then who will surrender?' He had been in the Second World War and he had surrendered to the Germans. He said I should surrender and go with the Pakistani prisoners of war.

I and three others surrendered to Lieutenant Colonel OP Sharma of the Indian Army. They knew that the American missionary and Red Cross knew about us. That is why they did not bully us physically but of course psychologically we were tortured.

We were taken to the cantonment which was occupied by the Indian Army and there we met the officers we had met at the Bishop's house and they were surprised. We shook hands and we introduced ourselves and they never expected to find a Naga like myself. It was from that time I came to know General Krishna Rao. Later when he became Governor and he took oath, he was asking about me from SC Jamir and Jamir was surprised how I know him and I said we were battlefield friends.

Then they took us to Tripura in a plane. We went standing up because there was no seat. Then we were in a Nissan car and the soldiers kept saying China, and from that I understood they thought we were Chinese.

We were taken to Shillong and there the guard was Nepali and he cut himself while slicing a bamboo and was bleeding. I said I had the best medicine which I had brought from Kohima, and I bandaged his finger. The bleeding stopped and the wound healed. After that we became friends. When they cooked goat, he would give me the intestines and liver.

From Shillong we were brought to Guwahati and from there taken to Calcutta. We were kept in Fort William, the headquarters of Indian Army's Eastern Command, for a week. One Sikh officer of the rank of a Lieutenant Colonel told me it would be better if we spoke in Hindi. They had caught a Pakistani officer who had joined the Mukti Bahini and he had told them about me. Then we were taken to Delhi cantonment. There they kept asking me to tell them about the special training we got in China.

I told them we had not taken any special training and they beat me. They showed me a plan of special training which they recovered from my friend's notebook. I told them to ask him because I had not taken any such training. Then a General Naik came in civilian clothes. I saw his nose and recognized him from pictures in a magazine I had seen. It was Sam Manekshaw who was at the time G-O-C Eastern Army and later a Field Marshall.

The next day I asked the man, although I had no right to ask since I was a prisoner. He was surprised and asked how I knew and I said I had seen his photograph in the papers and magazine. I told Manekshaw that the man who had interrogated me the day before had been very rough and he had boxed me on my mouth. I said, 'How could he torture me in front of you?'

Then one Brigadier Major who was trained by USA special training was asked to interrogate me. His behavior was very rough. His name was some Sharma.

In Delhi wherever we went I was blindfolded. I was told Sam Manekshaw asked the Nagaland Chief Minister, Hokishe Sema, whether I should be released and he said no; and then I was taken to Tihar jail. I was also told that Kevichusa was the MP and he was asked to interview me but he refused.

General Mowu was also in Tihar and then he was moved to a special jail in Meghalaya. I was also taken to a jail in Meghalaya. The Nagaland government deputed a Khasi lawyer to argue my case. I do not remember his name.

I came out of jail on May 8, 1976 after the Shillong Accord was signed.

I read about the Shillong Accord in the newspaper while I was in the jail. In the five years I was in jail, I was never allowed to meet anyone. I read that the signatories to the Accord wanted to accept the Indian Constitution and secondly they do not want to use the word 'surrender.' They want to deposit the arms. These were the conditions before they would talk.

I thought if we wanted to accept these terms then the 16-Point Agreement would have been alright. But we had refused. The Peace Mission had also put forward a similar proposal but we refused that also even though it envisaged India making the highest political adjustment. Why should we accept the Constitution on our own volition? And why should we surrender our arms?

I was very angry. I was quarrelling with the newspaper since there was no one else. But it came to my mind—one day I will be released and then I will know the truth.

In my case the government of India could release me any time but I said I would come out only if my friends were also released. The jail was called special but there was nothing special about it. It was made with CGI sheets. Even the partitions inside the jail were made with the tin sheets. There was only one road. My friends refused to go to the court because they said they do not accept Indian courts. The court was attached to the jail.

At one time they read out the charges to the prisoners on two loudspeakers they had specially brought so that they could not say they had not heard! At that time, I was not with my friends at the Mawlai special jail but in Shillong district jail, but I was brought to Mawlai for the trial. I was brought in a jeep and I sat in front. One day they told me to sit at the back of the jeep and I refused. Then they had to bring two jeeps so that I could sit in the front in one and the commander could sit in front in the other.

When we came out of jail then we tried to find out what had happened. We could either go to Eastern Nagaland (Burma) or go to meet Phizo, in which case we would have to take an Indian passport. If we go any other way it would take a long time. For me it does not matter because I have travelled with a Chinese passport but it did not mean I had become Chinese; I had travelled with a Pakistani passport but it did not mean I had become Pakistani. So, if I travelled with an Indian passport, I would not become Indian.

We found out that in the East, Muivah and his group have condemned the Shillong Accord. But they had not condemned the NNC as a whole. There was a split in the NNC between those who supported the Accord and those who did not.

VS WUNGMATEM: COMMANDER-IN-CHIEF

General (retd) VS Wungmatem (Atem), joined the Naga Army in September 1974 and was the Chief of Naga Army from 1989 to 1999.

He has been a Kilonser holding important portfolios, and for a long time an Emissary of the Collective Leadership. He was included in the Collective Leadership in November 2015.

Atem has been involved in the peace process.

We interviewed him in Dimapur from July 5 to 7, 1999.

Testimony of VS Wungatem:

I was born in Talui[147] on April 7, 1950. At the time the Tangkhul areas were not affected by Indian Army operations.

I was born in a Christian family and we are seven brothers and one sister; I am the third son.

My earliest memories are of stories told by my parents about the Kukis. If I ever cried, my grandfather or grandmother would tell me to keep quiet so the Kukis don't hear me. I used to think even if it is a sin and wrong in the eyes of God, I want to be the one to deal with the Kukis.

My grandparents told me how the chief of Chassad village raided Tangkhul villages. The entire Ngahui village was wiped out during a Kuki raid. My grandmother told me how our people, the Tangkhuls, were persecuted by the Kukis who carried off the entire village and converted them.

My father used to tell me that the Manipur Maharaja had oppressed the Tangkhuls if they failed to pay taxes and sometimes the whole village was destroyed with the help of the British. My father used to lament over the timidity of the Tangkhuls who could not resist the oppression by the Manipur Maharaja, the British and the Kukis. I never met a Kuki as a child.

---

[147] Talui is the Tangkhul autonym of Talloi which is an exonym. Talui is the second largest township in Ukhrul district.

My grandfather told me stories about Jawaharlal Nehru's father, Motilal Nehru. My grandfather told me that at one time Motilal got angry with the British and he picked a fight with them. But the Britishers were too big for him so out of frustration he bit the ear of one Briton. I do not know whether that was true or not but my grandfather was unhappy with the British even though he was himself a lawyer.

My grandfather was one of the first students of Reverend William Pettigrew and one of the first Tangkhuls to get converted. So we grew up in the new village.[148] But since some relatives were not converted, we were in touch with the traditions and customs of the Tangkhuls.

My father was a pastor and had worked with the British as their guide and interpreter. He and Napoleon (a Tangkhul elder) knew Indian Army people but since my Uncle was in the national movement my father had to stay away.

I heard stories about Phizo and how he could do anything and be anybody and he was so clever that once when he was completely surrounded by the enemy, he asked the villagers put him in a coffin and carry him to safety. But it was only in 1960-61 when my Uncle Ramyo Zimik was arrested I came to know that he was imprisoned because he belonged to the Naga National Movement.

Ramyo Zimik was my mother's brother, my maternal uncle. We used to talk and he told me about Uncle Suisa but I did not meet Uncle Suisa because he lived in Dimapur. Tangkhuls loved Uncle Suisa and had high respect for him. My Uncle Ramyo told me that one day I would understand Uncle Suisa's proposal.

I was also influenced by my paternal uncle, my father's brother, Reverend G Mhiasiu Vashum.[149] He was a very brave person and because of that he rose to prominence. The Indian Army was obsessed with him because everywhere there was talk about Mhiasiu activities.

---

[148] Early converts to Christianity were thrown out of the old village and had to establish a new village since the Christians did not take part in traditional rites, rituals and festivals.

[149] Reverend Mhiasiu became President (Kedhage) after Scato Swu; he was very close to Phizo.

I have many friends in the Indian Army and they used to speak very highly of him and they told me that wherever Mhiasiu was seen, there was danger to the Indian Army because he would resort to firing.

Mhiasiu was not very tall, but he was not short. Physically he looked weak and even feeble. His voice was also low and he was a very humble guy. He was a prayerful person right from the 1950s and he served as an evangelist and was a pastor in the church and he joined the national movement and worked as a chaplain.

I saw Phungtha[150] only once when he came to the village but I was very young. People talked about him as if he was a demi-god. He was known as a sharp shooter. There was one Indian Army officer posted in Ukhrul subdivision called Samundra Singh, and wherever he went he tortured people and he challenged Phungtha—they called him Captain Phungtha. But during the 1962 border conflict with China he was withdrawn and Phungtha continued to ride high.

Phungtha was illiterate but he could instantly dictate songs. His songs are still popular in Ukhrul.

I do not know Phungtha's songs. I am not a good singer but in the 1980s when I was operating in the Tangkhul hills I asked one Wungcham, a singer, to sing me Phungtha's songs. Wungcham was from Sirarakhong and he along with his sister-in-law Remnu sang his songs for me.

I finished school and then I went to Shillong. I was blacklisted by the government because I took part in the national activities. I took part in the movement from Class Eight and even went to the battlefield as a village volunteer.

Volunteer in the Battlefield

Once a fight broke out between my village and Ukhrul; firing broke out near Paosaitung. This was in 1966. The firing continued for two or three months. I was there from the first day. In the middle of that,

---

[150] Captain Phungtha Horam (1920–1967) from Tusom village.

four CRPF (Central Reserve Police Force) vehicles strayed on to the road—at that time the Imphal-Ukhrul road was in a bad condition, and at the junction where there is a turn for my village the road was wider so they may have thought it was the road to Ukhrul. And so by mistake they went towards the post of the Naga Army. It was ambushed just outside the gate of the camp, so firing broke out and we heard the explosion of bombs in the dead of night. We got up and asked what was happening and at the crack of dawn national workers came to our village and asked for volunteers and asked for ammunition and rations. The Naga soldiers had no time to cook. There was a lot of smoke and so anyone could have been killed but I volunteered.

I took a new Chinese rifle which belonged to my Uncle Ramyo. The rifle was presented to him by the Manipur Maharaja Bodh Chandra. I think my Uncle had helped the Maharaja and so I stole the rifle and some ammunition.

At the time Mr Phanitphang was the Commissioner (in the underground government) and he said I was too small to volunteer but from my childhood I have been very arrogant and naughty so I did not listen and rushed to join the battle. My two older brothers were a bit timid-type, but as I said I was influenced by my Uncle Mhiasiu.

I had always admired the Naga Army. I had seen them with sweat, broken rifles and fighting for the freedom of their people without any salary. I thought, 'If these people do not deserve love, affection and respect than who does?' I used to admire them and so when the fighting broke out, I immediately went to the camp despite Phanitphang telling me not to go. This was in February 1966.

It was during that battle I had my first taste of capturing weapons and booty. I captured one rucksack containing seven hand grenades, some light pistols, ammunition and I captured three wrist watches from the vehicles of the CRPF.

The Naga camp was overrun by the Indian Army but on that day the Indian Army withdrew because of the heavy casualties. I do not know how authentic the figure is, but it is said 800 people died in that battle. But I remember that when the final assault took place the Indian Army, Assam Rifles, Manipur Rifles and CRPF combined against Naga Army. Their force must have been 5000 against the 200 or 300 Nagas. A lot of the Indian security forces were drunk, completely drunk. I could see that they could not stand properly and when they said 'Charge!' they were tottering.

The next year in 1967 the same thing happened. Firing broke out at the same camp and it went on for a month. Again the camp was overrun and again the Indian Army withdrew.

I was told to go back and finish my studies. This time the person in charge was Suisa, not Uncle Suisa but a Suisa from my own village. He was a Major in the Naga Army and he told me to go and study.

In 1968 I again volunteered but at that time entire Ukhrul was overrun by the Indian Army; only my village was saved and that was because of my father's friendship with Major General NC Rawley. At that time my village was blacklisted both by the Manipur Government and the Indian government but my father and Major General Rawley had been friends since World War II.

The ceasefire (of 1964) had practically broken down and so this fighting was going on. In my village there was an Indian Army post. I used to speak out against them. The army post commander would threaten me and I told him that it was not a sin to love one's motherland. Once there was an Assam Rifles post commander, Major Ghiani, and I asked him 'Is it a crime to love my parents?' And he said no. 'Then is it a sin to love the freedom of my mother? The British used to brand Gandhiji as a terrorist—was he not the liberator of India? And was he not called the Father of the Nation? So if I do a little service to the national workers and help them, what is wrong with it?'

The post commander would say Nagas are too small and you cannot manufacture even a matchbox, a cake or a soap, so how can you dream of being an independent nation? And I replied, 'If I can stand on my two legs and live by myself it is none of your business. Why should you forcefully occupy our land against our will?'

By the end of the 1960s there was discussion in the village about why the Nagas were going to seek help of Communist China. There was discussion that if we Christians go to Communist China, we may endanger our future instead of solving our problem. I thought, 'What is wrong if they could help us?'

Uncle Muivah

I had seen Uncle Muivah; his village is very close to our village. He used to come to our village. In 1962 right after his post-graduation he came to my village. That time he was heading towards Somrah and was enquiring after my Uncle Mhiasiu. On his return from China he came again to our house. I served him and admired him. He was such a wonderful speaker. He used to speak in the church. He would warn people not to open their mouths and talk too much and maintain their dignity.

I remember Uncle Muivah quoted from the life of Moses. Moses was brought up in the palace of the Pharaoh; he was provided the best of life, amenities, and best of education and he enjoyed life. But in his veins was the blood of the Jews and he never forgot that his people had been enslaved. So Uncle Muivah gave the example of Moses to tell the students and educated people that even if they were educated, and get good positions in service of government of India or even become Chief Minister, but you cannot change the fact we are not free.

I had vowed I would join the national movement even while in school. I was short-tempered but I valued the truth. While I was in Class Eight, I had read Gandhi's *My Experiments with Truth* so I wanted to imitate his life of truth.

Agitation in School

When I was in Class Ten I got into a fight with the teachers in my school. The teachers tried to suppress me and they expelled me from school. My village school was a private school run with grant-in-aid from the Manipur government and because of the Naga national movement the grants were suspended and the teachers did not get their salaries. The village was shouldering the burden of paying the salaries but we could not get good teachers.

I wanted to take up science, but we did not have Tangkhul teachers to teach science subjects so we had Manipuris and Mayangs.[151] For Mechanics we had to study from what we called tutor's books by ourselves and give the exams. For subjects like history, geography and English, people from our village taught us. Sometimes they did not know much and most were male bachelors and more interested in the girl students.

One day when I pointed out the mistake made by one of the teachers, he asked me whether I am challenging him and I was hot-tempered so I said 'Yes Sir, if you want.' The students separated us and I went to the Headmaster, Oja Phareng. He was not prepared to listen to me and he shouted at me. He was always critical of me because I was vocal and outspoken. I told him, 'Sir, I have come for justice not to listen to your orders. If I get out of school it will be by my choice, not by your order.'

The whole student community decided that the teacher should be punished and I made the students sign a memorandum. We boycotted the classes for three or four days. The teachers started pressurizing the parents who did not know anything, and I had the feeling that I was being unjustly punished so I started to destroy the benches and tables in the school. I could not control my temper. I even beat up my brother Sword who had come from Guwahati where he was studying. He had shouted at me and the teachers were his friends. I told him he knew nothing and he should first understand the issue. Then my Uncle Kashim came (he was later shot in 1981).[152] He was the secretary of the school. He was also an arrogant person and he asked me to confess my mistake. He started counting for me to confess and I took out a khukhri I kept under my pillow.

---

[151] A word, often derogatory, for outsiders. It has racist connotations since it is not used for the Mongoloid people.

[152] Shot allegedly by the NSCN (I-M).

My father told me, 'My son, I am pastor. Everyone in the village respects me. But now because of you I am disgraced.' He just said that.

I said I would not compromise, and if I lose I will fight and die. This went on for three or four weeks. I no longer felt like passing matriculation. I used to carry around the 12-point bore gun which we had and my father was worried because he knew I would use it. Then the Village Council intervened and so did the church and I was persuaded to go back to school and the school authorities also climbed down a bit.

This incident made a deep impression on me. Whenever I felt unjustly oppressed or victimized, I was not prepared to listen to anyone.

Another thing that made me very angry was that whenever we went by bus to Kohima, Dimapur, Imphal or even to Ukhrul or from Ukhrul to my village the Indian security forces checked us and held up the bus for two or three hours. I got angry with one havaldar and threatened him with my dao and told him I would cut him to pieces. Then one Bengali post commander spoke to me very softly and he told me the jawans are illiterate and he calmed me down.

All this was common occurrence and on top of that I was blacklisted because of my Uncle Mhiasiu so I was determined to help the national workers. So whenever they asked me to pass information or bring rations I was glad to do it.

Of course my parents supported me because they had been made to suffer unjustly and who does not love the freedom of his country?

I wanted to be a doctor. I was really interested. My maternal uncle (younger to Ramyo) was a doctor and is in the USA, and my mother's cousin sister was a doctor so I too wanted to become a doctor. I passed my medical entrance exam but the Secretary of the Medical Department, who was at the time a Kuki, intentionally misplaced them. So I went to Shillong in 1973 and continued with my BSc.

Protesting against a Hindi Film

I became active in the students' movement. In those days Naga Students' Federation was already there for many years. We had consultations among the students. I had lost interest in studies.

I was also a jealous type. I used to see most of the authors of the books and science papers were Chaudhury, Mukherjee or Mazumdar—all Indian names. I had an unreasonable prejudice against Indians. Without the blessings of the Indians will I not be able to survive? Even if I cannot get education of this kind I can live. Why should I have to read Indian authors?

Then in 1973 a Hindi film *Yeh Gulistan Hamara* came. Before the screening of the film we had read about the film in *Filmfare*. That magazine was very popular. After I read about the film, I realized it is politically motivated and I started campaigning against it. Dev Anand and Sharmila Tagore were the actors. Sharmila played a Naga girl and she was named Sekrenyi which is the name of a holy festival of the Angamis.

The actor was playing the role of a prince and he came with elephants to a Naga village. He brought sweets and biscuits to court the Naga girl and teach her writing and reading. And in the end the Indians conquered Naga country with the help of the forces. We said our country was never conquered by Hindustan.

The Naga students protested and tried to get the Khasi students to join us because the film also depicted Khasis as backward. But Khasis did not understand. On top of that, the Meghalaya government relaxed the entertainment tax also.

We Nagas submitted a memorandum to the Chief Minister of Meghalaya, Captain Williamson Sangma,[153] asking him to stop the screening of the film. I also went to the Governor, BK Nehru;[154] he

---

[153] Captain Williamson Ampang Sangma (1919-1990) was a Garo leader and founder Chief Minister of Meghalaya which was inaugurated on January 21, 1972 after a long agitation starting with a protest against imposition of the Assamese language.

[154] BK Nehru (1909-2001) was a member of the ICS and Governor of Nagaland

was the enemy number one of the Nagas: 'You think the Nagas do not deserve human attention. If you do not accept memorandum and take the necessary steps then there would be violence...' but he said he would send the police.

The Chief Minister tried to pacify us but he also failed to do anything. We met the Deputy Commissioner of Shillong. He was a Sardar. But he did not help. So we took to the streets.

We organized a silent procession on the streets and the Assam police (it was still there at the time), the CRPF and Meghalaya police and even the BSF (Border Security Force) were mobilized. Naga boys and girls were beaten up as if we were beasts. Many of us were injured. The executive members were in the front with the girls but they lathi charged us. Then we could not control our friends and the protest turned violent.

We tried not to turn violent but the students were angry and the students rushed into the Anjalee Cinema Hall and smashed it. It was the best cinema hall in Shillong; it was air-conditioned. The Nagas smashed the windows, chairs and the fans but did not set the hall on fire.

The fight between the police and students went on for three hours. We were a thousand Naga students and we snatched away the lathis of the police. They beat us badly and resorted to firing. We in the students' executive were in the middle and we got beaten by both sides. The students' union executive was arrested and we were very badly beaten up by the police. And the remarks they made against us, like 'Sala Naga kutta' (bloody Naga dog)—it hurt us. We were taken to jail.

I was Action Committee President and the Union President was an Angami, both of us were released the next day to facilitate the negotiations. We sent a telegram to the Nagaland government. Immediately the Speaker and the Education Minister promptly came. They did their best. They spoke to the Chief Minister and brought

---

from 1968 to 1973 during which time he threw out Harish Chandola, the intermediary for peace talks; also Governor of Meghalaya from 1970-73.

some financial remuneration for us because many were injured. One of my friends was run over by a police jeep and both his legs were broken. He survived. That police officer was nearly killed by the students. He came out nearly naked because his uniform was torn. Someone pulling from left, someone from right.

After that we went to Delhi to submit a memorandum to then-Prime Minister Indira Gandhi against the film. We submitted an ultimatum that if this film is not cancelled (the censorship board had already passed it) then throughout Nagaland we will boycott Hindi films.

Hindi films were already stopped in Nagaland. There were cinema halls in Dimapur, Kohima and Mokokchung. Tension was there. I also went to Delhi, met Indira Gandhi and she was kind and said, 'Nagas were no longer backward. And you have a right to feel hurt.' She said she would do her best and yes, the film was cancelled. That was in March 1973.[155]

I had lost any pleasure in studying. I knew I was blacklisted fully. I would be victimized in many ways so I went back from Shillong.

I thought the fight against *Yeh Gulistan Hamara* was a golden opportunity to lead away all the Naga students to the jungle. During the movement against the film I was campaigning for our national movement which was dying out. When the nation is suffering how can we go on enjoying in the cities, riding cars, wearing suits and neckties? Even if you go back as a doctor, engineer or MA, it will not help you.

I was actively campaigning among the students. Many volunteered. Many were ready to work. I told them that we should go back to our respective regions and work there. No one was guiding us. I went back to the Tangkhul area with seven of our Tangkhuls and the intention that if opportunity comes we can help the Federals.

---

[155] The film continued to be shown except that there was a notice at the beginning: 'The customs depicted in this film, folk dances, dress etc have no parallel with any of the tribes in Nagaland.' Also, the lyrics of the offensive song 'Mera Naam Ao' were altered.

We went back and met our leaders and told them we were ready. Mr Muivah had already come back and he said, 'Ash! Atem, you are one of the very few science students,' but I said, 'No! I will not go back. I have taken a decision and I am not going back for studies.' We discussed what we should do and what strategy we should follow. Three of the students were told to work among the Tangkhul students and I took them to Imphal. The leader was Jacob from Sikhiphung near Litan. He was made President of the Tangkhul Students Union, Imphal.

I shuttled between the Naga Army camp and the overground. My Uncle was in the Kohima area and others were in Tangkhul area. At that time my Uncle Ramyo and Uncle Muivah were on good terms. Mr Yangmaso Shaiza was also there. There were on good terms and I met them.

Ramyo Zimik

To be very frank, right from the beginning I could smell there was something wrong with my Uncle Ramyo. He had lost hope or confidence in the power of the people's movement. He had lost sight of our political objective and was not in touch with the people. He had confidence only on his own statesmanship and he did not encourage the Naga Army.

My Uncle would scold the brave commander of the Naga Army after he came back from an operation with trophies because any action by the Naga Army always invited a massive counter-operation and the Indian Army would start combing operations—sometimes an entire Division was involved. In those days it was so difficult. They would start at Song Song, the Mao village, and up to the Burma border in Ukhrul area. The whole jungle! And so it was difficult to find shelter for the Naga Army. That is why my Uncle felt like he did. But unless and until we have beaten the Indian Army in many battlefields, it was no use in negotiating because the enemy would take the upper hand. So negotiation would amount to accepting the terms and conditions of the government of India. I was not happy with my Uncle.

At one point of time I sincerely had a discussion with my Uncle Ramyo. I asked him, 'Why, uncle, instead of saying thank you to the Army Commander and telling him he has done well, you scold them? They have risked their lives and come back as heroes. They deserve honour and decoration. Instead you are scolding them? Uncle, this is not correct.' He would reply, 'You are too young, you will not understand.'

So, I was drawn closer to Mr Muivah because he was more militant and more forthright.

Uncle Phizo

Sometime in 1973 (sic) the Tatar Hoho had adopted a resolution asking Uncle Phizo to go to Beijing because his thirteen-year stay in London had not helped the national movement in any way. He was losing touch with his people.

Whatever instruction, suggestions, advice he had given to the Federal Authority were not always warranted by the situation in the country. And whenever the federal government of Nagaland refused to follow his instruction or take his advice, he tended to misunderstand. Uncle Phizo I think was entirely dependent on the feedback provided by his family members. But his family members were not involved in the national movement, except of course Uncle Kevi Yalley, his brother. So there was a growing difference between the home country and the NNC office in London. That is why the federal Hoho asked him to go to Beijing, because staying in Beijing it would not be difficult for the federal authorities to reach him from India.

In those days, it was so difficult for our people to have correspondence with London. So they wanted him to be in Beijing. He wrote back saying, 'Let Beijing invite me.' It was unimaginable.

The home authorities wanted Uncle Muivah to lead a delegation to talk to Mr Phizo. As I said there had been a slight misunderstanding between the federal authorities and Uncle Phizo. How could Phizo, who had been going with a begging bowl to sympathetic people, expect

China to extend an invitation to him when he had displeased them in so many ways?

In fact the Chinese authorities were not happy with Phizo. When I went to China, they openly told us that 'Your President speaks ill of China.' In 1962 Uncle Phizo had called China the aggressor and said he promised to the government of India that he would make 40,000 Naga guerillas join Indian Army to drive away the Communist Chinese aggression.[v] In 1959-60 he submitted a case before the International Court of Justice against China: 'Chinese Communist monster for killing 50,000 Tibetans.'

Yes, I have sympathy for the Tibetans. I used to tell the Chinese that they may not be happy but you cannot say Tibet is a part and parcel of China. I said hundreds or thousands of Tibetans have fled their country because they cannot reconcile themselves to the forcible occupation of their country. They told me I did not know the history. I replied that I may not know the history but the fact that the Tibetans had fled their country in such large numbers was sufficient enough for me to understand their sentiment and their stand.

So, Mr Muivah did not want to lead a delegation to Phizo. He had smelled something because he knew some of the home authorities were ready to negotiate with the Indians, because they were shaken and full of fear due to Indian Army operations. So Mr Muivah was not sure of their stability. The situation was so bad because the national forces were being beaten everywhere so it was unimaginable to start political dialogue at that stage especially now that our Vice President Imkongmeren Ao (1900-1979) was ill and on his deathbed. He could not be expected to properly assess the situation. He told the home authorities that if they were shaken in their resolve, then they would be blocking the wind for the future generations.

The people said they were not shaken and had been fighting for twenty to thirty years. They said they would swear in the name of God that we will stick to our word. Then Mr Muivah said, 'Alright, if you stand by the decision of our fathers that Nagas will be independent of any outsider and this decision was affirmed by the plebiscite of 1951 and reaffirmed in 1965, and you say you are not shaken at all and you are as strong as ever today, then we should affirm our stand at a National Assembly.'

In August 1974 I was asked to go to China.

We left our battalion headquarters on August 14 after celebrating Independence Day. We began at night and reached the general headquarters UN Seti on September 1. The National Assembly was held on September 4. The National Assembly had to be held because Mr Muivah was leaving for China.

National Assembly

A National Assembly can be convened only by the President, Vice President or General Secretary or all three together. The Assembly was attended by 3000-4000 people. Almost all national leaders were there but Uncle Ramyo could not come because of the situation. It was a big gathering. I do not know how the people managed to come despite the terrible situation.

The National Assembly venue was called UN Seti; it was held near the Iganumi and Lazami between Angami and Sema areas in the jungles on the confluence of two rivers, tributaries of Doyang river.

I do not know what UN Seti means, it must be a word from Chakhesang or Angami language so I rang up Reverend Nuh but he said the word was a spiritual revelation.

The platform was erected and it was very beautiful in the middle of the jungle. We could not even cut a small tree because of the sound. And we could not talk loudly, only in whispers, because of the presence of the Indian Army.

The National Assembly was held on September 4, 1974. I am not sure but it was code-named 'Man of Iron'. The resolution re-affirmed the national stand.[156]

---

[156] Resolutions passed in the Naga National Assembly held at UN Seti on 4 September 1974:

1. The unalterable historical facts stand that Nagaland had never been a part

Taxing the Public

Yes I used to weave moorahs (cane stools) and riphan (low cane dining table) and baskets for carrying loads. That was the only means for self-sustenance. I had been taught by elders so I was compelled to do that. That was the only way I could get money to buy rice. That was in 1973 and 1974.

But by 1974 the situation was better. I repeatedly told my elders we are fighting for our country, for our people. The people must sustain us. If they do not understand us yesterday, they must understand us today. We must go to the people.

Till that time, we did not take tax. Till that time, our elders were so much alienated from the people. Because the forces against the movement were so strong—by elders I mean people like my Uncle Mhiasiu. In 1973 they made a budget for the Tangkhul Battalion and the whole region was forty thousand rupees but they could not raise even twenty thousand rupees. People were afraid of giving rice or money because of the Indian Army. The atrocities were all pervasive. They did not have the courage to give rice. The earlier NNC system was virtually not working.

---

of India nor any other country, and a compromise of rights would do wrong to Nagaland, therefore the national assembly hereby reaffirmed that, the sovereignty of Nagaland is not negotiable. It is in the matter of relationships between India and Nagaland that a negotiated settlement is possible.

2. Nagaland is dedicated to our Lord Jesus Christ. Whereas the evil forces are also active in human affairs, the objective of 'Nagaland for Christ' could be attained when the political freedom of the country is securely safeguarded. In pursuance of the truth, the sovereignty of Nagaland shall be defended at all costs.

3. Therefore, any attempt to revise the national policy, or any attempt to deviate from the national right and stand, or any to compromise with the opposing forces in the issue of national rights will constitute a betrayal to the honour of the people and an act of treason to the state.

4. The national assembly hereby resolved that a Council of Nagaland Churches be established, covering all Naga-inhabited areas.

5. The National Assembly unanimously re-elected Mr Thuingaleng Muivah to be General Secretary of the NNC for another term.

I sold the baskets to sympathetic individuals but secretly at the dead of night. Our boys would go to the people and give them five or six moorahs and ask them to give whatever they could in return, money or rice. We had to accept whatever they gave. Some people were generous and gave us a tin of rice, others would give us vegetables like potatoes, others without taking the baskets would give us a packet of dry fish and with this we would eat.

But in 1974 I said no, I won't do this. I will not make moorahs. I will go to the people and speak to them. I was then just a private soldier, just a student leader. But my elders treated me very well, they always entertained my views and they listened to me.

We must go to the people. Yes, there are enemies within our people. Therefore we must clean up. Without that it is not possible to work. All the intelligence agents and informers must be cleaned up. I said whether the informer or intelligence agent is my father or brother, whoever it is must be removed if they refuse to repent. I think my village was the first to take that step. I struck my village first.

There was one informer I knew when I was in college. I told him, 'My brother, why do you do like this? The national workers are not working for themselves but for the whole people without asking for any remuneration. Instead of helping them or trying to understand them you are working against them.' I told him if you want to report what I am telling you, go ahead. He did not try to understand. The informers were paid.

I visited all the villages in the western area. I told the villagers openly that they must pay, and contribute rice. Every village was asked to pay twenty rupees per house but no one was taking it seriously. So I was compelled to arrest the village elders of my village and detain them in the jungles; for four days, I think in July 1974. And then the same in Somdal, Mr Muivah's village. I told the villagers to sort both the things; to get rid of the informers and start making the contributions of money and rice to the movement.

We covered many villages. Sometimes the villagers were thrashed. Mr Muivah scolded them like anything. And after this we collected around one lakh sixty thousand rupees in cash within three months. We got sufficient rice.

This money was not only for our China trip but for the Naga Army. So in that way we collected substantially and the people were also ready to fall in line with us. The elders of five or six villages were beaten up by me. And I dealt with four or five informers before leaving for China. They spoke ill of me because I was young but I did not care. But my actions were authorized by the government. After that the situation improved then things cooled down and people did not open their mouth against the national workers.

Before my departure for China when I was actively preparing for the trip, I nearly was caught in an ambush of the Indian Army. I escaped by the grace of God but I got hurt in my hand. So when I was told to go to China I was there for the National Assembly.

Taking Leave of my Family

I had told my parents that I am joining the national movement and got their blessings. I did not care for my two elder brothers. I told them they did not understand many things even if they were good at studies. One of them, Sword, tried for Indian Civil Service and I told him he must not join Indian Police Service and if he joined the Indian Administrative Service (IAS) don't be an Indian officer. Even if you become an IAS officer you must remain Naga.

At the time I left for China, Sword was working as a lecturer at DM College in Imphal. He had got into police service twice but I told him not to take it.[157]

My parents were very understanding even though we had many differences on many subjects. At the time of my joining my father said, 'Because of your sins do not allow any Naga to suffer, like Achan's sins

---

[157] Sword Vashum retired from Audit and Accounts service in 2009 and has stood for elections; he was first a candidate of the Naga People's Front and then joined the BJP in 2015.

which led to suffering of Israelites.'[158] That is what he told me and gave me his blessing. That blessing is still fresh and an unfailing source of strength.

Going to China

In September 1974 I set off for China.

It must have been the third or fourth trip. The first had gone in 1966 and reached in 1967, then the second batch went in 1968 and came back in 1969. That was the trip led by General Mowu and on their return they were betrayed by the Revolutionary Government and sent to jail.

And then the third trip was led by Colonel Vedai, a Chakhesang—which was in 1972 and came back in 1973. We sent many groups to China in 1967 and many did not make it. There was the trip led by Angam but he was arrested by the Burmese Army as they were crossing the Chindwin. He was handed over to the Indian authorities and later released from Imphal jail.

Then the troops led by Dusoi did not reach and some of them were headhunted on the way and the rest scattered. Several times the Kachins did not allow the Nagas to go past them so they could not reach China. For instance, Colonel Taka and his group were not allowed to proceed to China by the Kachins.

And we were going in September 1974. That was the fourth trip. A few months later the fifth trip went in December. Despite knowing

---

[158] Joshua 7 and the story of Achan: The chapter recounts how Achan stole some of the spoils of the battle of Jericho, even after God had explicitly commanded the Israelites not to do so. This disobedience causes a military defeat in Israel's next battle, at the city of Ai. God tells Joshua about the problem that caused the defeat, and Achan is confronted and confesses his sin. As a result, a punishment is in order. 'Fair enough,' we think, as there is no sin that does not have consequences—either in this life or the next. But the thing about this story is the nature of Achan's punishment, because it doesn't just involve him—his whole family (even his animals!) bear the consequence of Achan's sin. https://www.riverviewbaptist.net/pastor-joels-blog/304-achan-and-the-consequences-of-sin.

about all these setbacks, when we left for China in September of 1974 our mood was buoyant.

On the way to China

After the National Assembly on September 4, 1974, we left for China two days later. Before leaving, for four days we were living on half-ration. There were fifteen of us in one Mess. We had what Angamis called 'galho' or porridge. So we cooked only six cups of rice with vegetables and meat for the fifteen of us.

On the sixth we left without eating any food. Because it is Thanksgiving Day for us, a commemoration of the ceasefire on September 6, 1964, so we observe it as Thanksgiving Day.

We reached the 16th Battalion Headquarter and then on the eighth we started marching. We were about 200 of us and we had forty Point 303 rifles. From Tangkhuls we were twenty-five or twenty-six and between us we had just seven rifles. Because the General Secretary was with us so we were a little better-armed. So whole day we were walking.

The first day we did not carry rations; we were told we would get them the next day. But entire Nagaland was placed under curfew so we could not get rations from any village. We tried to push through. Had the General Secretary not been that tough with the troops, every mission would have failed. He said, 'Man does not live by bread alone. Eat any leaves or any fruits.' He does not brook any arguments so we kept going and passed the whole of the Sema area; no food, nothing, then Lotha area. Then we came to Doyang river, swollen with flood waters so we could not cross. We managed to cross small, small rivers. I was not afraid. I did not care.

For six or seven days we were held up. We tried to go across by raft but one Chakhesang drowned. Yes, one floated down and came up alive at Golaghat. Bamboo raft does not sink and he held on tight. But he took away five or six rucksacks with him. Then three volunteers tried to swim across with a nylon rope but they were swept away.

Then we looked for a wider space and thirteen of our men tried crossing thinking that place would not be deep; six or seven of them were washed away and seven survived. The current was very strong. We thought of storming the suspension bridge which was guarded by the CRPF. We were watching it. We organized volunteers but the CRPF men deserted so we crossed by the suspension bridge and we went through the Ao area. We were there for two or three days and we met Uncle Imkongmeren.

Imkongmeren was always carried on the back of a man; he could not walk. General Secretary took us with him to his camp to get his blessings. He had given his last words. And then we proceeded without incident.

We did not go by the footpaths made by the villagers; instead we cut through the thick jungle and most of the time we took off our boots to avoid leaving footprints and most of the time we marched at night. It took a lot of time and energy. We crossed the Dikhu river and arrived in the Chang area.

In Chang area we suffered. We were ambushed three times by different forces, the Nagaland Armed Police and the Indian Army. And in the Phom area again we suffered.

Because of the tough conditions and starvation many deserted the Naga Army; some had swollen feet, and if you do not get proper food you get many ailments. In Phom area we faced a surprise attack by the Indian Army. One of our Tangkhul non-commissioned officers died there. We Tangkhuls were all young and marching in the front so we suffered the most, but we were braver than most. We were organized by battalions and we were ten. Whenever there was danger Tangkhul Battalion was asked to go in front. Only five (including Hanshi, Markson, Mr Muivah and me) are alive from that group.

In Phom area we lost thirteen or fourteen of our men. Some were killed and some captured. It was because of the surprise element. They were killed in the firings but somehow we managed to escape. The next day we were hunted from all directions. We were fired upon from the left and we were fired upon the right and from the rear. We came to the

Dikhu river and we surveyed some bridges but they were all guarded. But we had an exciting experience.

On one side was the Dikhu river in full spate and impossible to cross. And in front of us was an open field. The General Secretary asked us: what should we do?

I said we should jump into the river instead of giving ourselves over to the Indian Army. And everyone said yes! Then the General Secretary said to Colonel Pamrei, 'Okay! Go!'

Pamrei was such a brave commander and he never cared for his own self. He was tireless and always in the lead. He was never found in the middle. When the situation was bad in the rear he would be at the back; when the situation was bad in the front he would be in the front. He would go to help his men. So when he was told to jump into the river he jumped first. And after taking about eight or nine steps he found the water came only up to the waist.

Others had rushed to the open field; the Indian Army started shelling us with two-inch mortars and light machine guns. And then everyone ran into the water. Colonel Pamrei said we Tangkhuls should stay back and give covering fire so the others could cross the river. So we gave covering fire and the Indian Army started firing but we returned fire and they ran back into the jungle. They did not try and cross the river.

All these days we had been walking barefoot without food. The jungle was so big and so vast we could not see the sky and we had not come in contact with anyone. We found ourselves going round and round and we were all hungry. Finally we found ourselves in a Konyak village near the border. There some of our people ate the wild beans. That nearly finished us!

During the British days the Chins had planted the beans and so when you burn them, they extract sulfur. And from the sulfur they made gun powder. The Konyaks planted these wild beans for fermentation to make wine or rice beer. They used very little. They also made gun powder.

The Konyaks had their own indigenous way of making gunpowder, nothing to do with the Chinese gun powder. The Konyaks put their pigs together in one place so they could collect the soil in which the pigs urinated. Then they would mix the soil with water and filter it and boil it till they extracted a yellow whitish powder and this was mixed with charcoal and the ashes of the wild beans which they burnt. All you need is a nitrate, sulfur and charcoal. It was indigenous to the Konyaks.

We tasted the beans which we found in the jhum fields and they were sweet. The taste is like other beans. But they made everyone sick with severe stomach ache and everyone collapsed. We were very sick and had to stay there for three days. The villagers could not come out they were under curfew so no one could come out. We took whatever we could lay our hands on and we left money in the huts; some two hundred rupees, three hundred rupees and sometimes five hundred rupees. We ate whatever we found—fruits, maize and ginger but no salt or chillies.

In a way it was good for us to stay there because we had swollen feet and infection in our bodies with lice. So, it was good we were held up. We could clean our clothes. But after that we had to cross the border because the Indian Army knew we were there, they just did not know our exact location.

It was getting more and more dangerous, a life-and-death situation. So one night we left. And in the morning we started smelling fire and smoke coming from the Indian Army camps.

We divided ourselves into two groups. The General Secretary told Pamrei to lead. We were also losing hope because we were told by the Holy Spirit that we would have to cross seven enemy lines. And exactly, we had to cross the enemy seven times.

Fire was burning in several places where the Indian Army had camped but the army was not there. They had gone to the fields to comb the area. Ash! It was the work of the Holy Spirit. We climbed up Veda peak, the highest in the Mon area. We went to the top and prayed and then we went to the Burmese side.

The next morning we arrived in a village. It was a wild village. And General Secretary warned us that it was in this village they had tried to headhunt the Naga Army in 1966. Everyone must be very alert.

We went into the village and got maize. But that also, instead of helping us satisfy our hunger, it nearly killed us. It was after three months of starvation: September, October and November. It was November 17 when we reached that village; in fact for us Tangkhuls it was longer because we started from our Tangkhul area on August 14 so we had not eaten since then.

After long starvation when we got the maize we did not know how to cook it. For rice we use a wooden stick to stir the rice, it helps to soften it, but for maize if we use spoon it will not cook. It will produce starch and become hard. It should be boiled and then dried. But we ate half-cooked maize and it generated gas.

After long starvation we should not eat much; little by little we should increase the quantity. We took pork and started eating that with half-cooked maize.

After three days one of our boys died. First he had gas, then loose motions and dysentery and then finished. He died.

Kachins

After that there was no major incident and we reached the Kachin area. When we reached there, we found the Kachin minds had been completely poisoned by Indian agents. The Indian agents went through Rangoon to Myitkyina.

We passed a big village with about 900 households. It is south of Myitkyina. The Indian agents infiltrated that village, most of them cultivators. The Kachins started bringing up all kinds of irrelevant and irrational points.

We reached in the first week of December but they did not allow us to pass till April. They held us up. The Kachins demanded that we concede that the whole of Eastern Nagaland is theirs. Khaplang was with them. He may have agreed. The Kachin Army is very oppressive and they treat their own people as if they are an occupation force.

The Kachins provided us with rice for which we paid. Only rice, nothing more than that. But now the question was not of food but the mental torture of not being able to proceed to China. It was unbearable. It was unbearable but the General Secretary did not lose his temper. He talked to them and convinced them to let us go.

We spent five months in the jungles. We spent the time repenting for our mistakes and praying to God, and also we had political classes. Our General Secretary never missed an opportunity to take political classes. Sometimes we discussed military strategies comparing the Burmese Army which was better-trained than the Indian Army but because of the terrain could not get reinforcements.

We discussed the treatment of the captured. For instance, we captured a Commander of the Burmese Army. I interrogated him. He gave us all information. But when warriors fight, one is bound to win and one to lose. We should treat them with honour but he was just eliminated after three or four days. It was unjust and criminal. They said he was trying to escape but he is a prisoner and has every right to try to escape. So we discussed that we should use his capture as an opportunity and try to hand him back through international channels.

As for Indian Army, the whole Naga area was surrounded by them. The Naga people were so scared and did not dare to do anything against the security forces.

Sometimes we discussed political matters such as the matter of boundary with the Kachins; they were demanding 32 per cent of the share of arms and money we got from China.

Mr Muivah told the Kachin Foreign Minister who was commander of the second brigade and controlled the jade mines, that the boundary had been made by the British and inherited by India and Burma. Neither the Kachins nor the Nagas were consulted, and both Nagas and Kachins are fighting against the Indian and Burmese States.

So, Mr Muivah told the Kachins that as true revolutionaries we should decide the matter between ourselves and not be bound by what imperialists had done. Mr Muivah said we could sit together around the table and solve the boundary issue.

Somehow the General Secretary persuaded them to let us go without conceding to their demands. We started for China and we reached the border. It was very cold and covered with snow.

China At Last

I remember it was on April 29 1975 we reached. That day I shed tears—we had walked some 600 kms and taken eight months to reach; most of that time we had nothing to eat and it had been cold. It had been a difficult time. Later, my father told me he had a nightmare on that day.

I was in China till January of 1976.

The Chinese were very good, very kind and very nice to us. But the first memory was bitter when we asked them for a place to worship and that too according to our convenience. In the initial stage they laughed at us and spoke derisively about religion. Some of the officials said if God is Almighty then why does he not help you? Why come all the way to China for help, just ask God and he will wipe out whole of India and give you independence. He may be trying to test us to see our temper. But it was irresponsible of him to speak to us like that.

Some of them made fun of us when we had worship service and when we prayed. They would ask whether we got news of someone's death if they saw us cry in church and if we sang they asked the meaning of the song.

Some of them discussed so-called scientific socialism. Instead of losing our faith it strengthened us in our faith. For instance, one day one of the officers told me that there is no such thing as eternal God. It is impossible. He said everything changes and the whole universe is changing. Nothing can remain the same forever. He gave an example of a stone; if we weigh it here and then take the same stone to Beijing the stone will weigh different because of the atmospheric pressure will be different and the gravitation force is different so the weight will be different. Everything changes.

The Chinese also discussed the theory of evolution. I have read Dr Darwin's *Origin of Species* but he also said there is God. He said according to the Bible the world is just 6000 years old but in fact it is millions of years old. I told him Darwin had said the origin of species could be by God. Also it was not within the power of the human being to understand God.

We had discussions one-to-one and sometimes in groups. But what I learnt from the Chinese was that they were very hard-working people and they respected dignity of labour. They practiced Chairman Mao's teaching about simple living and high thinking. That is why I used to tell our people that we read the Bible, but the communists practice its teachings. In the Bible it says he who does not work must not eat.

Maximum number of people loitering in the streets are in Nagaland and they are 95 per cent Christian. In Nagaland so many people sit idle and they say, 'Idle brain is the devil's workshop.' I was in China for more than two years but I never saw Chinese stealing anything.

A Theft

One day I had a startling experience. There was a woman working in the Tengchong military hospital where I was also working. She had two children. She was working in the kitchen of the surgical ward and it was alleged she had been stealing. But that evening she stole a lump of ginger and a piece of meat. Of course she had taken it without permission. She was caught.

The next day she was paraded with a placard around her neck and a dunce cap on her head, in front of everyone in the military hospital, about 2000 officers and men were there. They called her a reactionary, anti-people and anti-China. I cannot remember all the words. She was made to confess in every corner of the city just because she had taken a lump of ginger and a piece of meat.

In the military hospital, my surgical ward was growing thousands of apples, some falling down. But no one ever picked a single apple. Seeing this I was amazed. People were so poor but when we go to the market commodities were so cheap. One li is 450 grams. One li or half kg of pork would cost 15 fen!

One Chinese yuan is divided into 10 jiao and one jiao is divided into 10 fen. It's like half kg of pork for 15 paise!

One day we were told the General Lee who was in charge of Kunming City and had ten Divisions under him would be visiting us. We were all excited. We were elated. When he came he was wearing ordinary shoes, and his shirt had been patched up, like his pants. So simple. Ash! I could not help laughing.

In our hospital there was no chowkidar, no sweeper, no gardener. Doctors, senior or junior, and nurses did all the work, including washing, cleaning and sweeping. At first I suffered. I was put on duty to be a watchman and I rang the bell; and some did weeding in the field within our hospital compound. Some mowed the grass. Ash! In this respect everyone should learn from the Chinese. Their work culture is very systematic and disciplined. I remember one Colonel was in charge of our group. When everyone has gone to have a nap in the afternoon he would be cleaning the latrines. In the garden he would work meticulously. He must have been seventy years of age and he was so hard-working.

The Training

For the whole year we were engaged in military training. And we had political classes. We were taught who is a friend and who is an enemy. We thought the Chinese have bitter hatred for Indians and in those days, you know almost all of us took every Indian to be our enemy. But Chinese taught us in their political education classes that Indian people are not your enemy. It is the government and the work of few leaders; the general Indian masses of people are your neighbours and can be your friends and help you, that is what the Chinese taught us. It was a very positive attitude. I think they have changed our attitude to a great extent.

In military training we were taught Mao Tse-tung's teachings about swift attack and swift retreat; when we should attack and when we should not. Random attack is not helpful. It is a waste of energy and resource. Then they taught us the need for proper planning and proper co-coordinating. It was really exciting because it was not only teaching in class but practical classes in the high mountainous areas. It was exciting and thrilling.

I did not volunteer for medical training but in a way was compelled to do it. I liked it but I was also compelled. There was no one to take care of the sick and especially the injured; casualty training. Yes I also did surgery, sometimes more than forty a month. I assisted the chief surgeon even in appendicitis.

Back home I did surgeries but I did not have anesthesia so I could do minor ones with local anesthesia or spinal cord anesthesia. In Burma I had a box of surgical equipment.

Shillong Accord

While we were there in China, we heard of the Shillong Accord and we had sleepless nights. It was not totally unexpected because we had seen leaders had been shaken by Indian Army. We decided to go back and condemn the Accord and send a delegation to meet Uncle Phizo.

Isak Swu had gone to London in 1960s, not this time. We waited for some directions from Phizo: some word, some advice. The Home Government had collapsed but he kept mum. Till his death he never said anything.

We had to go back.

The Khiamniungan, Konyak and Leinong areas were intact. We sent our men to contact people in every region to see who was still supporting us. Colonel Pamrei went to Ukhrul. He organized our people and sent some of them to give us the information.

I remained in Eastern Nagaland. The area was in total darkness because there were no Christians. There were no schools. We set up churches and somehow we managed to convert some of them. Since I was the only medical officer, I went from village to village to mobilize people.

Uncle Muivah injured

We had to deal with the Burmese Army. We ran over many of the
Burmese Army camps. They tried to run over our headquarters at
Lahe and Uncle Muivah got injured. He went against the wishes of
the commander and he did not listen to them. The commander tried
to dissuade him from fighting; they told Uncle Muivah, 'Sir you are
not an army officer you are our leader and only one left, and if anything
happens to you where will we go? You cannot die,' but he shouted at
them. He said, 'Naga Army men are falling like leaves so if they can die
then why not me?' Muivah also must taste the bitterness of that.

The fighting with the Burmese Army was going on for a month
after our first encounter in which we wiped out the first force of 76
Burmese.

The Burmese Army sent a big reinforcement but that was also pre-
empted by our force. We allowed the men to pass our ambush but
at the back thirty-three mules were carrying their ammunition and
rations. I just captured all the mules without firing a shot and held
them up. I unloaded the mules and I told our boys to carry the load
and kill all the mules.

But we could not carry the load! It was too heavy. We called the
villagers and 150 villagers came but they too could not carry the arms
and ammunition. Ash! I realized my foolishness in killing the mules. I
could have led them safely but I killed them. Again the Burmese force
was forced to retreat. We got 20,000 rounds of ammunition. They
were also robbed of their rations.

So when we contacted over the wireless, Uncle Muivah must have
thought we were surrounded and he tried to relieve us from the back.
He was very confident of taking over the Burmese headquarters because
he thought most of the force must have left. That was also true.

But it was well-fortified camp and Nagas had knocked off nine
bunkers. Only one remained. And trying to take that last bunker five
of our boys died. The Burmese had rocket launchers and three or four
gunners were knocked out. They were fighting hand-to-hand with

hand grenades. Uncle Muivah was hit by one bullet in the chest but it did not pass through but he was knocked down. Our boys thought he had died, but he was angry and said, 'No I am not dead.'

After that he got up and charged again and he was shot and then he was down. They took him to a safe area and then they sent a message to me. It was already one and a half days after his injury. They should have sent the message to me immediately.

I was at a distance of six days journey and the moment I got the message I marched day and night and reached within three days but already he had been injured for five days.

One bullet was in the knee and one in the tendon so he could not climb. I saw his mettle then. I told him he needs to take rest for fifteen days but after that time he started practicing walking. He said we must go back to our headquarters. 'How are you going to walk when you cannot even go for latrine? How can you dream of going to the Council Headquarters which will take not less than six days?' He said, 'No! We cannot allow the enemy to take initiative.' I said we will make some kind of stretcher but he said no, that would start rumours like wildfire and that will gladden the enemy. So he got a big stick and we started.

We started at five thirty in the morning and walked till five thirty in the evening; ten hours every day. And he would cover the same as others. He gnashed his teeth but carried on till we reached the council headquarters. This must be around March 1976.

We had a hectic time to mobilize people and reorganize the government and take the mandate of the people.

National Assembly 1976

A National Assembly was called in August 1976 at a Khiamniungan village called Supao. The Konyaks, the Khiamniungan, the Leinong and Panmei tribes came; national workers from the west also came including the Tangkhul, the Aos, the Angami and many from Chakhesang also came. The Zeliangrong had recently joined us and they also came.

The National Assembly condemned the Shillong Accord. And the NNC was re-organized. We reaffirmed the leadership of President Phizo. And also we re-elected him as the President of the Federal government and the NNC. That was the only way to ensure the safety of the national workers. You see the federal workers used to function independent of the NNC which was against the Constitution.

It was during this time Chairman Mao died and also other Chinese leaders. We had a meeting in his memory but there was nothing extraordinarily memorable about the meeting. We had a condolence meeting and we prayed for him and Mr Muivah told us stories about Chairman Mao.

We also passed a resolution that President Phizo must condemn the Shillong Accord and Zashie's government. We also heard rumours that the Accordists were going to meet Phizo. We also passed a resolution that if Phizo met with the Accordists it would amount to collusion.

From 1977 we decided to go again to China, partly to communicate with the Chinese what has happened and also for treatment for Uncle. That time we stayed in China the whole year. It was during this time the Chinese were fighting amongst themselves against the Gang of Four. But People's Liberation Army remained intact.

The Cultural Revolution, according to my humble understanding, was a necessity but it was misused. The so-called Red Guards backed by Chairman Mao were very arrogant. They committed excesses. I saw that with my own eyes.

I did not go to Peking because I was learning surgery. We returned in February 1978.

Attack by the Burmese Army

The Burmese Army came to attack our headquarters in 1978. It was the funniest time for us. General Secretary Muivah was supposed to get married at that time. We had brought buffaloes and pigs and everything. We had captured rations from the Burmese. The Burmese were coming in full strength, there must have been 300 of them, so we attacked them from the back and front and the Burmese forces were disorganized. My own group infiltrated deep inside the Burmese. I asked for reinforcements to crush them.

The General Secretary got agitated and he said he must go. The others begged him not to go but he said, 'When my soldiers are laying down their lives in the battlefield, am I supposed to go and sleep with a woman? No! Give away all the pigs and buffaloes to the soldiers.' He came to our group. I said, 'Uncle, how can you come here?' He said, 'I will stand at a distance.' We started chasing the Burmese from village to village. Uncle Muivah said he will be at a distance but he came almost three days journey from the headquarters. Firing took place thirteen to fourteen times.

We returned to the headquarters.

Martial Law: August 1978 to May 1979

The NNC was going to have a meeting in Khonoma by the signatories to the Shillong Accord. The Shillong Accordists said Phizo had not condemned the Accord so if we condemned the Accord, we were condemning Phizo.

We had two headquarters in Eastern Nagaland: the Sector Headquarters and the General Headquarters which was on the Indian border. Our meeting was held at the Sector Headquarters.

We had to hold a meeting to clarify this confusion. Instead of holding at the General Headquarters the meeting was postponed and shifted to Sector Headquarters. Mayanger[159] had already come to the Eastern Nagaland while we were in China in 1977. He was one of the people who went to Lhasa[160] and was chased away by the Chinese.

---

[159] Mayanger Ao was later killed in December 1979, allegedly by supporters of Isak-Muivah-Khaplang.

[160] A group of NNC had tried to reach China via Nepal. They reached Lhasa in September 1976 and stayed till April 1977; they were not given any support or military training by the Chinese.

So, all the leaders proceeded to the Sector Headquarters but three officers stayed back. They were in charge of the arms and ammunition. One was a Chakhesang and two were Angami. While everyone was away these people looted all the arms and ammunition. You see our big, big guns and ammunition were kept in a hidden place which we called UG (underground) and they took it all from there. We did not suspect in the least.

The persons who were operating the wireless were their boys so they were freely operating between the General and Sector HQ. The one in the General Headquarters was an Angami boy and the one at the Sector HQ was an Ao. I was the medical officer as well in charge of the defence of the General Headquarters.

So cleverly on August 30 at 5.30 p.m. Mayanger and his men made the final assault and arrested all the national leaders who were at the Sector Headquarters and placed them under detention. And martial law was declared the same day and it would last till May 1979.

I was at the General Headquarters.

I was summoned by the martial law authorities. After the two leaders I was next in the line of the firing although I was then merely a Lieutenant. I was sore in the eye of my senior commanders because I identified with the soldiers, led them and looked after them.

I was told to reach the Sector Headquarters. As soon as I reached the Sector Headquarters, I was disarmed at gunpoint. That really hurt me. Then they asked me to give them accounts for the medicines and warned me if I spoke ill of the Shillong Accord I would face death.

I could not meet Uncle but I could communicate with him through some of the boys. The junior people were not disarmed. In my short stay at the Sector HQ I discussed the counter coup with our boys. And we were all for it. Then we asked for permission to get blessings from our two leaders.

The two Uncles said we know if you will do a counter coup you will win but many innocents will be killed. So you have to bear it and we have to be patient. So we were told not to stage a counter coup and we waited till the end of martial law in May 1979.

While Uncle Muivah was under detention he was writing the manifesto for the NSCN. I went to the council meeting. The meeting went on for one month discussing the manifesto. For the first week there was discussion about the aftermath of the purge, and the law and order situation. I was not there at the meeting the entire time because I was preparing to strike against the Accordists.

I confided to Colonel Nuri that I would be striking, and I confided to Brigadier Thungbo, the C-in-C, two days before because I was in danger.[161]

NSCN is Born

The National Socialist Council of Nagaland (NSCN) was born in January 1980.

Right after that I was involved in military operations. And Assam was burning[162] and I said we should exploit the situation. Till then the Nagas were fighting against mighty India single-handedly. So I said Assamese are rising up and they are disillusioned and dissatisfied with their association with India. So we have to properly motivate them. So I volunteered that I would go to Assam and speak to the people.

And in Imphal valley, the Meiteis were also rising up. There was PLA, PREPAK. This was the right time to reach out to these organizations.

By the end of 1980 our Collective Leadership asked me to take a group of operation party[163] to Tangkhul areas so that our people could

---

[161] Sixteen NNC leaders were eliminated in the counter-coup after Khaplang was briefly elected President of the NNC at the National Assembly held on March 12, 1979. It was alleged that these leaders were all pro-Shillong Accord. Some Naga nationalists against Isak Swu and Thuingaleng Muivah have argued that the conflict was really over rejection of the new socialist ideology espoused by Isak and Muivah. The National Assembly was called by the Naga Army while Isak and Muivah were still in detention; the latter challenged the power of the army to call a National Assembly.

[162] Assam agitation against illegal migrants began in 1979 till 1985; the United Liberation Front of Assam was also formed in 1979 with the objective of fighting for independence of Assam.

[163] A 'group of operation party' means an armed group.

be properly mobilized and at the same time help Mr Raising who has recently taken over as Chairman of the Tangkhul Region. He wanted me to be sent as commander of the region because I knew the area and was familiar with the elders.

In January 1981 I came to South Nagaland. I had to mobilize people, and also do some operations against the Burmese and the agents and informers; this included my father's first cousin Uncle Khashim Vashum. My Uncle Khashim was a 'chaar-sau-bees' (a cheat) businessman. He had been cheating the national workers since 1960s. He had been taking money from national workers to buy weapons but he neither bought the weapons nor did he return the money.

He had been given several warnings. I myself was there when he confessed but he did not pay back the money. So I was directed to eliminate him and that night in Ukhrul four or five other persons were also eliminated. This included a cousin, Stanhope Muivah, whose wife was related to me and she used to come to me to speak on behalf of her husband.

We do not hold a trial because before eliminating a person, we warn them two or three times and at that time they have ample opportunity to defend themselves. No, there is no possibility of us being wrongly informed except when there is a war-like situation and Indian Army is conducting operations and our people are mingling with them.

Ambush in Namthilok

By the end of 1981, I thought we had sufficiently reached out to the people by political preaching and there was a need for some sort of action. When political preaching is not backed by guns it loses its impact. By now I was around thirty-three years old.

I got intelligence information that the Sikh Light Infantry 21 Regiment was being trained for three months. The first batch had arrived between Christmas of 1981 and New Year of 1982.

I started preparing seriously for the operation from the first week of February 1982. At first we did not make a camp and lived in the village but then I took my boys into the big jungle and made a camp. We started preparing ourselves by fasting and prayers.

The government of India was trying to solve the Naga problem by crushing Nagas by military force and we wanted to show them that they could not do that.

I disclosed my programme to only six of us. Mr Angelus also wanted to come; he insisted even though he was not in the army. I told him if anything happens to him, I cannot take responsibility but he insisted on coming anyway.

First we thought of attacking an Indian Army camp which had been harassing the villagers. We went to see the camp on February 16. It was some 15 to 20 kms from Mahadev. We could have destroyed the camp but we would not be able to retreat. So I called it off. We went back to our camp.

On the eighteenth, we came down near the Namthilok area. I kept my team in the Mapicha jungle nearby. I asked a villager for a Tangkhul haora (shawl). I sat there on the side of the road. I was observing the speed of the vehicles. Through spiritual revelation I had got the ideal place for the ambush. As I was sitting on the side of the road, I saw three or four army vehicles were heading that way. I saw the place where the speed of the vehicles comes down to almost 10 to 15 kms per hour and that is the spot. That is where the vehicles came with speed but they slowed down at that spot.

I tried to find something for natural self-defence, like trees or rocks where we could take shelter, but there was none. There was only grass. Since it was a revelation nothing could harm us. I went back to my boys and I told them we will move out at night, make some improvised explosives to mine the road. At exactly eleven at night we moved out and we reached the spot at twelve. We dug up the road and I planted the mines. I distributed the positions to everyone. At around two a.m. there was no movement except for the bullock carts in which the Meiteis brought firewood from the hills in February.

I told the boys they could rest till five in the morning. But then there was heavy rain and I was worried about the fresh mud. We were completely drenched and could not sleep. We were casually sitting as if we were some hired labour. Then some BSF vehicles came down. There were only two. I had told the boys we should wait for at least three vehicles. One of our boys was in a position from where he could see from both sides; vehicles coming up from Imphal to Ukhrul and those going down from Ukhrul to Imphal.

So he shouted, 'Two Ukhrul,' I said no. I said leave it. That was around seven thirty. Then another vehicle came, this time Manipur Rifles. The sentry shouted 'One Imphal.' I said leave that also. Then buses from Ukhrul to Imphal were passing. People saw me and I was completely drenched. Since it was winter, I was wearing an Indian Army coat. I was drying myself sitting in the sun.

At nine the sentry shouted, 'Four Imphal.' I said ready, take biscuits and fire. I told Angelus to press the remote at exactly one-yard distance but he pressed it earlier. The explosive was so powerful.

I saw the army jawans trying to jump down but they could not. They looked like pregnant women trying to come down. I was giving orders to my people, 'Shoot the people, shoot the people.' Within ten minutes it was over.

I saw some jawans hiding under the vehicle. I heard them shouting: 'Pakar, pakar,' and I tossed hand grenades and they tried jumping into the nalas and the moment they jumped the mines started exploding. I told them raise your hands but they were just saying 'Ram, Ram.'

I told my boys to give me covering fire and I jumped down and got a light machine gun and fired ten-fifteen rounds. Then there was silence. It took us fifteen minutes to take all the weapons since we were only six of us. I told everyone to take one weapon each but take as much of ammunition as you can carry. Because our boys were carrying their own weapons also; they cannot carry more.

We went up 150 metres up the hills and prayed and gave thanks to God. We took about twenty-five minutes from the time of the firing to going up the hill. Since we had not slept the previous night, I told the boys to rest till four in the evening. I could see the Indian Army sending reinforcements but I knew they would not come to the top of the hill.

Our attack had been at nine thirty in the morning and the reinforcements arrived at around twelve thirty in the afternoon.

We walked towards Imphal and reached Mapou village area and passed some Kuki villages and we were in our uniforms and walking quite openly. We did this to mislead the Indian Army. At one point when we came to a bridge, I told my boys to take off their jungle boots and then we applied perfume we were carrying on our feet. This was to keep away the sniffer dogs the Indian Army would use. Then I sprayed chilli powder so that if the dogs came they would get the chilli in their nostril and refuse to co-operate with their masters.

Then we changed direction and instead of moving south we went back north towards Ukhrul. We walked 30 to 40 kms that night and reached a village in Senapati district at around five in the morning. Then Angelus and I took a bus to Senapati and from there to Imphal and there we met our friends and they told us that the PLA (Meitei group) had struck at Namthilok. I laughed.

At that point they had still not heard of the NSCN.

I travelled through Silchar and Dibrugarh and met the Assamese leaders and finally I reached the Council Headquarters in April first week and reported everything.

So Namthilok operation was carried out of political necessity to mobilize our people effectively and also give a signal to the government of India that Nagas were not finished by Shillong Accord.

Ambush and Arrest

In 1983 I was in the West and I was called by the Council Headquarters in Eastern Nagaland. On the way I was ambushed and trapped by an entire battalion. I tried my level best to escape because I thought I should not be caught alive in their hands but I was injured and I was in fact praying in my mind to God that allow a bullet to hit me, but the bullet hit me on my knee and I fell and they were pounding me till I fell unconscious.

I was taken to the military camp. I was captured around 4 p.m.

and I recovered consciousness the next night. It was the 28th Madras Regiment that captured me in Mon.

I was very badly tortured. Throughout the period of interrogation, I was hung upside down for almost forty days. I was beaten with batons and rifle butts. I was given the roller treatment and my spine was broken so I could not run away. A bucket of water was put through my nostril every day and I was subject to electric shocks. My ribs, my teeth and jaw were also broken.

During interrogation I was asked where I had kept the weapons I captured at Namthilok, who gave us shelter, who gave us rations and who gave us money. I repeatedly told them I have nothing to say. It is a national struggle and it is a people's movement. And we ask the Village Authority to collect money for us. I was interrogated by army officers. I said there was not a sin to love one's motherland and fight for freedom. It is never a crime to serve the people.

They tortured and tortured and tortured me but I gave them no information. At last they produced me before the Deputy Commissioner who was the Magistrate. He was one RS Pandey. I spat on his face. He knew I had been arrested and yet had not insisted on my production.[164] I was brought in a stretcher since I could not walk. He sent me to police custody and then the Nagaland government handed me over to the Manipur Government. No, I did not have any lawyer. And they did not take me to any hospital in Mon. They did not have the courage to take me to a hospital; but they brought doctors to the lock-up.

The Manipur government put twenty-three cases against me and I was in jail for several years.

In 1986 Major General PN Kukreti came to see me in jail. He had brought a cake. I said I was not hungry and if I needed a cake, I would

---

[164] Under the law the army is supposed to hand over the prisoner to the police without delay and the police is supposed to produce the prisoner before the Magistrate within twenty-four hours. This provision in law is supposed to protect the prisoner from torture.

ask my wife to get me one. But if he wanted me to taste it, he should eat it first so I was sure it was not poisoned.

We had a quarrel. He told me that India would never be broken and I told him I had read Indian history and it had never been a united country and it was a creation of the British. It was they who had united it and made it the size it was. I told him his soldiers were no match for our NSCN soldiers.

I was finally released without any trial because they could not prove any case. They took eight thousand rupees as surety. But I was arrested again and in 1989 I escaped from jail in Nagaland.

NSCN after Khaplang

In 1991 we had no money and no weapons[165] and I set a target to my boys to capture weapons and money. Our government (the GPRN) did not give me a single rupee. I just went to a friend and borrowed ten thousand rupees and then we started working. We managed to capture money from banks and I had sixty lakhs and I gave the boys ten lakh rupees to boost their morale and told them never to beg anyone for anything. I built up the army again from scratch.

Yes, we have feelings against the Meiteis, the Kukis and Indians. The Burmese government is giving a false hope of a federal solution. We want freedom so we can stand up on our own.

NH: What is your vision for a future of Naga society?

Atem: I must be very honest: I did not dream much about what the future Naga society would be like.

---

[165] This was just after the fratricidal war between Khaplang and Isak-Muivah which left the latter totally decimated.

KHULU EUSTAR: THE SOLDIER-WIFE

Eustar (Khulu) Chishi Swu joined the Naga national movement in August 1971. She was among the first batch of women to go to China. She married Isak Chishi Swu, the Chairman of the NSCN.

Eustar is a member of the National Socialist Women's Organization of Nagalim (NSWON). She has been elected as the President of the Council of Nagalim Churches in February 2017.

She was married to Isak Chishi Swu for forty years and they had five sons and a daughter. Eustar can speak several Naga languages, including Angami, Chakhesang and Sema languages.

This interview was conducted on April 30, 1998 and May 4, 1998 in Bangkok. Isak Chishi Swu translated from Sumi Naga to English.

Testimony of Eustar Chishi Swu:

About my childhood? Thank you so much for asking that, I have always wanted an opportunity to express about our problem to the outsiders but we rarely get that opportunity.

I have one brother and two sisters; I am the second-eldest.

I had a very bad start in life because when I was just five or six years old, the enemy[166] occupied our village. And they started harassing people and my mother happened to be the chairperson of the village women's organization. Our village is called Lazami and it is the biggest in Sema area.

Lazami has got historical background. Because it was one of the biggest villages in Sema area, so it used to control a number of villages around it and many minor tribes had to pay tax to our village. And that is why it became a target of the British government who set up an Assam Rifles post in that village. At one time when I was young there were three posts, now there are none.

---

[166] The NSCN always refer to the Indian Armed Forces as the 'enemy' among themselves.

So the Indian Army occupied the post and they would chase people and arrest people so we did not have any happiness or peace of mind.

My mother used to go around the village to collect rice and vegetables or the villagers would bring those things to our house. Then my mother would cook for the national workers and send it into the jungles. My father would stand outside as a guard while my mother cooked inside. Many people would come to our house to eat and some would take package into the jungle. I was very young so I do not remember for how many people she cooked.

I saw the Indian Army harass our people. I saw them put people inside sacks and bind the sack and then throw it into their vehicle; sometimes people were thrown into a poisonous bush; my mother used to treat them in the jungle and sleep in the jungle and come back next morning.

The entire male population used to be taken to Pughoboto, a small town near our village. My father would also be taken. The womenfolk would gather up the children and sit in the sun. That is what I remember.[167]

So in such an atmosphere I could not go to school or get a proper education. I studied up to Class Six only and in 1971 I joined the movement so I could help the nation one way or the other.

I started working in the office of the Sema Regional President of the women's organization. The president was also from the same village. The regional women's organization President was called Lhovili; at that time the President of the whole Naga women's federation was Shitoli, she was also Sema. Shitoli was the longest serving woman president and she went to jail also. She also got a bullet injury when their camp was attacked. In those days whenever the camp was attacked, the women used to stay and load the guns in the jungles.

---

[167] The practice of keeping villagers grouped together, whether in their own village or re-located to another place is part of the counter-insurgency operations of the Indian Army in North East India causing immense suffering to the people.

Well in those days among the Semas we didn't have any doctor. But when we were in the eastern side it was a miracle that the Spirit of the Lord showed many medicinal herbs to our Oracle. Dr Unice was shown many kinds of herbal medicine by the spirit.

Sometimes she had intense pain and then she was told by the Spirit to apply a particular plant and she applied and she was cured. In this way practically she learnt and then she trained many people, how to use plants and also to research in the jungle. We learnt about bark of trees, fruits and leaves. We came to know that God has made so many wonderful things.

We discovered that some plants Japanese don't eat but the Chinese eat, and some that the Chinese eat we don't eat. And so we learnt that so many plants can be eaten. The Chinese also taught us a lot about medicinal plants.

Soon after I joined, we had a big meeting to elect the Tatars and President of the Federation. The meeting lasted three months near Tullo river, one of the biggest rivers in our area. I sat in the meeting and also collected clothes for the national workers. At that meeting which took place from July to September Zashie Huire was elected as the President of the Federal Government of Nagaland. It was at that meeting a group of fifty people were chosen to go to China.

The Indian Army surrounded us and took position and our people also took position. Isak and his group had just returned from China so we had a lot of arms. The villagers told the Indian Army that we had peculiar arms and a single bullet from a Chinese pistol can destroy the entire army. We also had a rocket launcher. The Indian Army was frightened. So no one fired from either side and the meeting continued.

It was rainy season but we had made shelter for everyone with thatch and plastic.

My work was to maintain office files. We had records of how much money was collected and how much ration had been distributed and also how many people had surrendered. That time many had joined the Revolutionary Government [168] and they were surrendering.

In 1974 we had another big federal meeting and a spiritual programme. It was at another site. This meeting also lasted three months and we were kept busy because we had to serve tea and cook the meals and arrange for clothes. My brother was arrested at this time and very badly beaten.

Soon after that meeting I left for China along with Mr Muivah's group. We were nine women. Before we started God told us that we will face many hardships on the way, and we will not get rations and the enemy will continue to chase us and we may not even have clothes to wear and some of us will not reach. All this was foretold by God through the Spirit speaking through the chaplain Kipfelhou who was a Chakhesang.

We started from UN Seti camp on September 4, 1974. Before that we had spent three days at another camp nearby. We had to prepare the clothes and rations.

The very first day of our march the enemy attacked us. At that time we were not given any weapons. Only experienced fighters had weapons.

The enemy had occupied all the villages and we could not get rations. We didn't get rice from any side. We were near a village near the Doyang river in a dark bungalow. The river was in full spate so we could not cross it. So we held back and had to stay for a week. We found a hut in a paddy field where the villager had kept paddy. We put some money for him and took it.

But in order to husk the paddy and take out the rice we had no mortar or pestle, so we dug a hole in the earth and put a hat in there which acted as a mortar and then we pounded the rice with a stick and stored the rice in a basket we made from bamboo.

---

[168] The Revolutionary Government was formed by Sema leaders on November 2, 1968 and it finally surrendered to the Indian State in 1973 when it was merged into the Border Security Force.

We also made a raft with bamboo and tried to cross the river—one person fell into the river and floated down. But he did not die, he was still on some bamboo and he floated to Assam.

So, since we could not cross at that point, we went to another point to cross the river. We tried to cross by holding sticks with seven people holding on to one stick. The level of water become higher and higher as the river became very deep and the water came over their bodies. One person was taken away by river and he died. The other six knew how to swim so they could reach the other shore.

We cooked the rice and put some meat inside and wrapped it in leaves and threw it to the other side for the six of them.

So with difficulty we made a kind of bridge with sticks across the river and then we could all cross to the other side and we came to a Sema village but we did not stop and continued to an Ao village where the women's society cooked for us and brought us food, and we continued past Mokokchung town and kept walking through the night. It was raining so there were so many leeches. In the morning we came across a hut in the jungle and the ladies were asked to rest there. When we took off our shoes there were so many leaches but they were dead. They had sucked out our blood.

Then we came to the Dikhu river which was one of the biggest obstacles for us. There we asked some Chang villagers for rations but instead of bringing the rations, some bad people among the Chang attacked us.

We were also being chased by the Indian Army so we were told to walk by the stream so the footprints were washed away; as a result we had to walk barefoot. But since there were so many of us, even that did not help because the water got muddy and the enemy could detect our movement. In the enemy attack many of us were killed and many scattered and we lost them. There was no question of getting any rations and we marched barefoot for security reasons. It was terrible. Our legs were swollen and got hurt with the stones and thorns.

We went completely without food for forty-seven days. We were carrying some salt and we boiled the leaves with salt and ate it. We could not hunt because the shots would have alerted the enemy.

Then we came to Lao Naga village, the biggest in the Konyak[169] area. They are different from us. They had body tattoos and had long, long daos and even menfolk had long hair. So they were quite peculiar. They still did headhunting. This was the first time I had seen Konyaks.

At the time we were passing one of the biggest Konyak villages and they had not yet converted to Christianity and it was a very tough village responsible for the death of many, including Naga Army which had passed through the village previously. So when we were passing by we prayed to God to keep us safe. God told us the Konyak will not be harsh with us and we would be safe and so we met the village elders and Konyak national workers.

Some of the Konyaks spoke Nagamese. When they saw us women, they felt pity because we had not eaten. The menfolk went up to the village and we were scared but then the womenfolk came and welcomed us. So because of the presence of women the situation changed.

We had not eaten but the only thing they had was maize and millet. They grow very little rice which is only for the babies. So we ate the maize and many of our men started suffering from stomach trouble. But by grace of God, women did not suffer. All of us were alright.

Then we came to the Chindwin river. One woman drowned in the process of crossing the river. The Burmese Army ambushed us at that spot and we lost one lady and a Captain of the Naga Army.

When we reached the Kachin area, they would not allow us to pass because there was a dispute between the Kachin and us over the ownership of the land. The Kachin said we could not go ahead unless we gave in writing that we renounce our claim over the area. Because of that dispute we were detained there for one month. They even separated us from our leaders. So we started fasting and praying and finally God heard our prayers and we could proceed forward to go to China.

---

[169] Law or Lao Naga are often included as Konyaks. They are in Sagaing Division near Lahe township in Naga-inhabited area of Burma.

We were so excited and we got ready and started marching to
China at midnight. So when we reached the China border they
came out and welcomed us and they had brought horses and asked
the ladies to ride them. But the ladies preferred to walk, so the
sick people were carried on the horses. We reached Molong in the
morning around nine o' clock.

We looked like sub human beings with our torn clothes and so
run-down in comparison to the Chinese who were so healthy and
well-dressed. So we were ashamed to meet them. Before our arrival the
Chinese had arranged everything for us, from clothes to toilet stuff for
each person. All our old clothing was thrown away and we dressed in
the new clothing. They had prepared food for us and they were so kind
to us. So we forgot all our hardships and trouble on the way and we
were so much excited.

After changing into new clothes and having a hot meal we were
taken in a truck to the training camp. We reached at around seven in
the morning the next day, but we slept almost all the way.

At the training camp everything was kept ready for us. We were
told to give our full attention on the use of different arms. At first we
were worried because we had not used arms before but once we started
firing all fear disappeared. We felt no fear at all.

So we were given pistol, submachine guns, light machine guns,
hand grenades and semi-automatic rifles. I tried the submachine gun
and liked it. We women were better than the men in target shooting.
The Chinese told us that when they had competition among the men
and women of their People's Liberation Army, their women were
better.

We were given different kinds of training from target shooting,
to first aid, and how to improvise if a person is wounded, even how
to operate and do acupuncture, and how to give injections. All the
women were given medical, political and military training.

When we had political discussions, they used to put questions to us.
They asked why we had come to China. So we told them our stories,
how the Indian Army ill-treated the women and how they burnt down

our homes and destroyed the crops. We told them about the suffering of our people.

They had all kinds of interpreters: English interpreter were mostly used, and Hindi interpreter and Assamese also. The Chinese told us the stories of how the Chinese people had suffered in the hands of their landlords, the Emperor and Japanese occupational forces; and how they had liberated themselves from all three.

They told us that when the Nagas first came they did not bring the womenfolk but this time we womenfolk also joined the campaign so now the Nagas will win the goal, because woman are half the nation. Both men and women must fight together for the nation.

The Chinese also told us about the sufferings of the Chinese women before their Revolution. When the husband died the Chinese women were not allowed to marry again, they were just kept as servant for the whole life and also when the women gave birth they were not allowed to breastfeed their babies because the milk was taken by the landlords or the Emperor. That was the kind of miserable life they lived. They told us also about how the feet of Chinese women were bound so the beautiful women could not escape. Even today there are old women with bound feet.

Whenever a Chinese woman spoke out about women's rights, the men would say that she is just like a hen who does not take care of her chicks and makes noise. They said the only duty of women was to make bread and wine. But when Mao became Chairman, he freed the women from their bondage and set them free and they were given liberty.

Chairman Mao started teaching woman to participate in all the activities and they were allowed to drive vehicles, become managers in the factories and were treated equal to men.

The Chinese women said they were very sad to hear about how the Indian Army was mistreating us and they said all the Chinese women were behind us.

We were also shown films. We saw films about how Chinese women had bombed the enemy. So after watching the films we thought the

Chinese women in the films can do it so we Naga women can also do it. We got confidence in ourselves like that.

We were in China when we got news of the Shillong Accord and by then we had five months training which was very short. But then it has taken us eight months to get to China. The Chinese authorities told us that since our government had failed, we should go back home.

Our leaders were also very unhappy. So anyway we were compelled to go back. But our leaders took a wise decision to stand up for the national rights so when we returned to Eastern Nagaland, and crossed the Chindwin on the night on 6 January 1976, we reached Khiamniungan area and we set up our camp there.

Well, the training given by the Chinese and their attitude towards us was very good. They did their best to give us the best ideas, education and political lessons. They supported us wholeheartedly. Even the arms they gave us—they told us we should take what was necessary for us and they were very careful in giving also. They told us why some weapon would be useful while something may not be useful. We even discussed with them the idea of carrying the weapons by horse so that we could carry more weapons. But the road conditions did not permit even use of mules because we have to cross the high mountain ranges at the border. And if we went by the plains the enemy could easily attack us. They said they could not allow us to parachute across the international boundary. They were very strict on this.

Before we started our march back, the Chinese had examined our route in detail: the part where there are snakes and leeches, where it is likely to rain and how steep would be the slope we will climb, and how thick the forest will be and whether there will be any bamboo, and finally the kind of ration we should carry with us. They also taught us how to deal with the public and they were experts in this.

The Chinese sent their men personally to examine the route. They told us that the Burmese Premier U Nu had given the Chinese some

Kachin land without the permission of the Kachin people so they were angry.[170]

We stayed in the Khiamniungan area for about two years. I had my first baby in that camp. We set up a caretaker government. The women's organization worked in full swing, we went to every village and we established one mission centre, one ME school and three or four lower primary schools. When our work was in full swing, the Shillong Accordists came and joined us. They said they had come to support us but they staged a coup and imposed martial law.

They arrested my husband and I was left there with around ten others. I was pregnant with our second child. Our second son was born in Khaplang area.

My husband and Mr Muivah were kept under house arrest. The treatment given to them was very bad. They were not even given porters to help carry their luggage when they were shifted from place to place. But I did not know then. I was separated from my husband and I did not know whether he was dead or alive.

So now I had two children to look after and the Khaplang people had been told not to help the families of the two leaders. The Khaplang people and Shillong Accord people guarded all the villages. So in the jungle we were driven from one place to another, and we had to build our huts with bamboo and leaves. The moment we had finished building the huts we had to move.

---

[170] The border dispute between newly-independent Burma and China over a large stretch of un-demarcated border was a longstanding one, dating back to the time of British colonial rule. China had never accepted the boundary. The Chinese claimed that the three Kachin villages of Hpimaw, Gawlam and Kamfang, lying east of the divide, belonged to them. The claim was based on the fact that the villages were once Chinese trading posts. U Nu, anxious to appease, was all for handing over the villages, but the Kachin state government was adamant about not giving up any Kachin land. In fact, the Hpimaw issue, as it was commonly referred to, became one of the chief reasons why a group of Kachin university students decided to take up arms against the central government and form the Kachin Independence Army (KIA) in 1961.

There were ten of us, including four men. I had a pistol but I hid it and we had one gun. I managed to write one letter to my husband but I had to write it in Nagamese. I wrote quotes from the Bible and below I managed to tell him that we had a son.

I quoted from John: 'You were of the world; it would love you as its own. Instead, the world hates you, because you are not of the world, but I have chosen you out of the world.'

Khaplang was playing a double game. In a way he protected my husband and Mr Muivah; on the other hand, he moved them near the Indian border from where the Indian Army could have got them.

I and the nine people with me were also moved from place to place and they did not help us carry the load or my babies. I used to carry one baby at the back and one in my arms and pray to God. The first was one year old. I had no other person to depend on, no reliable person so I relied only on God and hoped He would answer my prayers. I was praying all the time to God, asking him to send some prophet or spiritual person to see me.

Finally, Brigadier Vedai found me in the jungle. He and his wife who was a spiritual lady accompanied by one more person found me. He had also been arrested but was released so he had come in search of me. At that time we were in the thick forest near the Arunachal border with big, thick jungle and wild animals. So I lived in the camp with him in the jungle. All of us prayed seriously and I felt my spirit reviving. I felt no fear in me.

I decided to go, do-or-die: I will just go in search of my husband and General Secretary.

I started off and reached one village where Khaplang people and Shillong Accord people were staying. We were stopped. They told me it was no use trying to meet the two because they had 'become public' (sic) and no longer held any authority. I questioned the Major and asked what he thought was the mistake the two leaders had made, and if they had made mistakes then they must be charge-sheeted and put on trial. I told them they could not detain the two just like that. In fact, the two had united the Nagas when the enemy had tried to divide the Naga people.

So the Major became very angry. I told him that even if they die what they have sown would come up afterward. And if they are to sacrifice for the truth, I don't care.

I was told we had to go a long way to meet my husband and it would be a lot of trouble for me to carry my pistol so I should leave it behind.

Luckily one Captain returned from western side and he joined with us. We took eighteen days to reach the place where my husband and Mr Muivah had been detained. We had to go through the forest but we reached. I was reunited with my husband.

Then my husband, Mr Muivah and Khaplang had a meeting. I was not there but it went on for nine days. They discussed the plan to eliminate the Shillong Accord supporters and finally after nine days they came to some agreement. Then they signed an agreement that they were no longer in Khaplang's custody and then they had three months of more discussions and finally they decided to form the National Socialist Council of Nagaland or the NSCN.

We in the women's organization started working again and we went from village to village to teach the villagers better ways to weave and cultivate. We opened schools and the General Secretary's wife was the Headmistress of one school. We opened fifteen schools and three Mission Centres.

National Socialist Women's Organization of Nagalim (NSWON)

We from the NSCN decided that we should tell younger women about the kind of suffering and hardships we faced when we went from Nagaland to China.

Regarding scientific socialism, we did not understand. We only teach women to play their role in society and how to contribute to their families.

Our main concern is to understand the basic stand of the nation and teach every woman member of our organization that they should never surrender their rights to other people. They should never imitate others' culture. They have to maintain their own basic values. We also discuss about equal rights between men and women within the Naga society.

One of the points we explain is that women's rights were very much suppressed under the traditional Naga religion. And so there were many kinds of taboos against woman. For instance, women were not even allowed to touch the dao because it was believed that if a woman touches a dao then it became powerless. The same was true for the spear and all the weapons.

But slowly our society has started changing and people don't believe in such things after Christianity came. So looking at the present Naga movement, now the women also participate in the alee command, we call it foreign campaign. So women also marched along with the men up to East Pakistan and they went to China also. And whatever circumstance or condition or trouble or hardship the men face on the way, women also face the same thing. And so we say we can also do what men can do. So we express our rights as women.

So, in the past society the Naga women were very much suppressed but after the national movement started, the women's organization was established in every village, every range in the region and also at the federal level.

We in the NSCN are trying our best to uplift the position of woman to be equal with men, so that women's participation in the movement is equal. During the NNC time there were no women Tatars (Members of Parliament) or Kilonsers (Ministers). But now we have a Deputy Minister who is a woman in our Parliament. At present we do not have women who are qualified enough or with experience to be Ministers.

Naga women don't have rights to land; since this is traditional, it is not easy to touch. So we would like to lay down the foundation of our organization first and then slowly discuss the necessary problems. From our religious point of view, according to our Christian doctrine, woman must respect her husband and there is no doctrine that woman can be the head of the house. But that does not mean it is right for man to suppress woman all the time.

AVULI: THE BAREFOOT DOCTOR

Avuli Chishi Swu is a symbol of a patriotic Naga woman. She joined the Naga Army at the age of twenty-one in September of 1974.

After joining the Naga Army, she went to China twice—once in December 1974 and the next time in 1976. She underwent both arms and medical training.

After serving eight years in the Naga Army she retired in 1997 and then she took up a civil position in the NSWON where she worked in the capacity of Vice Chairperson from 1984 to 1989 and served as Chairperson from 1990 to 1991. She is a mother of five children.

Presently she is serving as a Steering Committee member of the highest decision-making body in the NSCN.

We interviewed Avuli on June 28, 1999 at Dimapur. She spoke in Nagamese and translation was done by Phungthing Shimrah.

Testimony of Avuli:

My name is Avuli and I am from Shesulimi village. We are nine siblings; two brothers and the rest sisters. I am the eldest.

When I was growing up, I saw the Indian Army operations. My village was burnt down nine times. I saw the time when it was burnt down the last time. It must have been around 1959-60 when I was still a child. I remember some people ran away to Zunheboto but my father took us into the jungle. I remember a small six or seven-month-old baby being carried by its sister because the parents were both killed. We could not go to our fields because of the operation.

The Indian Army did operations on southern Sema areas where the Naga Army had supporters. Both my parents were serving them. When my mother was serving the Naga Army, she sometimes did not have time to look after her own children.

All the villagers were involved in the movement. They all supported the Naga movement. The Naga Army would come late at night when everyone was sleeping and wake up my father and ask to deliver a letter.

At that time there was no vehicle so and he had to walk miles and miles to deliver the letter. So every now and then my father would go off to deliver a letter.

Once when my father was going to deliver a letter, he was caught in the middle of an ambush by the Indian Army but luckily he escaped and he told us his story.

On one occasion my mother was picked up by the Indian Army because she was the chairwoman of the village women's wing. At the time my brother was just a ten-month-old baby. But because of her baby she was allowed to return.

The whole village was made to suffer. They were not allowed to eat for two or three days and even children and old folk were not allowed to have food. I saw people hung upside down and smoked chillies were put under their noses. They were beaten very badly and then some of them were imprisoned for nine or ten years. They came back to the village after nine years.

During the Indian Army operations no one could go to school because they would come and group us, or carry out their operations. I began schooling only in 1964 when the situation was a little better because of the ceasefire.

I studied up to Class Five. Then I went to Pughoboto and did Bible Studies but I did not complete the course because I went to the jungles and joined the Naga Army. Many people from my village went for arms to East Pakistan. Although the national workers were underground, everyone in the village knew who had gone for arms training because the whole village was involved in the movement.

I remember the date on which I went to the jungles; it was on September 21, 1974. I was twenty-one years old.

I was inspired to join the Naga Army because of one incident. One day the whole village was rounded up and my mother was kept separate. The children were crying and the Indian Army gave the women half an hour to cook for their families. How my mother managed to cook in such a short time I do not know. My mother called my father and told him to eat but the food was so hot he could not eat it. The Indian

Army came and my mother put the rice in the pot and tried to close the door so my father could eat peacefully, but they shouted, 'Jaldi, jaldi,' (hurry up) and beat my father with the rifle butt.

Seeing the way they treated my father I was very angry. Then I thought: if only I was a boy, I would take revenge. I wanted to bite the Indian Army officer. It was from that time I decided I would join the Naga Army.

Even though I had no education I wanted to serve the nation and work for the people and I joined the Naga Army in 1974. Our village was surrounded by the Indian Army during a combing operation because they heard the Naga Army members were present in the village. The Indian Army called out the names of all the villagers to ensure their presence in the village. They did this exercise repeatedly. Two times they called out my name and I was present but during the third round of checking I had disappeared!

I left with my woman friend, Viqhali. We both went to the school headmaster and told him that we were leaving. We asked him to pray for us and we left the village on September 20 and reached the Naga Army camp the next day.

On September 21, 1974 we reached the camp and I met Isak Chishi Swu. The chairwoman of the Sumi area came and took us. We stayed in the camp till December.

We were the second batch going to China under the leadership of the Chairman Isak. The first batch of women went with General Secretary in September 1974 and we were the second batch of the same year. Eustar, the Chairman's wife (they were still not married then) had gone with the first batch.

The chaplain, Kipfelhou, prophesized that the Indian government would try to capture all the Naga Army. Before we left, he said the Spirit has said the Naga nation was very different from other nations and India cannot win with force of arms. Those who have faith in God will reach but many will die on the way. Only those who are strong and courageous will reach but those who smoke or have tobacco or want to eat will not reach China. He also prophesized

that the Federal Government was over. This was at the camp called
UN Seti.

On December 10, 1974 we started our march to China. When we
started, we were ten girls but some died on the way and some were
arrested and only five of us finally reached China.

Many of those who could not come with us, either because they
were sick or some other reason, were captured by Shillong Accordists
after we left.

The prophecy with us was a Chakhesang woman, Vechisalu. She
said that we should go through East Nagaland. The prophecy guided
the route. The chaplain went with the General Secretary two months
earlier. By the time we left, word had already reached the Indians that
one batch has left for China so they had already started the operations.

We reached the Ao areas but we could not go further as we could
hear the Indian Army blowing whistles. We did not sleep the entire
night and we climbed up the hill and climbed down but found
ourselves in the same place. We had gone round. Three times we did
that and the sun came up. We did not understand how that happened.

In the morning one man from the village brought us rice. One of our
members fired by mistake and the man was hit in the leg. They could
not take him back to the village and they could not give him medical
treatment so they kept him on the road. Everywhere the Indian Army
was present. We could not move. We were without food or water for
two or three days and we were exhausted by the time we moved out. I
do not even remember the name of the village.

In another place an Angami Major said he would get rice from the
village but when he went to the village, he found the Indian Army and
they arrested him. There was an exchange of fire but by God's grace we
were not hurt.

We could not cook because the Indian Army was all over so we just
had a little rice we were carrying with some leaves from the jungle. Even
in that time there was firing and one of our men was killed in a firing.

We could not take off our shoes and we had to keep walking with
our shoes even through small rivers. The skin of our feet peeled off

and our feet were swollen and bleeding. In the Ao area we had four encounters with the Indian Army.

I was not carrying any weapon because I had no training. I was not carrying very much when we were going, but coming back it was very tiring because we were carrying weapons.

There is one incident I remember. We had not eaten for eight days and we crossed a rivulet and came upon a jhum field with tapioca. We were so hungry we ate it on empty stomach and we all got diarrhea. Even the Chairman got loose motions and he was so weak he was carried by one of the men.

The prophecy had told us not to go right or left but march straight. But the person who was leading us ignored the prophecy and turned to the right and landed into an Indian Army ambush. Many of us were captured and some died.

When the Indian Army started firing, we ran in all directions and there was no jungle to hide in. A few of us climbed up a hillock and escaped but we had to stay there all day while they carried out combing operations. We stayed absolutely still the whole day and the whole body became numb. The Indian Army came very close to us but they did not see us. We prayed and we remained hidden from our enemy.

At night we crawled out. All this happened in Ao area near Changtongya.

We had started with almost 200 of us and only thirteen survived. Others were killed, injured or scattered. Many of us who had run off had dropped their rucksacks and even weapons and the Indian Army picked up these things.

One of our officers, Jekto, a Sema, was holding a submachine gun. The Indian Army saw him. He dropped the SMG and he was captured and now we were just twelve of us with only one Point 303 rifle with five bullets. No other weapons.

We crossed a river full of leeches. We tried to pull them out and we were bleeding. It was as if I had been cut by a knife. For one month and four days we never saw rice. The Indian Army were like ants everywhere so we could not cook because the smoke would have betrayed us. We were carrying salt and we had that with leaves.

Then we came across a Konyak village. I do not know the name of the village; it was the first time I had been to the Konyak area.

We saw a banana tree and we wanted to eat the bananas. We thought we would cut the bananas, eat them and then leave the money there, because we cannot steal in our culture.

At that moment three Konyak men carrying daos saw us. After seeing our condition, they felt pity. They must have seen how our eyes were sunken and looking at our pitiable state they must have felt for us. They were carrying a little rice in a banana leaf. They gave it to us and so the twelve of us shared the rice meant for three of them.

One of the Konyaks had been tortured by the Indian Army and had been in jail; he and the Chairman could speak to each other in Nagamese. The three Konyaks took all of us to a nearby village. By that time, we did not even have salt. So we bought about 3 kgs of salt from the village for two hundred rupees. The village kept the salt in a basket. Then we asked for rice but they said they had no rice. The village had been burnt by the Indian Army so they had no rice left. So we roasted a wild boar and ate it with salt.

In that village we found some of our people who had been left behind from the first batch which had gone with General Secretary Muivah. They had stayed back because they were not well or weak. Then there were people from the village who also wanted to come with us so there were now thirty-five of us who continued our journey to China.

We started looking for a Brigadier Ngamlu of the Naga Army who lived in that area. With the help of the Brigadier we were able to cross the border to Eastern Nagaland. We stayed in a village across the border for two days and we began our journey again. There was a big thunderstorm and we slept in a hut in the middle of a poppy field. That night the prophecy said we must cross the Chindwin river that night. But we did not know how to cross the river at night so we waited for daylight.

Just before dawn, around four in the morning, the Burmese Army ambushed us. In that ambush my Sema friend Ashili was shot dead by the Burmese Army. Two others were also killed in that ambush. My other friend Viqhali had already been arrested by the Indian Army at Changtongya.

When my friend Ashili was hit, I had also been thrown on the ground; my eyes were full of sand. Everyone had scattered and I did not know in which direction I should go. For four days we were searching for each other. After four days we found the Chairman and some of our people. They were cutting down bamboo to make a raft to cross the river.

While we were crossing the river, one Konyak fell from the raft and he drowned. We crossed the river. For eight days we were not able to make out the way. Just when we thought we were reaching Kachin area we realized that we had come back to the same spot where we had started.

We were lost. It is a very thick forest so we could not see the sun and the ground was swampy. We had no food for nine days. Even our salt was finished. There was no water to boil. We could not find any leaves to eat. In the swamp we found water collected in a depression created by an elephant. I drank from the puddle.

After having water from the swamp, I got fever. The Chairman knew if I was left behind, I would die. But everyone was too tired to carry me. So I kept walking and then I collapsed, then someone picked me up and I walked with determination and then I collapsed again.

Then I was put in a boat and taken by some Kachins to a camp. I did not know what was happening. The Chairman and the rest of the party came by foot. I was in the village and I vomited everything and then by God's grace I was saved.

I do not have words to express how much I suffered.

The prophecy said the Commander, Brigadier Vedai, should be changed. He should not lead and he should be at the back and he should cut the roots. So we changed our commander who was a Konyak. On the tenth day our new Commander found the route that had been taken by the General Secretary; our General Secretary had marked the trees.

The Prophecy said we would be given food on that day. That day we came across a river and we found five tortoises. We had a little salt left so without rice we cooked the tortoises and ate the meat.

The next day we reached a river. While crossing that river we met some Kachins looking for gold in the water. We bought some rice from those people. This was in the Shimpuyang area, which is a Naga area. This is our Vice Chairman Khaplang's area.

The Chinese also come there for gold mining. Nagas also go.

We had two pairs of boots but both were worn out so we were walking barefoot. We did not even have slippers and our feet were bleeding. When we reached Kachin land, the Chairman bought slippers for each of us and with those slippers, we reached China.

I was really sick. My eardrums were giving me problem and I was very weak. After I reached China, I was given very good medical care in the hospital and after that to this day I have never been sick!

I was given some roots and leaves to boil in an earthen pot and some other medicine. I do not know what leaf; it was dried up.

When we reached the boundary between Kachin and China then new clothes were brought for us and all the old clothes were discarded.

We reached on August 14. The others had celebrated Independence Day, but we reached that night.

Medical Training

I was sent for medical training. For one week we were taken to the forest and given training, also shown pictures of the leaves so we could identify the medicinal ones. Atem and Puni were also there. But we were not allowed to bring back that list.

We have these leaves in our land but we are not using them. I also learnt acupressure. All my needles were taken by the Burmese during a raid but the Chairman brought it for me again and I am still using it.

It is very good for paralysis, malaria and diarrhea; also for body ache and headache.

One Nagaland police was about to be dismissed from service because he was ill and not attending to his duty. They brought him to me. I was able to cure him and he is now well.

The Chinese treated us very well. Everything went smoothly but all we were thinking was when the Chinese will give us arms so we can go home.

We had a hall which we used as a church and there we were shown movies about the Chinese revolution. I remember a very inspiring movie about a revolutionary girl who led an ambush and had the courage to do what menfolk could not do; another movie about Chairman Mao and the hardships he faced. Even though he was Chairman he had served the public humbly. That's what I remember. We also visited Kunming.

I had arms training and after that I did medical training. People will think I am boasting but once the training master saw me with all officers including General Secretary Muivah—we were doing target shooting. One machine gun was fixed and everyone was asked whether it has been positioned correctly and everyone said it was. When I was asked, I looked at it and said it was not positioned correctly. It was too low for the target. The instructor said I was correct!

Everyone praised me. We were given eight bullets to shoot and all of us girls could shoot but some men could not shoot accurately. General Secretary cursed the men for not doing as well as we girls did in target shooting.

We could not interact with the Chinese because we did not know their language. I was told when the first batch of Nagas came and there were only men, the Chinese said the Nagas were not ready for revolution because there were no women. But when we went the Chinese said now the Nagas were ready.

Sometimes the Chinese would ask us about Nagaland and we told them how Indian Army tortured our people and raped our women.

We heard about the Shillong Accord while we were in China. The Chairman and General Secretary wanted to go and meet Phizo but they were told that Phizo had already accepted the Accord and everyone at home has surrendered. Now only we were there to fight for our independence. The General Secretary was in Peking when he heard the news and he came to Yunnan, where we were.

After hearing the news, the Chairman and General Secretary started preparing for our return. The Chinese gave us arms and ammunition and we started our journey back.

When we were going back, we women were made to carry one pistol with 150 bullets and extra TMT rifles and bullets. We also carried dynamite, our own stock of rice and army equipment, and a commando knife. Since I was in charge of the medical unit, I had to carry medical equipment and some herbs in addition to my clothes. It must have been 15 kgs. I found it so heavy someone had to help me put it on my back. We were carrying both sides, on the back and front.

When we reached the Kachin area, we had to face the Burmese Army.

We came down to the Khiamniungan Naga area. After getting back to Nagaland we had to go back to China to get more arms. The Chairman stayed back in Eastern Nagaland but the General Secretary went back and I went with him.

The Second Time in China

The second time I went to China in 1976, it took us just three months. We came back in August of 1977.

This time we were many but I do not how many we were. The majority were from Eastern Nagaland. We were five of us women. Many young people went.

I took arms training and medical training because the previous time I had not been able to finish my training.

While going back from China, the Kachins said the Burmese Army was coming and we had to run. We were carrying heavy loads while the Kachins were not carrying anything. It was pitch dark. I tripped over the root of a big tree and I collapsed and I could not breathe. My collarbone was broken. The others had gone ahead but I managed to catch up with them. The reason I could catch up was that they had to cross a very small bridge over the river; they had to go one by one so it took the whole night before everyone could get across. It was very cold.

We had to spend the night near the river. We bought a basket of fish from the fishermen. The Burmese Army must have seen the smoke when we were cooking the fish or some people may have informed them; while we were sleeping, they fired two-inch mortars in our direction. But nothing happened to us.

We crossed another river. It was so cold. We did not get time to dry ourselves. At one point the only way we had to go through a swamp was to wade through waist-deep mud and we could not pull our legs out and we were crying. The Kachins who were leading us were also crying and the whole night we were in that swamp and only in the morning we came out with our whole body full of mud.

After that we reached the Chindwin river and we had to make rafts. We had to cut the bamboo without taking off our loads. But when we were on the bamboo the load was too heavy and it sank so we could not cross. We found one boat and we had to cross in small groups. They were 400 of us so it took a long time for all of us to go across.

We were to reach a village in Eastern Nagaland but we found it was already occupied by the Burmese troops. The Burmese firing started from three in the morning till the next day noon.

Many people were sick. I was attending to them so I missed the meeting in which they gave us instructions on what we must do during an attack. So when the next morning the Burmese attacked again I did not know what to do or where to go.

I fell down and I was still on the ground when a two-inch mortar landed just a few feet away from me and burst. If I had been standing, I would have been injured but since I was lying down, I was okay but my eardrums got affected. For two months my eardrums were affected with water coming out. Even now I have pain in my ears. Many people were injured and I had to patch up the wounds of the officers and others who were hurt.

Many of the Burmese troops were also injured. They were bombarding the villages thinking we were there, but we were in a village on top and we could see below.

General Headquarters in Burma

We reached the General Headquarters (GHQ) and there the men would have to fight the Burmese troops. The Chairman had established the GHQ. Women had to carry the rations and do other work. It was around March 1978.

I was the Battalion Surgeon Major and there was an Angami adjutant who kept asking me for a list of arms every now and then. I told the Chairman and said there was something wrong. Even Mayanger asked me to make a list of arms so one day I went to his quarter and gave him a list. The conspiracy was being hatched.

In August 8, 1978 the coup took place. At the time I was in the Mess with the Chairman. They captured all of us but they did not detain me; they kept only the leaders. They even dug a grave for the leaders.

The Chairman told me to go to his wife who was about to have a baby. He asked me to tell her that he could not come to look after her.

Khaplang, who was still with the supporters of the Accord, harassed us. We had to cut the trees and make the camp and then move to another place.

I was with the Chairman's wife along with one Sema man who was a Captain. He insisted we get married even though I was not keen. We got married there. He was my first husband. My first son was born there in the jungles.

After the Chairman and his wife were reunited, I was sent to the Khiamniungan on the Eastern side with my husband. It was difficult to get into the Western side. We were supposed to teach there in the school because people did not know even A-B-C; and my husband also acted as pastor. We had no contact with our people.

Both of us decided to ask the village for a piece of land and my husband cultivated the land. I had another son. I would take my boys and go from village to village to mobilize people.

One night I was alone in my house. My husband had not come back from the field and I was cooking food for the pig[171] I was rearing when I heard a commotion outside. The whole village was awake. I had a pistol my husband had taken his pistol and rifle. I did not know what the commotion was about that night. My husband had not come back; I had not realized he would never come back.

In the morning the church deacon asked whether I had cooked. He told me cook fast. I asked what was wrong but he did not say anything. The deacon came back with his wife even before I had finished cooking. I asked him what was the matter. He drew a circle and said, 'Today you will go to your parents.' He meant today I would be killed. They ate the food but I could not eat.

I thought I could go off, but then I thought my husband will come back and wonder whether I had been killed. He would search for me. So I packed my rucksack and waited for him.

I could not sit idle. They were waiting for the night. But I did not know what to do. So I took my pistol and hid a dao in a basket and decided to go to the field where my husband was. But I did not know the way so I asked someone who I knew. The father in the family said he could not send anyone with me as there was a festival and no one was allowed to go out of the village on that day.

I asked them to send a child with me to show the way. I was desperate. At that time there was human sacrifice; headhunting was still going on there. I suspected that they were planning to sacrifice my husband. I had to go back to my home.

When I was going back to my place the whole village was watching.

---

[171] Nagas give the pigs they rear cooked food in the belief that it makes the pig tastier.

I was walking back alone. I thought if I die, I will die in my home. I thought I would give food to my pig. I gave some leaves to it. The villagers thought I had run away and they started giving a war cry.

I was hiding in my home. Then I heard that the Shillong Accordists had come and they were shouting at the villagers for not catching a woman. I thought if they try to kill me, I will also kill one of them. But I thought what was the point so I got up and went out and shouted, 'Who are you searching for, who do you want? What have I done?'

They were all surprised to see me. The men fixed a bayonet and charged at me. They came to my house and started taking everything and then the boys saw a new shawl and they quarrelled over the shawl. I was feeling really bad and felt like crying but I controlled myself. I told them, 'You must have been sent by someone. You are not doing this on your own. If someone has sent you, what wrong have I done? And if you want to take my things why are you doing it like a thief? Why are you quarrelling over a shawl?'

They arrested me and took me to another village. I was put in a house with guards outside. They used to tie me with a rope. The villagers were keeping watch on all roads so I could not escape. When the Burmese Army came the Naga Army ran away. But the villagers guarded me so I could not run away. Then they took me to a field and I made a thatched roof and slept there. I was there for quite some time.

I did not know my husband had already been killed. They did not tell me. They kept saying he was alive. Finally, I asked them: why have you killed my husband because if he was alive, he would have come. Then at last they told me that he was the lips, eyes and ears of Isak and Muivah. That is why he was killed.

Before my husband and I were sent to the Khiamniungan village we had been told that if there was any problem, they would send a message to them. Three times the Chairman sent us messages warning us but we never got the messages. It was much later I learnt that the messengers were ambushed on their way and stopped from reaching us.

The Burmese Army came and the villagers told me to hide and I said I will not hide. I will die in the field where my husband died. Then they took me to the camp of the Accordists and there I was told that no one was supporting Isak and Muivah anymore because they were communists. I was told everyone has left them except some Tangkhul girls. They asked, 'So do you still think Isak and Muivah are right?' I said I don't think the allegation against them was correct.

They asked me to surrender to the Indian Army and I said I would not. I told them I had joined the movement to serve my people and I would not surrender. So I was kept in the jail. They had planned on killing me but then they killed my husband. I was in their custody for six months. They knew I had been to China.

Then one man told me that they were discussing what to do with me. The Accordists were saying if I go back to Western Nagaland then I would be left; but if I say I will rejoin Isak and Muivah then they will kill me.

Two women were sent to escort me to the Nagaland border and I was supposed to surrender to the Indian Army. When we reached the border, I said I was very tired and wanted to rest. I did not want to cross to Nagaland because I knew it would be very difficult for me to return.

I told the village headman that I did not want to surrender and it is not safe for a woman to surrender. I persuaded him to hide me. I was wearing the Naga Army uniform. I had no other clothes.

I was in hiding in a schoolmaster's house. The Accordists were looking for me. The master's wife was very sick so I helped to look after her. I went to fetch water and on the way I saw lots of the Burmese Army but I thought they were the Accordists. I was very frightened so the Master told me to hide in the wife's bed. I was still in the Army dress. I was so frightened.

Aftermath of the Shillong Accord

After the Shillong Accord everyone in Western Nagaland had surrendered. The movement was kept alive by the Nagas on the Eastern side.

I met the General Secretary and Chairman at the Jordan camp. They explained to me what had happened and why we had faced this crisis. They said despite the death of so many we have to move forward. We must not get disheartened and we must re-organize ourselves.

Now I have five children; three girls born here in Dimapur, and two boys who were born in the jungles.

I was not well and for some time I retired and in 1997 I was asked to come back by the prayer cell.

I am in NSWON (NSCN's women's wing) and we educate people on women's contribution to society. We discuss our problems within the organization. We say women must be given equality. Now there are women in the Naga government and the Naga Army. This was follow-up from our suggestions. Now there are many women officers, including a Major.

It is the Naga women who have stood up, and have contributed to the movement. The menfolk are not very steady. Women must come up.

Life in the underground is difficult. In 1996 my second husband was arrested. At the time I was taking my youngest daughter to school. He was beaten up very badly. He was put in jail in Jodhpur along with Angelus. I went to see him in jail.

The man who accompanied me to Jodhpur was picked up by the police and put into the lock-up. I did not know what to do; I did not know the language and it took me four days to somehow contact the SP Police in Nagaland and tell him to get the man released.

The best part of being in the Naga national movement was that I saw different places like China, despite the fact I had no education. But life in the underground was full of hardship.

I have suffered so much and I had no education, but for my children I do not want them to suffer. I want my children to have education. I tell them my stories so they know and learn from my experiences.

RAMYOLA: THE SOLDIER-WIDOW

Ramyola from Paorei village, Ukhrul, is a soldier in the Naga Army and lived in Burma for several years.

Ramyola's husband, Colonel Pruining, General Staff Commanding Officer, was murdered by Khaplang's men.

She spoke in Tangkhul, which has been translated by Phungthing Shimrah.

Ramyola was interviewed at Dimapur on June 30, 1999.

Testimony of Ramyola:

My name is Ramyola and I am forty-three years old. I have had no schooling at all. We were ten brothers and sisters, six boys and four girls, and I am the fourth eldest. I did not go to school because we worked in the paddy field and looked after the younger siblings and also my brother's child.

During my childhood I saw the war (sic) and the fighting between the Indian Army and the Naga Army. In our village a lot of people from the Naga Army came and stayed. They used to go from our village to Nungbi and Kalhan and when they went, we heard a lot of sounds of war. I also saw the war in Phungcham and in our own village.

The Semas turned into tigers and they found out the position of the Indian soldiers at various posts and would report back to the Naga Army.[172] I cannot remember the year when all this happened but I was around twelve or thirteen years old. It was in the 1960s.

I do remember in the 1970s when Awo (Uncle) Mhiasiu and Oja[173] Pamrei led a group of people and they passed through our village. I took food for them in the jungles. And these two leaders stayed in our

---

[172] Lycanthropy is widely prevalent notion among the Nagas and there are innumerable stories about Nagas who turn into tigers by night.

[173] 'Sir,' used for teachers.

house. Once I saw them celebrate Naga Republic Day in the jungles. Now that place has been taken over by the Indian Army.

I came to know Mhiasiu properly only in the 1970s. He used to come along with a prayer group. He has died. He had three sons and two daughters. One daughter got married and died during delivery of her baby; the second son joined the underground and went down the wrong path and was killed by our own people. The others are married and the youngest daughter is studying. They are related to Atem's family.

So one day Pamrei said to me 'Ayola,[174] so you want to join the movement?' He asked just like this.

I thought and said: 'Do you think you can lead us? We are women, what can we do? Moreover, what can I do in the war?' That is how I answered him.

He replied: 'No! There is nothing like that. Men and women are alike and equal. There are a lot of women from Eastern Nagaland and also from Nagaland who are in the movement.'

Then I thought and thought and prayed and prayed for the cause. I prayed for a long time. Then I saw in my dream Oja Pamrei and his cadres looking so happy and enjoying themselves and I saw them climbing high up a mountain and climbing down and they suffered so much as they crossed the mountain. I saw this dream like a vision and I came to understand that this life is also for me. I came to know that yes! I can bear it and I felt happy.

The next time when Oja Pamrei came I told him I will surely join the movement: I have seen your way and how good and happy it is and how deep you suffer. I have seen the high and low and I will come with you. I will go wherever you all go and I will die where ever you will die. I know all your hardships wherever you go and how much you have sacrificed whenever required. I will follow you on that path.

Then Oja Pamrei said 'Oh! Ayola, oh no! I was just joking. There is too much suffering and you will not be able to bear it. It is a very

---

[174] Diminutive for Ramyola.

tough life and I will not take you with me. I will not let you come with me.'

Then I said: 'I will surely go. I will follow you and I have understood exactly what it is like and you can never stop me. If you don't take me along, I will be very disappointed and I will not serve you food, I will not feed you and I will not be happy.'

I had made up my mind to join the movement. I heard the news that some of my friends are going to join and I told my parents that I am going to join the movement. My parents said under no circumstance can I join the movement. My elder brothers said if I tried, they would beat me with a stick and they were ready to start beating me.

But since I had made up my mind and taken a decision, I was determined to join the movement. Then in December 1976, I heard that some people in our village were going to leave to join the movement so I said I was going to collect pinewood for Christmas from the forest and there I met the people who were already in the movement and joined them.

On December 22, we all spent the night in the forest, which our villagers called Kongchai Lui. The next morning Oja Ngathingkhui and Oja Pamrei and many more men and women were there. We started our journey on the morning of December 23, 1976.

At that time we did not know what Shillong Accord meant. All we knew was Uncle Ramyo had joined the Shillong Accord.

After we left, we found that the parents of all those who had joined the movement were captured and put into jail by the Indian Army. They picked up the fathers because of us.

Yes, my father was also picked up and put into jail. And they hoisted a red flag over our house. They hoisted a red flag over every house from where someone had joined the underground.

My father spent six months in jail. He was a farmer and not used to sitting doing nothing all day. They beat him and tortured him, disfigured him and when they brought him home, he was very sick. And slowly he died. I did not see him dying.

That night on December 23 we walked and walked. We crossed our village mountain and went to Kalhang and then to Somrah side in Burma. There was curfew because of the Naga movement. We were not able to cross to Somrah so we spent the night in the forest at Ngahui[175] mountain. There was an Indian Army post right there.

We crossed at night and we were very tired. The situation was very bad and the security was very tight. We spent two days in a village in the Somrah area. We recouped there and also prepared food and then we reached Tezi river and after crossing we fasted and prayed and gave thanks to God for bringing us safely through a dangerous area. We had a prayer meeting. The first session was over and Lieutenant Colonel Ningon was about to begin the second session when we heard shots and two of our men were killed. We heard firing by the Burmese Army and we ran here and there, not knowing who is firing and what has happening.

From that day onwards we had no food and the Burmese Army chased us and they ambushed us and put up road blocks. After that under the leadership of Ngathingkhui, thirty of our group escaped and we went under the leadership of Oja Pamrei.

In our group there were two Meiteis, one was called Oken[176] and the other was Sanayaima.[177] Oken is now KYKL now, I think and Sanayaima is older and he belongs to UNLF. Both of them came

---

[175] The Tangkhul name for Awong Kasom.

[176] Kanglei Yawol Kanna Lup (KYKL), meaning 'the Organization to Save the Revolutionary Movement in Manipur' is a Meitei militant group formed in January 1994 following merger of the Oken faction of the United National Liberation Front (UNLF), the Meiraba faction of People's Revolutionary Party of Kangleipak (PREPAK) and the Ibo Pishak faction of the Kangleipak Communist Party (KCP).

[177] The oldest Meitei insurgent group in Manipur, the UNLF, was founded in 1964 and is led by Rajkumar Meghen also known as Sanayaima. The armed wing of this outfit is called the Manipur People's Army. The objective is to establish an independent and socialist Manipur, a state the UNLF claims was 'annexed' by India in 1949. In 1990, the UNLF along with other NE insurgent groups like ULFA, NSCN (K) and the Kuki National Army floated the Indo-Burma Revolutionary Front to wage a 'united struggle for the independence of Indo-Burma.'

along with Mhiasiu and they wanted to cross to Burma. I do not know anything else of why they came.

The Burmese pursued us so that one point we had to spend nine days deep in the forest and we collected leaves and mixed it with a little rice and we ate that. That is how we survived for those nine days.

We decided that we cannot keep staying in the forest because we will suffer more and more. So we started walking again but I do not remember the names of all the villages we passed. There was one woman called Shimtharla, we called her Achon Thar, from Phadang who was brought by Mhiasiu. She was climbing up a cliff holding on to the roots and the root broke and she fell upside down and she got hurt very badly so we had to nurse her.

We had to wait and then we proceeded very slowly and we reached the Khiamniungan area by March 1977. We were not wearing uniform, some of us wore long pants, others wore sarong. We reached the village called Chemeyon, but I am not sure of the spelling. It was a non-Christian village and it was uncivilized. They did not have plates. We ate on bamboo stem.

When they brought out the food, we had never come across it. We said: 'Oh! How can we eat this!' It was just leaves, beans mixed with rice and sesame seeds. It looked like food for a dog. We were shocked to have such food. We said we would not eat it.

Then Ngathingkhui scolded us: 'You monkeys! You have come to teach them and you are running away from them—come back! Eat happily and enjoy the food otherwise it will hurt their feelings. Don't hurt their feelings and humiliate them by not taking their food. They are poor.'

This was the first time I met a non-Christian Naga who is not civilized. The Somrah people were a little better and wore more clothes. Here they were naked. Later Oja Khakhui was the first Pastor. He was from Sirarakhong village. He was also a school teacher. At that time, he was the Education Minister.

We were not allowed to stay in the village and we were sent to the camp and we stayed there in the jungle for three months.

Then after that we again shifted to another place and we stayed
in the forest for a long time. It was near Sephao village. It was only
in October 1977 that we were ready to go to China. During that
time, we learnt to read and write and each of us carried our Bible,
songbook and handbook.

On our way to China we were not disturbed and we reached
Kachin area. When we reached, our commander Oja Pamrei got sick.
He suggested that we should not eat anything from the forest, the
leaves or the fruits, because the climate in Kachin land and Nagaland
was very different.

Oja Pamrei did not get better and he was so sick he could not walk.
We left him near the India-Burma border[178] and continued marching
to China. The Kachin did not want us to go to China so they did not
take us to the Brigade Headquarters but made us walk through the
jungles. And finally they did not allow our group to go to China.

Then we came along a river and at that point the guards who had
gone with Oja Pamrei said he had died. They had buried him and came
to tell us.

We were crossing in a boat which was in a bad condition and it
overturned. We fell into the water and we did not know how to swim
so I swallowed a lot of water. One boy from Ngaingna village called
Philip died also. He had insisted on carrying our things and so when
the boat overturned, he submerged because he was carrying so many
things. He was a very nice person and very disciplined. He floated away
and we were not able to find him. But the next day we found his body
and we took out his dead body and we found his eyes, ears and parts of
his face had been eaten by the fish. We got back the luggage, including
the guns. We gave him a nice burial.

I was very sick because I had swallowed all that water. I was so sick
I was carried from village to village in the jungle. My condition became
worse. At one place the Kachins sent a doctor and he gave some

---

[178] They had crossed into Burma from Manipur and now they had perhaps reached
the India-Burma border near Arunachal Pradesh.

medicines and I got better and by that time Mr Muivah had come back from China. It was during Christmas.

I still feel angry that the Kachins did not allow us to go to China. We were so disappointed that we had to go back. I was angry in my heart with them, even if I did not show it. The feeling still lingers and even now the thought comes that we were not able to go to China. The feeling is called 'ning mathi' in Tangkhul, it means a thought which keeps coming back and you can't put it off.

I was so sick I cannot remember how many of us...but it was forty to fifty who did not go to China. Those who were healthy were sent back to Nagaland section by section.[179] After Uncle Muivah came back, the sick group was taken care of by Sister Avuli since they had got training in medicine and they took care of us. So we went along with the group that had gone to China.

We were all suffering from malaria or typhoid. At the same time the Burmese were chasing us. It is a long story of how we came from the Kachin area to Nagaland. In between we came to a village where the British had built a hospital and a school. The Burmese did not utilize either the hospital or school very well. That village had many CID because they had a lot of information so we killed the three CID people and then continued our journey because the Burmese Army was still after us.

With great difficulty we reached Chiyang village.[180] It is a Konyak Naga village. When we reached, we heard a story about the visit of the Naga Army in the 1960s, the story of when the first batch went to China. There were 150 of them and they marched from Western Nagaland and crossed to Eastern Nagaland and arrived at this village. It is not far from the boundary. They were very hungry.

The Naga Army tried to tell the villagers that they were Nagas like them and they had come from India and were in a very poor condition and needed food. Since there was no common language, they

---

[179] She means Naga-inhabited areas of Burma or Eastern Nagaland.
[180] She is not sure of the spelling.

communicated with hand gestures. So the villagers divided the group
and sent one soldier to one house and that is how they divided them.
So for every one Naga soldier there were two male family members. If
there were four male members then they put three Naga soldiers. Then
the Angh (Chief) killed a fat pig for them. The meat was distributed
to each home. He said he would ring the bell so they could eat together.

The food was cooked and distributed and the soldiers were in
different homes. So when the soldiers were praying or just putting food
in their mouths, their heads were chopped off. Only two or three were
able to escape. They ran for their life and did not know where to go
since this was their first time in the area.

The two of them who escaped were very hungry so they went to
a jhum field to see if they could find some maize or vegetables to eat.
Then they went down to the river and were looking for crabs and two
women saw them. They told the Naga soldiers that it was the season
for headhunting.

But when we joined Uncle Muivah after he came back from China,
we went to the village to take action against them. We wanted to find
out what happened but the Angh had told everyone to remain silent
so no one said anything. Then the Angh of seven clans was killed by
us. And the Burmese Army attacked us and we went to the next village
and there too they attacked us. Some of us escaped but some died. One
fellow from my village died in a bomb blast. His name was Ringphami.

We women and some sick managed to cross the battlefield and reach
a village; I have forgotten the name of the village. In the process one
bullet hit Avuli. One Brigadier was also hit and he was carried across.
There was so much fighting and fighting and then one helicopter came.

The helicopter was blasted and it fell. Then another helicopter
came to take away the wounded Burmese. Then a jet fighter came and
bombarded the village and their granary was burnt. I do not know how
many died. Many people in the Burmese Army also died.

Finally we came to Chonkhao village in the Khiamniungan area
and we set up our General Headquarters and we were divided into
Sector 1 and 2.

I was sick throughout this period and I had nose-bleeding and I had become very weak. I could not take hot rice because then my nose would start bleeding. I had to take my food lukewarm. Sister Avuli injected me with a medicine three times a day and the nose bleeding stopped but the pain in my body did not stop. One side of my body has pain even now.

Martial Law

Then the leaders started preparing for a meeting and then Khaplang also came. The leaders went to Sector Two for the meeting and we were also called to go there. It was in the Leinong area. The meeting was to discuss how to handle ourselves since Mr Phizo did not come and had not advised us on what to do. But the meeting could not proceed further because six of the leaders, including Isak Swu and Muivah, were arrested by the other group. Mr Khaplang was not at that meeting, he was in his area. They made the leaders sign that they were giving over NNC charge to the military and martial law was declared. Oja Ngathingkhui also went to support the Accord.

Then all of us were also detained and made to go from one village to another village. They had planned to kill the leaders but the Commander-in-Chief, who was a Konyak, said not a piece of hair should be touched of the leaders. They released four of them but two, Isak and Muivah, were kept in a smelly place and the people were so dirty that there was disease and when someone died they did not dispose of the body properly. I did not see all this but my husband told me.

The villagers gave the two leaders food and the martial law people scolded them for that. They were kept in a home jail.

I along with a few others were made to work in Khaplang's medical department. He had a doctor and he gave us training and we looked after the sick.

We met Khaplang and he could speak Tangkhul because he had lived in the west. From my point of view, I can't say how knowledgeable or clever he is, but from the women's point of view he is not good. He used to ask us to massage him and tell us to massage his stomach and go lower and lower. He said he had pain and he would hold hands with women and I have never seen that type of shaking hands. So many women hated him. Even if he might be a good leader, he was not clean with women.

We had a camp with the Tangkhuls and we set up a school and some of them were teachers and the church was managed by the Somdal village.

Sometimes there were joint operation between the Burmese and Indian Armies then we suffered. The two leaders were kept in a hut very near the India border.

Life in the NSCN Camp

We shifted to our new headquarters and the leaders discussed that since NNC has gone completely wrong we have to finish this government and form a new one.

Finally our leaders came out and NSCN was formed and I was posted at the General Headquarters (GHQ). Our Army had to kill the Accordists.

Our daily routine was: we got up at three in the morning to wash, cook and eat by 6 a.m. Then from 8 a.m. we do our work inside the camp like cleaning the compound, collecting firewood etc. Then at one in the afternoon ration is distributed. And we will cook by two. The cooking is done group wise. In some Mess there will be two or three, sometimes twelve and some go up to forty and fifty. We do not cook for everyone together because that would require bigger pots and longer time; so we cook for small groups, sometimes two or three people, sometimes twelve and occasionally up to fifty people. In this way we can cook faster and have smaller pots to carry if we are attacked by the Burmese Army.

We used to get rice, salt and chillies but for vegetables like bamboo shoots or leaves and herbs, we have to gather from the forest. For long periods we did not have rice and ate maize, millet or sweet potatoes and beans. We cooked it all into a kind of porridge. In some of the Mess they made the food very hot with five to ten king chillies.

Sometimes we stayed near a brook or stream but sometimes we had to walk into the jungle to fetch water. We always tried our best to stay near a stream.

After our meal at two we rested. Sometimes we read the Bible, sometimes some of us sang songs or chatted and some of us studied. It depended on you. We had political lectures on special days like our Republic Day or during budget session. Yes we were told what socialism means. It means you cannot say yours-and-mine and greediness cannot be there. Socialist means equal and the government is not greedy for land. And people cannot acquire more and more land.

My Marriage

The leaders arranged my marriage with Pruining. We married in the church and it was done by Reverend Mhiasiu. He was the chaplain in charge. We killed a pig and everyone was called for the feast in the courtyard. All the three leaders came: Muivah, Isak Swu and Khaplang. I put on a yellow sweater and a Burmese lungyi. I could not get a Tangkhul shawl. He had come after a successful job from home so he had a good suit. No, he did not bring anything for me. We stayed together for six or seven months at the headquarters.

Since I was not well and staying at the headquarters was very tiring, the leaders asked us to shift to a village called Keisan Chanang[181] and my husband acted as Pastor. We helped the villagers clean the homes and the compounds. We taught them the happiness of being Christian and slowly converted them. He was able to convert thirty to fifty to one hundred and twenty people.

They had all kind of practices and observed taboos. They made offerings to keep away evil spirits. They kept chicken, piglets in the

---

[181] We have not been able to confirm the spelling.

middle of house. We taught them how to pray before eating food, before sleeping.

I taught them how to raise money by keeping aside a little rice and selling it. We taught them how to weave and how to sew and make a sweater. Since we did not have a scissor for cutting, we used a knife and drew with a charcoal since we did not have chalk. The most difficult was to teach them how to sing. It was very difficult and tiring.

The village had a Longshim. Before the boys used to go to the ladies' Longshim, and ladies also went and slept in gents' Longshim. We stopped all these dirty things and now it is used by old people who spend their time weaving baskets and making tea. It is no longer utilized by the youth.

We taught them how to pray in the morning and in the evening, how to have family prayers and how to keep a fast. They converted and they even get visions. My husband led the work putting all his effort; in the same way I followed my husband and I led the women and taught them with all my heart.

My eldest daughter was born in that village. We stayed in the village about four and half years till the crisis came. Just before the crisis we were asked to go to the council headquarters so we were there at the time.

Split with Khaplang

The entire army along with the children went to the forest and even the children did not get any food. The Khaplang people started taking the weapons from the Tangkhuls. My husband was very sad and he said, 'How can we defend the nation if you leaders start doing like this?'

Mr Muivah had come back from China but the Chairman was in Kachin land. They called a meeting but Khaplang did not come. They called him to the council five or six times and sent two officers to meet him. But he did not come. But he captured all the arms and stopped the villagers from selling food to Isak-Muivah group. He had already given that instruction.

At the time I had my second baby and it was just three months old and I had to carry the baby on my back. Then we women and children were told to go by the main road and the men went into the jungles. But Khaplang men robbed us of our belongings, even utensils, and we walked some 10 kms to the council headquarters empty-handed.

One of the soldiers of Khaplang told us, 'You Nagas from the West side with such pride and vain attitude have come here to show us your richness and boast.'

So on April 31, 1988, the Khaplang soldiers came in and there was a lot of noise. Ashiho came there carrying his baby on his back; without suspecting anything he asked what was the noise about. We are not allowed to make noise in the Mess. It is a rule of our army. And he saw the Khaplang soldiers and they had lots of newly recruited men.

Then they told one of our officers Johnson from Somdal, 'You are Muivah's dogs and we are searching for you people only.' They hit him with the rifle butt and he fell unconscious. And they fired from AK 47. The bullets hit Ashiho and his child and Johnson. They all died there.

My husband was in the latrine and he came out and we all packed our things and took the two children and we went into the forest. The General Secretary was also there and we were altogether around a hundred of us and we climbed on top of a hill. Then we went to a village to collect rice near the roadside but the Burmese Army attacked us.

So my husband along with eleven of us ran separately. There was an Angami and people belonging to another tribe. It had been decided if we got separated and scattered, we should regroup at a village called Kako.

There was nothing to eat and we could not give anything to the children. There were two men, one was a doctor who had never faced such hardships, and they made a rope with roots and tied their stomachs to help them bear the hunger.

We found some paddy in a field and we pounded it on a piece of cloth and managed to take out a bit of rice for the children. Then we crossed the river and as soon we crossed the Khaplang men captured three of us. By that time, we were only three of us and our two kids. The others had scattered.

I was carrying the baby so there was no chance for me to escape. So first of all they captured me and my baby, then they captured the Angami lady and my husband who was carrying the other child. He ran towards the river but they captured him and dragged him. The small child due to the noise of gunshots was lying as if dead and I asked him whether he was dead and he said no. Then they tied my husband's hands and made the Angami woman carry my other child, the one my husband had been carrying.

They led my husband to the hills. And so the time came for my husband to be killed. My husband tried to talk to the Commanding Officer whose name was Karang.

The officer said, 'You Tangkhuls have treated us very badly and thought we were very low. Now you get your share.' Then he told my husband if he had any last words he could send through his wife and we could meet and speak to each other. I told my husband, 'Let us pick up one child each and run and let them kill all of us. Let us die together.' I asked him, 'What is the use of living? I had married knowing and understanding that I would face this kind of suffering and I am ready to sacrifice my life. I am not scared, let us die together.' He asked, 'Can you really do that?' And I replied 'Yes! I can do that, that is why I am in the movement.' He said no, you go back and report to Secretary Muivah what is happening. You have to go back. You must live.

My husband said: 'I hope, Avakharar, I hope you have escaped.'

Those were his last words and then they shot him.

They beat me and led me to a village where there were two other women. Then they brought the son of one officer. The child had seen his father dragged away and he had heard a shot and then his father did not come back. The child was just three years old. I saw with my own eyes the pain in the child's eyes. He came and put his head in my lap and cried. Just see how a small child can feel and express. Because we are not his parents and we are strangers so he could not cry out loudly. We did not know how to console that little child.

I have seen lots of suffering, difficulties and pain, but seeing that child was unbearable. During the day he would play with my two children but when he came back into the house he was downcast again. He thought Khaplang men were Burmese Army and he would say when he grows up he would take revenge. He could not speak but he managed to express himself. We were kept in that house for one week.

They took everything from us except the clothes we were wearing. Then they took us to another village and kept us in home detention for a month. The Angami lady was looked after well and she had a separate Mess.

Then lots of people were getting sick and one child was sick, and I told the soldiers that I want to meet Khaplang. I kept insisting and since I was the wife of a senior officer, I and a few others were allowed to go to his home. And at last we met him and I asked why he was doing like this.

Khaplang said a lot of things to me but still I did not understand. Then he answered, 'Yes! You will not be happy because your husband has been killed. But your husband did not listen to the Collective Leadership. He was Muivah's right-hand man and he was sent to Mon to meet Rajesh Pilot.'[182] Khaplang said it was a collective decision to kill my husband.

I told Khaplang that my husband had never done anything wrong and he had always followed orders of the Collective Leadership. I asked him for the charge sheet against my husband. Khaplang said Muivah was planning to surrender. And whatever Mr Muivah does Isak follows, he is Muivah's dog. He is Kong Titi (a kind of bamboo which flows with the current). When I asked Khaplang for my husband's charge

---

[182] One of the allegations made by Khaplang was that Isak and Muivah wanted to betray the movement by agreeing to talk to the government of India. NSCN denies that Pruining went to meet Rajesh Pilot. But it was Pilot who made the initial contact with Thuingaleng Muivah at the beginning of the peace process with the NSCN (I-M).

sheet he answered like that. He blamed Muivah and he said Muivah manipulated everyone.

Then I said what has happened has happened. But he should not allow the sick to die. I told him he was not able to look after the sick, or provide us with food and medicines, so it was the same as slaughtering the children.

Sanayaima heard me and he said 'Ash! Achon we really feel pity for you but what has happened has happened.'

Sanayaima was in the UNLF but Oken was in jail in Manipur at that time, I think. They and the Assamese were with Khaplang. I told him: 'You are on the same side, why don't you encourage him to set us free to go back?'

Then I left. After that we were sent for treatment one by one. Before I left, Khaplang said your husband has been killed and you have a child so you will be discharged. So I put in my discharge papers and I was sent home. I went to Dimapur. I reported to Raising and asked whether I would be discharged and he said we do not recognize Khaplang and told me to go on one month leave to take treatment and so I went to Imphal.

Then I was contacted by Mr Muivah's wife, Pakahao, who reached Western Nagaland by 1989, and the Chairman's wife, Eustar. They both revived the NSCN's women's organization. I was one of the executive members. We started mobilizing again.

A Fund for Widows

I worked in Dimapur and organized the rations and the Mess. At that time the government (GPRN) could not afford to give us more than one thousand rupees for seven or eight people and we managed with that for a month. We used to buy a kilo of potatoes and rice with salt and chillies. Most of the time we ate a curry of leaves.

None of us had money to take a rickshaw if we wanted to visit family or friends and we walked. Sometimes we did not get even that one thousand rupees; that was how difficult it was for us during those days.

Then on Republic Day we all walked to our camp and I met Atem's wife. We are very good friends. We share everything and tell our stories to each other. I told her my difficulties and she said she can understand because when her husband was in jail, she too lived the life of a widow. And I said it would be good to have an organization for the widows, and she and her husband started one in 1994.

The name of the organization is Naga Freedom Fighters' Widows Federation. This is for the widows after the Shillong Accord only. At present there are around fifty members. In August 1996 we had a meeting and I was chosen as Chairperson, one Angami was the Secretary, one Mao was the Accountant and a Sema woman was the Treasurer. We took up a project of fisheries and then weaving.

My youngest child died in 1995. I had brought him to Dimapur to educate him. It was a Saturday during the rainy season in August. He saw lots of fish in the stream when he was returning home and he went to catch the fish and he drowned. He was around seven years old.

Even now I am in touch with the people from Eastern Nagaland and I have translated 200 songs for them. It was with difficulty we raised the money to translate and then to publish the songbook. We made a calendar and sold it to raise money.

Now the main problem in the movement is the leaders are after money and the youth is undisciplined.

One day I had gone to phone when the Indian Army came and found a lot of bombs in my house. The town commander had left them in my house. There were bullets also and five bundles of wire for explosives. And that day Raising's wife and son had come to my place on their way to meet him and the Indian Army arrested them. Another NSCN girl was also arrested. The Indian Army released Raising's wife and son after they said they had come to meet her husband who was in hospital; but the girl was tortured and given electric shocks and even now she is not well.

After that the Indian Army never came because now we have ceasefire!

CHAPTER FOUR

Culture, The Church and China

I hate, I despise your feasts,
and I take no delight in your solemn assemblies.
Even though you offer me your burnt offerings and grain
offerings,
I will not accept them;
and the peace offerings of your fattened animals,
I will not look upon them.
Take away from me the noise of your songs;
to the melody of your harps I will not listen.
But let justice roll down like waters,
and righteousness like an ever-flowing stream.
—Amos 5:21-24 English Standard Version (ESV)

The relationship between the Naga national movement and the Christian church has not been smooth for a number of reasons.

In pre-colonial times the Naga culture and Naga religion were inextricably linked to the agricultural cycle. With the coming of Christianity, the link between the culture and religion was broken. The Nagas who converted to Christianity gave up their old religious beliefs and thus lost much of their culture and cultural institutions, such as the morung.

However, the missionaries developed the Naga languages, mainly for the purpose of translating the Bible and Christian songs into local languages.

Under the impact of Christian missionaries during the colonial era, much of Naga culture has been lost. There is not even an inventory of the cultural heritage stolen from the Nagas during the colonial rule; much of it now lies scattered in museums across Britain and parts of Europe.

Even after the British left, the process of cultural loss continued due to the coming of mass media, the globalization of culture and impact of the market. The Naga national movement has not come out with any policy on the problem of preservation of cultural heritage and ways to evolve the cultural resources of the Nagas.

Many Naga youth struggle to reconcile a pride in their cultural heritage with belief in their religion (predominantly Baptist Christianity) which rejects that cultural heritage as pagan.

One way the early Naga nationalists addressed this problem was by claiming that Christianity did not come to the Nagas via the missionaries, who were in colonial times all from the West.

Phizo emphasized that the Nagas had always remained 'outside the influence of any other nation' and they had preserved that purity. In his speech of May 16, 1951 before the historic plebiscite, Phizo claimed categorically that Christianity among the Nagas was not a foreign influence.

He said: 'Someone may tell us that Nagas are Christians following a foreign religion. The Indians publicly say this. We do not take Christianity as foreign religion any more than we consider the light of the sun as foreign origin from outer world. There is a father-creator (Ukepenopfü) as we call it. He is God. The message of the Gospel fulfils our Naga conception of religion—Nanyü—which literally means 'anguish of mind' for which we do worship. Once we came to know that there is a personal Saviour to whom one can talk or pray directly, the real light dawned on us, and the weight of man's 'anguish of mind' greatly vanished away. It is the end of the beginning of our personal realization in relieving the anguish of mind in this world and for the next world after death. Whatever the Indians may say of us, there is no foreignness in relationship between father and child; that is, between God the Father and His children.'

Like Phizo, many Naga nationalists claim that Christianity did not arrive with the foreign missionaries but by the Holy Spirit acting through dreams and visions which led to conversion and then people were formally baptized by the missionaries. The story told by Isak Swu of his father's conversion dramatically illustrates this; as does the story of Shatkamla or Unice the Oracle.

The 1962 Constitution of the Naga National Council recognized traditional Naga religion and Protestant Christianity as the official religions of Nagaland.

Although the overwhelming numbers of Nagas within India are Baptist Christians, there are substantial numbers of Nagas who belong to other denominations such as the Seventh Day Adventists, Catholics and many Nagas are are not Christian. These non-Christians include the Nagas in Myanmar who are mostly Buddhist or practice their own religion. It has been alleged by several writers that many of the Burmese Nagas were forcibly converted to Christianity when the NSCN had made its base there. Some of those converted had to return to the Buddhist fold in order to stand for elections under the Myanmar law.

What is forgotten in these debates is that a significant section of Nagas are not Christian; for instance, the Nagas living in Myanmar and also those who continue to follow Rani Gaidinliu (1915-1993) and their Haraka religion.

In 2015 the Indian Prime Minister, Narendra Modi, announced that the centre would honour the Rani on her birth centenary by building a library and museum in her honour in Kohima where she stayed after she came out after fourteen years of imprisonment. But the move was opposed, primarily by Angami Public Organization, on the ground that the Indians were trying to impose the Rani's religion on the Nagas. The BJP claims Rani's legacy and Haraka religion as a part of the larger Hindu family. The Haraka temple in Mbaupungwa was demolished by church workers just as the British had demolished Jadonang's temple a century earlier.

The fight is as much between the Baptist Christians and non-Christians (Phizo opposed the Rani even before she went to jail) as it is about inter-tribal rivalries between the Zeliangrong people (Rani and Jadonang belonged to the Zeliangrong tribe) and the Angamis (Phizo was an Angami).

The NSCN Constitution of 1980 does not recognize Naga religion. It states: 'We stand for the faith in God and the salvation of mankind in Jesus, the Christ, alone, that is 'Nagaland for Christ'. However, individual freedom of religion shall be safeguarded and the imposition of this faith on others is strictly forbidden.'

This change reflects the fact that by the time the NSCN emerged on the political scene, more than 90 per cent of the Nagas had converted to Christianity. The overwhelming number of them are Baptist Christians; the Catholics form a significant minority.

The NSCN Constitution also expresses concern with the growing influence of Hindu culture and calls on the church leaders to take up the challenge of fighting the influence. It specifically mentions the challenge posed by the Ramakrishna Mission. The Hindu missionaries had spread the word that Christian missionaries were a threat to the traditional way of life of tribal communities in the North East.

The hostility to Hindus was also rooted in the way the Indian Armed Forces had desecrated the churches by using them as detention centres during counter-insurgency operations; there were incidents in which pastors had been tortured and some even died as a result of the beatings.

Christianity has been a major source of inspiration and strength for the Naga national movement. The NSCN's People's Army has a chaplain attached to each battalion, an independent Ministry of Religious Affairs and a separate Council of Nagaland Churches. A publication of the NSCN makes the objective of the Naga national movement clear: 'One of the main objectives of our revolution is to make our land for Christ and in order to construct a Christian state it needs an army who trust in the Lord...Nagaland for Christ shall be built by those soldiers who trust in Him.'[ii]

The Naga nationalists who went to China were very proud of the fact that they had successfully negotiated with the communist Chinese and got a hall for their weekly worship and they also insisted on not working on Sundays. Later the Chinese gave them material and space to construct a church. That is why they felt betrayed by the church leaders who accused them of becoming communists.

A section of the church leaders in Nagaland criticized the Naga national movement for taking help from the Chinese and accused them of leaning towards the socialist ideology. Leading this section was Reverend Longritangchetba Ao (1906-1981) popularly known as Longri Ao. He wrote a circular in May 1968 enumerating the dangers of communism to the church. For him communism and Christianity were irreconcilable.

Longri Ao was known for his efforts to bring peace in Nagaland. He established the Peace Mission, later came to be known as the Nagaland Peace Council. It was the work of this Peace Mission which led to the signing of the Shillong Accord.

Even before the signing of the Shillong Accord, Phizo's Federal Government accused the church leaders of siding with the Indian government against the Nagas. In a pamphlet published on February 19, 1970, entitled 'Nagaland and Church' the Federal Government condemned the role the church leaders were playing in the name of trying to bring peace:

> It is impossible to believe, but we have just witnessed it. Why does the church which calls itself an organ of peace in the world help the aggressors as they deliberately open a wound that will make peace impossible or at the very least put it off a very long way? With the anti-communist falsehood and propaganda that the Indian press and radio are pouring forth every now and then, Nagaland is turned today to witness another theatre of war. Many thousands of innocent villagers are being tortured in the most inhuman way, or tortured to death, womenfolk are not free to move about...and the nationalists shot down like animals. What makes it even more scandalous is that the church is silent when such crimes against humanity are being committed in this part of the globe. Who has raised the voice against the Indians' conduct in this matter?

This statement was signed by seven members of the Federal parliament headed by the Speaker, Dubo Gwizantsu.[iii]

The Baptist church (and the other church leaders as well) seldom condemned the human rights violations by Indian Armed Forces despite the fact the churches were made into detention centres and pastors were often arrested and tortured. The Naga nationalists believed that some of them were working with the Indian intelligence.

Indian intelligence worked through many church leaders by whipping up the anti-communist sentiment. It became a part of their counter-insurgency strategy.

During the early days of the Naga national movement Indian intelligence agencies thought that the foreign missionaries were encouraging the Nagas to separate from India. The Indian state banned American missionaries from entering the North East in 1956 but later they allowed certain kinds of evangelists such as Billy Graham to visit Nagaland in November 1972. He was allowed to conduct a crusade in Kohima. The crusade, organized by the Nagaland Missionary Movement from November 17 to 22 was attended by more than 100,000 people from all over Nagaland and beyond.

A few years later in 1976, the White House and the Central Intelligence Agency admitted publicly that overseas missionaries have been regularly used in information gathering. The then-Director of Central Intelligence, William E. Colby, and Philip W. Buchen, White House Counsel, stated that the use of missionaries violated neither the law nor the integrity of the missionaries.

The Americans continue to play a significant role in Naga affairs through the peace process. A large number of church leaders have been trained in the theological institutions in America and many of the village level church leaders have attended Bible schools and Bible colleges affiliated to American churches and institutions. The impact of the Americans on the ideology of the Naga national movement needs to be further studied.

In recent times there has developed a sharp divide between the Baptists who are in the majority and are backed by the NSCN (I-M), and the Catholics who are a small but growing minority. Villages all over Naga-inhabited areas have passed resolutions that there must only be one denomination within each village; Catholics have not been allowed to build their churches or even bury their dead within the village.

The case of Ritah Haorei was just one example of this growing divide. The dead body of Ritah Haorei, wife of Yangmi, lay in the Catholic church of a Tangkhul Naga village of Hundung in Manipur from August 7 to September 18, 2017 while there was an angry debate on the pros and cons of allowing a Catholic burial in a village which passed a resolution in 1973 banning all other denominations except Baptist Christians from practicing their religion. Several delegations of Catholics petitioned the National Socialist Council of Nagalim to intervene in the situation. The NSCN allowed the burial on humanitarian grounds. When Ritah was finally laid to rest in the village it was on humanitarian grounds and not as the right of Catholics to practice their religion. Her husband was told to withdraw the case he had filed in the courts and when he refused to do so, he was kidnapped and his body was later found. Ritah and Yangmi's child had been orphaned.

Religious intolerance is the hallmark of the times as is being demonstrated by the political developments in both India and Myanmar, and further afield in America. Unfortunately, the Naga nationalists have not been an exception to this trend.[iv]

PUNI: THE REVEREND

Reverend A Puni Mao, forty-five at the time of this interview, is from Song Song village, Mao Maram Tehsil, Senapati District, Manipur. He is from Mao Naga tribe.

Reverend Puni went to China two times. He was the Chaplain at the NSCN Camp, Eastern Nagaland.

At the time of this interview, Puni headed the Ministry of Religious Affairs in the Government of People's Republic of Nagalim (GPRN) and was also the Convener of the Steering Committee.

Reverend Puni has been a part of the Collective Leadership of the NSCN (I-M) since 2013.

Puni was interviewed in Dimapur on June 25, 1999.

Testimony of Reverend A Puni:

I am from Song Song village in Senapati District of Manipur. We are a poor family with my parents and their eight children. I am the third child of my parents.

I did not hear any folk stories because my father was always out of station and mummy was always busy in the field. Whenever she came home, she was tired and sleepy. She was the only one supporting us. My father did some contract work or business so I did not have much contact with our mummy and daddy.

My mummy was a practical woman—she did not teach by theory. Even now I have not forgotten what she taught me. She always said we have to prove ourselves practically. It was a great lesson for me.

I had to go to school at Mao Gate but when I came to my village, I worked in the paddy fields. I finished my matric in that school. The most difficult thing for me has been that I am not well-educated. From the very beginning I was religious minded. I went to a theological college.

My uncle, he was very close to us, he warned me to not experiment.

Don't try and taste (sic) women like a lottery system. So I am a happy man.

I am serving the purpose of God so I am a happy man.

In Search of God

I had a conception of religion. At that time I thought I would not go to church unless and until I see Jesus Christ for myself. I must have knowledge, otherwise why go to the church holding a Holy Bible and being a hypocrite?

I used to go into jungle in search of the real God. And the whole night I did not sleep. I went to the hills which were very cold and I did not wear proper clothes and I did not care if I died. I challenged Jesus and I said, 'If you are a living God give me a signal. I cannot put my faith in Jesus just because someone has told me to; that will not be satisfying.'

Such thoughts gave me very much pain.

Then a Sema Reverend came to my village. He brought a tape recorder. He put on the recorder and his father was praying in Sema language and bitterly crying. The Reverend told me that he had found that he would meet his father in Paradise along with my brothers and sisters. Seeing the future had made him sad.

My father said no one could see the future and he chased the Reverend out of the house. But the Reverend said to me, 'Don't you want to know the Word of God?' and I said yes, I want to know. He said, 'Your father does not know the Word of God that is why he does not want to share these thoughts. But if you want to know the Bible then you will be the happiest man.' He wrote down for me the address of the Bible college in Bangalore.

Then I went to Bangalore for theological studies. I studied in Berean Baptist college at Bangalore. I went there in 1969.

But I did not see the torture because I was away in Bangalore. I was told about all this when I came back. But in Bangalore we Nagas discussed the situation and when we got together, we discussed about joining the Naga Army. We were few Nagas, one Tangkhul fellow, one Sema fellow, two or three Aos and some five Mao Nagas. There was no feeling of division between Nagas from Manipur and Nagas from so-called Nagaland. We were all Nagas. Now the Nagas in so-called Nagaland say they are the original Nagas and Manipur Nagas are Kacha Nagas.

But we did not discuss about the Nagaland State because if we discussed then divisions would have come up.

The other Nagas came from the same kind of families. They were all cultivators. In those days we felt Naga and loved each other. I used to tell them that I will go to China after my studies. I told them this long before I actually went. My friends told me to write to them from China and ask them to join me. So my letter did not reach because of security in China.

In my college I told my Indian brothers that I would be a missionary in China. I challenged them, you know. They said, 'No! No! Mr Puni you are too weak, you cannot go there. How many missionaries have been murdered by the Communist Party?'

I said, 'What a pity your faith with Christ is not enough. You will see one day, in the newspaper, I will be in China.' They used to laugh at me. But from my childhood I have determination about going to China to preach the Gospel there.

Athiko Daiho

My father told me story of Daiho[183] who was my Uncle and from the same village as me. He was the first graduate among the Mao. He studied in Guwahati. I think he had more knowledge than Uncle Phizo, who had studied only up to Class Ten.

Phizo met Uncle Daiho secretly and told him about the Naga issue. Phizo took a lot of money from Daiho before he went abroad to East Pakistan. Daiho was the first revolutionary; he started by not

---

[183] Athiko Daiho founded the Naga National League in 1946. See Chapter One.

paying taxes to Manipuri Raja. The Mao people supported him and Mao people said we want freedom. We have been free from times immemorial but since Manipuri are a little bit more advanced, they could control us.

Once the Manipur Raja sent army to arrest Daiho but Mao people surrounded him and did not allow his arrest; and they even fired and four or five people died. Mao people were going to fight because they had Japanese rifles left over from the Second World War but Uncle stopped them and he was arrested and he was put in jail for so many years.

In those days no one understood what Uncle Daiho was doing. Khathing[184] was very much Indian and he had influence. So people did not understand what Uncle Daiho was saying. He was alone.

Later, Daiho became a Finance Minister in Union Territory of Manipur. When I met him, I asked him for his advice and he said he had nothing to say to me. Once he wanted to speak and they did not want to listen to him, especially the Angami people. They said he surrendered by taking up job with the government of Manipur. But he still supported the Naga cause so no one is allowed to mention him. He wanted to explain his mistake but no one wanted to listen to him.

I showed him the NSCN manifesto. I also showed him what Gandhi had said. He said he had tried to get the official account of what Gandhi had said but he could not find it.

Daiho said if we allow China to come to our area it would be very dangerous.

First Indo-Naga encounters

In my childhood I saw an ambush by the Naga Army in which one Indian soldier and one officer was killed in my village. That is when I

---

[184] Ralengnao Khathing, a Tangkhul Naga, (1912–1990) popularly known as Bob Khathing, was an Indian Army personnel, civil servant and diplomat and the first person of tribal origin to serve as an Ambassador for India.

first saw the fighting. It must be around 1960. This was the first action in the Mao-Angami area.

This was the first incident by the Naga Army. The SDO was carrying a lot of money and the Naga Army wanted to capture the money. The Naga Army shot but unluckily the driver was not killed.

I must have been around twelve or thirteen years old and I watched the incident with my own eyes. We were watching. The topi (hat) of the man who was killed was kept there to mark the spot.

After that the Naga Army escaped and went into the thick jungle and the Operation did not continue. Six of our Mao people went to join the Naga Army but four were shot dead on suspicion of being spies for Indian Army.

Then the Indian Army came down and they stayed in our village for so many days. They came accompanied by the Manipur Rifles but in those days they did not harass anyone or burn down our village.

Even while I was in school, I had met many people in the Naga Army like Lieutenant Colonel Nelie. Nelie was my cousin brother, his father and my mother are brother and sister so we were of the same blood. I helped him in many ways.

I would carry rice and meat for them into the jungle; we were a very poor family so we could not give money but we would help them with food. They would call us into the jungle.

But in 1970s when Nelie killed one CRPF Captain, the Indian security forces came to our village and many people were tortured. My father was also tortured and he had to be hospitalized. My father's eldest brother was even more seriously tortured. He was also hospitalized because he was hit on the head.

The Indian Army Commander came to my father who was a Pastor and asked him to pray for him. He said he kept seeing people beaten up and he could not sleep. The Indian Army Commander asked my father to forgive him. So my father asked God to forgive the Indian.

I do not remember the name of the Indian Commander who asked my father for forgiveness, but he was not Christian. But the Captain shot down by the Naga Army was called Ram Singh.

This Ram Singh had threatened Nelie and said he would arrest him and not rest till he had shot him down. So Nelie took the challenge and got his boys to kill the Indian Captain. One day the Naga Army shot dead a member of the VVF[185] and then the VVF came to our village and tortured the people in my village. The VVF are Nagas but in Indian service. Those who came to our village were Poumai.

Many people in the Kaito party joined the VVF. That was before the Shillong Accord. They were reactionaries and so they joined the Indians.

Joining Naga Army

My younger brother ran away from home and joined the Naga Army. My father was left alone in the hospital and he called back my younger brother and told him that he was supposed to serve his father. But my younger brother said he was so angry that he wanted to take revenge. But my father told his younger son that he was still too young to join the Naga Army.

In those days everybody respected the Naga Army. The Naga Army was very forceful and everyone was afraid of arms. They had never seen such guns. So if the Naga Army kept something people will not touch it; everybody will be afraid. Even if the Naga Army drop something on the way people will respect them and return it. Because the Naga Army called it 'Nagaland for Christ' and they were fighting for the people.

So, from the bottom of my heart, from my very childhood I wanted to join the Naga Army. But they said I should get some education so I finished my matriculation from the Bible college and came back and

---

[185] Sashastra Seema Bal, created in 1962 to guard the borders, came up with an innovative idea in 1965 of raising Village Volunteer Forces (VVF) to protect the villages, deprive support for insurgents, and also assist in counter-insurgency operations of the Indian Army and Central Paramilitary forces. Bob Khathing helped organize the VVF.

served as a pastor in Kohima for a year. After that I wrote to the Sema Reverend and thanked him for telling me about salvation in Jesus. Now I believe in salvation.

After I joined the Naga Army my battalion commander told me that Mr Muivah would be leaving for China so if I wanted to go, I better go with him. I went straight to my parents and asked their permission. My father was angry and he rebuked me; he said he had spent so much money on my education and I would go and preach to the trees and stones in the jungles. He said I should preach to human beings. But I told my father: Nagaland Army means Nagaland for Christ and not only must I join but he too should join to proclaim Nagaland for Christ.

My father refused to give me permission so I asked my mummy to bless my decision to go underground. My mother started crying and she had a problem with blood. If she saw blood she would faint. She told me before joining the Naga Army I should kill her.

But my brothers were enthusiastic. They said it was the right time to join. My elder brother encouraged me. He said, 'You have finished your college life, it is time for you to join the Naga Army. If you don't join the Naga Army it will be a shame. We are four brothers and if we could not give one for the nation people would laugh at us.' He told me if I did not join, he would go instead and I would look after the family. I told him he has many children so I should go.

But my father did not give permission. My commander told me he would give me three days to convince my father and mother. If not, they would not accept me. He said I need my parents' blessings.

So I used to call my whole family for family worship to pray for me and if it was God's will, He would open the way. I had full confidence. I did not fear and I was determined. I knew I must join the Naga Army because it was Nagaland for Christ. Now I have got a little bit of theological knowledge so I must go among the Naga Army and give them the salvation of Jesus Christ. If a person does not belong to Jesus Christ, they will misuse their power. The people will start to hate the Naga Army. Then everything will be upset.

I must go there personally so I could witness the good news personally. And if they know they will be saved, they will not be afraid to die. People are afraid to die because their life is not secure. If they are not sure of their salvation, they will be afraid of death even when they know that it is the right cause and they must sacrifice. They should know that even if they die, they will be in paradise. This knowledge must be possessed by every Naga.

Then on the last day, the third day, I called my brothers and sisters and gave a lecture in the common room and told them to open their minds and pray for me. And if God is willing, I would always be in the service of the Lord. We had a nice prayer and everybody was very much sincere. Everybody prayed because my father and mummy were very hard.

Then on the last morning my father came into my bedroom and told me to stand up. He said he would pray for me. I asked him, 'What happened, Daddy?' My father said he saw his father and his father asked him, 'Athiu, Athiu, why don't you open the door? It is time to open the door.' Athiu is my father's name.

Then my father started worrying that he was the man who is blocking my way to join the Naga Army. He said, 'My son, maybe this is God's word. I know life in the Naga Army is not easy, you may not get enough sleep, you may not get enough food, or a comfortable place to rest. It will be raining and all the time you will be in trouble. You are a young man and you consume a lot of rice and in Naga Army you may have to fast, and you will not get enough food.'

He said, 'I know, my son, Naga people are suffering.' Then according to custom, he put his hand on my head and he said my fingers are straight and like that my life must be straight. He blessed me. My mother had to agree because my father is the head of the house. So she also blessed me.

The moment he blessed me, I brushed my teeth and put on my clothes and I went straight to the battalion commander to join the Naga Army. I went to the Naga Army camp and along with Mr Muivah went straight to China. I went to the UN Seti camp. I do not know what the word meant but the Head Chaplain Kipfelhou had prophesized that it was the safest place for the Naga Army. It was in the Sema area.

Marching to China

Before joining the Naga Army, I had no training except for the training from the NNC in school. We had learnt to march and to shoot. But we Nagas by nature are trained since we hunt, so without any training I went to China.

We began our march to China. We were 135 of us. We could not walk in the daytime so it was always at night and we took eight months to reach China because we had to face so many encounters with the Indian and Burmese armies. We started in August 1974. There were eleven women with us, including the woman who married Chairman Isak.

The Indian Army was everywhere except in the jungles but in the jungles there was no water. We could not go anywhere to get water, either to a river or a paddy field, because the Indian Army was there.

We had to live for forty-five days without food and four days without water. I used to preach that we must love one another and share with one another. I would preach about brotherly love and how Jesus sacrificed all and we are one in Christ. But I forgot whatever I preached, especially one day in the jungles without eating for forty-five days, I prayed to God to show me eatable things. God gave me a banana tree with ripe bananas and I ate up all the bananas without sharing with my brothers.

I again prayed, that the day before yesterday You showed me a banana tree and You fed me. Again, God, show me something to eat. I thanked God for showing me the banana tree which saved my life.

I asked God to show me the direction and he told me to go right and I went and found a lot of fruits and I filled up my stomach. My motive was to fill myself; it is selfish.

I thanked God for showing some wild vegetables and fruits even if we did not have proper food. Then I filled my stomach and the remaining I brought for my brothers and shared it. But my motive was first to look after myself.

We reached the border and about to cross it near Saramati. We were on top of a hill and on that day Mr Muivah took out from his bag four packets of glucose. He had kept it in his pocket for forty-five days and had not eaten it.

Then Mr Muivah shared the glucose by giving each of us one spoon of it. He gave me one spoon but I could not eat it. I started thinking, this must be Jesus; otherwise no one would share their food in this way when he had been without food for forty-five days. I took the spoon and I remembered my past life. How I had preached with my mouth, not my heart.

I had finished the fruit of one banana tree without sharing. And I remembered how I had preached to people to love one another, share with one other. I had preached just one month ago. And here was Muivah giving me his glucose. He was truly a man of God. My fellow men ate that glucose the moment he gave it to them but I did not eat for a long time. It was a wonderful thing like a mystery. I thought a mere man cannot do this unless the spirit of God is with him. I realized Mr Muivah really cared for his people. He cared for me—I am nothing, just passed my BT (Bachelor of Theology). He cares for me, just a soldier, then how much he cares for the Naga cause. Then I took the decision that if he has to face an accident, I would jump in front of him and I will die and save him so he can fight the Indian Army.

Just after taking that decision I prayed to God and I ate the glucose.

After we took the glucose Muivah said that we would cross the border and so if you want to go you can go. But no one went. We felt there was an unseen hand which gave strength to our life, otherwise how could we survive forty-five days without food and successfully avoid the Indian Army?

We could not contact the villagers because they were surrounded by the Indian Army. There was curfew for four months. They knew that Mr Muivah was going to China and they had blocked all roads.

We were on top of the hills. Their idea was that if they blocked every source of water, how would the Naga Army survive? But by the grace of God and because of Mr Muivah we felt strengthened. We knew he would guide us.

Normally it takes us three months to reach China from Nagaland; but we took eight months. There was terrible fighting and sometimes we got lost but Mr Muivah helped to find the way.

We lost a few people. One Tangkhul Sergeant Major was shot; one Chakhesang was lost when we crossed the river, but one who fell into the water floated down all the way to Assam and survived! A Chakhesang got a boil in the thigh. It was very big. He could not walk so Mr Muivah carried him. But finally we had to leave him in a safe place and he surrendered because he could not walk.

This fighting was all on the Indian side. It took us more than a month to cross. But the Kachin Government detained us on the Naga-Kachin border and demanded that we give them 50 per cent of the arms we get from China. Finally we came to an agreement. Then when we reached China it took the Chinese two months to make arrangements for our accommodation, for 400 of us; since we were so many, we stayed with the Kachins on the Kachin-China border.

Rice Eating Competition

After reaching China, Atem and I were in the medical department. You know Atem is the kind of person who will never surrender to anyone. He is a very strong man. He will not surrender in sports, reading or writing or walking. I used to consume a lot of rice but he did not eat as much as I did. Seeing my style, he competed with me in eating rice. If I ate eleven bowls, he would eat twelve; if I ate twelve, he would eat thirteen.

Because you know after so many days without food people used to consume a lot of rice. Very funny. The Chinese gave us a bucket of sweets every week and we finished it and then bought more from the market. The China people made fun of us.

And two of us could consume one big dog. The villagers would laugh at us and say, 'You eat meat like a tiger. Even a tiger cannot eat a full dog in one go.' There was an interpreter who would interpret for us.

When we first went, we ate with spoons and we made a lot of noise. Most of the Naga Army was from Burma and they made a lot of noise while eating. So many people eating with spoons sounded like thunder in the dining hall. Most of the Naga Army from Burma did not know how to use spoons. I felt ashamed.

It was also the first time we saw noodles and it was so difficult to eat them. Then we learnt how to eat with chopsticks. In the beginning it was very difficult and the two chopsticks would meet. Now most of Naga Army can eat with chopsticks. It is very easy once you learn.

Political Training

The Chinese gave lectures in Chinese and there was an interpreter and some of them knew Hindi and Urdu very well. We speak simple Hindi but they speak complicated Hindi. But English we somehow managed.

When I saw the China people, I was very much inspired. I felt ashamed because I did not have the qualifications to be a revolutionary. They told us a revolutionary must have relationships with the people. We were told to have self-reliance and to fight with courage.

They taught us about military tactics and a lot about ambushing, attacking camps and suicide squad. They taught thoroughly and we had lectures on the military subjects and in the evening they showed us films. If anyone felt sleepy and stayed back in his residence and did not go for the film, they were not happy. They said no one can understand only by listening to lecture but had to see the practical side in the film.

Then they would ask our opinion about the lecture. They will write our name, tribe and answers. They said the reports will be kept. We will keep the report till Nagaland is liberated.

They gave very much respect to the Naga Army. They stood in line on both sides and as we passed, they would clap and say we were heroes and they encouraged. They said Nagas understand their motherland. They gave us practical and theoretical to make us good revolutionaries. I felt very much embarrassed that we were not qualified to understand what is revolution. But I got a lot of knowledge from them, both political and military knowledge.

Political knowledge I got was to recognize who was our enemy and who was our friend. They taught us according to their ideology. They said we must be able to distinguish between our friend and our enemy otherwise our politics will fail. They used to have a picture of a Chinese commander who was a capitalist fellow and they used to shoot his picture for practice.

Daily Routine

Our daily routine was that early morning we got up and had tea. Then we had PT or just running. Then washing and breakfast; sometimes noodles or khichri, sometimes boiled rice.

Then our classes began—sometimes military class, sometimes political class. Then we had lunch and some rest, and then more training. In the evenings we were shown films and sometimes at night training for ambush and sometimes physical marching. On Sunday we worshipped. We had worship service also on Saturday evening. We asked them to build a church and they said we will build the next time you come. So we had service in the cinema hall.

During our political class the Chinese said they had a volunteer force to help world revolutionaries. They asked whether we would like some volunteers. I said yes, that would be good. I ran to Mr Muivah and said, 'Let us get the Chinese and we can destroy Delhi, Calcutta and Bombay and Madras.'

Mr Muivah told me to sit down and he asked me whether I knew about the Vietnam war. He said there was no Vietnam war—it was a war between the Americans and the Chinese. If we invite the Chinese volunteers, there will be a Third World War because democratic country and communist country will always clash. So Naga people will be finished.

Mr Muivah told me that we should get training and material help but we should not invite the Chinese into Nagaland. So then I stopped asking them.

When I look back, I realize our Naga people do not know who is their friend and who is their enemy. That is why we cannot stand up to the last. I learnt from China that we must not compromise with our enemies. I should always be with my people because my people are my friends and they will care for me whenever I am in difficulty. I teach this to our friends and so politically I learnt a lot from China. And even now I tell our friends we should not forget what we have learnt from the Chinese.

I never went to Peking and Chairman Mao was already dead by the time I went to China but they still taught his work. They taught us Chairman Mao songs. But I have forgotten the words now.

Politically I improved. I did not go to Peking but I went to Kunming city.

Shillong Accord and Second Visit to China

I went to China two times: once I stayed for nine months, and the other time I stayed seven months. The first time when I went to China, I heard of the Shillong Accord and we came back in December 1975. Then we established our camp in Burma, condemned the Accord and Uncle Phizo and then we went again to China in 1976.

I left for China a second time. There was no leader but there was a Commander: Ashiho Chao Mai. He was then the deputy of the Chief Commander of Naga Army. Mr Muivah had already left, he was injured in the knee.

This time I stayed in China for seven months. It took us less time to reach.

The first time I had army training they did not teach martial arts, only a little. The second time in China I was partly in the medical department and partly in wireless interpretation from English to Nagamese. So I did not get full doctor training.

I learnt mostly herbal training. And first-aid. They taught us more than 1000 herbs. We had noted it down and due to the fighting, I lost the list but Atem may still remember because he has a good memory power.

We learnt acupuncture. It is very effective. Within ten days malaria will subside. It is wonderful. It is effective with needles, without medicine. Sometimes we used to go to the Chinese hospital in Tengchong so that the doctor could examine how we practice. They asked us to talk to patients and diagnose the disease.

When we were in Burma, we had established a nice hospital. It is especially effective in joint pain and for those who cannot walk or have pain in the knee. Acupuncture is very helpful for underground people.

We had one lady, Avuli. She also had medical training and she also had midwife training—she was an expert on delivery cases in China. In Burma, Atem was in charge.

Mr Muivah can sing and play guitar. In the camp we played volleyball and basketball.

Preaching the Gospel

We were not always at the hospital even though we were trained in China. I had to go preaching because the people in Burma were in the dark. I used to preach the Gospel. Nobody knows who is Christ. No, we did not use gun to convert. We would save their souls.

Our General Secretary taught us that animism and Christianity will be our Naga religion. Actually according to our manifesto, you know we try to convert them because if they practice their own tradition and custom there will always be an economic crisis. Because they have to celebrate so many things, kill so many buffaloes and cows and make huge amounts of wine.

We recognize the belief of the Zeliangrong who are not converted to Christianity. But this is our faith in Christ and our propaganda also. In our manifesto, we believe that every Naga should be converted to Christianity. That is the aim.

According to their will, let them join Catholic. Our manifesto does not say what kind of Christianity—it only says faith in Christ. We cannot force them to join a particular denomination. Our aim is just to inform them to have faith in Christ only.

So whether they belong to Catholic or Baptist, we just worship one God. We used to say, come down and let us pray together. But we want to be uniform. We should not particularize. We should worship together in one church since we are in the underground. We cannot make it a Catholic church or Baptist church; otherwise we will have so many categories. But we should have uniformity. We should not kneel down or do shouting and praising. If you are Catholic or revivalist, make a little bit of adjustment. Let us adjust. Let us not be doctrinaire.

But Nagaland for Christ means we want everyone to be Christian. The slogan was there during the time of the NNC; because of that I was interested in joining the Naga Army.

Our church has become capitalist. The rich become richer. It is very difficult because within the NSCN also some want to keep their property selfishly. Our two leaders rebuke them and teach them socialism, but Naga mentality is always selfish. In our manifesto we have mentioned Christian socialism.

Aftermath of the Shillong Accord

When I came back from China the second time, the two leaders told me to go to my Mao area and explain about the Shillong Accord. I went back home. I found I was alone; the national workers had surrendered and supported the Shillong Accord, even those who had been in the movement when I was a child.

I went straight to our General Secretary's elder brother Shangreihan and he helped me with money so I could establish myself.

I went all over the villages and told people if they love the Naga National Council, they must condemn the Shillong Accord. We had sent a delegation to convince Phizo but we could not.

I said Uncle Phizo was still our leader. I talked to them about the NNC and told them only Mr Muivah can lead us. But there was jealousy.

Our Mao people have been in the movement from the beginning. But we never had a national leader. Government comes and government falls but Mao people are there, always following other leaders. We are not policy makers.

We supported NNC, then we supported Hongkin Government, and Phizo, but we never had a national leader. Mao people killed and we fought among ourselves during the Kaito time.

Day and night, I went to preach to them about Shillong Accord. I said people must condemn it but we are the NNC. That is only party. A few did not sign it.

Four to five years I worked to convert the Shillong Accord people. Nobody understands what is socialism. It is not easy to understand. I just explained about Naga issue.

I lived in the jungle and I converted them. I began in the Poumai area because I could not enter the Mao area immediately because it was the stronghold of the Shillong Accord supporters.

I challenged some Shillong Accordists with the help of our Tangkhul brothers and shot dead ten Accordists. Finally our people started fully supporting us. The Mao Council passed a resolution that we will support only the NSCN group after NSCN was formed in 1980.

I challenged the people to call the Accordists to the church and let the public hear a debate between me and them, and then they can decide.

Meeting my Parents Again

I was Regional Chairman and so I was in the area but I stayed in our camp in the jungle, and I had to go to our camp in Burma. I went to meet my parents. I told them about our life in Eastern Nagaland. I told them we had established more than 200 churches there and set up more than ten Mission Schools. And many of the Burmese Nagas had been given water baptism.

I narrated to my father that now the Eastern people are happy and they have hope and they know they will be in paradise. I told my father I praised him that he had allowed me to go. My father said, 'I praise God, it was the voice of Jesus when I allowed you to go.'

Then my father and mother told me not to visit home very often because it was not safe: 'We know you love us but your life is more important and you should stay in your camp where you will be safe. Try to do your level best for the Nagas.'

The Indian Amy went to my parents' house and harassed them very often. They would break the window or door. My parents never locked the window and door. They encouraged me that you must never surrender even if you die.

Arrest, torture and prison

In May 1985, on my way to Burma side, I was in Dimapur staying with a Sema brother and he betrayed me. He had a huge amount of arms in his house but he was not arrested. I was arrested on May 22, 1985.

I was kept in military custody for three months. While in the military custody they interrogated me. They wanted me to tell them about Mr Muivah's vision. They said if I told them they would not beat me or torture me.

I told them Mr Muivah does not want to fight India if India re-organizes Naga nation. But if you come with arms Mr Muivah will not remain silent. I told them that the Chinese had offered to send Chinese volunteers into India and all the younger men wanted to accept the offer. But Mr Muivah refused.

The Indian Army man said Muivah took the correct decision. He told me if Chinese came Christianity would disappear. They left.

I was tortured. They stretched my body till it was full of sweat and my long pants and shirt were wet. I was shivering so much. I could not hold a book in my hand because I was shaking. And the beating was such that my whole body was black. I did not feel the beating but it was the stretching of my body that was bad. Even today I feel weak and suffer from nervous disorder.

After keeping me in military custody for three months, I was handed over to civil authorities and kept in jail for more than two years. I was in jail in Allahabad, Shillong and Imphal; they kept shifting me.

In Imphal jail we had an argument about Greater Mizoram. The Meitei underground people in jail opposed the idea. Then I asked Oken and he said he supported Greater Mizoram demand. The Meiteis will surrender one day. They have no future because Imphal valley is surrounded by Nagas and Mizo.

Some Mao people got me a lawyer in Imphal and I was bailed out. Then when I came out of jail, one of the men who signed the Accord was also released and he and I had a public debate so at last people were convinced. Mao people said they were convinced.

Then I was arrested in Nagaland when the police called me to the police station. I was out on bail and had to report to the police station every day. The SP called me and said, 'I am sorry, Mr Puni. You are under arrest.' I was in jail for a year.

So during the Khaplang crisis I was in jail; I did not know what was happening. When I came out, I reported to Mr Raising and I was elected Regional Chairman. People were so confused because so many divisions like Hongkin Government, then martial law, Kaito, then Shilling Accord and now the split with Khaplang. So much tribalism and people no longer believed we could achieve our sovereignty. Naga mentality is such: one tribe cannot control others. Phizo could have united the Nagas. But he betrayed us, even though officially he did not sign the Shillong Accord.

After the Shillong Accord

Then Mr Muivah called me to Kathmandu and I went there. I stayed there for two years. I was a station officer.

In 1989 I got married in the Burmese camp. My wife was also in the Naga Army. One Reverend came from Nagaland to conduct our marriage ceremony since I was the only reverend in the camp and I could not conduct my own marriage ceremony, could I?

We married in the church. Food was supplied by the villagers. She is Tangkhul but living in Thiva which is in Senapati. She speaks Poumai and Tangkhul language.

She was a go-between, a messenger between the Naga government and the region. My first daughter was born in Kathmandu and the second in Dimapur.

Steering Committee

From 1990, we in the NSCN started contacting people abroad.[186] During the period of 1990 to 1996, our boys were clean and honest. They were disciplined. Every church prayed for the NSCN cadres. They prayed with tears.

The corruption and indiscipline started after the ceasefire in 1997. They felt free. Before the ceasefire the cadre could force people to pay but they were disciplined. After ceasefire there is no discipline and there is corruption. Among our NSCN cadres, we have a habit that we teach others but we do not teach ourselves.

We have resolved to set up a Steering Committee to deal with the problem of corruption and indiscipline. The members will be senior people. Most NSCN cadres do not understand NSCN ideology. They will be socialists. They will have authority to check anyone, whether in the Naga Army or even a Kilonser, and even check revenue collection. We want transparency. I am the first Convener of the Steering Committee.

If revenue collection is done the cadres have to submit the money within a month. Otherwise they will be arrested. Army people don't

---

[186] This is the time when NSCN leaders could be seen at various UN Human Rights fora as well as indigenous people's rights forums; also, other Western-funded NGOs.

listen to the civil side. The army and civil sides have parallel set ups so do not listen to each other. Now with the Steering Committee, that mistake will be corrected.

Now we have only four Kilonsers instead of eleven. The four are Defence Ministry, Home Ministry, Finance Ministry, Industry Ministry. Only four. The Religious Affair Ministry is under the Finance Ministry. It is a bit complicated. I have made a complaint and asked that Religion should be under the Home.[187]

Christianity means to fight against corruption. Christianity means to fight against power abuse, Christianity means the fight against immorality.

I argued with Mr Muivah for supporting Khaplang because he drinks, he takes drugs, he is always after women. But both Isak and Muivah remained silent when we were in the camp.

If any junior officer in the Naga Army drinks or misbehaves with women he is punished even up to capital punishment. But Khaplang is on the highest body of our organization and so I challenge Muivah to take action against Khaplang. I said there should be equal treatment because everyone is equal before the eyes of God. God will not be pleased with you. God will never accept your leadership to liberate the Naga nation.

I criticize the church leaders for making money. Kuldip Nayar wrote an article that 75 per cent Nagas are Christian. I took the article and told people I have not seen any true Christian. They are supposed to fight corruption but they did not. They are supposed to fight injustice

---

[187] However, with time and the need to have representation from all tribes, the Council of Ministers again rose to fifteen in 2010: (1) Kilonser of the Ministry of Kilo Affairs; (2) Kilonser of the Ministry of Chaplee Affairs, (3) Kilonser of the Ministry of Mineral Resources, (4) Kilonser of the Ministry of Forest & Environment , (5) Kilonser of the Ministry of Keya Affairs, (6) Kilonser of the Ministry of Information & Publicity, (7) Kilonser of the Ministry of War Victims' Welfare Affairs, (8) Kilonser of the Ministry of Arts, Culture & Tourism, (9) Kilonser of the Ministry of Education, (10) Kilonser of the Ministry of Lota & Horticulture, (11) Kilonser of the Ministry of Health, and four Kilonsers without portfolios.

but they do not. Once Jamir said the church leaders asked for money and he asked them whether he should steal from the government for their missionary work: 'Can you pray for me even if I steal for your missionary work?'

I told them, 'Even though you know Jamir is a corrupt Chief Minister you still go to him and ask for money and pray for him. You will compromise with Satan also.' They remained silent.

Hope of Peace

Now we have negotiations with India. I have great hope that there would be a settlement if India is sincere. Our leaders have already committed themselves and Indians have promised to respect our unique history, i.e. we never signed that we would become a part of the Indian Union and we have our plebiscite when 99.9 per cent voted for independence. Gandhi also said he respected the Naga demand.

UNICE: THE ORACLE[188]

Unice Shatkamla, from Somdal village, Ukhrul district, Manipur, was
born around 1936; she said she was sixty-three years old at the time
of the interview.

Unice was the Oracle who accompanied the Naga Army in
December 1976 to China. She went with them up to Eastern Nagaland.

Unice was the first President of NSCN's women's organization, the
National Socialist Women's Organization (NSWON).

Interviewed in Dimapur on July 1, 1999.

Translated from Tangkhul to English by Phungthing Shimrah.

Testimony of Unice, the Oracle:

I was born in Shogran village.

My earliest memories in Shogran village are of the Japan war. We
called it the Japan War, not Second World War. I remember seeing the
Japanese troops and planes flying in the air. The Japanese called us to
their camp and gave us food. They were fond of us. At that time, we did
not even have proper clothes to wear.

I saw the Indian Army around the time I was ten years of age. But
they just passed by; they did not stop at our village. I heard about a
Naga Army around 1961. We heard that they did not have any house
but were living in caves or in hollows of trees in the forest. I was very
curious to see how this Naga Army lives and keeps themselves safe
inside the forests. I heard that they did not come out during the day,
and in the night when they came they would cover their heads with a
thin shawl.

I remember one night my brother brought a man from the Naga
Army. My brother introduced the man as Ngayan from Hemi village in

---

[188] Nagas call the oracle a 'Prophecy' i.e. a noun. The oracle or prophecy is a
person considered to provide wise and insightful council or prophetic predictions or
precognition of the future inspired by the Holy Spirit.

Burma and told me to quickly cook him a hot meal. That is how I first met a member of the Naga Army. Even when we took the food into the forest for the underground, we did not meet the Naga Army; we just left the food under a particular tree and went back and then they would take the food. At that time the entire village did not cook for the underground; we cooked for three-four people and left the food in the jungle.

I was not born in a Christian family. When I was young my parents drank rice beer.[189] But I did not want to drink it so I had only water. In 1952 there was a division in the village and the Christians had to move out and settle outside the village. My brother and I were converted to Christianity even before the division so we moved out and stayed with the other Christians. My mother died and I had just one brother. My father lived separately with my stepmother and younger brother.

So my brother and I lived in one house. My brother brought Naga Army-men into our home and I started cooking for them. Even at a young age I would take food for them into the jungles. At that time no one knew who was in the movement and who was not. The people in the movement did not wear any uniform or carry guns. They just moved as if they were going to the paddy field or out on business.

I noticed that normally when villagers met each other they exchanged greetings but the Naga Army did not talk like other villagers. They used to hide and meet people and later I realized that Uncle Muivah too was doing that.

And soon the Naga Army would come looking for me and asking me for help. That is how I got involved in our movement. Whenever I did weaving, I made cloth for the Naga Army also.

By 1962 I had already joined the underground. Uncle Suisa is from my village and although he had left the village to stay in Kohima, he visited the village. I knew he was already involved in the Naga national movement. On one occasion when he came to the village, he invited

---

[189] Baptist Christians are forbidden from drinking alcohol, including the traditional rice beer.

me to a prayer cell of the underground. I did not tell anybody that I was going to the meeting and left quietly. That was in 1961, before the Indo-China war.

I started praying and during the prayers I had a vision that I had got tickets for the Nagas. I saw myself holding tickets and, in my vision, I saw that I had to distribute the tickets. That is when I realized I must serve the Naga cause.

In 1961 Uncle Suisa brought Chuba Ao and Samuel Lotha to preach. Suisa was working for Christian revival movement and he told us that there was no other way to achieve our goal than to pray. He said we must pray and if any family member objected to my work and chased me away, I could stay with him.

I started thinking that even though I am not educated I could still serve my people through prayers. So I decided to go to Uncle Suisa and ask his advice on how I could be of service to the movement.

I went in search of Uncle Suisa with two of my friends. Uncle Suisa welcomed me and said it is good that I had come. He said it would have been better if educated people had offered their service but he felt it was the will of God that I had gone to him.

Uncle Suisa told me to go to every village and pray for every pregnant woman; pray so that the baby in the womb, whether he is a boy or a girl, the child when born will know God and know his or her people. He said: 'You go and pray for them.' Uncle Suisa told me that it was not only with guns that we must fight for our freedom, but also power of our prayers.

Uncle Suisa said womenfolk must awaken for the sake of the nation, that a mother has to pray and her prayers should help the baby in her womb, whether a girl or boy, to develop a national consciousness and so the baby will be born a nationalist and will be able to serve the people. He said womenfolk must fast and pray for the nation and national peace.

After listening to Uncle Suisa I started touring all the Tangkhul villages from 1961. I went to other areas as well although I did not know their languages. I went to Wokha and Mokokchung; I went on foot and was accompanied by a man called Ramkathing from Sanakeithei village who acted as my translator. Ramkathing was a disciple of Uncle Suisa and it was Uncle Suisa who told him to accompany me.

At that time when I was going from village to village, the Indian Army was carrying out operations in every village and so I could not have any political discussions with anyone. The moment I spoke to anyone, the Indian Army would ask what we were speaking about and where we would be going next.

In the midst of this tension I would continue to pray and God gave me strength to continue. I would remind myself that even though I had no education or knowledge and I did not understand the language of the people in places like Wokha, I had a precious gift from God. And I was guided by the visions I had. I knew what would happen next so I could move around without being caught.

In Wokha, the Indian Army operations were going on everywhere and after six in the evening we were not allowed even to speak or move around.

I remember seeing burning houses in villages set aflame by the Indian Army. I remember that some villages were burnt twelve times and people staying in those burnt, thatched homes. They had nothing in their homes. They did not have even a mug to give us a glass of water so they cut from bamboo and gave us water in the bamboo. There was nothing to sit down on, not even a moorah; the villagers cut a big bamboo into half so we could sit on it.

Even though I saw these things I did not fully understand the extent of pain the people were suffering. Then I began to be more conscious and I began to feel more and more pain and also love for the people, pity for what they were suffering.

I went for a meeting at Wokha but I do not remember exactly which village, and there I saw a play which showed how the Indian Army was torturing people. In the play they showed how two people could not sit together and chat. The play showed how one woman was praying and the Indian Army came and dragged her by the hair and killed her; and a pastor was buried alive up to his chest. After seeing the play, I realized the extent to which our people were suffering.

Uncle Suisa told me that God does not differentiate between those who know English and those who do not know. He said the only thing that matters is that if we pray and God answers our prayers. He told me to go everywhere to pray. He sent me along with two elders. Uncle Suisa made all the arrangements for us.

Once when the Indian Army came and found us praying and asked who were the people who had come from the Tangkhul area, I did not understand what they were saying but all I said was 'Hat! Hat!' The Indian Army asked what are you doing, and we told them we are praying for each other, and we are here to share the pain and sorrow of everyone. So we were going everywhere, praying everywhere, praying for everyone and for one another. That's what we told anyone who asked us what we were doing.

On one occasion I was asked by Uncle Suisa to meet him in Dimapur. He gave me a letter to deliver to Ramyo Zimik in Kohima. He told me to deliver the letter and spend the night at Ramyo's house and come back to him in Dimapur.

So I went to Kohima along with the letter to Ramyo Zimik and, like I had been told, I slept the night at Ramyo's home. Then I went back to Dimapur and Uncle Suisa asked me, 'What did you dream that night when you slept at Ramyo's house?' I told Uncle Suisa that I had dreamt that Ramyo had not been baptized yet.

Uncle Suisa said 'Oh!' but I did not understand what he meant or the significance of my dream. Then he asked me to deliver a letter to this Yangmaso Shaiza and to spend a night in his house. So I did what I was asked and when I came back Uncle Suisa asked me what I had dreamt in Yangmaso's home. I told him I had the same dream that Yangmaso was not yet baptized. I did not know the meaning of my dreams. Uncle Suisa said, 'Don't worry about the meaning, just tell me and I will tell you the meaning.'[190]

---

[190] Both these people, according to the Naga nationalists, were traitors to their cause so not baptized.

I do not remember all my dreams. I could not write down my dreams since I am not educated. But I remember that sometimes when I went to a village, I would dream that a tiger has been born in the village. Uncle Suisa told me that this meant there was an informer in the village.

When I moved around the village, I felt someone was guiding me and, in my dream, I would see an event that would soon occur or the coming of the enemy.

I joined the Naga Army in December 1976 when they were leaving for China. But I did not go all the way—I stopped at Kachin area and stayed in Eastern Nagaland. Till then I did not prophesize and did not allow myself to be possessed by the Holy Spirit. Nobody knew about my gift, not anyone in the village or even my family. I kept it a secret. Only Uncle Suisa knew. He said I must do what God asks of me. Only when I was in Eastern Nagaland I began to listen to the Spirit and to prophesize.

We left on Christmas Eve in 1976. We had to leave because of the Shillong Accord. We were told that Mr Muivah had already left. Pamrei called us and we left secretly. We started from Shogran (Somdal), walked through Phungcham to Paorei and crossed to Somrah in Eastern Nagaland across the India-Burma border.

Feeling happy that we had crossed the boundary we had a fasting there.[191] Then we started trekking through the thick jungles. I could not take my boots off for several days and my legs began to get swollen and my nails grew long and when I took off my boots, I could not put them on again because my feet were so swollen that the boots would not fit.

In Burma side I was praying while they were having a meeting and I saw a vision of the Indian Army and a bullet hanging from the neck. So I went and told the leaders that something is wrong: when I pray I see this vision.

---

[191] Thanksgiving through fasting and prayers is a common practice amongst the Baptist Nagas.

But they scolded me and told me that I was scared and they told me to go and pray. So I went, prayed again, and I saw the same thing and I went back and told the Commander again. He got angry and told me that people like me dishearten others by being fearful. He told me to go and pray.

So I went outside and prayed and then I heard a lot of noise in the village side, and the dogs were barking around so I went back and said, 'Oh! Something is wrong, what is happening? Everyone is making a noise out there and the dogs are barking.' Again the Commander told me I was too scared; that's why I was reacting like that. He told me that the villagers were having a festival and he told me to go back and pray again. But this time I didn't go, I stayed in the room where they were having a meeting. Just then the man guarding outside was shot dead by the Burmese Army. The Burmese Army is very cruel, more than the Indian Army.

After that attack everyone scattered and the village was overrun by the Burmese troops. We had nothing to eat for a week. We were on the run and the Burmese were looking for us all over and they said they would catch the women alive.

We escaped into the hills but the way was full of rocks. Sometimes it was difficult to climb so we used ropes to help us climb up the hill. And sometimes we used ropes to climb down the hill as well. We could not go into any village because everywhere, in every village, the Burmese Army was waiting to ambush us. After many days we reached one small village and when they saw us women in the Naga Army, they felt pity and they said they would cook for us. When they were cooking and everything was finished and we were about to eat, they saw the Burmese Army coming so we left without eating any food.

Then we went to another village. Once again, the village saw us women and they said they could cook and started preparing our food. I was so tired and exhausted and I fell asleep. Then I saw a vision of the army again so I went to Commander Pamrei and warned him that I had seen the enemy coming again. But the Commander told me I was always scared and that is why I was always seeing the enemy but I told him, 'Whenever I have seen the enemy, they have attacked us for real.' He said, 'No! You are too scared so just sit down.' Then just as we were about to eat, he got a message that the Burmese Army was coming up to the village so we had to leave the food and make our escape.

So it went on like that, every time we had to run away and make our escape. I could not keep up with the rest of them. I could not walk fast because my feet were hurting. The rest of the group were ahead of me and they had already crossed two or three streams. I was left behind and I followed them by following in their footprints.

They sent two persons to look for me. I was praying to God to allow me to serve the nation. I don't want to die even before I have served the nation. I prayed to God to save me so I could serve the nation. Then I heard two people calling me from the top of the hill. They took me with them and the Burmese Army was chasing us.

So we could not walk on the footpath and we had to walk through deep jungle and we came to a place which was very cold and it was snowing heavily. We were not carrying anything, no blanket or woollens. We had just some thin cloth to cover ourselves; there were no leaves to cover ourselves because the trees were bare and even the birds were lying dead because of the cold.

We were moving through a thick forest so we had no idea where we were. We were going along on a path and we came across a river. The menfolk crossed the river and bent the branches of a tree for us to hold and cross the river and climb a steep rock. One of our men slipped and he dislodged a rock which went rolling down and hit the head of one woman whose name was Shimtharla. Shimtharla fell and started rolling down but luckily there was a creeper growing on the cliff and she got entangled in the creeper and lay there unconscious.

It was very difficult to reach her and bring her up to the rock where we were all standing. We did not have place to sit. With great difficulty they carried her to the cliff and then some of us volunteered to stay with her to nurse her. Others had already gone ahead. We were praying for the woman.

One of the men who volunteered to stay back was Livingstone. We had not eaten for so many days and we were all tired and exhausted and weak. So Livingstone said how can we stay like this; he announced that, 'Today toh I will get meat, so I'll go and hunt.' So when he was about to leave we were shouting 'Bring meat! Bring meat!' And he jokingly said that he would bring a deer.

Livingstone was so weak he could not even climb up the cliff to go into the jungle and he told us to shove him up. And his friends pushed his buttocks and heaved him up. He had a rifle with a broken butt.

After sometime, just ten or fifteen minutes after he left, we heard shots being fired and everyone was happy—ah! he has killed something. He had killed a deer but he was so weak and exhausted that he could not carry nor pull it up to where we were camping. But somehow he managed to carry up to some distance near the cliff and then he called out, 'Come and help me, I cannot carry all.' Everyone wanted to go to help him but were just too weak. At last one man went up and then without even carrying just pushed the deer down to where we were.

The deer fell. But then the problem was cooking the deer and we needed water. To fetch water, we had a small pot and one of the men had to go down to the river to get the water. And we managed to cook the deer. There were no leaves which we could use as plates. We just ate with our bare hands. The deer lasted two days. We prayed to God to give us energy, especially to the wounded woman, so that we could move on.

All of us were very tired and so they could not carry the woman and had to make her walk or drag her. Since she had been hit on the head, she felt giddy and after walking a few steps she complained of a headache and she felt like vomiting and then she said she needs to go to the latrine. Finally, she collapsed and fell down.

They would climb up a tree and see if there was a village. The group which had gone ahead had marked the tree for us. After two or three days we saw a village which was far away. We were happy and we kept asking whether we were reaching and whether we were nearing the village.

We reached a Khiamniungan village. The General Secretary had already left. We stayed in the village for almost a week. The woman who had been injured could not survive because we could not give her rice. The village had only maize.

When I reached, I realized how much pain I had and my feet were torn with thorns. I had walked without boots and they had to take out thorns from my feet and legs.

We were exhausted and our leaders said we womenfolk could stay back. They took down all our names and told us when they came back, we could return with them. But then one of the women said that the decision could not be taken for them. Each of us must be personally asked and we must decide for ourselves. She said she had given up everything and she would not go back. So we all went ahead and camped near a river in a Khiamniungan area.

Then we went to a Leinong Naga village. I was shocked to see that the people were all naked. We were backward, but compared to us, these people were really backward. The men had long hair. I had heard that my grandfather used to be naked. And we found they eat only yam, maize and millet, but no rice. I wondered how we would stay with them and work with them.

At the camp everyone got another pair of shoes but there was none left for me. I was afraid of thorns and snakes because I had to go barefoot.

I was determined to go to China because I thought even though I am not educated, I will do whatever they tell me to do and I kept praying. While crossing the Chindwin river, one boat with three men and three women got a small hole; those who were able to swim could save themselves but those who could not were carried away by the river. One boy who died was Philip from Ngainga village.

Then we had to cross another river. The boy who was rowing was not an expert and he kept rowing backwards and one girl jumped off and went to the riverbank where she was caught inside a sinking sand and she started to sink. She was alone and she kept sinking but she managed to get out and reach the group. By then the rest of us had already had our meal and were preparing to go. They had thought she had been swept by the river and died so no search party had been sent to look for her. So, she had to keep marching without any food.

The guide who was taking us to the Kachins purposely took us round and round so what should have taken one day took five days. He wanted to make us tired. So, by the time we reached the Kachin headquarters and contacted the General Secretary he said they were coming back. It would be no use for us to go because there would be no time to get training. The Kachins said the agreement was to allow Nagas to go to China only once, not two to three times.

Our Commander Pamrei died of malaria in Kachin. They tried to save him and carry him, but he went into coma and he was buried in a small Kachin village.

Going back we all wanted to go in Mr Muivah's group. He said we should divide us into two groups because if we were too big a group, the small villages would not be able to feed us all. But we all wanted to go with him and we said it does not matter if we cannot eat.

Then we proceeded towards Western Nagaland. The Burmese were still chasing us. At one point when we were trying to cross a river, we saw lots of footprints so we knew that the Burmese Army was nearby. So we avoided the larger villages and went through the jungle's paths instead of the roads. By this time our rations were finished. We passed a small village and we saw that the Burmese troops were there so very quietly we passed through and the Burmese realized we had gone and they again chased us.

After a long journey we came to a village, if I remember rightly it was called Tauggyi. The Burmese had set up a hospital there. There were Nagas there so when we reached where they lived, Mr Muivah told the people that we are Nagas and they too were Nagas. He reminded them that when the Naga Army had passed through some months back the people had betrayed them to the Burmese Army and as a result some Naga Army had got killed. Mr Muivah told them if they confessed to their crime then they would be forgiven. But the villagers denied their involvement and so their leaders were picked up and their hands tied and they were brought before the villagers, but they kept denying. But we knew that Naga Army had been killed here. Finally, in front of the villagers three of their leaders were shot dead. Then we took the medicines from the hospital and destroyed the hospital since it was built by the Burmese in a Naga area.

Two or three times we set up ambush for the Burmese Army and we took positions but they knew the area well and they did not come. They kept chasing us. Then we came to a village Chuiyang. It was a place where there was a dispute between the Konyak Nagas and Pangmi Nagas. So the General Secretary said the area would be our general headquarters and so it will not belong to either the Konyaks or the Pangmis. It was there that the villagers had killed twenty of the Naga Army. That was the first batch which had been sent ahead to find the route to China. Mr Muivah explained everything to them for three days and asked them to confess their crime but they refused to accept. It was in this village the Naga Army had taken shelter and they were resting after returning from China and each one was taken to a different house. When they entered the house each one was killed by spear. The chief of the village had lots of heads of the Naga Army (kept as trophies).

Even after telling them that we knew what had happened, they refused to confess so they were rounded up and all their weapons were taken, including spears and daos; seven of their leaders were arrested by us. It was a big village and they made guns. The seven leaders were taken to the river and they were told to confess or they would be shot. But they continued to deny. At last one man said they had killed two, but we knew it was twenty. Finally one man confessed and he was allowed to go but the other six were shot dead.

Then we left that village and reached another village. I think it was called Tonkho. Here we took rest and the villagers said the food would be ready by midnight. The Burmese Army was coming but this time General Secretary said we would stay and fight, and we took position. The Burmese Army came at two in the morning and started firing. The

General Secretary took the lead and was in front encouraging everyone to fire. He was shouting 'Fire! Fire! Fire! Are you not a man? Fire!' Mr Muivah's guards were looking for him and he was right in front and it was dangerous because the Burmese Army was on higher ground. The guard told him to come away and he was refusing. The firing went on from 2 a.m. to seven in the morning. Finally the guard found him and told him to go at the back and asked if he was to die who would lead the movement? The guard told him that it was not the duty of the General Secretary to be on the frontline. The whole movement depends on him.

So the General Secretary was told to go ahead with the womenfolk. After they left, the Naga Army thought they should quietly withdraw instead of wasting bullets. So they started withdrawing. At that time the commander was Vedai. He is no more. And there was a boy from Phungcham called Ringphami. Ringphami's stomach was hit by a bomb and his intestines spilled out. He called out for the General Secretary but Mark told him that Mr Muivah had gone far ahead. There was no chance of the boy surviving, so they had to leave him and he died.

Many Burmese died and they sent a plane to pick up the dead bodies. I heard many of our leaders also died in that battle.

We kept going and the Burmese troops were always behind us. At one time a helicopter was circling over us and another time a plane dropped a bomb on a village—everything was destroyed but no one was killed except one pig. But we all got separated and were given different duties and we could rest for a while.

It was at this time Mayanger Ao came to our camp and arrested Mr Muivah and the Chairman. The Aos kept changing the camps so we had to cut bamboo and make the camp five times. My hands got cuts because of the bamboo. I was sent to cook food for Mr Muivah. It was at that time I got a vision that I should work with herbs. I had this vision before also but I kept refusing.

Finally one day I accepted it and decided I must do as I am told by the Spirit. At the time my eyes were paining and I could not bear to sit near the fire because of the smoke and I could not go out in the sunlight because my eyes hurt. I had a vision in which I saw a plant and I found it behind one house in the village. I cut it and put the juice into my eyes and my eyes began to burn and I thought I would become blind. It was as if chillies had been put into my eyes. But after a time when I rubbed my eyes, I found I was feeling better. Then I got dysentery and, in my vision, I saw the bark of a tree. I boiled the bark and drank it and it cured me.

Then I realized this was a way for my training and that I must try the medicines on myself before I start to give it to others. Then I was called to a house and there an old man was lying half-paralyzed. He had been paralyzed for twenty years. I told him I could not do anything for him but the man became very sad so I gave him some medicine and prayed for him and went home. Then at midnight someone called me. They said the old man insisted that I come immediately. I went back and the old man said I should pray according to my faith. I put my hand over his head and prayed. And his head became very hot. Then I moved my hand over the paralyzed side of his body which was cold and as I moved my hand it became warm and by the time I said 'Amen,' he said he could walk again. I told him it was not I that had cured him, but Jesus.

The old man said he wanted to be a Christian and I taught him how to be one. He said he would follow me but I said he should stay in the village and teach the others. When the villagers heard he had become Christian they told him if that year the harvest was not good, they would chop off his head and cut his body into half and dry one half and bury the other half. The old man asked me what he should do and I told him nothing would happen and slowly the whole village became Christian.

By the grace of God, I cured many people—two leprosy patients also. They called me Vikhoo, or Avakharar, the eldest mother.

Atem gave training to many girls on how to use herbs but at that time I was not well so I could not attend his training. Later he met me and saw the herbs and bark I was using and he asked me who had taught me. I said no one had taught me; I had seen these herbs in my vision. Finally he believed me.

After the NSCN was formed around 1980, the General Secretary and Chairman asked me to become the first President of the women's organization. I started to cry and asked the General Secretary why they wanted to put a blind person in the driver's seat. I had no education or knowledge about running an organization. They told me I would not be alone because God would guide me. Then I remembered I had a dream ten years before. In that dream I saw a big church and people were coming out of the church and one man came to me and gave me a big shoe and told me to put it on. But in my dream, I refused and said it was too big for me. But he gave me the shoe. It was because of that dream I accepted the job of President of the NSCN Women's Organization.

I began by preaching the word of God. I spoke in Nagamese but people did not understand so I got the children to translate for me. After the prayers the villagers would ask, if they became Christian would they be sent to China? And they asked whether we would give them free cloth if they became Christian. Talking to the villagers was almost like talking to stones, walls and trees. Then I persuaded the elders to translate for me because people would listen to elders. I told the elders they could be Deacon and Head Deacon.

It was a difficult time for me but also for the villagers. They never had enough to eat. So, at no point were they satisfied, they were hungry all the time. They just had a little maize and yam.

At the time of the Khaplang crisis I was not there in the camp. If I had been, I would have been killed since I used to cook for the Chairman and General Secretary. But I was ill and had been admitted to hospital at Jorhat. But before the crisis I had a dream. I saw the whole place was in total darkness and then there was a huge tree with lots of fruits and leaves and lots of people had come with knives and spears. They were throwing stones and trying to remove the fruits from the tree. A lot of fruit fell down. Then they tried to cut down the tree when a voice came that people should not cut down the tree. I discussed the dream with Mr Muivah and then I left for Jorhat.

I did not get better in Jorhat so I went to Dimapur. But there was a lot of security problems so I went to Imphal because I had to find a way to earn something to live on. I was really short of money by then. From Imphal I went back to my village but all this time I had no news about the General Secretary or Chairman. I did not know whether they were alive or dead.

I had to work for daily wages and sometimes elders who had been with the NNC and knew my work gave me rice. It was so shameful because I had to borrow rice but there was no curry to eat it with.

Then I heard that the General Secretary was alive.

I also heard the story of one Khaplang boy called Karang who was told to shoot the General Secretary. So he was chasing Mr Muivah and at one point he came very near. Mr Muivah and his group were resting. Karang aimed and shot. The bullet did not come out. He shot two or three times but the bullet did not come out. Then he shot for the fourth time and the rifle burst and the boy lost his hand. Then he realized that truth was on the side of Mr Muivah.

I was so happy to learn Mr Muivah was alive and I felt peace of mind. I could not meet him immediately but finally I did go to meet him in the company of his wife. We went by vehicle up to the Bangladesh border and then walked from there.

Even in the midst of the crisis with Khaplang, Mr Muivah's elder brother was supporting Khaplang's son and looking after his studies.

What do I remember most? There was an incident when we were on our way to China when one of the men did not know he was bitten by a snake. But his body was swelling and he could not proceed. So we had no choice but to leave him with a little rice and some water. Ahead we told some villagers to look after him. But by the time the villagers reached him he was already dead. The villagers found a little money in his pocket. And the villagers ran after us for two days to return the money they had found in his pocket.

Another time the villagers found the body of one of the Naga Army who had drowned in the river. The fish had eaten his eyes and ears and the villagers took him out and gave him a burial. They found money in his pocket and they had to walk for a week to catch up with us and return the money. We told them they need not return the money and could buy tea for themselves, but they said no, we were doing so much for them and suffering so much—it was not right to keep our money.

The villagers shared their food with us, even though they were so poor. But there were days when we had nothing to eat and we were all hungry. And then we would tie a cloth around our waists tightly and it helped us to bear our hunger. Sometimes when we were hungry we would ask each other, have you eaten? And we would reply yes, someone would say they had meat, others would say they had phaoren rice, and then we women would laugh and we were told not to laugh because the Burmese Army would hear us laughing.

Now I see that Nagas are fighting Nagas. There is no stability on earth and the earth is shaking and there is a landslide. I see people trying to build a big church but it will not stand because the land is sliding down and people are scared and holding on to the branches of trees to prevent from sliding down. Whatever I have seen I have shared.

I liked this interview. Thank you.

CHAPTER FIVE

The Tribe, Tribalism and The Nation

Grandfather constantly warned
That forgetting the stories
Would be catastrophic:
We would lose our history,
Territory, and most certainly
Our intrinsic identity.
So I told stories
As my racial responsibility
To instil in the young
The art of perpetuating
Existential history and essential tradition

—Temsula Ao

In Burma, Naga tribes were called Na-Ka, which in Burmese meant people with pierced ear lobes. The piercing of the ear was the most important initiation rite for young boys entering manhood.

But it was not till the end of the nineteenth century that the most important institution for the Nagas became not their tribe, but their village. As M. Horam points out:

> It is important to note that the Naga villager of the period up to 1900, was not aware that he was part of any greater social unit other than the village. It is to this community to which he was bound in solidarity from birth onwards. Though loyalty to his clan is a significant factor

throughout his life, it is the ruling and law as set out by the village
Council of elders to which he must abide.[i]

The story of how the villages joined together to form a tribe has
still to be written, but by the time the Naga national movement began
the toughest challenge before the movement was to unite more than
sixty different tribes and communities spread over four states in India
and across the international border into Myanmar.

Nagas generally think that the most significant contribution that
the Naga National Council under Phizo made was to bring together
the Nagas under one political organization. There are anecdotal
accounts of how Phizo travelled all over the Naga-inhabited areas in
India and Burma, often incognito; how he held meetings and instilled
his people with pride in belonging to a Naga family.

Unfortunately, we do not have much documentation of the process
by which the Naga National movement brought together the Nagas
whose primary loyalty was their village and then tribe. The emergence
of tribes itself is of recent origin, and is a continuing process. But the
greatest challenge before Naga nationalism has been to deal with
tribalism. Horam observed:

> This (tribalism) has been one of the main sources of tension and
> instability and in fact, has led to inter-tribal rivalry and killing in
> Nagaland during the past 30 years... If anything of the movement
> for Naga independence has during many a crisis, boldly accentuated
> the disunity of the Nagas and the recent rapid developments in its
> disintegrating ranks are ample proof of this.[ii]

At various points in Naga history, one tribe has found itself being
condemned as 'anti-national' or a tribe has felt that its role in the
national movement has not been sufficiently recognized.

The Naga national movement has tried to address this problem by
creating pan-Naga organizations such as the Naga Hoho (Parliament
or Assembly) or the United Naga Council.

The second problem is the challenge of trying to give representation to the smaller Naga tribes, some of whom have just three or four villages. In the past, these tribes came together to form a larger entity but now the individual tribes are asserting their own separate identities.

In our interview with Angelus Paiza Shimrah (1946-2007) a senior member of the NSCN on June 28, 1999 in Dimapur, the NSCN leader said: 'Naga identity is built through the process of different tribes coming together. Smaller tribes assert themselves and their identity. This is a process which will continue even after we achieve our national objective. As long as the smaller tribe has a sense of belonging to the larger Naga family, such assertions are not a threat to the Naga nation. Individual tribes have every right to assert themselves and develop themselves.

'For the present, actually in the name of administrative convenience, we are trying to group some of these smaller tribes and we do not call them smaller tribes but full-fledged tribes. This is for administrative convenience but also to preserve the identity of smaller groups. We are also trying to have their representation within the organization (NSCN) apart from representation in the region.

'For instance, let us take Chandel district. It has seven tribes[192] and the region is supposed to send three representatives but we have provision for extra representation if there are smaller tribes. Even if the population is less than 5000, they will be sending one representative to the Consultative Committee.

'One Tatar (Member of the Naga Parliament) represents 15,000 people but in case of smaller tribe the Tatar represents even a community of 5000 people. Even at the administrative level we have such representations. In some parts we have Ranges where there is only one tribe but in Chandel we do not have a Range because we will ensure each tribe is represented. We want each tribe to have a voice. That is our vision. We want each tribe to identify with the Naga identity.'

---

[192] The seven Naga tribes in Chandel are: Maring, Anal, Lamkang, Moyon, Monsang, Aimol and Tarao. But this list is changing and it does not include the Purum.

The third problem is of reconciliation between the different Naga armed groups in the name of Naga unity. The efforts to reconcile have been largely been the work of the church leaders.

In recent years the divisions within Naga society have led to deadly clashes between the Naga armed groups and the breakup of pan-Naga organizations such as the Naga Hoho. Three major tribes, the Sumi (Sema), the Ao and the Lotha have disassociated from the Naga Hoho and formed a rival Central Nagaland Tribes Council in 2010. The disagreement was over the recognition of Rongmei as a Naga tribe in Nagaland State in 2013.

The most complex problem has been the integration of Naga-dominated areas of Manipur with Nagaland State. When the Nagas raised this issue in the 1950s and 1960s the problem was perhaps less vexed, but those opposing the integration of Naga areas are also backed by armed groups (many trained by the Nagas themselves).

Within Nagaland State there is growing resentment among those tribes who are considered 'backward' and those who consider themselves 'advanced'. Six Naga tribes: Konyak, Chang, Sangtam, Khiamniungan, Yimchunger and Phom living in four districts of Tuensang, Mon, Longleng and Kaphire within Nagaland have formed themselves into the Eastern Nagaland People's Organization or the ENPO and are demanding the formation of a separate state because they feel they have not got a fair share of the development pie.

Within Manipur too there are divisions among the Naga tribes and the Zeliangrong United Front, which was formed in 2011 with an armed wing named the Zeliangrong Tiger Force with the objective of having a united Zeliangrong state; but that organization too has split.

The four interviews here give some insight into the problems of tribalism and how the NSCN has tried to deal with this.

The NSCN maintains that much of this tribalism is the work of the Indian intelligence agencies. They point to the Joint Directive for Counter Insurgency Operation in Nagaland written after the creation of the Nagaland State.[iii] The section on Psychological Operations directs the security forces to 'divide, disorganize and induce defections of members of the hostile movement...'

If the Indian intelligence agencies are involved in this game, they seem to have been quite successful in turning the Naga national movement against itself.

MEDEM JAMIR: THE AO

Medem Jamir was born in Mokokchung District in 1946. He joined the NSCN (I-M) in 1994.

He has been a Deputy Kilonser and later a Kilonser holding different portfolios; he was a member of the Steering Committee of the NSCN and has taken part in the Indo-Naga peace process.

Medem Jamir was interviewed on June 24, 1999 at Dimapur.

Testimony of Medem Jamir:

I am now running fifty-three years old. I was born in Chungliyimsen village in what is Mokokchung District of present-day Nagaland State.

Right from my childhood we were taught we are Nagas who belong to the Ao community. So, we knew we belong to Ao tribe as well as to Naga nation. I did not have a chance to discuss these things with anyone because I grew up on my own and tried to answer questions on my own.

My father was a Gaon Burra. I have four brothers and three sisters. My oldest two brothers died when they were young—one in Kohima in 1957 and the other in Calcutta where he was a student of theology. Two of my sisters are married and the youngest is looking after my mother.

I do not remember my childhood very well except that I studied till Class One and then the school was closed down because of the national movement. We did not go to school for two or three years and we were just running around assisting the elders involved in the movement. Two of my Uncles were in the movement and the third was my mother's brother, he was also in the movement.

But I do not remember much except once I saw Assam Police come to our village and drag some people away. I saw them dragging them to the village gate which had been built from the time of the British. I was told that the underground had been having a meeting in our village and the police took them away. I remember as a child I wanted to look at these heroes who were fighting for our freedom.

When we saw our freedom fighters beaten, we started hating Indians.

On another occasion I spent a week in the field with my Uncle who was underground. And we had a very nice time in the jungles for six months when we were underground. The elders were making all kinds of things with bamboo, like baskets and bags. And sometimes we would be asked to take messages like intelligence work!

I also saw grouping of villages.[193] In my village people of two other villages were grouped: from Khar village and from Mongchen village. They were there for two years and many of the villages died of starvation. Khar was a big village and they were kept fenced in. For us children it was fun having friends from other villages but for the elderly it was difficult. I saw people crying and crying. And we were not allowed to go for kheti (cultivation) to our fields. The men could not roam about freely and if they tried to go out, they were beaten black and blue.

Schooling

Since the school in the village was closed, my Uncle who was posted at Tuensang as Area Superintendent with the government of India took me with him. This was in 1959. So I did my schooling in Tuensang.[194]

---

[193] Uprooting an entire population from a cluster of several villages and relocating it for purposes of counter-insurgency was first tried by the British Army in Malaya (as it was then), by the US Army in Vietnam and the Indian Army in the North East, mainly in the areas which later became Nagaland and Mizoram.

[194] Tuensang town is the headquarters of the Tuensang district, the easternmost and the largest district of Nagaland, bordering with Myanmar. The town was founded in 1947 for the purpose of administering the erstwhile North Eastern Frontier Agency (NEFA) that comprised the present day Tuensang, Mon, Longleng, Kiphire and Noklak districts. Nowadays, these four districts combined together are also known as Eastern Nagaland. And there is a demand for a separate state of Eastern Nagaland not to be confused with NSCN's Eastern Nagaland which refers to Naga-inhabited areas of Myanmar.

I went there with my elder brother and a Phom Naga boy who was brought up in our village by one of the teachers. He was married to my niece. So they took me to the Government High School at Tuensang.

I do not remember how we went from the village to Mokokchung but from Mokokchung to Tuensang we went in my Uncle's jeep. It took the whole night driving and I was sick. I vomited and vomited. You know I was very fond of chewing gum so my brother gave me chewing gum to subside the vomiting but after that journey I started hating chewing gum.

I passed Class Two from the school and I did very well in Chang language. We studied in Chang. I got the highest marks in Chang language and my relatives made fun of me, that, 'How can an Ao boy do so well in Chang?'

My uncle was transferred from Tuensang to Yimchunger area which was in the interior and there was no school there, so I was sent to Chungtia, which is an Ao village, where I stayed with relatives. I studied up to Class Three. After that I was sent to Alongchen along with my sister. I tried to run away twice to Mokokchung because my sister used to scold me. I was very naughty. I passed Class Four from Alongchen and then I was sent to Mokokchung.

In Class Eight I was put in boarding school because my relatives could not control me. My relatives liked me and I would go from one to the other; each one was willing to keep me but I would just go my own way. So they kept me in a hostel and I passed matric from Mokokchung school.

While I was in Mokokchung ceasefire was declared. That was in 1964. I must have been about fifteen or sixteen years old. At that time my Uncle who was a colonel in the Naga Army was the quartermaster so I used to get free rations from him and I was feeding my whole hostel with those rations. It was a time when there was no rice because people were not allowed to go to their fields. I got rice from my Uncle.

I was a very lucky boy. One of my uncles had a shop in the village so he used to come to Mokokchung to buy things. He would always give me something. My Uncle who was in Tuensang was a Circle Officer and he used to send me eighty rupees a month; I had a scholarship of twenty rupees after Class Six so I had a hundred rupees every month! I was a rich man.

At that time I still did not know how to smoke, drink or chew paan. But I was learning all this from my friends. I was very much enjoying drinks with my friends.

After passing matric I was sent to Shillong. But I wanted to go to Assam. My friends had gone to Assam and I also wanted to go. Trouble started from that time. I had never seen Assam. There was no bus at that time so people walked through the jungles nine hours to reach Mariani where they went for shopping and walked back nine hours. But I did not go to Assam then.

Further Studies

After passing Matric I was sent to Shillong. My villagers made fun of me because I was known to be absent-minded, and they said 'You have not even been to Assam, how will you reach Shillong? You will get lost.' I went to Shillong with my friends. We went from Mokokchung to Amguri by truck because there was a road, and from Amguri we went to Jorhat and slept the night there. From Jorhat we went to Shillong.

In Shillong I did my PU in science. I had many good Mizo friends and stayed in their camp. My Naga friends asked why I stayed with the Mizos in the Tribal hostel. In Shillong the Nagas and Mizos dominated.

I passed in 1969 and then I applied for engineering in Bombay and got admission. I studied there for two years but I could not continue because my brother who was the Runa Peyu (Chairman, Village Authority in underground administration) was captured by the Indian Army. That was in 1972. He was the one who was supporting me and so after his arrest there was no one to send me money. In order to go back to my village, I pawned my Rolex watch which I had bought for four hundred rupees. I got three hundred rupees from the broker and arrived back to my village.

On reaching my village I was arrested and beaten very badly by the Indian army. It was on 13 December, 1972. My hand was broken. I did not go to hospital but to a village doctor, and so I could not continue my studies in Bombay.

I taught at the school in Mokokchung and also finished my BA from a college in Assam.

Shillong Accord and the Church

Then the Shillong Accord came. I do not know whether my relatives accepted the Accord in their hearts or not, but they stopped working in the movement. They did not take a conscious decision but they just stopped being involved. Today they are against the Accord.

After the Accord was signed, people in Mokokchung were against Isak Muivah because they eliminated so many Ao people. At that time I was wondering, why was it like this? It should not be like that, no nation can go against a whole tribe or an entire tribe goes against the nation.

I think the Nagaland Baptist Church Council (NBCC)[195] were against Isak Muivah. The believers were asked to pray against these two leaders because the church leaders said the two leaders were going to bring communism. I felt there is something wrong because I could not believe they were going to bring communism.

But I could not discuss this with anyone because of the situation. I stopped going to church because the church was going against the national movement. So from 1978 to 1992 I did not go to church. So many girls and boys did not know what was happening and I also did not know what was happening to the Naga national movement.

In 1986 I asked my Uncle from my mother's side, General Sani, who was in the Naga Army, to tell me the difference between NNC

---

[195] The Nagaland Baptist Church Council (NBCC) has its origins in an American mission of the American Baptist Mission (American Baptist Churches USA) in 1839. It was officially founded in 1937 as the Naga Hills Baptist Church Council, changing to its current name in 1953. NBCC is not to be confused with the NSCN's Council of Nagaland Churches under their Ministry of Religious Affairs.

and NSCN and the Federal Government and the GRPN. He said the NNC is no more and he was supporting the NSCN in his heart although he did not join.

When I learnt of the crisis in the NSCN I was worried about Muivah. I wondered where he was and whether he was alive. And whether there was a design on his life by Indian intelligence led by an Ao, SC Jamir. So I was searching for the truth. I could see people were still struggling for freedom.

Deciding to Join the NSCN

Then there was my Uncle Tajenyuba Ao, an authority on Ao customary law. He told me to join the NSCN (I-M). Yes he was the first advocate from the Ao Naga tribe and is the author of *British Occupation of Naga Territory* (1993). He was very fond of me and he said it was important for a person like me to join the movement because I can make friends with everybody. But I felt embarrassed to join since I was a nobody.

My Uncle kept telling me I should join the national movement and do something; he kept inviting me to his house to persuade me to join the NSCN. I was interested but I kept thinking, what someone like me could do for the movement?

That was when I started going to church again to pray to God to change my Uncle's mind about my joining the NSCN (I-M). People were surprised to see me in church even at night. I started reading the Bible, going to church and having family worship but I did not tell anyone why. I did not even tell my wife that I was praying to God to make Uncle Tajenyuba change his mind about my joining the NSCN (I-M).

I could not discuss this with anyone else because if Khaplang's men came to know I was even thinking of joining NSCN (I-M) they would not hesitate to shoot me. The only person I did discuss my problem with was Yimsu, my neighbour; he was the first person to pass his PU from Ao tribe. But my wife got to know about my sympathies for NSCN (I-M) when soldiers started coming to our house. It was this neighbor and I who planned the first operation of the NSCN (I-M) at Aliba village. I did not of course go to the spot but I arranged everything at Mokokchung and my neighbor had a jeep.

The I-M boys started coming to our home and I was the person who arranged their shelter and my wife went to buy rations for them and cook for them. And the first person the Khaplang people shot in Mokokchung was my wife's brother's son. They called him an I-M boy. For three months I told the Town Commander not to come to our home because my wife was so upset—the nephew was like her own son.

Yimsu had joined the NSCN (I-M). He was already given an appointment but he said he would not join unless I helped him. I said: 'I'll help you, I'll help you, I will do all the writing and help from the outside.' Then he gave me the appointment as his Secretary. I did not tell my wife. But he has already sent my appointment letter to the government. They came looking for me.

Khaplang people suspected that Yimsu was working for I-M and they had beaten him black and blue; because of that he died in 1995.

I had been working with the NSCN (I-M) from 1993. I did not tell my wife. I used to find accommodation for them, identify the people who could be trusted, and tell them the geography of Mokokchung.

From 1994 I was in charge of the Ao area, so in 1994 I told my wife because I had to be careful and live outside my house.

The impact of my work with the Naga movement was on my children. I have six children and we could not afford their education and our relatives took them in and took care of them. One year I got a Christmas card from my children with just one line: 'Dear Dad, the way to freedom is too long. Come back home.'

Those years from 1989 to 1994 were very bad when Khaplang people were killing our people like animals.

Till that time, I had not met the NSCN (I-M) leaders except Major Ramkathing and Captain Johnnyson. Then Ramkathing took me to meet Mr Atem and Mr Atem took me to meet Reverend Puni who was the Kilo (Home) Kilonser. Like that, without fully being aware, I had joined the organization in 1994.

Just before I joined the organization, I took my wife and kids to my village while my father was still alive. I did not tell them anything but I knew that my days with them were numbered. It would be too dangerous for them if I visited them. It was on Good Friday that I met my father and mother. It was my last meeting with my parents who were good Christians.

Khaplang

One day I was called by General Sami but before going I went home and my wife asked me to have food. I said ok and while I was waiting for food, the Khaplang men surrounded my house. It was, I think, 18 June and it was very bright. I had no way of escaping because if I jumped from the window, I would land thirty feet below on steep rocks. I hid under my bed.

My house is very small. The Khaplang men searched for me all around and I was praying to God. I said for two years I have prayed that I may be saved from joining the organization and now I have joined and I am going to die.

They beat my wife and children putting the barrel of the gun to their mouth and they searched all over but they did not find me even though it was such a bright summer day and my house was so small. I can't believe they did not see me. But after fifteen minute of search and touring my house they turned everything upside down and then they left.

Tribe and Nation

It is only right to identify with one's tribe without forgetting we all belong to same Naga family. Some people are trying to take advantage but it is very beautiful to belong to different tribes; I am Ao, you are Tangkhul (*pointing to Sebastian*) and he is Sema. It is very beautiful.

We Nagas were separated by administrative boundaries and we were not given a chance to study the Nagas of Manipur, and Nagas of Manipur did not get a chance to study the Nagas of Nagaland. And the Nagaland Nagas do not know how many Naga tribes there are in Nagaland.

When people say Tangkhuls are not Nagas[196] I say to them, there are more than forty Naga tribes but only seven tribes participated in the plebiscite. That was also a great achievement for the Naga National Council leaders who walked through jungles on foot crossing all the mountains and ranges and through valleys. And with the passage of time the Nagas got united.

Konyak people did not participate in the plebiscite so does that mean the Konyak people are not Naga? Neither did the Chang, Yimchunger, Sangtam participated. Nor did Pochury who were under the Chakhesang in those days.

Even though Konyak did not participate in the plebiscite, but they were very much in the movement. Tangkhul did not participate but if Tangkhuls were not in the movement how come NNC during Phizo's time chose Muivah as the General Secretary?

The Naga Students' Federation has a good coverage of all Naga areas and the NSCN (I-M) are good friends with the NSF. Nation building has to be done with every individual contributing. The economic and the political problem has to be understood and the defence problem has to be understood. If we are strong in politics and economics then we can make progress and then the nation will be strong.

Yes the Nagas are now divided between rich and poor. SC Jamir may be the richest man in India. Who knows? He has remained in politics for so many years and he looks upon politics as a business.

The problem of tribalism has been created by different agencies like the Nagaland State. The Nagaland State government is under the

---

[196] A part of the divide-and-rule policy carried out by the Indian state is to isolate the Tangkhul Nagas of Ukhrul district in Manipur and say they are not Naga. They are special targets because Thuingaleng Muivah is Tangkhul.

Constitution of India, then how can it represent the Nagas? We have to face the Khaplang people, then the state government and the Indian Army. We know Khaplang is supported by the Indian Army because whenever there is a red ribbon on the barrel they do not attack. The villagers reported this to us.

We have started going to the villages and explaining all this to the people. We enter the village with a heavy heart. We have to be careful and with a little bit of wit and humour we explain things. It is the most difficult problem and also the most interesting. You meet all kinds of characters. After two days we leave with a happy heart. Some of the villages send us back with tears in their eyes. If we cannot satisfy them, we cannot step into the village again.

G GAINGAM – THE RONGMEI

G Gaingam, Rongmei Naga, born in 1942, was a Captain in the Naga Army.

He has been the President of the Zeliangrong[197] Naga Union.

At the time of this interview, he was President of the United Naga Council (UNC) the apex body representing the Naga tribes in Manipur; and one of the four Vice-Presidents of Naga Hoho (Parliament), the apex body for all Naga tribes.

In 2011 Gaingam became the Founder-President of the Manipur unit of the Naga People's Front,[198] a political party committed to integration of Naga-inhabited areas of Manipur with Nagaland State.

Gaingam was interviewed on July 15, 1999 at Dimapur.

Testimony of G Gaingam:

I was born in a very old village called Taodaijang (in the present Tamenglong District of Manipur). I do not remember much from my childhood but my village was burnt down by the Indian Army in 1957 because the underground people had made their camp there. We all had to go underground.

We had to give rations both for the underground and to the Indian security forces. The Indian security forces would beat up the underground.

Contributions of the Zeliangrong People

The Zeliangrong people participated in the Naga national movement[iv]

---

[197] Zeliangrong Naga tribe consists of four tribes: Rongmei, Liangmei, Zeme and Puimei spread over an area which covers Manipur, Nagaland and Assam. Zeliangrong Union was formed in February 1947 in Manipur.

[198] From 2003 to 2008, the Nagaland People's Front ruled the Nagaland State in alliance with the BJP in the Democratic Alliance of Nagaland (DAN), where it is the main constituent of the coalition.

expecting to get independence. The Imphal central jail was always full of our people; one came out another went in.

You will not believe how wonderful the spirit of the time was. The entire village participated. Every ten families had to give one youth for the Home Guards—at the time it was not called the Naga Army.

Then we had to enroll all the youth for standby Naga Army; the women below fifty years had to form a women's society; and all the village was under the Federal Government. We had to choose a Runa Peyu (Deputy Commissioner) and a Razzu Peyu (SDO). So the Federal Government reached everyone in the villages.

Even a widow with just one female pig would willingly give it away to the Federal Government. And if a family had two granaries, they would readily donate all their paddy to the Federal Government. So every family donated to the national movement and was also physically involved in the movement.

We organized a safe road to get Phizo from Silchar to East Pakistan. Tadingpau[199]—he knew the roads so well. He was the guide for Phizo as well as the Naga Army when they went to East Pakistan for arms training. I did not meet Phizo. I was too young. But I met Rani Gaidinliu.

There was some misunderstanding between Rani Gaidinliu and the Naga National Council. The NNC took her as being anti-Christian. Rani also recruited people and armed them, so NNC and Rani's men killed each other and this went on for two years. It was decided by our Zeliangrong Union that Ranima should shift deeper inside Nagaland side but later the Deputy Commissioner of Kohima made her surrender. No, NNC people were not involved in her surrender.

Later Ranima was involved in the unification of the Zeliangrong who are scattered over three states: Assam, Nagaland and Manipur. The area is contiguous. She took up this movement when the Naga national movement was going down.

---

[199] We interviewed Tadingpau in Dimapur on July 16, 1999. His interview is incorporated in Chapter One.

Our people suffered because of the Indian Army operations. Our people could not attend to their fields and suffered from famine. We also suffered under the Village Voluntary Force. They were very, very strong and they have done much more atrocities than the Indian security forces. Bob Khathing was in charge, but in our area it was the intelligence officer named Mohanty who was stationed in Imphal.

This was the time India had her first Five Year Plan but our people did not care about development. Only after 1972 did people of Tamenglong see some development.

Nagas of Manipur

Nagas of Manipur have our own customs and traditions. We have our villages which have come together to form tribal organizations such as the Zeliangrong Union or the Tangkhul Long. Other tribal organizations also have their own organizations. But we did not have a common platform for all the Naga tribes to come together.

The first organization formed for the Nagas of Manipur was the Manipur Naga Council. It was most probably formed in 1957.[200] The purpose was to unite the Nagas of Manipur to participate the Naga national movement. I do not know very much about that organization, but it was the first apex body of the Nagas in Manipur so Nagas could join the Naga national movement.

After the creation of Nagaland State, because most Nagas were left out, another organization came up called United Naga Integration Council. Rishang Keishing was the General Secretary and the main demand was the integration of Naga-inhabited areas in Manipur with Nagaland under one administration.

The United Naga Integration Council merged with the All India Congress Party on the basis of an Agreement signed in 1972.

----

[200] Prof. Gangumei states that the Manipur Naga Council was made on the initiative of R Suisa in 1960, Kumar Suresh Singh states that Daiho formed the Manipur Naga Council in 1956 and converted it to United Naga Council in 1957 and Vashum says the United Naga Council was merged with the NNC in 1957.

The agreement between the Congress Party and the Integration Council stated that the demand for the integration was not anti-national or unconstitutional.[201] The Naga National Council had nothing to do with this since they accepted the Constitution of India. As I said, I know very little about that and I was not a member. At that time I was busy doing contract work to support my family.

The United Naga Council (UNC) was started in 1984. The first President of the UNC was Meijinglung Kasom who was a Member of Parliament. But the UNC was not active till 1992 when it was reorganized.

I became President of the United Naga Council in 1995. We had to deal with the Naga-Kuki clashes from 1992 to 1997, but we also had to deal with the issue of Naga integration.

It was during my presidency that the United Naga Council became a part of the Naga Hoho.

Naga Hoho

We had village level organization, we had tribal bodies but we did not have one organization for all Nagas. The Naga Hoho is now an organization with all the tribes coming together as a federation. We now have a Naga Hoho and we are proud of it.

However, it took us a long time to make it the kind of organization we wanted. The idea of Naga Hoho was initiated by SC Jamir. But

---

[201] Joint Agreement for merger of the United Naga Council (UNIC) and the All India Congress Party signed on August 4, 1972 stated: 'Agreement on Political Stand: It is agreed upon that the Congress party does not oppose Naga integration movement and does not consider Naga integration movement as anti-party, anti-national, anti-state and unconstitutional activity. Further it is agreed upon that no Congress Party member will be subject to disciplinary action on the ground that he or she as the case may be is involved in Naga integration movement. It is also agreed that the Naga integration problem should be discussed and settled at the Government level. The party members can also discuss the matter at different party levels.'

his idea was to create an organization of Naga tribes confined only to Nagaland State.

Till recently the Naga Hoho did not have any representatives of Nagas of Manipur. It took three years to convince them to include Nagas of Manipur.

At their first summit meeting at Wokha on June 25, 1994 and at the Kohima Summit of 1995 the Naga Hoho passed formal resolutions to confine the membership to the Nagaland State only. It was at the Phek Summit that the Naga Hoho approved the participation of Nagas of Manipur, but with only two representatives from the UNC in the Liaison Committee. Then the Liaison Committee meeting held in January 1995 formally agreed to induct more representatives from four Naga districts of Manipur. Finally, in the Zunheboto Session (March 10-12,1998) finally the Naga Hoho agreed to having representatives from fourteen Naga tribes from Nagaland and fifteen from Manipur represented on the Naga Hoho.

The Naga Hoho is a federal body of all Nagas with representatives of Nagas cutting across artificial boundaries from Assam, Arunachal Pradesh, Nagaland, Manipur and townships in Myanmar. It represents approximately sixty tribes from India and Burma.[202]

Relationship with Political Parties

The United Naga Council has no link with any political parties. According to our Constitution, by virtue of the fact that a person is a Naga MLA (member of the Manipur Legislative Assembly) he is an executive member of the UNC. The President, Vice President and General Secretary are elected posts. They are directly elected by the general body of the UNC which consists of seven representatives from each of the fifteen Naga tribes in Manipur. All Presidents of the tribal bodies such as Tangkhul Long are automatically members of the UNC.

---

[202] G Gaingam was the convener of the Expert Committee which brought out the 'White Paper on Naga Integration' published in 2002.

A representative of Naga Women's Union is also a member. The church leaders have a forum which is represented in the UNC.

There are various groups in the village—women's society, clubs, so many others—but the village is represented by those authorized by the village to speak on its behalf. They will speak on behalf of the village; a group cannot say they will speak on behalf of the village. Likewise, the Naga Mothers' Association represents mothers and not all Nagas, the Naga Students' Federation represents students and not all Nagas, the church represents the church and not all Nagas. Isn't it?

The UNC and the Naga Hoho are apex bodies, like a father within a family. Children have to come together and they cannot deny their father, good or bad.

Relationship with the Underground

As for our relationship with the underground: sometimes they appreciate us, sometimes they are critical. According to us the NSCN (I-M) is a Naga national political organization and represents the Naga national movement, whereas the Naga Hoho is a social organization representing the Naga people and it does not have a downfall; because people come together according to their custom and tradition and it brings together all the tribes.

The Hoho also represent the people—the tribe and the village. Hoho is a federation of Naga tribes. Naga Hoho is not an NGO. But yes, there is some confusion about the role of all these organizations and no clear understanding.

The NSCN (I-M) is not only a political organization, it is also a government. The Naga national groups are divided so NSCN (I-M) cannot say they represent Khaplang, isn't it?

But there will be one group which will have the mandate to represent the people in a national struggle. There can never be a perfect consensus. So I am confused with the what people mean by Naga unity. There are so many meanings of the word unity.

That is why Naga Hoho openly says we support the present political dialogue between the NSCN (I-M) and the Indian government. That is clear.

Even after settlement we need unity. There is nothing wrong to talk about unity. But some people are shouting for unity with different intentions and to cause confusion. To us it is clear there are two kinds of unity. One unity is for all Nagas whether underground or overground. The other unity is unity of the underground groups.

Boycott of 1997 Elections

As the President of the United Naga Council I see the main task before us is to initiate dialogue between the Nagas, Meiteis and Kukis living in Manipur. But before such a dialogue can start, we have to create the basis for such talks and that is why during my presidency we called for the exodus of Nagas.[203] We also called for a boycott of elections.

The problem between Nagas and Kukis or Nagas and Meiteis cannot be discussed in the Assembly; in a house of sixty seats, only nineteen are reserved for tribals (one for scheduled caste) and the rest for the Meiteis. So it does not allow us, Nagas or the Kukis, to have our voices heard. Meiteis can thus suppress the aspirations of the Nagas.

At present we want a solution, a final solution—not an election. Every Naga family in every village has faced death, torture, misery, jail, beatings and arrests. We have faced from both sides: the Indian Army and the underground. No one man can remove this problem, neither the MLA nor the Chief Minister. This problem can be solved only if we have a solution to the Indo-Naga conflict. Every man, woman and

---

[203] In the background of clashes between Nagas and Kukis and tension between Nagas and Meiteis throughout the 1990s, the United Naga Council in August 1997 called for the Nagas living in the Imphal valley (where the Meitei majority live) to go back to their homes in the four Naga-inhabited hill districts of Ukhrul, Tamenglong, Senapati and Chandel. The Kukis were demanding their own district, Sadar Hills, which they have been given by taking a part of the Senapati district. The Meiteis called for unity between the hill and valley people and integrity of Manipur.

child has been living in a war-like situation; we cannot sleep soundly in the village. We do not want to prolong this problem for the next generation and we do not oppose elections but for now we want a solution, not an election.

Our call for boycott of elections, resignation of MLAs and withdrawal of candidates was not appreciated by the sitting MLA, or by Jamir. And the aspiring candidates do not appreciate us because we said we don't want election but a solution, the Indian Army also does not appreciate us because they say we are giving the call for boycott for elections on behalf of the NSCN (I-M). The NSCN (I-M) accuses of being pro-Jamir, and so no one appreciates us. I say that means the United Naga Council is working without trying to please any one organization or one leader! That is one point.

The second point is that our members do not go after money and we do not go after any position like MLA or officer. We are doing work in our own capacity. We have no relationship with outsiders, and we are fully independent.

Even if we take part in the elections, those who represent the Nagas cannot speak out in the Legislative Assembly.[204] There are advantages and disadvantages in participating in the election process but those who are supposed to represent the Nagas, like the MPs and MLAs and ministers, have so many compelling situations and circumstances that stop them from speaking out. That is why it is be better not to participate.

It is a part of the government of India's policy to make Nagas participate in the Indian elections so that Nagas can represent the opinion of Indians to the Nagas. To some extent they have succeeded.

---

[204] The Manipur Legislative Assembly has sixty seats out of which forty are for the hill areas (four Naga-inhabited districts and one which is Chin-Kuki-Mizo). Therefore, the tribals in general and Nagas inhabit much larger area but have far fewer seats in the Assembly which means they cannot effectively influence the decisions because they are a numerical minority.

Lobbying Delhi

We took a delegation of the United Naga Council to Delhi to explain
the situation to the Central government. We wanted to tell them the
ground reality. We told them the valley area of Manipur is only 10 per
cent of the land where the Meiteis live. And they try to suppress the
hill people who live in 90 per cent of the land. The Meiteis dominate in
all government departments and in the University (the department of
tribal studies has been closed down).

The Minister thought that Meiteis were settled all over Manipur
but we explained they live only in the valley. In fact, we Nagas are a
minority. I think they listened to our viewpoint.

At first they thought the Naga problem is nothing since it is a tiny
state with a small population. They thought they can suppress us with
military might. But when they understood the ground reality, even
Inderjit Gupta[205] listened.

We said the ceasefire must be extended to Manipur.[206] I led a nine-

---

[205] Inderjit Gupta (1919-2001) was a member of the Communist Party of India
and the Union Home Minister from 1996-1998 in the United Front Government
under Prime Ministers Dewe Gowda and IK Gujral.

[206] The issue of extension of ceasefire to Manipur has been the most contentious
issue in the peace talks. When the ceasefire was first announced, it was said that it
was 'without territorial limits' which meant it extended to all areas in which the
NSCN operated. Manipur State objected and said the ceasefire should be confined
to Nagaland State. They said the extension of the ceasefire to Manipur amounted
to endorsing the NSCN claim to parts of Manipur. The NSCN (I-M) maintained
that a ceasefire confined to Nagaland State would mean they could carry out armed
operations outside of the state, and also they would not have impunity from arrest
which they had under the ceasefire rules. In 2001 when the Government of India
finally extended the ceasefire to Manipur, there was a massive protest by the Meiteis in
the Manipur Valley. Thirteen people were killed and over fifty wounded in police firing
as demonstrators protesting the Naga ceasefire extension set ablaze the Assembly,
Chief Minister's Secretariats and government buildings, leading to imposition of an
indefinite curfew in three districts: Imphal East, Imphal West and Thoubal on the last
day of the sixty-six hour state bandh. The Indian Army staged flag marches in three
districts and additional para-military forces, including commandos, were rushed to the
troubled parts of the State.

member delegation and we met many people from October 17 to November 20, 1997. We met intelligence officers because they are the ones who feed wrong information to the Home Minister and damage everything. We also met Vinod Misra.[207] He suggested many positive things to us, like talking to Indian leaders and also having joint action with other North East people. We met Jayant Rongpi who was then the Member of Parliament from Karbi Along.

We even met the Indian Prime Minister Narasimha Rao in July 1995[208] and he also said our demand was reasonable. He said there was no reason why the ceasefire should not be extended to Manipur.

---

[207] Vinod Misra (1947-1998) belonged to the Communist Party of India-Marxist-Leninist (Liberation).

[208] PV Narasimha Rao (1921-2004) was Prime Minister from 1991-1996.

SHANGLOW: THE KONYAK

Shanglow, a Konyak from Mon District, was the Vice President of Naga Hoho at the time of this interview.

He was a part of the Naga Hoho team which went to Kolang village (Burma) to meet NSCN (K) Chairman SS Khaplang on April 19, 1999. At the meeting the NSCN (K) agreed with the proposal initiated by the Naga Hoho to form a peace committee represented by all Naga groups.

Interviewed on July 16,1999 at Dimapur.

Testimony of Shanglow:

I am a Konyak Naga, the largest Naga tribe. And I am from Wakching, the largest village in Mon district. Konyaks have 107 villages and in each village there is a different dialect, but the Wakching dialect is the common language for all Konyaks. Wakching is the oldest town in Mon district. It was the first place where Christianity came and also education.

We had a literacy campaign in other villages to stop tattooing and to stop putting dead bodies on top of trees and bury them in the earth instead. There was theological activity and then the underground people came from Kohima and Khonoma. Konyak people joined the movement from 1950.

During the plebiscite some leaders from Konyak took part, not the general public. I met some of the first leaders who joined the movement, but that generation is already gone. I have been with the Naga national movement for the last thirty-forty years.

Early Memories

I was born in 1952.

In my childhood my mother carried me into the jungle because the Indian Army burned all the houses. All the villages were affected. My mother was carrying me on her back and carrying her other children as well. My father and other children went ahead because they were carrying the other things. We went some 5 or 6 kms deep into the jungle. I do not remember how many days we spent in the jungles but Wakching was not burnt. It was saved.

I remember once the Indian district authorities organized Indian Independence Day at Wakching. They had ordered food and told all the villagers to attend the function. They warned that anyone who did not attend the function, the government would take action against them. On the other side the underground had said if anybody goes to the Indian government function they would be killed.

So, our villagers did not know what to do. They came up with a solution. All the villagers set off for Wakching but some stayed behind and set fire to an old house. Seeing the fire, everyone returned. So no one attended the function. When they were asked by the Indian Army why they did not come they said a fire had broken out. That is how Wakching was saved from being burnt down by the Indian Army!

All Konyak villages were burnt down in 1956 by the Indian Army and from that time Konyaks have supported the Naga independence movement. We do not know how this Shillong Accord has been done. No Konyak signed it. No Konyak participated in the Shillong Accord. Also in 1964 we do not know how ceasefire has come to Nagaland and how NNC and NSCN separated. That also we do not know. But after some time there was NSCN (I-M) and NSCN (K).

We Konyaks stand on principle and now also the Konyak people are approaching all the Nagas to become one to unite; we stand in the same position. Konyak is the largest tribe in Nagaland and we have about 100 to 200 (sic) villages in Burma.

Konyaks divided by boundaries

In Burma we are called Eastern Konyaks; in Arunachal Pradesh side we are called Wancho who have forty to fifty villages and in Nagaland we have 107 villages. So Konyak is the largest tribe in Nagaland.

The demarcation between India and Burma by Nehru and U Nu[209] resulted in one village, Longwa the Angh's house has been divided between India and Burma. So, the Konyaks have been divided into pieces.

When the students' union has a meeting, we call the Konyaks from all sides.

Cultivation

For us, we depend on the market for rice. We have to buy it from Assam. We who live on the lower side have sufficient rice, but on the Burma side they do not have enough rice and they have to eat maize. The whole year we go to the fields for cultivation but we do not get enough rice from the fields so we have to buy it from the market. Sometimes we have millet.

But for the Naga Army we do not provide millet—we provide rice even if we do not have enough for ourselves. When they come, we provide good food for them with meat because they do not come often. The Runa Peyu provides the food.

Education

I started schooling in 1963. I went to school in Wakching up to Class Five, then from Class Six I was in Shibsagar in Assam and then Class Seven to Ten I studied in Mokokchung. The situation in Assam became bad because of the Assam movement so I shifted to Nagaland and then I went to attend college[210] in Calcutta for two

---

[209] The British drew the boundary between India and Burma but in common Naga perception it was Nehru and U Nu who drew the boundary. At one point on the international border the boundary runs through the house of the Angh of Logwa Village so half his house is in India and the other half in Myanmar. Longwa, one of the biggest villages in Mon district on the India-Myanmar international border, has a road connecting it to 'Loji' village in Myanmar's Sagaing Division.

[210] Class Eleven and Twelve is often in a college called PU.

years. I passed Class Twelve from Calcutta. After passing I went to Japan for a few months for training in a printing press. Then I came back to Nagaland and started some industries and then I went to the USA, France, Malaysia and some other countries to learn about the industry. I have a printing press and a plywood factory. I am now planning to start a vegetable and fruit processing unit in Dimapur and a sugar mill in Mon district.

In 1987 I was back in Dimapur and I graduated from a college in Dimapur. I could not study Political Science in Nagaland so I went to Dibrugarh University and joined there for my post-graduation. I am still studying there. There is a rule that I have to attend ninety days of classes, but for the last two years I have been active in the Naga Hoho so could not attend even the ninety days and I could not take my examinations. I am hoping to take the exams this year.

I have five children, the oldest three are in college, and so you see we are all students!

Konyak Guns

Yes, Konyaks made guns from iron. We used to buy pipes from the tea gardens in Assam but the police would chase them so they had to hide and go back to the village. Once, six or seven of the villagers purchased ten pipes and they covered it with cloth and put bamboo inside the pipes they put akhuni (fermented soya beans which have a strong smell which could pass off as putrified flesh). When the police stopped them, they said a friend had died and they were carrying his dead body back to the village. The foul smell is from his body. So they crossed the police camp.

The tea garden factories made very good quality pipe which can take a lot of pressure, and when they condemned some pipes we took them. It was very helpful to make guns. Even the old pipes are good. They last a thousand years. The guns were used for hunting and also for fighting with the enemy.

For the gunpowder, we use different kinds of firewood to make charcoal and then make it into powder and then we mix with fish bones. It is better you go and see for yourself.

Konyak Lands

The British took the land for their tea gardens and they paid tax to the Konyaks every year but we do not have it in black and white. We just went to collect the money. In Wakching we had documents and we used to collect every year but in 1964 fire broke out in the village and the documents were burnt. So we request Assam to give us the documents but they did not. It was a large tract of land of which some belonged to our village and some to tea garden and some to Assam, but Assam has claimed it all since we do not have any documents.

Konyak Culture

The Konyaks are very different from other Nagas in custom, culture, lifestyle. It is similar to the life of the Jews in the Holy Bible. We are like the Jews in every way.

We are different from the other Naga tribes. We have kingship and a rich culture. We have so many songs, so many stories, and so many systems of worship and rituals and rites during festivals. If we announce that the village will go fishing tomorrow, the whole village will come and attend the meeting at the Angh's house. But at the meeting fishing will not be discussed because everybody knows their duty.

Or suppose someone dies: everyone knows who will dig the earth, who will make the box (sic) and who will carry the body. On Christmas suppose I kill a pig, I will put it in front of my house and an old man will take it. The old men collect the hearts of pig from every house and then distribute it and eat it.

Or suppose you have an accident on way to my village and I did not inform my friend, then I will be fined for not informing him about the accident. And if I informed my friend and after knowing he did not go to the accident site, then he will also be fined.

We have a Konyak literature society. They have published a Bible in Konyak language. And a Konyak songbook. Konyak language can be taken as a subject up to Class Eight.

Konyaks in Burma

Naga people are enjoying their lives because they got statehood and all facilities. But in Burma it is different. In the month of April, I went to Burma side to meet Khaplang and on the way I could not climb up. After I was in jail, I could not walk that much so villagers carried me.

When we stopped to rest, the Nagas from Burma told me that they were working every day for Naga independence but the people in Nagaland are enjoying life and did not know what it was to work in the national movement. I feel sad seeing Nagas on the Burma side. They have no food, no communication, no facilities and even no jungle animals—people who have an empty stomach want food first then everything else. After getting food they will decide what we will do. [211]

When I met Mr Khaplang he said he could not compromise on this sovereignty. He said he has been fighting for thirty-six years and has been underground for all those years fighting for freedom. If you meet him it will be very nice. He can tell you many things. You will be carried up. (*Last two sentences addressed to us*).

Khaplang will not agree to settle for a Naga state within Burma. He wants full independence. Khaplang was trying to form the Indo-Burma Revolutionary Force but I think that has also failed.

I asked Mr Khaplang to unite with Isak Muivah again. I said Naga people want unity. He said okay, I will have unity, but then Isak and Muivah said that Khaplang attacked the Council Headquarters in 1988 so Khaplang must first confess to the wrongs he has done. Until and unless he confesses, we cannot have unity. And then there are the

---

[211] Shanglow is making a comparison between the Nagas of Nagaland who live in relative comfort whereas the Nagas of Myanmar often have nothing to eat, not even animals to hunt, so their priority would be to get the basics before they decide on other political issues.

Accord people and those who support the 16-Point Agreement and
Khaplang people always staying with the Ministers in Nagaland.

Khaplang says he has been staying in the jungles for the last thirty-
six years so why should he confess? He said he does not want to talk
to Naga Hoho. He said he would apologize for past mistakes but not
mention this-or-that incident.

Role of Naga Hoho

This is the role of the Naga Hoho—we are trying to bring unity among
the Nagas. We in the Naga Hoho think there should be unity first and
then we should go for talks. But Isak and Muivah say they want to get
something concrete and then there would be unity. They say if they get
something from the government of India then everyone will benefit.
Like Mahatma solved the problem with the British and all Indians
enjoyed it.

We Konyaks are all behind the talks. I feel we should leave behind
the Shillong Accord and the 16-Point programme and support Isak
and Muivah for the talks. Government of India is not bringing up the
Shillong Accord or the 16-Point Agreement then why should we?
They are willing to talk to Isak and Muivah and they will do something
good for the people.

I do not know why people say Konyaks support Khaplang. The
Konyak people are for sovereignty. When Isak-Muivah split from
Khaplang and their people scattered all over, the Konyak villages gave
them shelter, food and clothes and took them in our vehicles and
reached them to Dimapur. We do not know how this faction came
about but we did good to them and we provided them with food.

Many Konyaks were killed in their fight but we Konyaks do not
belong to any factions. We support them when they are united.

Every tribe has a union and we also have a Konyak Union;
unofficially the Burmese Konyaks are also members. And we are
members of the Naga Hoho. I have been a member of the Naga Hoho
since 1997. Before that Konyaks were not members of the Hoho. I

insisted that we Konyaks be a part of Naga Hoho otherwise we have been slightly isolated from other Nagas.

The Naga Hoho started in 1994. At that time there was no Konyak member. Then the President of the Konyak Union attended the meetings of the Naga Hoho as an observer. His name is Mr Huka. At that time we did not join because the Naga Hoho decided that we should not participate in the elections but the Konyak people decided that we should take part in the elections. At the time they took vote and eighteen members were against the elections and only three were for the elections.

Elections

Till we are in India we should participate in the elections and it should be left to the people, we should not interfere. That is my personal opinion. This time the call for boycott of election has been given. The resolution was passed in December 1998 so we cannot go against the resolution. I have already made my speech two or three times in the Naga Hoho, that we should not oppose this election. We do not have to support the election but we need not oppose it either.

As for the Nagas of Manipur and Nagas of Nagaland: we are one. The Nagas of Manipur were supposed to be a part of the Nagaland State. The 16-Point Agreement was a mistake. Now we are under separate administrations.

Mr Jamir was one of the persons involved in setting up the Naga Hoho which did not include the Manipur Nagas. We have decided to work together for Naga integration but Isak and Muivah say that once we have a solution then automatically there will be integration of all Naga areas.

Naga Hoho is not a political party, but a social organization. We are not fighting for sovereignty—Isak and Muivah are. Things are moving forward and we will become one. The underground factions will come together and Naga tribes should become one.

Konyak Demands

The Konyak students are demanding a radio station in Mon with Konyak language programme; 33 per cent reservation for the backward tribes (which include Konyaks and others in Mon and Tuensang districts) and they are also trying to stop opium cultivation. It is grown mainly by the Konyaks on the Burmese side. We cannot say what the solution should be but it is ruining our children. We do not know what the alternative source of income for them is; let them sell it to others, not to us.

The money that comes from the Centre is taken by advanced tribes and we Konyaks have been fighting for independence for the past fifty-three years. So people are suffering and we have been working for the national movement but there are too many collections every day. I cannot run a business because I am asked for donations from the underground groups.

ZARSHIE NYUTHE: THE POCHURY

Pochury is a Naga tribe of Nagaland, located in the eastern part of the Phek district, around the Meluri town which is about 166 kms from the state capital Kohima.

The Pochury identity is of relatively recent origin. It is a composite tribe formed by three Naga communities: Kupo, Kuchu and Khuri. The word Pochury is an acronym formed by the names of three native villages of these tribes: Sapo, Kechuri and Khury. The British classified the Pochury communities as sub-tribes of the 'Eastern Sangtam' or 'Eastern Rengma'.

After independence of India, the Pochurys campaigned to be recognized as a separate tribe. Nagaland State recognized the Pochury as the sixteenth tribe of Nagaland in April 1990; and the Census of India recognized the Pochury as a separate scheduled tribe for the first time in 1991.

Zarshie Nyuthe (Peter) joined the NSCN (Khaplang) and later he joined the NSCN (I-M). He lobbied within the GPRN to get recognition of his tribe.

Zarshie has been the Keya Kilonser (Defence Minister) GPRN. He has also been a member of their Steering Committee and Speaker of the Tatar Hoho (NSCN Parliament).

Zarshie was interviewed on August 14, 1998 in Goa.

Testimony of Zarshie Nyuthe:

I was born in 1952 and am around forty-six years old. I am from Pochury tribe; although it is small and backward, I love my tribe.

My family is poor. I have one older brother who is physically handicapped and two sisters. They are both married; I am also married to an Ao lady and have children. My villages had 400 houses.

Childhood

As a small child we played without any clothes; we played games in which we would be Indians versus Nagas and the loser will always be Indians. Or we would go roaming and shooting birds with catapults.

My parents are Christian but my grandparents were not and I don't even know their names. During my childhood there were 50 per cent Christian and 50 per cent non-converted; now twenty-five are still not converted. We Christians established our own khel (Clan).

During the NNC time, the Indian Army told us to make fences. It was time of grouping. One plane was shot down by the NNC. I remember the incident.

I started going to Government School at the age of nine at my village. My own classmate and best friend was a Gurkha, Kailash Thapa; his father was in the movement.

I was not bad in studies. I used to get first, second or third position. In Class Six I got a prize for getting the highest marks.

But I did not get time to study. I had to go to fetch water from a long distance, collect firewood, look after the domestic animals. I had to go to the jungles to get leaves to feed the pigs and like everyone else we also had cows. We do not tether our cows so they are allowed to roam around and I had to go and look for ours and bring them home. We did not have Nepali servants[212] so the cows were not milked but kept only for meat. We had no servants to help.

I had to pound rice when my sisters went to the paddy field and I had to cook. After doing all these activities, I was tired and could not study at night. Many other students suffered the same hardships. We opened our books in front of us for namesake but could not study.

My Uncle in the Movement

My parents did not tell me about the national movement. They were not educated. Only my father's younger brother was forcibly arrested

---

[212] For many Naga tribes, drinking milk was taboo and they did not have knowledge of dairy so they employed Nepalis to look after the cows for milking.

(sic) by the Federal Government and he worked for them, and he used to tell us about the national movement. But I was too young to understand. National workers used to come to our house.

My father's younger brother, Churtho, is still alive. He studied up to Class Seven during the British period. But then he was forced to join the Federal Government to work as a clerk in the office. Became a Magistrate and an SDC in NNC and became a Pantong, which is same as Deputy Commissioner.

He used to tell about the national movement. I could not understand much. My home environment is a simple house. There is no education or political talk.

My Uncle Churtho used to live all alone in the jungles. The reason was that all other Pochury who had joined the NNC had surrendered to the Revolutionary Government formed in November 1968. But my Uncle refused to surrender. He believed that Nagas will become independent one day. Our clan used to quietly look after him. But after four or five years the clan got fed up.

The clan asked my father to give back the money they had spent in looking after my Uncle. We sold our field and some guns and gave back the money to the clan.

For three years my Uncle was alone, then one person was with him in the jungle. The Revolutionary Government people hunted him like anything, so he had to live in a solitary place where no one could find him.

My Uncle was all alone in the jungle doing nothing all day. This affected his mind. He started thinking he was being chased by Punjabis (Indian Army) and he would close all doors even when we would say no one is behind you; but he would say, 'Punjabis are coming.'

So one day he ran away from our house. The whole village went to the jungle to look for him. The second day he was found and taken to church. He always carried a Bible with him.

When our villagers took him to the church it was evening. The church elders surrounded him and placed their hands on his head. He told them he had done nothing wrong and they should pray for themselves.

If some people tried to give him money he would not accept. One MLA gave my Uncle five hundred rupees after he was better, but my Uncle said he will not take any money. The MLA insisted so he accepted the money but he just kept in the loft. He would check it from time to time. My younger sister's husband took the money.

When I decided to join the underground, my parents were not willing to let me go, but my Uncle told me I should be careful because I would get killed on my way to their camp. He said if I found the way to Isak-Muivah then he would join in my place so I could continue my studies.

Joining NSCN

I became political when I went to Kohima to do my PU.

When I was in Kohima Art college I was the only senior student from my community and we discussed politics. We used to discuss the position of my tribe which was not recognized at the time. We wanted to enjoy the status of a tribe but it was not allowed by the Chakhesang. Every time they blocked any move by any government to recognize the Pochury as an independent tribe.

So we discussed that if we could not get recognition from the Nagaland government at least we should get recognition from the national government, so somebody should join the national movement. This was in 1978. I took the matric exam but I do not know if I passed or failed because I left to join the movement.

We heard the news that Naga National Council had capitulated and under Isak-Muivah-Khaplang a new party was formed called the National Socialist Council of Nagaland to save the Naga nation.

In 1981 at our Pochury Students' Conference there was a request from the NSCN that we volunteer for national service but no one volunteered. Then again the next year there was a request from the NSCN (I-M) for volunteers and especially from families with good number of boys, but no one wanted to join.

The recruiting agents told us life in the jungles would be good.

There are a lot of jade stones and one elephant cannot pull the jade because it is so big.

I volunteered so I could represent my tribe. At that time I was studying for my PU final exam.

My parents were not willing. I have only one brother and he is physically handicapped. My family is poor and their condition is very bad. Even now it is. My parents are getting old and there is no one to look after my handicapped brother.

Looking at the condition of my family I had second thoughts but my parents said, 'You have already promised so you must go.' At least I can do good for the village, tribe and nation. There were two more volunteers with me. The other two were Nyumasie who was working as an LDC (Lower Division Clerk) in the office of the Assistant Deputy Commissioner, and Chulekhu. Nyumasie informed me that he has got a line to reach the headquarters to Isak and Muivah.

We were told to take what was absolutely necessary, not even extra pants or shoes. But we were told to take rice for six days.

Eastern Nagaland

So in June 1982 we started from Dimapur and reached the Naga Army headquarters at Longchang in Eastern Nagaland by July 15. There the GSO (General Staff Officer) was Colonel Ashiho and the Adjutant was Captain Hao who was later killed. When he died he was a Lieutenant. They both encouraged us and we stayed there for a week.

In Eastern Nagaland we got only maize and millet, and sometimes there was no maize. There were times we did not get even salt or chillies.

Then we started for the consular headquarters. In July 1982 I met the Chairman and General Secretary and I was assigned to the Chairman's Mess where I had to fetch water, firewood and search for wild vegetables in the forest.

Although we three were not well-qualified, they were happy to have us. Brigadier Vedai had prophesized that three people were coming to help the government. We stayed for a week and then I accompanied the Chairman and his wife, with Vedai and his wife to the Leinong[213] area. There were about thirty of the Chairman's bodyguards also with us.

It was the darkest place in Naga territory and no one wants to follow Christianity. From their community very few are educated and the Burmese government does not reach them.

We went there and baptized them. So much so we forcibly baptized them and some of them were beaten by us because some of them said they won't get baptized. So there was controversy. It was said that we should not go to that extent.

When they kill, they keep the skulls and decorate the whole house with them. We broke the skulls, and spoiled their vessels and their millet. We were directly attacking their way of life. The Burmese heard about this and they ambushed us at one place near village Mophin. The fighting went on for a week and a huge number of Burmese died and two or three of our men also died.

In that fight we were able to capture arms and we asked for reinforcements from the GCH which was not very far but no reinforcement came so we also got injured. Three of us were not allowed to fight since we had not taken any training, not even basic training. But Captain Nyumasie died.

Our training begins

Then for six months we were not given any work. We were not given any salt, chillies or vegetables. We had to collect vegetables from the jungle and survive on that. We were not even allowed to take part in church activities and we just stayed and were under observation. My stomach was demanding meat.

After that we were allowed to go the nearby village. We went to Kesam Chanlam village and bought a pig for thirty rupees. We paid

---

[213] Leinong or Lainong Naga live near Lahe town and their population is are mostly Buddhist.

the driver fifteen rupees. We killed the pig and cooked it and finished it all. That is how we spent our first free day!

We had a little money with us. When I first came, I sold one paddy field and got a few thousand; then my parents gave me one or two thousand rupees; and my friends had brought ten thousand rupees. The village also gave us some money and one of my friends was given ten thousand rupees from the MLA.

The organization got money through collection of taxes: house tax, military tax, and other taxes. Sometimes rich people gave donations and then we captured money. The Indians call it looting but we did not invite their banks on our soil or ask them to illegally occupy our land. And we did not ask India to establish the self-styled government of Nagaland.

That year the Chairman was to give a feast for Christmas but the Burmese attacked us so there was no celebration.

Recognition of Pochury Tribe

Then we had a discussion on the Pochury tribe with the Collective Leadership, all three of them. The Pochury are a very small tribe *now* but at the time of the NNC we were spread over a big area. So the Collective Leadership said we should combine with other smaller tribes and become one, that way we would be bigger and stronger.

But we argued that we joined the movement to sacrifice for the Pochury tribe so by any means they must recognize the tribe. We quarrelled with the leaders and even exchanged bad words but the leaders did not give up. They said Pochury would still be there even if the small tribes combined to make one bigger one.

They said that five tribes: Pochury, Sangtam, Makury, Para and Yimchunger[214] should combine together. They suggested we should

---

[214] Yimchunger consists of four sub-tribes: Tikhir, Makuri, Minir and Chirr each of which has their own dialects of the same language.

In the year 1989, some Tikhir members, constituents of the Yimchunger tribe, eventually joined the 'Tisary Region' of the NSCN (K) and simultaneously demanded call ourselves the Tisary—'Ti' is for Tizu river in Nagaland, 'Sa' for Saramati, the 'Ry' is for all of us—Pochury, Makury, etc.

The Collective Leadership also wanted the small tribes in Chandel district of Manipur to come together under the name of 'Khurmi.' They had a ceremony to rename the tribes and AK Lunglang was the Chief Guest.

But this was beyond our capacity—to accept the merger of Pochury into Tisary because this would unmake the Pochury. So we decided that we should go back to our tribe, so we went back and discussed for several months. Our people went to discuss this with other tribes.

I came back from our area and gave my report that most of our people did not agree to combining with other tribes.

I said it may be a good thing but not immediately. Maybe we can do this after some time. I was deadly against the idea.

I was told to represent the Tisary unified area but after I went back to our village I resigned as Regional Secretary as I could not represent the Tisary since I was against combining the tribes. But my resignation was not accepted by the Centre.

The Chairman, the Education Kilonser (Angam) and Khaplang came to me and requested me to withdraw my resignation: 'You will be alone. We feel pity for you.' I told them, 'If you want to kill me, you can kill me but I came here to make a mark for my tribe and if you kill me then I would have made a mark for my people. So you can sacrifice me. Just finish me.' I went to that extent.

Then one morning I was called early one morning by our honourable Chairman. That time he sent a boy to call me. He scolded me. 'Zarshie,' he called me by my name, 'why are you not writing this report?' I said I cannot twist the truth. He said they would have to take action against me for going against their decision on the Tisary issue.

---

a separate region for the Tikhir dialect. However, the demand was not granted and as a result in the same year they again defected to the NSCN (I-M) since 1990. The NSCN (I-M) approved the 'TIMACHIR' region; whereupon the members of the Chirr and Makury dialects protested.

Then I got angry and said, 'If you are supposed to take action against me out of pity, you are violating the law. There is no question of pity and I am not afraid to meet anything.' I challenged him. He became quiet.

Khaplang also insisted for unification and took much interest in the issue.

One of the two boys who had come with me, Chulekhu, also went to talk to our people. He stayed in the jungles alone and sometimes he slept in the paddy fields. I stood firm. I came to sacrifice for the Pochury and not to destroy them. And I did not want the name of Pochury to get lost forever.

But Captain Nyumasie agreed to the idea of Tisary. He said we should not think only for our tribe but also the nation. Each tribe will be able to claim the entire territory as theirs, so whole of Tisary territory can be claimed by a Pochury or a Yimchunger, and he said there are historical facts that in the past we were one. Our customs are same, only language is a bit different.

I used to be the only person opposing the idea of Tisary whenever we had meetings of the Tisary. I said then others can claim Pochury villages within the Tisary. This problem was there even before starting of our revolution (sic). That is why our central government took interest in the problem because it had become a headache for them to make the boundaries and each will claim the area as theirs. So the central government wanted our unity.

I was under unwritten suspension; they did not give a written suspension order but I was not invited for feasts or for official activities, and I was not allowed to participate in the church activities. Even my attendants were taken away from me. I was totally isolated.

But I was brave enough. I was the only one who opposed the idea of Tisary till the end. Somebody told me you have resisted enough. Some friends and Kilonsers said we know you. You have made a point. So I said you are witness to my stand and then they accepted my resignation and I was appointed section officer within three days. I was posted in the Chaplee (Finance) Ministry. So I gave up.

Accepting Tisary Identity

But I am happy. Now I realize that the idea of forming Tisary was the best idea for both the central government and for each of us tribes. Even now many people want to stay separate but less people are opposing it. Now students are also supporting the idea—it was a new idea so it took time for me to accept it.

After one or two months I was sent to Meghalaya to mobilize along with a Garo friend. I recruited five persons and brought them to the headquarters for their training. Then I went to Tripura to contact TNV [215] to help in the mobilization.

I stayed with the Tripura students in Shillong when I heard that our leaders were quarrelling. [216] I felt sad. I got the news in 1987. I was told that there would be talks between India and Nagas.

We thought if there is a quarrel then we have lost everything. We were so hopeful because NSCN had Isak from so-called Nagaland State , Muivah from Southern Nagaland and Khaplang from Eastern Nagaland: they were like the three stones in a fireplace.

Khaplang was very aggressive and if he lost in badminton, he got angry. We had to tell the ULFA and UNLF to lose.

I wanted to play the role of mediator. I had no alternative but to join Khaplang because I had no way of contacting the Chairman and General Secretary who were away in the Kachin area. We were told that Isak and Muivah are ready to negotiate with Suisa proposal.

Socialism

Nagas can never be scientific socialist because money and rations are not equally distributed within the organization (NSCN). We are all

---

[215] Tripura National Volunteers Force was a Tripuri nationalist militant group in the Tripura that launched an armed struggle in the early 1980s to separate Tripura from India. TNV was led by Bijoy Kumar Hrangkhawl. TNV surrendered in 1988 and integrated themselves into a political party.

[216] Reference to the differences between Khaplang and Isak-Muivah leading to the break in 1988.

given rice, dal, aloo and chillies but some people can buy chicken and pork while others cannot afford to eat meat. The ULFA and UNLF are much stricter about controlling the money.

It was not only us who ate rats; Meiteis and ULFA also ate rats. We took out the intestines and dried the rats and sold them. Small dogs would sell for thirty rupees and ULFA would buy big dogs for one thousand rupees.

I like Hindi films because there is action; English movies have too much talking inside the rooms. I like Shatrughan Sinha, he is not so much handsome but he is brave.

By Way of a Conclusion

I thought that my voyage had come to its end at the last limit
of my power, that the path before me was closed, that provisions
were exhausted, and the time come to take shelter in a silent
obscurity, but I find that thy will knows no end in me, and
when old words die out on the tongue, new melodies break forth
from the heart, and where the old tracks are lost, new country is
revealed with its wonders.

—Rabindranath Tagore

It was a truly historic moment in the annals of Indian democracy when the Prime Minister of India PV Narasimha Rao met the Naga leaders, Isak Swu and Thuingaleng Muivah, in Paris on July 15, 1995 and they discussed the possibility of initiating a peace process.

It took another two years before the peace talks began after the then Prime Minister of India said in Parliament on March 4, 1997:

'I made a public announcement inviting the underground groups for discussions without preconditions, in order to find a political solution which would ensure durable peace in the region.'

An elaborate ceasefire monitoring system was put in place and the peace talks began on the basis of the following principles:

1. The talks would be unconditional. According to the NSCN leaders this meant the talks would not be within the Constitution of India—something they were totally averse to.

2. The talks would be held at the highest level. This meant that from the Indian side the interlocutor would directly represent the Prime Minister of India, and the NSCN would be represented by its General Secretary who was the Ato Kilonser or the Prime Minister in the Government of People's Republic of Nagaland (GPRN).
3. The venue for the talks would be outside India.

The peace talks have continued on and on but there has been no resolution. The talks took place outside India till and Thuingaleng Muivah was arrested in Bangkok in 2000 and after his release the venue for the talks shifted to India. Then on August 3, 2015 it was announced that the Government of India and the NSCN (I-M) have agreed on a 'Framework Agreement.'

The Indian Prime Minister Narendra Modi paid rich tributes to the Naga society rooted in village-based democracy and to the courage of the Naga people. He also acknowledged that the NSCN had held the ceasefire for two decades. He said the resolution to the conflict would bring peace and development to the Nagas.

It is now been more than four years but there has not been a final settlement.

There should be a book on the ups and downs on the peace process which started from 1990s to the present moment; and there is an earlier history when there was a ceasefire in the 1960s. This is not that book.

Although we have been deeply involved in the human rights movement, this book does not deal with the problems of human rights violations committed by the Indian security forces in the course of the counter-insurgency operations. We have dealt with that subject in our earlier book, *The Judgement that Never Came: Army Rule in North East India*.[1]

As human rights activists, our stand was simple and clear: there can be no military solution to the Indo-Naga conflict. It can be resolved only through dialogue between the two parties to the conflict.

It was only when we got involved in the peace process that we discovered how complex the problem was. The complexity was compounded by the fact that neither party to the negotiations seemed to have any idea what the final settlement would look like.

The resolution of the Indo-Naga conflict is a challenge to Indian democracy. And for the NSCN (I-M), it too needs to define its vision for the future of the Nagas as a people.

Prime Minister Modi, like Prime Ministers before him, emphasized that the resolution to the Indo-Naga conflict would lead to peace and development. But he did not spell out what kind of development he envisaged for the Nagas. The NSCN (I-M) too have not spelt out what kind of development they wanted.

This question is vital because Nagas are now no longer a casteless, class-less tribal society as they were in Phizo's times. Phizo had claimed in 1951:

> There is no pauper in Nagaland. There is no social 'out-cast' in our country. There are no professional beggars up to this very day. There is no families who are houseless anywhere throughout Nagaland. There are no landless persons among us. We do not pay even land tax, which is always a crushing burden to the mass citizens in many other countries. We have no unemployment problem. Economically, Nagaland is on a strong foundation. And, no Naga wanted the Indian immigrants to migrate in Nagaland. It will not help India in any way; not only that, it will disturb the whole Nagaland.

Today these words are no longer an accurate description of Naga society. Naga society is deeply divided between rich Nagas and the poor who do not have land or money enough to educate their children or have two square meals. Many Naga youth have migrated to cities and town all over India and abroad and become migrant workers in search of jobs.[iii]

So, the first question that needs to be answered is kind of development do the Naga nationalists envisage which would ensure that the growing gap between the rich and poor Nagas is substantially narrowed?

The second question that emerges from these interviews is the question of Naga identity. Naga identity is increasingly becoming religious and fundamentalist. Do the Nagas support growing religious intolerance not only towards people of other religions but even towards Catholic Nagas?

The third question which we raised with the Naga leaders—but their answers were not satisfactory—was the place of women in Naga society. There is conflict between Naga traditional values (and also between Christianity as practiced by Nagas) and women's rights, but patriarchy is not seen as problematic by the Naga nationalists.

The fourth question that has been central to the Naga national movement has been the efficacy of armed resistance versus other forms of protest. To some people, like church leaders, it is a question of principle while others think of armed resistance as a matter of tactics and strategy. There needs to be a robust debate on these issues. The complexities and ethics of armed resistance are questions which are at the heart of the Naga national movement but unfortunately outside the scope of this book.

Lastly, there has been no debate on the allies and alliances of the Naga nationalists within India and abroad. Many alliances are solely for the purpose of procuring arms and getting a passage to smuggle them.

But it is not clear whom the Naga nationalists consider their friends and whom they consider their enemies. Early Naga nationalists were inspired by the Indian freedom struggle and had friends among the Indians. However, later the Naga nationalists have treated both the Indian State and the Indian people with suspicion and even hostility.

Indian society too has treated people who eat certain meats as inferior, making it impossible for the Nagas to be accepted as equals within large parts of caste-based society.

Instead the Naga nationalists have sought to work with Western NGOs and American Baptist churches, citing the common religion as the basis of this trust. They have not questioned the politics of Western funding and been slow to acknowledge the fact that Indian state's track record of treatment of indigenous people is far better than the way the Americans treat Native Americans, or how Europeans treat refugees and outsiders.

According to Indian sources the Naga national movement continues to have links with China. But it also has the support of the Unrepresented Nations and People's Organization (UNPO) which was founded in 1991 with Tibetans as founding members; the Secretary General of the UNPO was Michael van Walt van Praag, the legal advisor of the fourteenth Dalai Lama.

The Naga nationalists seem to have set themselves on a path of self-destruction; having lost their political direction, they are caught in the world of realpolitik.

Naga youth feels disillusioned with the Naga nationalists but has yet to debate and discuss these political and economic issues, which go beyond defining Naga identity based on race and religion. Perhaps this book will inspire more debate.

Can they once again take their destiny in their own hands? Only the future will tell.

Appendices

I) SPEECH BY AZ PHIZO, PRESIDENT OF NAGA NATIONAL COUNCIL, MAY 1951

Uncles, aunties, friends, brothers and sisters,

Today is a great day for our people. Throughout Nagaland our people are ceremoniously observing this day May 16 as the day of our Plebiscite Day, which we are going to record by taking the thumb impression of our people. This we are doing to show India and the world of our aspiration and that there is an effective unity of the people in Nagaland.

We have been living as a subject nation for the last seventy years. Our country was an independent country before the British conquered us with superior force of arms. The British left our country and India in the year 1947. Without making any special arrangement for our country the British abandoned us and we found ourselves under the mercy of the Indian people.

Our Naga people (the British subject Nagas) have demanded independence from the British on many previous occasions. Unfortunately, we never put it on record as our people are not accustomed to writing. The only written record submitted by our people to the British Government was submitted in the year 1929 January 10 when 'Simon Commission,' under the chairmanship of Sir John Simon, came here in Kohima seeking our people's opinion about the 'New Reform' as it was called. Our Naga people demanded Independence and said, 'Leave us alone, and when you—the British—leave us we shall be free and independent again.'

A long struggle has followed with the march of history and we have fully kept pace with it. When the Japanese Imperial forces smashed the British defences and reached Burma, some of us took full advantage of it. The

Japanese forces along with the Indian National Army, better known as the INA, fully co-operated with us and as a result of our concerted action most of Nagaland as far as Kohima was freed from the dominating control and influence of the British. In this connection, I may say a word concerning strategy. Our country was and still is supposed to be a strategic area. The experience of the last war (World War II) has belied this popular belief. Strategy depends more upon the people, it is not merely a question of geography or location.

I am not going into details of our past experiences with India especially since 1947. Prior to the transference by the British of their administrative authority and controlling over—that is, military and police—into the hands of Indians, we had talked to the British for our Independence. But there again we made a mistake. We had not put it in writing for record. Anyway, we the Naga people declared ourselves Independent on the 14th of August, 1947, and on the same day we informed India by telegram, and cabled to UNO for information and record.

Since then, we have tried to settle our political issue with India on various occasions. But we have not been successful. As a result we have gathered here together in order to try to convince India of our inherent right to be free and equal to any other nation as a distinct people. This time, and from now on, we shall put everything into writing. We shall see to it that our talk do not end in mere words.

In the name of the Naga National Council and on behalf of the people and citizens of Nagaland, I wish to make our stand and our national position perfectly clear. We are a democratic people, and as such, we have been struggling for of a separate sovereign State of Nagaland in a democratic way through constitutional means as it is so called. We shall continue to do so.

On many occasions we have been accused by the press in India that we were a troublesome people and that our 'movement' for Independence must be stopped. Many Indian leaders told us that we the Nagas are 'Indians' and that Nagas can never be allowed to become independent. Some Indian leaders say that even Hyderabad had to submit to the Indian Union just as the rest of the Indian princely states, which number over 500, had to submit.

When we examine those rapacious assertions, accusations and misapprehensions we find that the Indians do not know the Nagas. India tried to stop our Independence, they are still trying; and, they will probably continue to do so. The British tried to keep Indian Independence in their own hand. They thought they could remain in India forever to come, that was why they, the British, built such cities as Bombay, Madras, Calcutta, Delhi and the rest of all the modern Indian towns and cities. Roads were constructed, railways were laid out, and companies with capitals running into millions of pounds in gold came into existence. All those are now in the hands and under the authority of the Indians. Such is history. Simply because a strong people got the control of political administration of a country over a weaker people it does not mean the end of history. The history of progress and freedom have been written and will continue to be written. Most of the histories of human freedom were recorded in human blood. Most of the foundations of free nations were built on human bones and crushed skulls. But we want our national independence to remain holy and pure. We do not want to mix freedom, and our independence, with human blood. We do hope we shall not be compelled to live on a structure founded on human skulls and bones. We are determined to extricate our self, clear with understanding, by goodwill and through reason, so that we may continue to live in freedom and enjoy national independence.

We want our Indian brothers and sisters to know that we are not their enemy. We want the world to know that there is civilization in Nagaland. Academically backward though we may be, it is up to us to show to the world that we are not a people which has lost its raison d'etre. We are alive.

We never feared India; and, of course there is no reason for the Nagas to fear India in this human struggle for maintaining our political independence. Just as much as you cannot see a black spot in clear water, likewise, we cannot have a black spot of fear in our mind of clear conscience. I always have a feeling that God, our Heavenly Father—our creator—is with us and guiding us. What is there for us to fear? Only a murderer and people of evil intent can have fear and suspicion in his mind. We do not belong to a criminal race. And there is no ground for the Nagas to be worried or to fear the millions of Indians in this struggle to retain our Independence. We also appeal to India to be sane and wise. We appeal to them that they should be human and not brutes. We appeal to India to be a free people with a real feeling of independence in which there is no place for suspicion or fear. The Nagas do not ask Independence from India; indeed, we do not want anything from India. India has nothing to give away to Nagaland. We are Independent and sovereign in our own national right. What we ask is not to interfere our administration but leave us alone and allow Nagaland, the national State of the Nagas, to continue to exist in peace and make progress without hindrance.

The present discord between Nagaland and India is not a natural consequence of inevitable history conflict. It is the result of the break-up of the British Empire in the East and the issue is entirely of British creation but more of the callousness of the British government toward the Asiatic people of their contemptible subjects that we have been. Now that India is free, we appeal to them to exercise their sovereign right to let the Nagas continue to remain free and independent which, in verity, is in keeping with the precept of Mahatma Gandhi's creed of 'non-violence'. Should we seek a better example than of the British who granted political independence to India? The British possessed India and ruled over it for a long period stretching over 200 years; whereas Nagaland, it is not an Indian colony.

As for the question of race, the less we talk the better. It is an undeniable fact that the Nagas are not Indian. We distinctly and unmistakably belong to the great Mongolian family. Strictly speaking, the world has come to know that the question of nationality is not a question of racial purity of a people. Also, the most important thing to consider is not merely one of politics but it is rather a problem of biology and psychology. To live together in peace different people must have the same attitude and the same feeling: there must be tolerance. Between the Indians and the Nagas, I am sad to say, these are lacking. Nagas found it impossible to tolerate the Indians. This is our experience in the last seventy years ever since our people came to know them. The Indians have no human feeling in them and their attitude is anti-social. There are, undoubtedly, many good Indians who understand us; but we do not live together with those good men.

The question whether the Nagas will or will not be allowed to maintain our independence remains to be seen. If free India wishes to be a leader in this word's affairs, particularly in Asian affairs, India cannot sidestep the voice of Nagaland upholding the national right of the Nagas. It is not merely a claim. If India honestly believes that 'Truth Triumphs' (which is inscribed in the official Emblem of the Republic of India) the truth of Naga existence and the need of freedom cannot be buried in secret. India cannot ignore the national state of Nagaland and continue talking Mahatma Gandhi, non-violence and Democracy.

The position of Nagaland and the Naga case have no comparison anywhere in the word where a human race newly emancipated like India try usurp its neighbour country of a sovereign state like Nagaland all because of the vast wealth of mineral of resources in our country which the manumitted Indians have come to know and they wanted to grab it by any means. Leaving aside the distinctiveness of our nation as a race and Nagaland as a country, our native right over our own national territory that had been clearly demarcated 400 years ago cannot be superseded by India. The Indians have no vested interest in our country and there is not a single Indian nationality who own an acre of land in our Nagaland. Prior to 1947, that is, when the British were yet here, no Indian is allowed to enter Nagaland without a special permit and that good regulation (which was in force before Naga territory was annexed) still happily prevails up to this day.

If this world is to have peace and goodwill toward one another, the will of the people and nation must prevail.

India puts forward various arguments in their attempt to confound us:the first argument is about the 'menace' of China and Burma. They always say this trying to scare us which we do not have the least thing to worry.

The second argument is what they called 'strategy' for security of India. Just as much as India needs precaution for her security, other countries also require the same precaution. At least Nagaland cannot permit India to build up military strategy in our country against Burma or China whose people are our own blood relatives. We have another neighbour in the south west which is Pakistan. We have no quarrel with them. Whether China, Burma or Pakistan, these neighbours have not given us any trouble and we are certain that they have no evil design to annex Nagaland. Whatever it is, we cannot allow India to build up military defence in Nagaland not only against our good neighbours but for our own safety as well. Our country can easily become a graveyard and we, on our part, are determined to prevent it.

The third Indian argument is about economy. The Indians saythat Nagaland cannot maintain itself economically as if we are a sort of just crawling out from a hole. Their talk is nothing but insult. The truth is, Nagaland had never been dependent on India at any time in history. These are problems decent people do not argue and try to grab other people's territory. In matters of maintenance, or to be more precise, the question of finance for a state, I cannot do any better than quote His Excellency Shri C Rajagopalachari (the former Indian Governor General known to all of us) who said in his famous book that:'The notion that any state can be self-sufficient in resources is illusory. It is born of the habit of thinking in terms of property. Sovereignty does not exclude trade and communications and commerce. The right to rule one-self should not be mixed up with economic independence.'

Fortunately, Nagaland is a surplus country in matters of food and in other daily necessities that makes life happier. We have a vast area of oil deposit and we have been burning oil long before the British appeared in our country. The Indian government have already brought in other foreigners: of oil drillers and geologists and they have shamelessly started exploiting our oil resources. Many of you have seen, and all of you know that drilling has been going on in Chumukedima, 37 miles from here. Drilling is being carried out against our strong protest. We hope it shall not turn out to be another Anglo-Iranian sort of affairs. The position is very serious. We have foreseen the danger long before. There are coal deposits throughout Nagaland. The present coal mine is only a small fraction what we have. For oil we just dig with hand and draw out, that is why we call it 'digged-water' (to tzü). Our people still continue to manufacture salt for culinary purpose for its effect on health though not on the same scale as in the ancient days due to cheap salts in the market which are imported. Yet we need not import even salt in this landlocked state of ours. We have mica, gas, lime, iron ores, nickel and many other essential materials for which India has an eye on our land.

What worries us is not poverty as every one of our citizens knows this fact. Overabundance in natural resources of modern military which exist in our country so plentifully causes us much concern. The simple fact is that Nagaland is not yet internationally recognized and free India is trying to take advantage of us.

The Indians insolently told us that China and communism may take possession of Nagaland sooner or later, therefore, India must occupy it first! This line of argument is grossly vulgar on their part. Simply because India is afraid that China may take possession of Nagaland or 'may come to wield influence over the Nagas,' as they say, will it be the right thing for India to deny us our birth right and deprive us our independence?

Being a nation the Nagas have their own distinct way of manners and living; and it is quite possible that we think differently in many respects.

In our country, land belongs to the people as private property, and every family possesses land. We uphold every person as sovereign: man and women alike. Every family is a landlord; but there is no landlordism in Nagaland.

Democracy is the very spirit in our country. Land being so owned by the people who are in their person sovereign, there is a sound economic basis and there is no room for anyone to grudge or complain against social injustice. If our Naga civilization is not destroyed there is no possibility for any section of our people to become servile or entirely dependent on someone.

Over and above these, the system of our Naga community organization, which is rooted in the humane principle of individual responsibility, sharing collectively the common weal and woe together, had stood the test of time without waver throughout those centuries of great changes.

The system I refer to is our village and community—group (Thino) organization. Who is there among us who does not feel proud of this national institution of ours? The organization is not only a social system of a kind. Our community-group system is a living and dynamic institution which makes you love your country and your nation so intensely. Out of this we grow and our society generates a spontaneous feeling that gives you real sense of happiness. There is a compelling sense of responsibility in us toward our fellow citizens which our people happily share in common. It arouses a joyous urge to be of service to others and give our help the best possible. Do our people feel satiated with life? This had not been our experience. We are very happy as we are. We feel joyous with our social institutions and we want to safeguard it and preserve it. It is precious to us.

We never hear of suicide in Nagaland. There must be a reason. Not only in youth alone but you are never a finished product even in your old age because there is an undiminished consciousness of the social link of youthful bloom in the perpetual companionate association with your fellow man day after day, month after month and with the change of seasons without end, singing even in your work regardless of how heavy the work may be. In fact, the heavier the work the more joyous we sing together. In all things, your community-groups stand by you, laugh and cry with you, so you are with them, throughout life. You enjoy your life's span till the last day comes to leave this earth. Was there any Naga who was ever abandoned on the day he died? Not that we know of even a single instance, it is unthinkable to our society: because we are a proud people, proud in the sense that we respect human personality, the personality that makes the fragile man altogether a different creature from the rest of powerful animals.

To abandon the dead is irreligious, a dishonour to the Creator. To ignore the living is still worse, it is a disgrace to the community and nation. It mocks human personality. Indifference toward human personality, the abode of man's soul, is not only ignominy to our society's viewpoint (themia pese kechü-a kenyü) but it inflicts injury to one's sense of love and justice which are the hallmark of a mature people.

We do not like to mention about the Indians at all at any time. We have nothing to do with them. But it is only for them alone that we are taking all these unnecessary troubles. The Indians repeatedly tell us that we cannot manage our national state,and all that. But what we see in India? Their dead bodies are abandoned to the jackals in the fields. Those who die in the hospitals, even their own relatives very often refuse to claim them! Millions of their sons and daughters are pitifully roaming about in the streets in their awful cities begging and stealing. Why? No work, no land, no self-respect. The sturdier woman becomes prostitute and even then it is considered as an honourable profession to give happiness to their male population. The Indian mind greatly differ from the way we judge things. We refer to their society, their national characteristics, and not to the weakness of individual person. And this is not to traduce them but they must know that Nagas are not 'fools' to be bluffed or frightened to give away their fatherland. Their society is absolutely their own concern. We thought helpless humanity is to be pitied whatever race they may belong to; but when these hopeless races wanted to grab our national state and usurp our birth right by sheer force of preponderant might, why! It is entirely a different matter. It is a challenge to human integrity. No amount of sacrifice is too high to save one's national honour and preserve one's hearth and home so that the posterity may continue to live in honour and in peace and enjoy their birth right.

Nagas do not want to be associated with, much less to become citizens, of a people who have no sense of human honour in their make-up, and no human compassion even toward their own sons and daughters. We must yet believe that the Indian leaders will adhere to Mahatma Gandhi's doctrine of 'non-violence' and fulfil Gandhiji's promise to the Nagas that India will not attack the Nagas; yet, Mahatma Gandhi is no more. And, we must look into the background of the Indian civilization and see the heart of their people: the core of nationhood in being.

It is a practice in India to kill their daughters because they cannot marry them; that means, they have no tolerance, no consideration even toward womanhood who is the very fountain of their posterity. Their men are so selfish that they will not marry unless the wife-to-be brings wealth which they call 'dowry' for the price of marrying her, and, it is almost always the case that the girl does not know the man who is to be her husband. A man old enough to be her grandfather is often represented to her as a handsome young boy. That is the way the Indian do business and they consider such tactics as skilfulness! The selfishness reveals more tragically on the last day the man leaves this world. His wife is burned alive on his funeral pyre. All these go to prove that the core of their heart or the basis of their civilization is intolerant.

What we see in other established institutions in India? In their courts of law the learned lawyers are there whose profession is to defend their clients. To defend another person is a most noble mission, but instead of looking to the human side of helping and defending their clients it become rather a general practice to mulct their clients through various dubious means who place themselves at their mercy ready to bend and pay any fee within their means. This is especially done by dragging the cases calling it 'postponement' and the law becomes expensive for the poor; thus, the lawyers failed in their responsibility, never trying to obtain a quick decision. Or all the professions, the lawyers and the pleaders hold the highest respect in the Indian society, but these learned man instruct their clients to tell lies to outwit their opponents. This learned and noble profession was so prostituted that the former British regime in our country never allowed the Indian lawyers to come to courts of law in 'Naga Hills Excluded Area' and our Naga people have been saved from the immoral practice of telling lies to deceive one's opponents like in India. And we are to take note that almost every Indian leader is a lawyer, and these learned people, who search for a flaw in legal system or try to produce one when there is none, are the leaders of their great country today. This is the danger. We already see their tactics.

In the 'Charitable Hospitals' also the Indian doctors are there who see the patients as a diseased body and not as fellow human being who need one's tender care. Every one of us knew all these. What is the lot of the Indian cultivators? They are mere tenants in their own soil and not the sovereign owners of their own land as in our country. Most of the Indians live in rented houses in all the towns and cities though they may appear to the onlookers as 'big gentlemen' behaving and speaking very good English like the British. Leaving aside other considerations, the whole trouble with the Indians is they are not trustworthy. They never keep their word. In the last World War also our people have been cheated crores of money in labour and contract works. Many of you have suffered tens of thousands of rupees and you have failed to recover it.

What substance is there in the Indian civilization? Anything to yearn for? The Indians are not a happy people. It may have nothing to do with race as much, but they have miserably failed to develop a civilization that makes their people happy. We have nothing to do with them but we the Nagas do not want them to disturb us. We dearly love our pristine nationhood which should not be tarnished with a world splitting culture, which divides man, and not unites them.

We would not have gone to the extent of mentioning all these things about the Indian society and about their country what is patently known to every one of us so long ago, had they not shamelessly told us again and again that the Nagas cannot exist without India! We do not like to talk about India: let them be anything, we simply do not need them and we do not want them. A self-respecting people understand these human feelings but we have to watch India. We hear the Indians say in Shillong: 'Naga log machines gun se khatam kardena hoga.' (The Nagas shall have to be finished by machine guns).

Whereas Nagaland ought to have enjoyed unruffled peace for generations to come without end, being surrounded by world's biggest nations around us (in matters of human population), it is unfortunate that the Indians, who alone are one-fifth of world population, seem to be determined to quarrel with so small a nation even like us.

In 1879 the Indians came and killed our people as the British mercenary soldiers. There are our fathers here standing among us today who personally saw the battle. In the last World War II again how they behaved is fresh in your memory in spite of stern discipline under the British officers. These are bygone experiences. But, now that they are free and independent, and they threaten us that they have three million men under arm, which is quite possibly as high as five million—if police force is included, these are terrible things even to hear them talk. We wanted to avoid any sort of a clash if humanly possible. And, it remains to be seen what Indian government will do as the government of the one of the eldest family of civilized people on earth.

It is needless to say, we love to retain our Naga age-old culture of classless society as we are, in the spirit of true sisterhood and as brothers to one another.

We like to follow our own form of civilization wherein one need not worry for his and her needs or fear another person. Neither does our Naga society dehumanize another person and force him or her to resort to begging. We have no lawless problem to deal with and we are happy to see our citizens for all these.

There is no death sentence in Nagaland and we must hope and work for it that this will continue. Life to us represents prestige and honour: it is not merely an animal body of flesh and blood for self-enjoyment. Life is such a serious matter that wanton killing can easily precipitate a local clash. Even a small boy among us understands the implications that involve human integrity.

Being a democratic people, our Naga people are highly disciplined. This did not come easily, that we all know. We are strong enough to be very individualistic but we also know that man cannot live by himself alone. We had to abide by community and public opinion and our fathers struggled hard for all these good things our nation enjoys today. We have learned that every individual citizen has a responsibility toward others, not alone to be kindly but give our best possible help to each other. Nagas uphold that every human being is sovereign and equally precious regardless of his and her social position. We never needed police force to maintain peace, law and order because we are ready to defend ourself and always ready to defend others. As it is, our country is so calm and peaceful that we cannot imagine if we will ever have to worry for personal danger even in future. It is not so secure in many countries. We uphold that it is an honour to recognize the dignity of personal responsibility, and we consider as a privilege to be of service to others which our culture has given the expression we call 'mhosho'—to excel (mho: overhead; so: touch). Was there any Naga citizen who has ever fallen into trouble and left to his and her own fate? This did not happen in our memory. Wherever a need or trouble arise, is it not the responsibility of that community to attend to it wherever it may be? Every citizen realizes his and her responsibility toward fellow countrymen and countrywomen without fear. To do good to others, to stand by them and be ready to live or die together if need be, is the highest culture any nation could wish to have. You and I find it difficult to love our enemy; but to get an opportunity to help that enemy is a rare privilege in trying 'to excel' to do good to a fellow man. I call this a great civilization. These are expressed, to be sure, not in the spirit of boasting our national culture but for certain necessity because there are people who have a wry notion about us and we want them to come and see our country with their own eyes.

In a truly democratic society police seems to be somewhat out of place as in a small country like ours. Whatever may develop in future, our community must be sensibly alive all the time as in the past. We must see to it that no section of people be dehumanized to the level of begging or condemned below the social statues of other fellow citizens to be content with his or her helpless lot. This is a responsibility our 'community-groups' understand and we must be all the time on the alert to stand by others.

There is no pauper in Nagaland. There is no social 'outcast' in our country. There are no professional beggars up to this very day. There is no families who are houseless anywhere throughout Nagaland. There are no landless persons among us. We do not pay even land tax, which is always a crushing burden to the mass citizens in many other countries. We have no unemployment problem. Economically, Nagaland is on a strong foundation. And, no Naga wanted the Indian immigrants to migrate in Nagaland. It will not help India in any way; not only that, it will disturb the whole Nagaland.

In 1948 also we have informed the Indian government that Nagaland cannot accept the Indian excess population. Our country is too small. This is not an issue on a question of humanity. What all of us know need not to be repeated. Even if we do give away our country to India, it will not do any good. It will not solve Indian problem; it will not serve the world or create an atmosphere for world peace in which every nation is deeply interested including our country.

Indian immigration to Nagaland by force will only create tension, a problem which did not exist in the last thousand years of human history. We do not want any tension to arise between India and Nagaland; and, we do not want India to create situation in Nagaland.

India is already too congested. While we look to the birth of a child to a family as a great blessing, the birth of a child to the Indian family is a curse to their parents because they cannot feed them; particularly, a girl is considered the greater curse, and very often these daughters are killed by their own parents. It is a paradox that the only thing the Indians produce in excess is more Indians whom they themselves do not want, but they cannot stop producing them more and more. We all know that India as a country is a vast country, a very big country, in itself. It is almost three times as big as the whole Great Britain, France and Germany combined together. But their race have been multiplying so fast that their country cannot feed its population instead of producing more than enough foods by such a vast family of man. When a river rises up the danger is not in the riverbed but damage is done to the surrounding bank of the river; that is where we found our self today.

India wanted to dump her excess population in Nagaland as well as exploit the rich natural resources in our territory. This is so dangerous that it threatens our very existence. Being a small nation (almost a thousandth part of India), we can easily be submerged and get lost: our culture, our civilization, our institutions, our nation and all that we had struggled and build up as we are today will be perished without the least benefit to mankind. And, these we shall lost it not happily but in anger and in perpetual sorrow. If such a day were to be forced on us, God forbid it would have been better none of us were ever born into this world.

We have been threatened with violence.

And, we have weighed and considered everything carefully and all of you know our position. To give away Nagaland to please India is not the solution. You all know that our Naga Delegation met His Excellency, the Governor General of India, Shri C Rajagopalachari at Government House in Shillong, only eighteen months ago, on November 28, 1949, and we stated to His Excellency: 'Nagas shall not buy friendship with their territory.'

This is not an individual family matter: it concerns one whole nation— and a very small nation at that—it needs great precaution. The crisis facing our nation concerns not only of this generation but it concerns our posterity. As our fathers braved in their generations and handed us down a heritage we are all proud of, we are here to reaffirm that we are the worthy children of our fathers who sacrificed their lives for us, of whom we are their posterity. We want our nation and our posterity to continue to live in honour and in peace. Is it anti-Indian to state the living fact that we want our nation to live?

We intensely value our way of living even in so far as land ownership is concerned; and, we yearn nothing better leave alone our social institutions of pure democracy in a classless society where each regard the other as brother and sister, parent and child. We are not just a bunch of human beings called citizens.

The Indians openly say that communism may take possession of Nagaland but there are communists in India while there is no communist in Nagaland. China is the only communist country near us but we do not think China will ever bow so low to annex our territory. As for India, we cannot yet say. We have no quarrel with communism as an economic or political expression; whatever it may be, we never worried about it. Nagas do not favour communism as a way of life.

There is no political party in Nagaland. We do not need it. And we hope we shall not be pushed to a position in which we have the least desire to shift our stand even so much for an expedient measure. All things considered, Nagaland need not imitate or adopt foreign institutions like India in matters of political organizations.

The basic structure of political organization in Nagaland had withstood the change of time all these centuries because it is based on the democratic principle of sovereignty of the people over land ownership as private property. It needs no substitute.

Socially, our community is built up on a system of social alliance and this national institution, which is really three in one whole (Thehu, Thehsü, Thino) has the greatest influence on each and everyone of us.

Economically we have nothing to worry. There is no room for anyone of us to complain against any sort of injustice since he has the same equal freedom with everybody else to own land and to better his position. Nothing prevents him and her. What help he needs the community is there to stand by him for advice, protection or actual supply of material needs. Naturally enough the whole conception is based on sympathy, love, pride (in the spirit of 'mhosho') and human conscience.

If Nagaland is not disturbed, our country will remain an oasis of peace in the present form of purest democracy in this corner of the world. This is what we like to see it continued.

Someone may tell us that Nagas are Christians following a foreign religion. The Indians publicly say this. We do not take Christianity as foreign religion any more than we consider the light of the sun as foreign origin from outer world. There is a father-creator (Ukepenopfü) as we call it. He is God. The message of the Gospel fulfils our Naga conception of religion—Nanyü—which literally means 'anguish of mind' for which we do worship. Once we came to know that there is a personal Saviour to whom one can talk or pray directly, the real light dawned on us, and the weight of man's 'anguish of mind' greatly vanish away. It is the end of the beginning of our personal realization in relieving the anguish of mind in this world and for the next world after death. Whatever the Indians may say of us, there is no foreignness in relationship between father and child; that is, between God the Father and His children.

Our nation is emotionally fascinated with our way of Life. It makes life cheerful. We are not unaware of other people's opinion of us: they call us 'primitive'. Yet, with all our primitiveness, you see smiling face spontaneously beaming on you wherever you go. I say spontaneously because it is not cultivated as an education. There is an instinctual feeling of self-confidence in you and you know it. A sense of security is reflected in your behaviour. What is the source of this happy outcome? It is in the foundation of our 'community' system (Thino); and, secondly which is equally important, it is in the land and your ability to cope with life.

We do not say that we have everything or do not need any other thing. That is sheer folly. But the important thing is we have all the basic needs in political matters, for country's administration, community organization, economic set-up (uki-ulie); and these institutions we have in the way we need it. These are not problems in Nagaland. It is not a grafted growth. Our fathers had laid down all these in their time and we are just restating the fruit of their labour we enjoy today which are natural enough to their ingenuity in the process of developments to our nationhood. And, the best thing is, it fulfils the requirements of the present-day changes; no alteration or adjustment needed. All sound principles stand throughout the ages. Time and situation cannot defy it. Need we stress it again how truly we love our native institutions of people's democracy where none is the master or servant but all are as parents and children, brothers and sisters.

There is still another argument the Indian Authority put forward which is of recent origin and it is very dangerous for which we are hers today. They now say that the Nagas are not united and that there is no substance or basis to defend the independence of Nagaland. This is a strange argument. The Indians are trying to outwit us because they already got their armed forces entrenched in our territory. This unhappy situation arose through the 10-Year Agreement the Government of India entered into with the Naga National Council in 1947, which took place here in Kohima on June 26, that is, three years, ten months and twenty days today. But the Indian government officially repudiated the Agreement one year six months and eight days ago (today) which they made it known to our Naga Delegation on November 8, 1949 at the Government House in Shillong. These facts are known to you. Seeing that they cannot deceive the Nagas, as they thought they could browbeat us, have resorted to dirty, shameless and unmanly tactics. We are to note carefully that present tactics of argument placed Nagaland not as a national state of a people. India is trying now to argue the existence of Nagaland a political matter (of Indian concern)! But how can this be? Whether we call a national state or a country, both concerns the same thing: it concerns the territory of a people. Nagaland is the land of the Nagas; it is Naga country and nobody else. We are not refugees or immigrants in this beautiful land. Our own language tells exactly what a country is. We call country 'Ura' which literally means 'we are first' (u, we; ra, ria, first). The root meaning of territory also developed from the same word; namely, 'theria' meaning 'self-first'. And our Naga language is certainly as old as human tradition and history cannot contradict us. No man can argue with fact and existence of Nagaland (Nagara) is a natural fact.

What confronts us just now is not a political matter as between a colonial government and the subject people. We are not Indian subjects. Only when there is controversy problem will arise. But, in our case, Nagaland is not a controversy.

The Indians went so far to tell us that 'the talk of Naga Independence is the voice of only a few educated Nagas'! The Indian government have come to know that they cannot move the mass Naga citizens in any other way except to say that it is the voice of the educated Nagas. What of it? Where India will be without their educated class? Their talk is not only to confound us but they are trying and preparing the way to confuse the world opinion in their favour. Here our mass citizens who are directly concerned with land, as all our people are directly concerned with land but particularly those of you who are cultivating your fields, you are far more acutely conscious and much more feelingly touched of our national problems because it hurts you in a very personal way. All of us realize that it is not merely a crisis; it is a question of life and death, and for a small nation it means annihilation and extinction from the face of this earth. This is a terrible aspect. With a united voice we shall explore every possible means to avoid getting entangled.

One thing we shall not make a mistake is that Nagaland is not a problem. It is not a controversy between the Indians and the Nagas. It is not a case. Strictly speaking, it is not an issue; at least, not yet.

The Nagas have nothing to do with India. And the Indians have nothing to do with Nagaland. This is the exact position. Historically, Nagas and the Indians did not have a common tradition. Racially, Nagas belong to the Mongolian family while the Indians belong to entirely a different race of their own. Politically, neither the Nagas nor the Indians know each other, that is why trouble is just about to start. Legally, it is non-existent. There is absolutely no like. Culturally, the Nagas and the Indians never had occasion to meet each other; and, there is nothing in common. Socially, the Indians abhor the Nagas and the Nagas despise the Indians. It is better to face fact now. Religiously, the Indians are Hindus; and the ancient Naga religion is 'Animism' having nothing to do with Hindus. As it is, there is nothing in common between the Nagas and the Indians. The difference is too varied, the feeling is too deep, and the attitude is too wide and too malignant for the two nations ever to think to live together in peace much less to become 'Indian citizens'. The only way to live in peace is to live apart. Economically, Nagaland had never been dependent on India. All these have been so ever since and long before human history began. Nagas and Indians do not speak the language. Why, we do not eat even the same food. It was very good that the Indians never allow the Nagas to go near them because they hate our people.

So, what connection is there between the two people? Whoever tries to implicate us and confuse the existing or rather non-existing state of affair, he tells deliberate lies. It is folly for India to attempt to subjugate the Nagas. On our part, our fathers even in their illiterate stage never implicated our nation with India; that is why we are so distinctly alive as individually a distinct family of nation. This generation will not blunder. We shall not tarnish our honour.

Since our Naga people take word seriously as an oath, I stress these things once again so that you all will bear in mind that our nation and those of us who are in the Naga National Council for our national affairs have not made a mistake in dealing with India. Naga National Council tried and continue trying to find a peaceful solution with India for Nagaland to continues to live in peace without harassment. We have no secret. Nothing is hidden from you. And, whatever may happen, you will that our nation had tried her best to avoid it, the rest, it is beyond our power.

Now, we are here today to reaffirm the stand of our Naga nation that we do not need India and we do not want her. We are here today to prove to India and to the world that Nagaland is united and that our nation aspires the same conviction to continue to be independent as a distinct nation as we are and have always been in the sovereign national state of the Nagas of Nagaland.

We have never doubted and we never worried about the question of our unity, which is an internal affair of Nagaland alone. This was never a problem and India has no business to interfere us. But the menace of India is there because she wanted to grab our country saying one thing or another like the well-known story of the 'Tiger and the Lamb' in the Aesop Fables who had painted the worst type of cannibalistic humanity.

We are here united as one nation for the common cause of our nation's freedom, which is in jeopardy. Nagaland is independent state. We are as independent as any country could be; yet, we are not free and we cannot be free because the Indian government ceaselessly interferes our administration with their armed forces. They have been harassing our citizens all the time.

The presence of our people here in a big group in several thousands from all over our country certainly relieves the awful sense of oppression and persecutions. We are already here about six thousand people and more are still coming. Your presence here willingly to stand by our nation in peril dispels the Indian argument of disunity among us.

We all know that the Indian government have strongly entrenched their armed forces right inside our territory and they threaten our very existence to 'use all the forces at my command to crush you' as their Prime Minister Jawaharlal Nehru put it to our Naga Delegation who went to New Delhi seeking a peaceful solution to live side by side as friendly neighbours.

We shall do all what is humanly possible so that we shall not have to go down in history in shame or live in sorrow and disgrace; what else we cannot do, we leave it to God's own mercy and to His care and pray that we do not become a victim of the Indian imperialism.

We are here to commence our voluntary plebiscite to put on record and to express our mind, our national policy, in the form of Thumb Impression. It is five months now that our nation has been given time to discuss about this plebiscite voluntarily offered by us to prove our unity and our spontaneous willingness to continue to live on as a distinct nation. In the past five months I have visited every region of our area and met every one of you. What we do now will go down in our history. We shall have enough time, especially this is being a busy season for our people and many of you will have to be disturbed for this national work. Not a single village will be left out as each and every one of us will like to let our posterity know what we do now for their freedom, for their glory, and for their happiness which they must continue to enjoy as free man.

This plebiscite is not whether Nagaland should become a part of India or not. This is only to show India and the world of Naga unity as one effective nation in order to let India know the position of Nagaland. However, those who wish to show their differences in preference to join the Indian union, we welcome their expression of full freedom of choice. Nobody need worry or fear his and her safety in expressing oneself freely. All will be put on the record in the form of fingerprint. We are making three separate copies for historical document and one copy shall be presented to the Republic of India.

Lastly, let me state that the Nagas' stand for independence, that is, the continued existence of Nagaland as a sovereign state, is not a political challenge to India. We stand on, and try to reaffirm, our own right as a nation. We Nagas are not against Indians. We never wanted enemies. We only hope that India shall not become our enemy.

Let me enumerate my speech again:

Why Do the Nagas Want to be Independent?

1. We want to feel that we are absolutely and unconditionally free as a nation. Nagas belong to a distinct people and live in a country entirely of their own. We want to remain outside the influence of any other nation, be it white or brown.

2. We want to develop our own culture unhampered in the way we like, without having to worry for a possible mixture of alien blood.

3. We want to direct our own education through the establishment of our own universities.

4. We want to keep our own land in the possession of our own people for our own people.

5. We want to live our own lives. There should be no room for any possible interference, directly or indirectly, whether now or in days to come.

6. We want to keep in our possession as a heritage something which is exclusively of Nagaland; something which is bound to vanish and be lost to the Nagas if they were to live under an alien direction; these are our national institutions of –

    a) Community Organization.

    b) People's sovereignty over ownership of property and land.

    c) Our culture: a culture of love with a true respect for individual personality, a society that admits no strata of social class, caste or creed, religion or race.

7. We want peace, real peace put into an abiding practice in the lives of men. We do not want war. And we do not want to see another war in our land. We do not want to make our country a defence line. We do not want to let our children live in battlefields.

8. We want to make our country a place of happiness, of security and rest. We hope and we cherish that we can make our country a meeting place of the East and an understanding centre of the world.

9. We believe that we shall become a better friend and that we can remain a better friend to India and the outside world if we are left to ourselves – unmolested and unexploited.

10. We believe that it is not only for Nagaland but for India and other surrounding countries as well that there is a better chance of creating and retaining peace and goodwill with a sovereign Nagaland being in existence.

Above everything else, we want to be free as a distinct nation—and we shall be free.

II) MANIFESTO OF THE NATIONAL SOCIALIST COUNCIL OF NAGALAND

Relevant Extracts

Nothing is more inalienable for a nation, big or small, than her sovereignty. No moment, either, is more challenging for a people than the time when their free existence is challenged. The Naga National Council has failed. The sovereign existence of Nagaland is more at peril than ever before. It is high time for the revolutionary patriots to declare their national principles, their views and their aims.

Nagaland and the Naga National Council

We live in a world of constant change. But the forces causing the change are not always the same. They develop and perish according to the different given conditions, stages and times.

To us, the forces that defend the righteous cause of sovereign national existence and further the just cause of the people along the inevitable course are alone patriots and revolutionaries. All forces standing in opposition to this are traitors and reactionaries, in that they try to pull the wheels of history back. All the reactionary traitors lean upon one another; all revolutionary patriots stand as one, supporting one another; there is no via media.

The Naga National Council was the only authentic political organization of the people of Nagaland. It was this council that boldly took up the historic national trust, that is, the safeguarding of the right of the sovereign existence of Nagaland. With all its resoluteness, the Council faced ups and downs and it was never deterred by setbacks here and setbacks there. It has withstood the bitter period of the past three decades or so, turning neither to the right nor to the left—although there had been marked degeneration in its integrity and vigour. Our country could exist and we owe it to the National Council and to the thousands of patriots who have unsparingly laid down their lives and to the unprecedented endurance of the people, thanks to the leadership Naga National Council had given to the people in their past trials and tribulations till the time of its failure to condemn the treacherous Ministry and the accord of treason of 1975.

The sober reality, however, is that our country is still under heavy occupation of the enemy troops. What are to do with this? The enemy will never withdraw of its own accord. In no circumstances should we allow ourselves either to count on the sensibleness of the enemy. Because it is always suicidal. History has sufficiently warned us against the possible repetition of such error. Politics is successful but only when backed by arms. We are safe so long as we fight to save ourselves. Therefore, we have to fight... If negotiations, however, would be indispensable, they should be done only from a position of strength. Any attempt, therefore, at negotiated settlement at the moment would undoubtedly mean doing away with oneself, if not, it is traitorous in motive.

Facts must be acknowledged in spite of whatever turn the world might take; people must be told the truth so that they may understand their country and know what is what. The enemy is superior, therefore, our war will have to be a protracted one. We are in the course of active defence. Who will lead us through this long war? It is the most decisive issue. Is this the Naga National Council still? It has got to be reasoned out.

True, facts must be admitted and it is a fact that the most ignominious sell-out in the history of Naga people ever since the time the first bullet of freedom was fired, is beyond dispute the notorious 'Shillong Accord'. That Accord deserved an outright official and open condemnation by the Ministry that surrendered arms and consented to such sell-out. This failure left the country in a dangerous political mess. Nationwide danger was thus brought about. Any earnest appeal in a time like this for guidance, and letters of determination to fight to the last were never vouchsafed; no imperative given. The helpless unyielding were left entirely to themselves.

What existence must our society have in this material world is the cardinal issue before us. We are to know that it is the world where there is the problem of exploitation of men by men and we are not an exception to this. It is altogether due to the system we live in. Therefore, it is true that the problems of disparity and poverty, and the concomitant evils which have resulted from exploitation cannot be solved by any amount of benevolence and benefactions. It is the system that has to be abolished and lead the people into a new one where there is freedom from the fear of economic exploitation and political domination and suppression. Of course, we shall not struggle for the stage of perfect equality, simply for the factual reason of impossibility.

Nagaland and the National Socialist Council

The world is changing fast but the Naga National Council has failed to keep pace with changing conditions. It has not understood the world and Nagaland; it has isolated itself from the people; it has not promised the people any future from the danger of the forces of domination, exploitation and assimilation. All the old forces have yielded and are drowned without a trace and any contrary claim is just a claim to save one's own face, and not to save the nation. All have fallen and Nagaland remains to be saved. Where is the way to save our nation now? Where is the Council that upholds the cause of the sovereign Nagaland and the salvation of the people?

We declare we are revolutionary patriots. Let no traitorous nor reactionary bounds be on us. To us the sovereign existence of our country, the salvation of our people in socialism with their spiritual salvation in Christ are eternal and unquestionable. It is because life has meaning and that is in freedom alone. Only the revolutionary patriots are diametrically opposed to all the anti-national, anti-people forces. Because we refuse Nagaland to be gotten for gold; we refuse Nagaland to be weighed in term of silver, wine and women; we refuse Nagaland to be valued for one's status. Indeed, our Nagaland shall forever refuse to perish together with any leadership or organization that has failed and betrayed her cause, that has no promise of future for her people. Time moves on, and we have to move along, although the Naga National Council does not, for we have to redeem Nagaland. Therefore, in this irreconcilable world, our National Socialist Council declares:

National Existence

We stand for the unquestionable sovereign right of the Naga people over every inch of Nagaland whatever it may be and admit of no other existence whatever.

Political Institution

We stand for the principle of people's supremacy, that is, the dictatorship of the people through the National Socialist Council and the practice of Democracy within the organization.

Economic System

We stand for Socialism. Because it is the only social and economic system that does away with exploitation and ensures fair equality to all the people.

Religion

We stand for the faith in God and the salvation of mankind in Jesus, the Christ, alone, that is 'Nagaland for Christ'. However, the individual freedom of religion shall be safeguarded and the imposition of this faith on others is strictly forbidden.

Means

We rule out the illusion of saving Nagaland through peaceful means. It is arms and arms alone that will save our nation and ensure freedom to the people. However, if India and Burma sincerely realize the folly of the use of brute force and stop killing and torturing the Nagas, we shall not fire a single shot as we did for a decade before the start of our violent resistance. (*Last line added in November 1993*)

Self-reliance and the Policy of United Front

We stand for the practice of the principle of self-reliance and for the policy of United Front with all the forces that can be united with.

Sons and Daughters of Nagaland, ask not what the Maker has in store for us. In His righteousness, He has given us all that is ours. Let us understand our country and our freedom and hold them fast, for what have the people that doubt their freedom and that of their country? They are only fit to be ruled, nay, they are already ruled. They are the people to be pitied most. Without her freedom Nagaland too has nothing. Truly, when freedom falls, everything falls. Your country is challenged; your freedom is in peril. Arise and look! It is time, it is our today; we should never fail her, for no amount of sermons and lamentations can save her tomorrow. We have chosen Nagaland and here freedom forever; we will never part with them. Indeed, it is the war we have to fight; it is the war we have to win. We shall access no summons to bow down;

our Nagaland shall never put her hands up. We shall live only in freedom. This alone is the way to our salvation. Praise the Lord! We hold the promises of history.

LONG LIVE NAGALAND!
LONG LIVE THE NATIONAL SOCIALIST COUNCIL
OF NAGALAND!

Oking: 31 January 1980

Source: Luingam Luithui and Nandita Haksar, *Nagaland File: A Question of Human Rights* (New Delhi: Lancer International, 1984).

III) SPEECH BY NARENDRA MODI, PRIME MINISTER OF INDIA, AUGUST 2015

(Text of PM's remarks after witnessing the signing of the historic agreement between Government of India and NSCN).

Shri Rajnath Singh ji, Home Minister, Shri Muivah and all senior leaders of the National Socialist Council of Nagaland.

My warm greetings to all those present here today on this historic occasion!

I wish that Shri Isak Swu, who played a leading role in reaching this agreement, was present today. He could not be here because of poor health. I wish him speedy recovery. Just as his contribution to this agreement has been huge, his guidance will remain crucial in the times ahead.

The Naga political issue had lingered for six decades, taking a huge toll on generations of our people.

I sincerely thank Shri Isak Swu, Shri Muivah and other Naga leaders for their wisdom and courage, for their efforts and cooperation, which has resulted in this historic agreement.

I have the deepest admiration for the great Naga people for their extraordinary support to the peace efforts. I compliment the National Socialist Council of Nagaland for maintaining the ceasefire agreement for nearly two decades, with a sense of honour that defines the great Naga people.

My relationship with the North East has been deep. I have travelled to Nagaland on many occasions. I have been deeply impressed by the rich and diverse culture and the unique way of life of the Naga people. It makes not only our nation, but also the world a more beautiful place.

The Naga courage and commitment are legendary. Equally, they represent the highest levels of humanism. Their system of village administration and grass-root democracy should be an inspiration for the rest of the country.

The respect for the infirm and elders, the status of women in society, sensitivity to Mother Nature, and the emphasis on social equality is a natural way of Naga life. These are values that should constitute the foundation of the society that we all seek.

Unfortunately, the Naga problem has taken so long to resolve because we did not understand each other. It is a legacy of the British Rule. The colonial rulers had, by design, kept the Nagas isolated and insulated. They propagated terrible myths about Nagas in the rest of the country. They deliberately suppressed the reality that the Nagas were an extremely evolved society. They also spread negative ideas about the rest of India amongst Naga people. This was part of the well-known policy of divide and rule of the colonial rulers.

It is one of the tragedies of Independent India that we have lived with this legacy. There were not many like Mahatma Gandhi, who loved the Naga people and was sensitive to their sentiments. We have continued to look at each other through the prism of false perceptions and old prejudices.

The result was that connectivity between Nagaland and the rest of India remained weak across this divide. Economic development and progress in Nagaland remained modest; and, durable peace was elusive.

Since becoming Prime Minister last year, peace, security and economic transformation of North East has been amongst my highest priorities. It is also at the heart of my foreign policy, especially the 'Act East' Policy.

I have been deeply concerned about resolving the Naga issue. Soon after entering office, I appointed an interlocutor for talks with the Naga leaders, who not only understood the Naga people as also their aspirations and expectations, but has great affection and respect for them.

Given the importance of this initiative, I asked my office to supervise these talks; and I personally kept in touch with the progress. I want to especially thank my senior colleague, Home Minister Shri Rajnath Singh ji, whose support and advice was invaluable in bringing us here today.

Today's agreement is a shining example of what we can achieve when we deal with each other in a spirit of equality and respect, trust and confidence; when we seek to understand concerns and try to address aspirations; when we leave the path of dispute and take the high road of dialogue. It is a lesson and an inspiration in our troubled world.

Today, we mark not merely the end of a problem, but the beginning of a new future. We will not only try to heal wounds and resolve problems, but also be your partner as you restore your pride and prestige.

Today, to the leaders and the people of Nagaland, I say this: You will not only build a brighter future for Nagaland, but your talents, traditions and efforts will also contribute to making the nation stronger, more secure, more inclusive and more prosperous. You are also the guardians of our eastern frontiers and our gateway to the world beyond.

Equally, the rest of the nation will join you in shaping a future of dignity, opportunity and prosperity for the Naga people.

Today, as you begin a new glorious chapter with a sense of pride, self-confidence and self-respect, I join the nation in saluting you and conveying our good wishes to the Naga people.

Thank you.

The Government of India and the National Socialist Council of Nagaland (NSCN) successfully concluded the dialogue on Naga political issue, which has existed for six decades, and signed an agreement today in the presence of the Hon'ble Prime Minister Shri Narendra Modi.

Government's Interlocutor for Naga Peace Talks, Shri R.N. Ravi, signed the Agreement on behalf of the Government of India. Shri Isak Chishi Swu, Chairman and Shri Thuingaleng Muivah, General Secretary were the signatories on behalf of the NSCN. The entire top leadership of the NSCN (I-M), including all members of the 'Collective Leadership', has fully endorsed the agreement and was present during the ceremony.

This agreement will end the oldest insurgency in the country. It will restore peace and pave the way for prosperity in the North East. It will advance a life of dignity, opportunity and equity for the Naga people, based on their genius and consistent with the uniqueness of the Naga people and their culture and traditions.

Notes

Chapter One:
The Naga People, Their Land and The Movement

i.   KS Singh, *People of India: Nagaland, Volume XXXIV* (Kolkata: Seagull Books, 1994), 47.

ii.   For a detailed account of the origin of the Nagas, see William Nepuni, *Socio-Cultural History of Shüpfomei Naga Tribe* (New Delhi: Mittal Publications, 2010).

iii. Asoso Yonuo, *The Rising Nagas: A Historical and Political Study* (New Delhi: Vivek Publishing House, 1974), 39; also see RR Shimray, *Origin and Culture of Nagas* (New Delhi: Pamleiphi Shimray, 1985), 26-7.

iv.   Sir James Johnstone, *My Experiences in Manipur and the Naga Hills* (London: Sampson Low, Marston and Company, 1896), 199.

v.   See NN Acharya, Chapter XII detailing Ahom-Naga relations in *The History of Medieval Assam* (Guwahati: Omsons Publications, 1966) (Reprint, 1984); also see Lakshmi Devi, *Ahom-Tribal Relations: A Political Study* (Guwahati: Lawyer's Book Stall, 1968) (Reprint, 1992).

vi.   'The Naga Political Scene,' *Naga National Rights and Movements* (April 1955), 48.

vii. 'Thuingaleng Muivah on the Naga Issue—An Interview with Subir Ghosh' (July 17, 2009). https://northeasterner.wordpress.com/2009/07/17/thuingaleng-muivah-on-the-naga-issue. Accessed on 1 May, 2019.

viii. Rai Saheb Golap Chandra Barua, *Ahom Burranji: From the Earliest Time to the End of Ahom Rule* (Guwahati Publications, 1985), 45.

ix.   Verrier Elwin, *Nagaland* (Shillong: P Dutta for the Research Department Advisor's Secretariat, 1961).

x.   T Aliba Imti, *Reminiscence: Impur to Naga National Council* (Mokokchung: Self-Published, 1988), 17.

xi.   Ibid., 39.

xii.   Sir Robert Reid, 'The Excluded Areas of Assam,' *The Geographical Journal*, Vol. 103, No. 1/2 (Jan-Feb 1944), 18-29. http://brahmaputra. ceh.vjf.cnrs.fr/bdd/IMG/pdf/Excluded_Areas_Reid.pdf.

xiii.   Luingam Luithui and Nandita Haksar, *Nagaland File: A Question of Human Rights* (New Delhi: Lancer International, 1984).

xiv.   Imti, 10.

xv.   Imti, 57.

xvi.   Luithui & Haksar, 170.

xvii.   Pieter Steyn, *Zapuphizo: Voice of the Nagas* (London: Kegan Paul International, 2002), 55.

xviii. Ibid., 63.

xix.   Sushil Pillai, 'Anatomy of an Insurgency: Ethnicity & Identity in Nagaland.' http://www.satp.org/satporgtp/publication/fauL ieutenantlines/volume3/fauLieutenant3-genpillaif.htm.

xx.   On the fiftieth anniversary of T Sakhrie's death, his clan Lievüse Khel decided to forgive whoever was involved in his death. See Ahu Sakhrei, *The Vision of T Sakhrei for a Naga Nation* (Kohima: Dr Kepelhusie Terhuja, 2006).

xxi.   Murkot Ramunny, *The World of Nagas* (Delhi: Northern Book Centre, 1993), 84.

xxii.   Harish Chandola, *The Naga Story: First Armed Struggle in India* (New Delhi: Bibliophile South Asia, 2012), 182.

xxiii. R Suisa's proposals were given by him on his deathbed to his personal assistant, and published as 'The Legacy of Suisa;' quoted extensively by UR Shimray, *Naga Population and Integration Movement: Documentation* (New Delhi: Mittal Publications, 2007), 123-4. The proposals were also put forward in a letter dated January 5, 1967, to the Indian Prime Minister Indira Gandhi and Prime Minister of the Federal Government, reproduced in Biseto Medom Keyho's *My Journey in the Nagaland Freedom Movement* (Self-Published, 2000), 64-5.

xxiv.   BN Mullik, *My Years with Nehru* (New Delhi: Allied Publishers, 1972), 313.

xxv. For a reproduction of JP's peace proposal, see Jayaprakash Narayan, Chapter V about Nagaland and the Plan for Peaceful Settlement in *Nation Building in India*, ed. Brahmanand (Varanasi: Navachetna Prakashan), 353-5.

Chapter Two: The Political Leaders

i. W Shapwon, *Nagaland and Th Muivah's Terrorist Activities* (2005). https://www.burmalink.org/wp-content/uploads/2014/08/Th.-Muivah-3..pdf.

ii. Mohan Ram, 'Nagaland: A New Dimension,' *Economic and Political Weekly*, Vol. 14, No. 40 (November 17, 1979), 1873.

iii. Rustem Galiullin, *The CIA in Asia: Covert Operations Against India and Afghanistan* (Moscow: Progress Publishers, 1988), 85.

iv. Cited by Dinesh Kotwal in *The Naga Insurgency: The Past and the Future*. https://www.idsa-india.org/an-jul-700.html; Dinesh himself has taken the quote from VK Sarin *India's North East in Flames* (New Delhi: Vikas, 1980).

v. M Horam, *Naga Insurgency: The Last Thirty Years* (New Delhi: Cosmo Publications, 1988), 145-6.

vi. Isak Chishi Swu, *Kushe Chishi Swu A Chosen Vessel for Semaland*, December 1996.

vii. Ibid.

viii. Muivah did not give us the details of his time in Vietnam or North Korea, but the fact of his going is mentioned by AS Atai Shimray, ibid. (2005) and by Dr Timothy Kaping in the article 'Thuingaleng Muivah as I know him,' *Asian Tribune* (February 3, 2009).

ix. A reference to Mao's article written in 1926 analyzing the friends and enemies of the Chinese revolution: 'Who are our enemies? Who are our friends?' in *Analysis of the Classes in Chinese Society, Selected Works, Vol. I* (March 1926), 13.

x. For organizational structure of the NSCN (I-M) see Shimray, ibid.

xi. Amitav Ghosh has accounts of the exodus from Burma on his blog. http://amitavghosh.com/blog/?p=432.

xii. This is the visit when Nehru went to Kohima in 1953 along with PM U Nu, and the Nagas boycotted the meeting because the NNC was allowed to hand him a memorandum by the Deputy Commissioner. See an account of the meeting by Harish Chandola, ibid. (2003), 15-9.

Chapter Three: The Naga Army

xiii. Owen L Sirrs, *Pakistan's Inter-Services Intelligence Directorate: Covert Action and Internal Operations* (Oxon: Routledge, 2017), 42.
xiv. Maloy Krishna Dhar, *Open Secrets: India's Intelligence Unveiled* (New Delhi: Manas Publications, 2005), 117.
xv. RN Kulkarni, *Sin of National Conscience* (Mysore: Kritagnya Publications, 2004), 115-6.
xvi. See Joshua S Horn, *Away with all Pests: An English Surgeon in People's China, 1954–1969* (New York: Monthly Review Press, 1969).
xvii. Ibid.

Chapter Four: Culture, The Church, and China

xviii. Nandita Haksar has dealt with this problem in her book *ABC of Naga Culture and Civilization: A Resource Book* (New Delhi: Chicken Neck, 2011).
xix. *The Two World Outlook* (NSCN publication, 1990) as quoted in AS Shimray, ibid. (2005), 166.
xx. Ibid., 147.
xxi. There is a small but significant body of academic literature critical of the influence of fundamentalist theology on the Naga national movement. For instance, John Thomas, *Evangelizing the Nation: Religion and the Formation of Naga Political Identity* (New Delhi: Routledge India, 2015).

Chapter Five: The Tribe, Tribalism and The Nation

xxii. M Horam, *Naga Old Ways and New Trends* (New Delhi: Cosmo Publications, 1988), 72.
xxiii. Ibid., 23.
xxiv. The document has been reproduced by several writers, including by Reverend VK Nuh in *Nagaland Church and Politics* (Kohima: Self-Published, 1986).

xxv. See Gangmumei Kamei, *A History of the Zeliangrong Nagas: From Makhel to Rani Gaidinliu* (New Delhi: Spectrum Publications, 2004).

By Way of a Conclusion

xxvi. Nandita Haksar and Sebastian M. Hongray, *The Judgement That Never Came: Army Rule in North East India* (New Delhi: Bibiliophile South Asia, 2011).

xxvii. See Nandita Haksar, *The Exodus Is Not Over: Migrations from the Ruptured Homelands of Northeast India* (New Delhi: Speaking Tiger, 2016).

Select Bibliography

The literature on the Nagas is vast. A large part consists of ethnological studies of individual tribes, or of the Nagas as a whole from colonial times to today. The second category of literature on the Nagas is by administrators concerned with governance and the third is the accounts of those concerned with intelligence and counter-insurgency. Most of this literature is available—much of it is on the internet or in form of printed books in libraries.

However, there is a growing body of literature on the Naga national movement generated by Naga national organizations in the form of pamphlets and brochures; also accounts written by Nagas and those who are close to the Naga nationalists.

The list below deals with books on Naga resistance from the time of Ahom rule, through to British colonialism and resistance to the Indian state. Many of these texts are self-published and thus not available easily, but to any scholar who wishes to go deeper into the subject of our book, this list could be a starting point.

Ahom-Naga Relations

Acharya, NN. 1984. *The History of Medieval Assam*. New Delhi: Omson Publications.

Bhuyan, Dr S.K. 1990. *Tungkhungia Buranji or A History of Assam 1681–1826*. Translated, compiled, and edited by Bhuyan, Dr S.K. Guwahati: Historical and Antiquarian Studies in Assam.

Devi, Lakshmi. 1968 (Reprint, 1992). *Ahom-Tribal Relations: A Political Study*. Guwahati: Lawyer's Book Stall.

Golap Chandra Barua, Rai Saheb. 1985. *Ahom Buranji: From the Earliest Time to the End of Ahom Rule.* Guwahati: Spectrum Publications.

Naga Resistance to the British

Ao, Tajenyuba. 1993. *British Occupation of Naga Country.* Dimapur: Naga Literature Society.

Imti, T Aliba. 1988. *Reminiscence: Impur to Naga National Council.* Mokokchung: Self-Published.

Jadonang and Rani Gaidinliu

Kamei, Gangmumei. 1997. *Jadonang: A Mystic Naga Rebel.* Imphal: G Lanshailu Kamei.

——— 2004. *A History of the Zeliangrong Nagas.* Guwahati: Spectrum Publications.

Yonuo, Asoso. 1982. *Naga Struggle Against British Rule Under Jadonang and Rani Gaidinliu.* Kohima: Leno Printing Press.

Documents of the Naga National Council and the NSCN (I-M)

Lasuh, Wetshokhrolo. 2002. *The Naga Chronicle.* Shillong: ICSSR and North East Regional Centre.

Luithui, Luingam and Haksar, Nandita. 1984. *Nagaland File: A Question of Human Rights.* New Delhi: Lancer International.

Naga National Council. 1993. *The Naga National Rights and Movement.* Dimapur: Self-Published.

Nuh, Reverend V.K. 1986. *Nagaland Church and Politics.* Kohima: Self-Published.

Naga Insurgency

Ao, A Lanunungsang. 2002. *From Phizo to Muivah: The Naga National Question in North East India.* New Delhi: Mittal Publications.

Chandola, Harish. 2012. *The Naga Story: First Armed Struggle in India*. New Delhi: Chicken Neck.

Horam, Dr M. 1988. *Naga Insurgency: The Last Thirty Years*. New Delhi: Cosmo Publications.

Iralu, Kaka D. 2000. *Nagaland and India: The Blood and the Tears*. Kohima: Self-Published.

Nibedon, Nirmal.1978. *Nagaland: The Night of the Guerillas*. New Delhi: Lancer Publishers.

Shimray, A.S. 2005. *Let Freedom Ring: Story of Naga Nationalism*. New Delhi: Bibliophile South Asia.

Steyn, Pieter. 2002. *Zapuphizo: Voice of the Nagas*. London: Kegan Paul.

Yonuo, Asoso. 1974. *The Rising Nagas: A Historical and Political Study*. Delhi: Vikas Publishing House.

Indian Response to Early Naga Insurgency

Ramunny, Murkot. 1988. *The World of Nagas*. New Delhi: Northern Book Centre.

Acknowledgements

We would like to first of all like to thank most sincerely the two leaders, Isak Chishi Swu and Thuingaleng Muivah, and their wives, for giving us their time, their patience and their trust. We are also grateful to them for taking such good care of us during our one month long stay in Bangkok, including the most memorable day when they escaped from their guards to take us out for lunch at a shopping mall. We feel very sad that we will not be able to give this book to Uncle Isak since he passed away in 2016.

We would also like to thank all the NSCN (I-M) members for giving us interviews and our sincere apologizes to those whose interviews we could not include in this book. We hope someone else will continue the task of recording the memories of so many more Nagas and their extraordinary experiences in the movement.

Two friends from our days in Jawaharlal Nehru University, AS Atai Shimray and Ahu Sakhrei, too have passed away. Both of them shared their insights and knowledge with us and welcomed us into their homes during the writing of this book. We miss you both very much.

In Dimapur we stayed with Adani and Roni for several weeks while interviewing the leaders in Nagaland. We remember with gratitude the warmth of your hospitality.

Our special thanks to Phungthing Shimrah for dealing with all the logistics of these interviews, arranging safe houses, providing transport, ensuring our safety and even doing the job of an interpreter when the the people we were interviewing did not know English. He did this despite his busy schedule as the Chairman of the NSCN Monitoring Cell.

Although everyone we interviewed was on the specific suggestion of the NSCN, at no time did they interfere in our work and were open in our discussions; unfortunately we could not include much of those discussions for lack of space.

We are also grateful for all the help given by Gapumkhai Grinder Muivah, the nephew of Thuingaleng Muivah, who had the thankless task of being the go-between the NSCN and the Government of India from the start of the talks till his death in 2016.

We are grateful to Sonia Muivah for introducing us to Mayori who took one year off and did the task of transcribing the tapes which ran into 3000 hand-written pages. Mayori passed away suddenly just a few months before this book went for publishing. She was so keen to see the book and if it had not been for her hard work this book would not have come out. We miss her deeply.

We have not forgotten the friend who first put us in touch with the NSCN leaders in Bangkok and we are grateful to him for his efforts, and are sorry that we cannot name him.

We would also like to thank so many of the young Nagas and Indian students who have encouraged us all these years and made our book feel wanted. We hope they will not be disappointed after such a long wait.

Temjem has been enthusiastically helping us with the proofs in Goa and we are really grateful for his help and support. And to Dr Felix for answering our queries on spellings, events, etc at all odd hours of day and night: a big thank you.

Our thanks to Ravi Singh, our publisher, for his enthusiastic encouragement, and to Yauvanika Chopra for her meticulous editing, especially of the footnotes, and saving us much embarrassment by spotting our mistakes.

www.ingramcontent.com/pod-product-compliance
Lightning Source LLC
Chambersburg PA
CBHW070244290326
41929CB00047B/2557